STRATEGY, INNOVATION, AND CHANGE

Strategy, Innovation, and Change

Challenges for Management

Robert Galavan
John Murray
Costas Markides

OXFORD
UNIVERSITY PRESS

OXFORD
UNIVERSITY PRESS

Great Clarendon Street, Oxford OX2 6DP

Oxford University Press is a department of the University of Oxford.
It furthers the University's objective of excellence in research, scholarship,
and education by publishing worldwide in

Oxford New York

Auckland Cape Town Dar es Salaam Hong Kong Karachi
Kuala Lumpur Madrid Melbourne Mexico City Nairobi
New Delhi Shanghai Taipei Toronto

With offices in

Argentina Austria Brazil Chile Czech Republic France Greece
Guatemala Hungary Italy Japan Poland Portugal Singapore
South Korea Switzerland Thailand Turkey Ukraine Vietnam

Oxford is a registered trade mark of Oxford University Press
in the UK and in certain other countries

Published in the United States
by Oxford University Press Inc., New York

British Library Cataloguing in Publication Data

Data available

Library of Congress Cataloging in Publication Data

Strategy, innovation, and change: challenges for management / [edited by] Robert
Galavan, John Murray, Costas Markides.
    p. cm.
  Includes index.
  ISBN–13: 978–0–19–923990–0
1. Strategic planning.   2. Technological innovations—Economic aspects.   I. Murray,
John A., Ph. D.   II. Markides, Constantinos.   III. Galavan, Robert.
HD30.28S7387   2008
658.4—dc22   2008000351

Typeset by SPI Publisher Services, Pondicherry, India
Printed in Great Britain
on acid-free paper by
the MPG Books Group

ISBN 978–0–19–923990–0

Contents

Part I. Understand your Situation

Part II. Develop your Options

Contents

Part III. Lead the Change

List of Figures

List of Tables

About the Authors

John Bessant Ph.D. holds the Chair in Innovation and Technology Management at Tanaka Business School, Imperial College, where he is also Research Director. He previously worked at Cranfield University, Brighton University, and Sussex University. In 2003 he was awarded a Senior Fellowship with the Advanced Institute for Management Research and was also elected a Fellow of the British Academy of Management. Author of fifteen books and many articles, he has acted as adviser to various national governments and to international bodies including the United Nations, World Bank, and OECD.

Cliff Bowman Ph.D. is Director of Research at Ashridge. He was formerly Professor of Strategic Management and Dean at Cranfield School of Management, UK. He has published extensively in the areas of competitive strategy, dynamic capabilities, strategy processes, and the development and leveraging of strategic assets. He also consults for a wide variety of leading international organizations.

Jay Conger DBA holds the Henry R. Kravis Research Chair in Leadership Studies at Claremont McKenna College and is Visiting Professor of Organizational Behaviour at London Business School. He is a world expert in interpersonal and organizational communication, executive coaching, leadership development, and organizational change and development. He has a distinguished track record in research and has authored over a dozen books and ninety articles. *Business Week* selected him as the best business school professor to teach leadership to executives.

John Cullen is a lecturer at the Dublin Institute of Technology. He has edited several texts on management topics and is currently engaged in a large leadership-focused research project. Previously he was senior management researcher with IMI.

Kasra Ferdows Ph.D. is the Heisley Family Chair Professor of Global Manufacturing and Co-Director of the Global Logistics Research Program at the McDonough School of Business, Georgetown University. His research and publications are in management of global operations. He is a Fellow and former President of Production and Operations Management Society, and has served as a consultant to many multinational companies.

About the Authors

Robert Galavan Ph.D. is Head of the Department of Business and Law and Associate Dean of the Faculty of Social Sciences at the National University of Ireland Maynooth. He is an accomplished executive educator, business consultant, and an award-winning researcher in the field of strategic leadership. He was previously head of Executive Education at the Irish Management Institute and Programme Director at the Trinity-IMI Graduate School of Management.

Rob Goffee Ph.D. is Professor of Organizational Behaviour at the London Business School where he teaches on the world-renowned Senior Executive Programme. He has taught executives from some of the world's leading companies, including Unilever, Nestlé, and Sonae, and consults to the boards of a number of FTSE 100 companies. He is a recognized authority on organizational transformation and leadership, and has co-authored the international best-seller *The Character of a Corporation* (1998) with Gareth Jones.

Lynda Gratton Ph.D. is Professor of Management Practice and director of the Lehman Centre for Women in Business at London Business School. She was named by *The* (London) *Times* as one of the world's top fifty business thinkers and ranked in the top two of *Human Resources Magazine's* Most Influential poll. Her best-selling books include *Living Strategy* and *The Democratic Enterprise*, her latest book is *Hot Spots*. In 2004 she was appointed a senior fellow of the UK's Advanced Institute of Management Research.

Gareth Jones Ph.D. is a Fellow of the Centre for Management Development at London Business School, a visiting professor at INSEAD, and former Professor of Organizational Behaviour at Henley Management College. Gareth was Director of Human Resources and Internal Communications at the BBC and Senior Vice President for global human resources at Polygram. He is co-author with Rob Goffee of the famous HBR article and book *Why Should Anyone be Led by You?* Gareth serves on the Editorial Advisory Board of *People Management* magazine and is a trustee of The Work Foundation.

Andrew Kakabadse Ph.D. is Professor of International Management Development at Cranfield School of Management, UK. He was recently the H. Smith Richardson Fellow at the Centre for Creative Leadership in North Carolina, USA, and Visiting Professor at the University of Ulster, Ireland. He is co-editor of the *Journal of Management Development and Corporate Governance: International Journal of Business in Society.* He has published over 25 books and 150 articles.

Nada Kakabadse Ph.D. is Professor of Management and Business Research at the University of Northampton Business School and co-editor (with Andrew Kakabadse) of the *Journal of Management Development and Corporate Governance: The International Journal of Business in Society.* She is a researcher and prolific author with over 8 co-authored books, 50 book chapters, and 100 articles published.

William Lawler Ph.D. is a Babson Leadership Professor of Strategy & Accounting at the F. W. Ohlin Graduate School of Business, Babson College, and Director of the Consortium for Executive Development at the Babson College School of Executive Education. His teaching and research focus on the financial footprints of business unit strategy and the impact of new technologies on cost systems design. His primary focus is on aiding operational managers in understanding the financial consequences of their decisions.

Linda Lee-Davies is a Senior Lecturer in Business and International Management at the University of Northampton. She researches and publishes in the field of leadership and management and runs a suite of management courses from certificate to MBA tailored for local business people at Northampton Business School.

Dermot McAleese Ph.D. is Chairman of the Consultative Board, Institute for International Integration Studies (IIIS). He was Whately Professor of Political Economy, Trinity College Dublin, 1979–2004, and was a director of the Central Bank of Ireland for over seventeen years. He is currently Pro-Chancellor of the University.

Rita Gunther McGrath Ph.D. has been Professor of Management at Columbia Business School since 1992. She works extensively with leadership teams in international companies to address challenges of innovation and growth. She has published extensively in *Harvard Business Review* and other prestigious journals and is co-author of two leading business books, *The Entrepreneurial Mindset* and *MarketBusters: 40 Strategic Moves that Drive Exceptional Business Growth*.

Andrew McLaughlin is a Senior Specialist at the Irish Management Institute and director of the M.Sc. in Organizational Behaviour at the Trinity-IMI Graduate School of Management. He has held senior posts in the Irish Civil Service and in the EU in Brussels. He has worked for the OECD and the EU in consultancy assignments in Europe.

Costas Markides DBA is Professor of Strategic and International Management and holds the Robert P. Bauman Chair of Strategic Leadership at the London Business School. He has published extensively in the world's most prestigious journals. He has published several books and his most recent, *Fast Second: How Smart Companies Bypass Radical Innovation to Enter and Dominate New Markets*, was shortlisted for the F/T-Goldman Sachs Management Book of the Year Award in 2005.

Seán Meehan Ph.D. is the Martin Hilti Professor of Marketing and Change Management at IMD in Switzerland. He specializes in helping companies enhance their levels of customer orientation. He has published his work in, among others, MIT *Sloan Management Review, Business Strategy Review, strategy+business*, and *Marketing Research*. He is co-author of *Simply Better: Winning and*

About the Authors

Keeping Customers by Delivering What Matters Most, published by Harvard Business School Press, which was 'Marketing Book of the Year' in 2005.

John Murray Ph.D. is Professor of Business Studies at the School of Business, Trinity College Dublin. His research and publications have addressed the strategic challenges associated with organizational renewal and managing in the public sector. Currently his focus is on the dynamics of global business systems. He has served as faculty member with business schools in Europe, Asia, and North America and as consultant to multinational companies.

Gerard O'Brien is an economist in the Policy Division of Enterprise Ireland. He is currently engaged in developing and evaluating state supports for Irish enterprises engaged in international business development.

Kathleen Reardon Ph.D. is Professor of Management and Organization at the University of Southern California's Marshall School of Business, Visiting Professor of Philosophy at University College Cork, and was named distinguished research scholar at the Irish Management Institute. She is a best-selling author and her latest books are *The Secret Handshake*, *The Skilled Negotiator*, and *It's All Politics*.

Richard Schoenberg Ph.D. is Senior Lecturer in Strategic Management at Cranfield School of Management. He previously held faculty positions at the Judge Business School, Cambridge University, and Imperial College London. He is an active researcher, holding a prize-winning Ph.D. from the University of London, and teaches across Cranfield's MBA and executive education programmes.

Willem Smit Ph.D. is a Research Fellow in Marketing at IMD in Switzerland. He obtained his Ph.D. from Erasmus Universiteit Rotterdam in 2006 with a thesis on the topic 'Market Information Sharing in Channel Relationships: Its Nature, Antecedents and Consequences.' At IMD his research focus has broadened from a specialization on 'market information sharing' to many other usages of market intelligence of firms in their strategy making.

Donald Sull DBA is Professor of Management Practice in the Strategic and International Management area at London Business School. He is a highly accomplished researcher and has published several books including *Made in China* and *Why Good Companies go Bad and How Great Managers Remake Them*. Prior to joining London Business School he was Assistant Professor of Business Administration at Harvard Business School.

Dave Ulrich Ph.D. is a Professor at the Ross School of Business at the University of Michigan and Partner at the RBL Group. He has written over a dozen books and a hundred articles on human resources, organization as capabilities, and leadership. His work bridges academic theory and research and management practice. He is co-author of the global Human Resource Competency Study.

Introduction

Robert Galavan, John Murray, and Costas Markides

The idea for this book emerged from the executive development and master's classes provided by the Trinity-IMI Partnership in Dublin where **Robert Galavan** and **John Murray** have had the pleasure of working with most of the authors as they engaged with leaders of industry, commerce, and public sector. Together with **Costas Markides** who has been a great friend and supporter over the years, we expanded our reach and connected with colleagues at London Business School who have a similar dedication for developing ideas and influencing people who can make a difference.

We invited all of the authors to contribute to this book because of their special ability to engage with, not just the concepts, but also with the application of strategy and leadership. When these authors teach they engage in the most lively debates that connect research to the real-world issues of management. This book is a collection of the reflective work of these scholars which integrates their thought leadership with the practice of leadership.

Management is by its nature an eclectic subject and the range of contributions to this book reflects the rich diversity that makes it so engaging. The connecting theme of the contributions is not just a subject theme, but also the common ability of all the authors to take their years of rigorous research and make it relevant to today's and tomorrow's organizations' leaders.

The three editors are strategy specialists and so it should hold no surprise that the book contains a strategic theme. Strategy is still clearly a developing subject and even within the past decade there have been a number of important articles addressing the question of 'what is strategy?'[1] We should be clear at the outset that this book will not address that question or resolve the argument. We are equally clear that if strategy is to help executives make a difference it cannot be an intellectual pursuit of concepts. Strategy in isolation has no life and no energy. We have brought together a group of contributors who breathe life into strategy through the connection of innovation, leadership, and change management. They are all passionate about their subjects and we know from experience with them that their thoughts make a difference to the people who make a difference.

All three editors recognize the enormously privileged roles we get to play. Our daily lives provide us with the opportunity to interact with the smartest, most talented, and innovative academics from around the globe and before we go home we engage with the best executives as they work to translate these ideas into commercial reality. This book springs from that remarkable space where innovative thought and reflective practice collides.

The book can be read in two ways. Each of the contributions is unique and complete in its own right. So readers should feel free to dip in and out of the book to read individual chapters if the topic captures their interest. The book can also be read in a more structured manner in which case the reader should connect with the discussion of the chapters that follows below. Each of the three sections in the book, 'Understand your Situation,' 'Develop your Options,' and 'Lead the Change,' relates to a framework of analysis, formulation, and implementation that underpins most comprehensive strategy texts. This book is not a textbook and while the framework is comprehensive, the content is not designed to give an unbiased view of the subject area. It contains the definitively biased views of some of the greatest contributors to their fields.

Understand your Situation

The rapid evolution of globalization is one clear anchor for the chapters in this section. Having transformed the world of manufacturing and traditional agribusiness it has most recently changed the competitive reality of service sector companies. In addition, as manufacturing companies have focused more on their component activities and processes, they have begun to disaggregate traditional manufacturing into its physical and service components. The latter are then subject to the global locational opportunities and pressures that affected whole subsidiary operations in the past. This 'great unbundling' of enterprise results in services being traded as actively as manufacturing.

Dermot McAleese and **Gerard O'Brien** open this theme with their observations on the gathering pace of globalization, its impact on business, and use 'Celtic Tiger' data to illustrate the interacting effects of global macroeconomics, national policy, and firm response at multinational and indigenous levels. The general pillars of economic policy that began to emerge in the 1980s are represented as a new, broadly shared, international consensus. The consensus is interpreted in varying ways at national economy level around the world, as illustrated by aspects of the Irish approach such as its use of social partnership agreements on incomes policy. Two issues raised by this chapter seem of special relevance to strategists. One is the fact that the current process of globalization is based on ideas that have currency across many powerful economies. These ideas began to impact policy and competitive reality from 1980's onward. It is wise to remember that such constructions of the world are in fact delicate and abstract fabrications and that their conversion into broad consensus and orthodoxy often leads to their own decline or translation into a new and contrasting consensus. Fukuyama's claim of the arrival of the 'end of history' should not be forgotten. So the wise strategist will appreciate fully the implications of the current, and still rising, tide of globalization but will also factor into long-term considerations the implications of a receding tide too. The second issue is the extent of differentiation in local interpretations and actions based on the 'new consensus.' For the strategist, there is no perfectly common ground within the consensus on a country-by-country basis. The search for competitive advantage remains significantly rooted in country-specific factors. Choice of location for the 'unbundled' firm's activities remains pivotal and drives competition between nations and firms. These realities are reflected in the authors' consideration of the manner in which national concerns about competitiveness have grown beyond cost factors to include more complex and subtle determinants.

At the firm level **Cliff Bowman** and **Richard Schoenberg** provide frameworks to assist management in understanding competitive positioning and options. They bring a strong emphasis on market and customer understanding as a starting point for strategy formulation. Their frameworks speak directly to managers in terms of how to visualize customer-perceived value and how to deepen their understanding of value-for-money as constructed by customers. They develop a series of strategic options for managing the price–value trade-off and draw out the potential performance implications. They also operationalize some of the concepts of value innovation by integrating them with their charting of perceived use value (PUV) and price. Finally they address the opportunities to challenge conventional wisdom about industry boundaries in the search for strategic innovation. These techniques support the manager in analyzing and elaborating strategic options in any competitive market and have particular strength in their focus on customer perceptions and choice behavior.

The possibility of dominating 'winner-take-all' markets has been a siren song for many strategists. The prevalence of significant new technologies and the vast increase in the potential size of such markets in a globalized world act as a lure to even more. **Rita McGrath** begins with a well-timed warning about the disasters that have struck many who have placed huge strategic bets on the assumption they were entering a winner-take-all market. To avoid such disasters she counsels managers in two ways: how to recognize a winner-take-all market and how to manage entry and positioning. In order to assess the potential for such market characteristics she asks managers to identify a substantive change in the basis for competition, the potential for customer lock-in, and the potential for competitor lock-out—and preferably a combination of these factors. Moreover, adding to the complexity of understanding such preconditions, she notes that they are significantly created by the strategies of firms and not provided as environmental 'givens' or structural constants. Furthermore, she notes that the means of entering and managing strategically in such markets depends on the continuing evolution of the product market—strategy is contingent on stage of evolution. This is a cautionary as well as an illuminating chapter in the context of the contemporary emergence of many technology and globalization driven markets that are seen as having winner-take-all characteristics and that tempt strategists to make enormous pre-emptive investments.

Bill Lawler takes up the storyline by showing us how to see strategy through a financial lens, in the process deepening our diagnostic ability and expanding our understanding of strategic performance and of strategic options. Every strategy, as he notes, has a financial footprint and a financial logic that must be fully understood. He urges the use of return on invested capital (ROIC) as the central measure, but more particularly its component elements that tell whether a business model is driven by margin or by asset turn. The reality that few firms are able to excel at both, and must therefore make choices, adds extra edge to his framework. The framework is illustrated through a detailed analysis of the strategic history of Compaq, since its entry into the PC market in 1982, that documents the evolving nature of competition and performance in this iconic industry. The strategic financial analysis is very revealing and will provide a fresh perspective on the dynamics of strategy for many managers.

Staying firmly with the perspectives and responsibilities of the top management team, **Dave Ulrich** provides us with a view of where the strategic contribution of human resource management to value creation is headed. He begins with the same view of the strategic context: technological change, customer diversity, new competition, and globalization. In these conditions HR is expected to contribute directly to competitive success and to create value for the firm. Such value must be delivered to employees, customers, investors, and managers. He proposes ten challenges that lie at the heart of the ability to generate strategic value from HR. For HR professionals to meet these challenges the HR function must be appropriately structured and the professionals themselves must behave appropriately.

Finally we turn to a context that has traditionally weighed less on the strategic management discipline: strategic public management. The context shifts from private to public sector practice. Interest in strategic public management is an outgrowth of the global wave of reform that has moved through government and public service systems worldwide since the 1980s, giving birth to public management and the 'new public management' in place of the earlier public administration. **John Murray** notes that many of the challenges now faced by senior public managers are remarkably similar to those encountered in the private sector. Public managers, managing strategically, are seen to have three essential tasks: delivering public services, giving advice and wise counsel to senior political decision makers, and providing stewardship of the values that are fundamental to good government and its legitimacy. New pressures on these managers come from a more demanding citizenry insisting on a 'performing government' and creating a new milieu of audience democracy where some of the buffers in traditional deliberative analysis and decision making are removed in favor of rapid reaction and decision making, propelled by media and powerful interest groups. Critical challenges relating to the three basic tasks are discussed and the exceptional contemporary pressures on top management leadership are noted. Public managers are now in the front line of change and transformation, as much as their private sector colleagues.

Develop your Options

This section of the book explores the theme of developing options in what has already been categorized as a globalizing, uncertain, and volatile environment.

Seán Meehan and Willem Smit argue that in today's globalized and interconnected world, consumers are not as easily persuaded by marketing messages as they once were. Far too many are convinced they have been let down by the product or service they bought. Widespread dissatisfaction and even rage about value propositions that do not deliver ultimately hurt the reputations of well-established firms. They examine the dark side of having active, well-informed, connected customers, provide an analysis of these trends, and recommend three strategies on how firms could respond. The first strategy is to improve the dialogue with the right customers by assessment of customer lifetime value and permission marketing. The second strategy is to improve the offering of the right value proposition through customer development programs and immersion strategies. And the third strategy is to reduce negative network effects of poor value proposition delivery by effective complaint management and by rewarding customers with positive word-of-mouth.

Not only does the marketing process of the modern corporation need a total rethink but so do the manufacturing processes of the multinational firm. **Kasra Ferdows**'s chapter takes many of the globalization and uncertainty arguments to a firm-specific level and focuses on global production networks. He notes the new challenge: where to perform the component tasks in the production process, rather than where to produce. It is already commonplace to have a product 'produced' in six different countries as he illustrates for a toy robot. It is not uncommon for twenty or more countries to be involved in some processes. So a distinct feature of our changing world is the growing dominance of multi-country production networks. The central challenge of such networks is, not surprisingly, coordination. As he points out, some of these are dramatically successful and some are disastrous. What strategic considerations should guide decisions about the design and management of global production networks? The logic and characteristics of footloose and rooted networks are developed and contrasted and a clear warning is sent to the strategist about making choices unintentionally through the accumulation of incremental decisions: the riskiest decision is a decision by default. A framework to support analysis, discussion, and decision making is presented. It arrays networks in terms of the degree of differentiation of the product on one axis and the degree to which the production process is proprietary on the other. The contrasting 'rooted' network and 'footloose' network are on the upward-sloping diagonal in this array while two 'slippery' positions exist on the downward-sloping diagonal. The challenges of operating in each of the four archetypical modes are developed as well as the nature of hybrid positions and strategies such as Zara's strikingly successful approach.

The contribution by **Don Sull** examines how the strategy process of the modern corporation needs to change in today's world. Don argues that the traditional approach to strategy is rather linear, passing through the stages of first formulating a strategy, then implementing it, and finally protecting the competitive advantage. This linear approach hinders managers from incorporating new information into action. His chapter sets out an alternative view of strategy as an iterative process known as the strategy loop, which helps managers act on new information that arises in the course of executing a strategy. Managers can put this approach into practice through formal and informal discussions, which are the key mechanism to coordinate activity within large, complex organizations. Uncertain markets make these discussions more necessary and, at the same time, more difficult. Despite the diversity of these discussions, they all follow the same fundamental logic and pass through four distinct steps of the strategy loop: discussions to make sense, make choices, make it happen, and make revisions. Managers who master the four types of discussions can notice new information and incorporate it into their strategy execution.

The last two contributions examine how the modern corporation must deal with radical innovation. First, the contribution by **John Bessant** argues that discontinuous changes can often be disruptive to established players. Their challenge is to reinvent themselves to allow at least a part of the business to behave as if it were an entrepreneurial start-up—and to hold back the conservative forces of the mainstream organization to let this happen. The big question for established players is how to develop the capabilities to handle this kind of innovation. One option is to set up their own version of new entrant firms, simply spinning off entities which they hope will be able to colonize and settle the new world. This is a low-risk option but may also mean that there may be little synergy or leverage to and from the core business. Another option is to try and develop a parallel innovation management capability within the mainstream business—but in order to do this a number of new approaches will be needed. The chapter explores the approaches that different firms are experimenting with in order to develop these capabilities.

The contribution by **Costas Markides** takes a different approach to the challenge of radical innovation. Markides differentiates between the creation of a new market and the scaling up of the new market into a big, mass market. He argues that big established companies should not be in the business of creating radical new markets. The innovation process that creates such markets and the structural characteristics of these markets in their early formative years are such that no established corporation could realistically succeed in creating them. What the big corporation ought to focus on is scaling up young markets by positioning itself to exploit the pioneering efforts of younger firms. It could do this by taking the new markets that younger firms have created and scaling them up into mass markets. This is the area where the older, established corporation has unique advantages over the small, start-up firms and should therefore be the focal area of their attention. This has serious implications for how the modern corporation ought to be structured and what strategies it should be following.

All the contributions in this section make it clear that the modern corporation faces several serious challenges. None of them can be effectively met without strong strategic leadership which is the topic of the third section of the book.

Lead the Change

The previous sections of the book identify the enormous challenges faced by contemporary organizations. The challenges are more diverse and dynamic than those faced by any previous generation of leaders. A defining characteristic of this modern organizational context is the challenge of developing and managing intangible assets. Where once the strategist could look to the balance sheet to identify assets to be leveraged, they now need to harness the collective tacit knowledge of their organizations. **Rob Goffee** and **Gareth Jones** open this section with a timely reminder that intangible assets now account for more than half the total market capitalization of public US companies and that a significant component of that value is derived from the 'tacit' skills of the 'clever people' in them. The embeddedness of these tacit skills and their importance to organizational success presents leaders with a difficult and at the same time unshirkable challenge. The solution Rob and Gareth propose is a type of leadership which promotes a culture capable of nurturing this tacit human capital. The central challenge of managing the 'clever' people arises from the fact that they don't particularly like to be managed or corralled. They live with a tension between the preference for freedom and expression and the need for an organization that provides a well-resourced and supportive network. In this world where we need the skills of these innovative beings, leaders need to find a new psychological contract, recognizing that clever people are not staying for the pension. Rob and Gareth suggest an insightful list of actions for clever leaders, including the creation of a simplified rule environment where these motivated people can figure out their own way forward. In this new contract it becomes the role of leaders to win the resources, time, space, and freedom for the clever people rather than control their actions. The act of leadership in this world is aptly compared to the role of herding cats.

The great diversity that leaders now face brings with it both opportunities and challenges. Strategy as a field has developed to a point where there is an emerging orthodox approach, at least from a planning perspective. This planning approach seeks to match the organization's external reality with its internal capabilities. **Robert Galavan** and **John Cullen** question whether these realities that leaders come to accept are simply mental prison bars. They suggest that rather than treat their environments and their organizations as embedded realities, that leaders need to recognize the discretion offered in these situations and recognize the limits to that discretion that are created by their own minds. At the most basic level we can see that optimists and pessimists will see the world in a different light. A central point to their discussion is that managers matter more in some (high-discretion) situations than in others, but that equally some managers matter more than others. It has been somewhat of a truism in organization behaviour discussions that these differences between managers can be largely ascribed to their experiences. However Galavan's recent research challenges this assumption and raises the somewhat forgotten perspective of the leader's personality. While this is in no way an attempt to reopen the twentieth-century search for the 'ideal' leader, it is an attempt to recognize that even if there is no ideal profile, personality still matters. It matters because it shapes a leader's perception of the discretion available to them, and describes the mental bars that imprison them. Robert and John go on to discuss the approaches leaders can take to understand the role they play through reflective practice and unlearning some of the 'givens' they hold to be true. In their discussion of the airline industry they discuss the counterintuitive benefit of not 'knowing' the industry which accrued to some of its new low-cost entrants in the 1990s.

Developing the theme of innovation in organizations, **Lynda Gratton** introduces us to the concept of Hot Spots in organizations. Using the metaphor of thermal imaging, Lynda describes how these Hot Spots are inflamed through igniting questions and visions of the future rather than the classical command and control approach to management. Examples of Linux software development and Google, together with more traditional organizations such as BP, are used to explain the challenge of managing in a more sophisticated manner. Connecting with the earlier contribution from **Rob Goffee** and **Gareth Jones** and the importance of intellectual capital, Lynda extends it to a group level through the development of social capital where it is not just the individual that matters, but also the depth and extent of the relationships in the team. The creation of Hot Spots in organizations is therefore dependent on the reinforcement of emotional capital, intellectual capital, and social capital. Hot Spots in this world are developed through idea sharing in deep relationships and through exploration that extends beyond traditional boundaries.

Andrew Kakabadse, **Nada Kakabadse**, and **Linda Lee-Davies** take on the topic of governance, an area that has been regularly addressed in the popular press of late. Their chapter takes a very focused perspective on the role of the chairman in the governance of organizations and in particular how the chairman's role as leader affects organizational outcomes. Andrew and Nada provide an interesting perspective on the different structures and expectations for the role of chairman that exist around the world and go on to identify eight issues that affect the nature and impact of the chairman. They identify the influence of role boundaries including intra-board relationships, external relationships, and relationships with the CEO as significant factors that place expectations on the chairman. Role duality of CEO/chairman is a recurrent theme in the research and raises significant issues relating to accountability, development of organizational vision, and the pursuit of appropriate governance. Other issues they address included the tenure, domicile, and recruitment of the chairman as well as the emergence of the counterbalancing role of Senior Independent Director (SID) being adopted in the UK and the Lead Independent Director (LID) in the USA. What is clear from Andrew and Nada's study is that we are in a state of transition with the role of the board, directors, and chairman. While our state of the art knowledge in this regard is limited and it is hard to come to conclusions on the 'best' way forward, their chapter nevertheless articulates the challenges and issues to be addressed. It is also clear that whatever shape the board of the future will take and however we will describe the role of the chairman, the effect of their leadership will be felt and must be understood by the strategist.

Leadership, at whatever level it takes place in organizations, has moved on significantly from the command mentality of early management approaches. If we are to embrace the leadership of clever people and the development of organizational Hot Spots then the emerging importance of the leader as negotiator proposed by **Kathleen Reardon** and **Andrew McLaughlin** must be addressed. In an approach that echoes **Robert Galavan** and **John Cullen's** call for reflective leadership practice, Kathleen and Andrew present the Negotiation Style Inventory as a practical mechanism with which leaders can gain an understanding of their own negotiation style. By understanding their style predispositions, leaders can recognize the situations that challenge them and so can plan to stretch beyond their current limitations. By turning cognitive detective, leaders can use the style inventory tool as an intelligence-gathering instrument. One of the great challenges to stretching one's style is the need to understand how. Many leaders find that their style works in some situations and not in others, but are at a loss to understand what to do about the deficit. In a very practical way, Kathleen and Andrew provide a description of how leaders can stretch their negotiation styles to attend to the needs of others and go on to provide an extensive discussion on the development of a comprehensive negotiation capability that is so essential in our emerging collaborative organizational world.

The section concludes with a practical approach to the development of leadership talent. Despite the growing clarity of the leadership challenge that faces organizations, **Jay Conger** expresses his dismay at the uncoordinated and haphazard approach to talent management that he sees in organizations. In his chapter he describes talent management as a critical element of organization behaviour which should be addressed as a core competence that is no less valued than the organization's marketing or operational capability. Part of the challenge in managing talent is the nature of the beast which Jay describes as mobile and demanding. The advances in internet-based recruitment provide a fluid marketplace opening opportunities to an expanded range of employers and employees. The need for broad experience and the diminishing face of employer–employee loyalty provides encouragement for employees to take up these expanding opportunities. Jay argues that to deal with this situation organizations need to develop talent management systems with the dual aim of satisfying the organization's needs and the need of the employee. In this chapter Jay provides a detailed agenda to guide the development of talent management systems dealing with issues from strategic alignment to feedback mechanisms. If, as most of our contributors seem to agree, we need more innovative and adaptive organizations to deal flexibly with the twenty-first-century challenges we must have a system to develop, manage, and support our twenty-first-century leaders.

Notes

1. Michael E. Porter (1996) 'What is Strategy?,' *Harvard Business Review*, Nov.–Dec.: 61–78; Costas Markides (1999) 'What is Strategy and How do you Know if you Have One?,' *Business and Strategy Review*, 15 (2): 5–12.

Part I

Understand your Situation

1   The Economics of Global Competition: Implications for Business

Dermot McAleese and Gerard O'Brien

Introduction

The pace of globalization shows no signs of slackening. Standard indicators on foreign trade and direct foreign investment show a continuing rapid integration of national economies. This has resulted in a profound change in the economic environment facing business. New business models have emerged and delivery systems to market have changed, with a consequent need for business and policy makers to formulate appropriate strategic responses.

The aim of this chapter is to analyze the changes in the global environment that are of strategic relevance to business and to explore the implications of these changes for business behavior, taking Ireland as a case study.

Ireland's experience is particularly relevant to this discussion. The Irish economy is a globalized economy *par excellence*. Its role as a global production and financial intermediary is reflected in exceptionally high export and import ratios, enormous two-way flows of foreign capital, and growing migration flows in and out of the country. The United States is Ireland's major supplier of intellectual know-how and direct foreign investment; Asia has evolved into a growing source of intermediate manufactured imports; while trade in final products is predominantly transacted within Europe. Foreign workers now comprise 10 per cent of the Irish labour force. All these factors make Ireland a useful case study to illustrate how business and economic policy makers can respond to the challenges and opportunities of globalization and to the relentless search for higher productivity, more competitiveness, and new areas of specialization that global competition demands.

The chapter is divided into five sections. The *first* section describes the key features of the new economic environment. These features include greater openness and liberalized access to world markets, lower corporate and personal tax regimes, and an enterprise-friendly climate on the one hand, and the discipline of unrelenting and often unpredictable international competition on the other. The *second* section analyses the emergence of competitiveness as an overarching policy concern. In the early stages, attention focused primarily on measurement of cost competitiveness. Nowadays the range of components of competitiveness has been greatly extended. Innovation policy and investment in the knowledge economy have become crucial factors in economic and business strategy. *Third*, we discuss the role of direct foreign investment in promoting growth and in influencing economic policy. The *fourth* section focuses on new policies to encourage domestic industries to develop, innovate, and grow. New evidence is presented on the role of foreign subsidiaries as generators of new start-ups and on the degree of success of new venture and seed capital schemes in promoting indigenous high-potential entrepreneurship. Attention is drawn to the importance of marketed service activities as a generator of employment and to the role of the new policy framework in stimulating their growth. A summary and conclusion is presented in the *fifth* section.

The New Economic Policy Environment

During the past quarter-century economic policies throughout the world have converged around three basic pillars: competition and the market system, macroeconomic stability, and globalization.[1]

Three Pillars of the New Consensus

The first pillar is *competition and the market system*. It signals a shift in priority from state intervention to free market mechanisms in achieving policy objectives. The underlying principle should not be seen as a doctrinaire opposition to state intervention *per se*; but rather as a willingness to give market forces room to resolve supply or demand imbalances and to resort to state involvement only when there is clear evidence that it will deliver an improved outcome. The new policy orientation has led to the adoption of comprehensive privatization programmes in countries as diverse as Chile, Ireland, New Zealand, Vietnam, and the United Kingdom and to a pro-business, pro-enterprise stance by governments replacing indifference, and sometimes outright hostility, to business success.

For the market system to function efficiently, however, complementary policies are needed. For one thing, business must be given a strong incentive to invest and to innovate in response to market opportunities. In practice this means lower personal and corporate tax rates, a positive approach by government to the accumulation of personal wealth, the provision of specific incentives, and targeted interventions in relation to R&D and productivity improvement. Accompanying these changes, one observes an increasing emphasis on competition policy. Penalties for breaches of competition law have been stiffened, competition authorities in one form or another have sprung up both in developed and developing countries, and monopoly and anti-competitive practices have been outlawed. The practical implications of competition legislation in today's business environment cannot be ignored.

The second pillar is *macroeconomic stability*. The new consensus identifies the achievement of a stable framework of price stability, controlled government spending (relative to GDP), low budget deficits, and a sustainable debt/GDP ratio as key requirements for a well-functioning economy. Price stability (defined as inflation in the range 1–3 per cent) is necessary in order to allow the market system to do its job of allocating resources efficiently. Consistent price stability sets a clear and advantageous platform for efficient long-run investment decisions and saves on transactions costs. To achieve price stability requires good management of monetary policy by central banks. It also requires stable public finances and a sustainable public debt/GDP ratio so that governments will not be tempted to use inflation as a way of reducing the real burden of debt.

This line of thinking has led to a radical reappraisal of the role of fiscal policy in stabilizing an economy. There is more awareness of the limitations of counter-cyclical fiscal policy and more scepticism about its effectiveness except in extreme circumstances. A recent comment of the chief economist of the OECD encapsulates this more critical approach to fiscal policy:

> In theory, fiscal policy is supposed to mitigate the vagaries of the business cycle and smooth the tax burden across generations. It is also supposed to reallocate resources in a way that increases the well-being of societies. Alas, in many countries fiscal policy is doing exactly the opposite. Because it often exacerbates problems instead of alleviating them, fiscal policy increasingly turns out to be a problem rather than a useful instrument. (Jean-Philippe Cotis, OECD Economic Outlook, May 2006)

From a business perspective, macro stability means not only stable macro prices but it has the further advantage of ensuring that governments will have the financial capacity to maintain a low tax environment.

The third pillar is *globalization*. In economic terms, this refers to increasing integration in the world economy, including the adoption of outward-oriented policies; rejection of import substitution, liberalization of foreign trade, removal of restrictions on foreign investment and so on. Emphasis is placed on export promotion and participation in the WTO's rules-based trade regime. With each passing year national economies, rich and poor, large and small, are becoming more integrated and interdependent.

The New Consensus and the Irish Economy

Successive Irish governments have adopted new consensus policies with enthusiasm. In many respects Ireland is a classic case study of a new consensus regime, with a strong link between policy change, structural reforms, and improved economic performance. Consistent commitment to globalization, macro stability, competition and the market system, and low taxes has been the hallmark of Irish economic policy for several decades. Yet within this broad canvas there are peculiarities that differentiate Ireland from other new consensus countries. *First*, the orthodox new consensus policy regime was implemented alongside a distinctly unorthodox commitment to incomes policy. The 'social partners' (trade unions, government, farmers, private sector employers) played a major part in determining pay agreements. Social partnership helped to ensure wide acceptance of the new policy orientation, understanding of its implications, and the consistent application of economic policies by successive governments. This policy consistency, and the absence of social strife, was to prove immensely important. *Second*, social safety nets were preserved. The number of people falling below the absolute poverty income threshold fell markedly. Replacement ratios were reduced as a consequence of higher pay and lower taxes (i.e. by reducing the tax wedge, which by 2006 had become the second lowest in the OECD), not through cutbacks in social welfare payment. *Third*, proactive policies were used to promote industrial development. The Irish authorities had no ideological inhibitions about establishing state institutions such as the Industrial Development Authority (IDA) and Enterprise Ireland, the former charged with managing the inflow of direct foreign investment and the latter focusing on the encouragement of domestic enterprises. *Fourth*, while the new consensus tends to favor flexible exchange rates (determined by market forces) Irish governments have sought fixity and certainty rather than flexibility and had no hesitation in joining the euro area. Thus, although generally conforming to a new consensus approach, the Irish model did not follow any textbook blueprint and responded in a pragmatic way to the particular needs of the time.

New Consensus Policies and Growth

The causal link between adoption and consistent implementation of the new policy regime and subsequent economic performance has been much debated. To date the weight of evidence supports the proposition that the policy framework was a major contributing factor, and some would say the dominant factor underlying the Celtic Tiger. This is not to deny the importance of accompanying factors such as benign economic conditions in the developed

economies during the transition period and the importance of the simultaneous coexistence of a shift in policy and these favorable circumstances. Thus,
luck played a part, as did the process of cumulative and circular causation or
self-reinforcing change, which economists such as Gunnar Myrdal identified as
critical elements in economic development. For whatever reason, the new
policy regime is seen to have 'delivered.' Employment has increased and
average income per capita has soared since the late 1980s. For the first time
in living memory, Ireland has become a full employment economy, with low
government debt and government expenditure ratios to GDP and one of the
strongest growth trajectories in Europe.[2]

Economic growth under new consensus policies has generated new problems as well as new gains. For example, although the rate of absolute poverty
has sharply declined the *relative* gap between rich and poor widened—as
happened in most new consensus countries.[3] This may be an inevitable consequence of cutting income taxes and incentivizing entrepreneurship. At a
business level, the new policy regime signaled good news for firms that could
adapt successfully to the new environment and could benefit from improved
access to foreign markets. However, many companies found themselves under
severe competitive pressure even during the period of fastest growth. Their
experience illustrates the problem of the pacing of structural change and its
relation to cost inflation and competitiveness (pp. 19–21 below). Also there is
the longer-run challenge of devising a strategy to ensure that sufficient new
enterprises are created and sufficient change within existing firms occurs to
replace the inevitable turnover ('churning') of the present employment profile
(pp. 27–8 below).

Competitiveness as a Policy Imperative

Competitiveness has become a global preoccupation. Virtually every government worries about its competitiveness and wants to do something to improve
it. The European Commission frets about falling behind the USA in the
competitiveness league. Many European countries have set up competitiveness
councils. Mirroring and to some extent feeding this concern is the multiplica-
tion of new international competitiveness indices. The IMD's *World Competitiveness Scoreboard* and the World Economic Forum's *Global Competitiveness
Report* are published annually and attract wide publicity. Their findings are
scrutinized with a fine-tooth comb by development agencies and government
commissions. Movements up and down the rankings attract media comment
and political flack. The 2007 IMD indicators show Ireland was in first place,
followed by a number of small European countries. Ireland is ranked 14th
(down from 11th in 2006). These indices are based on data provided by national

statistics offices supplemented by specially tailored questionnaires. The result-ant data is then compared with the average value of the comparable data in competitor countries (the benchmark).

The search for competitiveness can be viewed as an inevitable consequence of globalization and the new economic policy environment. Competitiveness benchmarking is used to identify competitive weaknesses and strengths in the economy, at both a macro and a micro level, and to recommend appropriate policy measures. Improvement in competitiveness is seen as crucial to achiev-ing growth and full employment and as the essential corollary of engagement in an integrated world economy.

Definition of Competitiveness

Competitiveness was originally defined in a narrow sense, focusing on trends in pay, productivity, and unit costs, aggregated into a cost competitiveness index. This approach stressed the role of pay bargaining, labor productivity, and exchange rates. The importance of maintaining unit cost competitiveness was heavily emphasized, and with good reason. Deterioration in a country's cost competitiveness can cause many problems.

Suppose cost inflation in a country exceeds that in competitor countries. Sooner or later, the country will lose export markets and will become less attractive as a location for investment. Eventually GDP growth will be cut back and employment will decline. The speed of this process is not well defined. For example, Ireland's inflation has exceeded the EU average in every year since 2000 and as a result its price level stood at 12 per cent above the euro area level in 2005. Yet the economy has continued to boom and to enjoy full employ-ment. While the decline in cost competitiveness is unsustainable in the long term, exactly when and how equilibrating forces will come into play is difficult to predict. In practice much may depend on factors other than narrow cost considerations that affect the rate of return on investment. These 'other factors' have prompted researchers to seek more broad-ranging indicators. Thus Ire-land's *Annual Competitiveness Report 2005* defines national competitiveness as encompassing 'a diverse range of factors that support the ability of firms in Ireland to achieve success in international markets, in a way that provides Ireland's people with the opportunity to improve their living standards and quality of life' (p. 2).

The World Economic Forum defines competitiveness in an equally broad sense as 'the ability to achieve sustained high rates of growth in GDP per capita.'

Competitiveness measures the degree to which a nation or a region can, under free market conditions, produce goods and services that meet the test of international markets while simultaneously expanding the real income of its citizens and their quality of life.[4] The broader definition widens competitiveness to include factors such as a country's taxation and regulation regime, its economic infrastructure, education and training, and innovation and research. It recognizes that a country's long-run competitive position can be profoundly influenced by its policy towards research and development (R&D) and by its success in innovation and technology, two key ingredients of a country's economic infrastructure.

Ireland's Competitiveness Challenges

In a small open economy, the need to maintain and improve global competitiveness ranking must be given high priority. Ireland is no exception in this respect. Since 1997 the National Competitiveness Council (NCC) has published an annual competitiveness report that provides a rich store of information on competitiveness indicators and an innovative methodological framework for analyzing them. The NCC competitiveness pyramid depicts *sustainable growth* as the outcome of competitiveness (Figure 1.1). The *essential conditions* supporting this competitiveness are the conventional cost factors (costs, productivity, prices, etc.) alluded to above. The base of the pyramid (the novel part of the methodology) refers to *policy inputs* that over time have significantly impacted

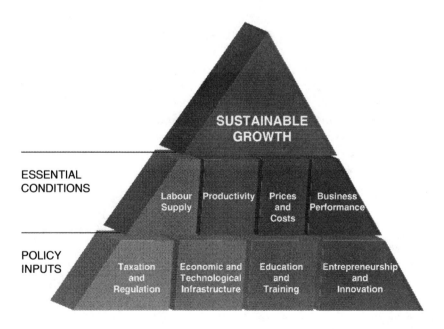

Fig. 1.1 The competitiveness pyramid

Source: National Competitiveness Council, *Annual Competitiveness Report 2005*.

on business costs. In the new policy framework, the design and implementation of these policy blocks plays a crucial role in determining how well the economy will function. An overriding theme of the Report, much in line with new consensus thinking, is the need to promote *a favorable environment for business* in order to remain at the forefront of international trade and competitiveness (*National Competitiveness Council Report 2006*, 8).

Formulating a policy to improve competitiveness is a complex task. *First*, competitiveness is a relative concept. Success in the competitiveness league depends on how well an economy is progressing relative to others. By definition if some countries rise in the competitiveness rankings, others must fall, even though all countries might have been growing faster, expanding employment, and enjoying better quality of life. The process of striving to rise in the world competitiveness ranking is a zero-sum game but, insofar as this process induces better economic performance, it has potential positive-sum side effects.

A *second* issue concerns the choice of benchmark. Should it be the average of all countries, or just the average of a selection of closely competing countries? And if the latter how to determine the criterion for deciding which country is a competitor? Ireland's NCC uses the average of fifteen countries as benchmark.[5] Interestingly, not one of these countries is a low-cost competitor. China and India are not seen as front-line competitors for Irish domestic producers; they compete with other low-cost producers not with Irish producers.

Third, the competitiveness ranking involves the use of a large number of indicators (170 in the case of Ireland). This involves a huge exercise in data organization and collection. It also gives rise to another important issue: the weight to be given to the individual factors that go into the competitiveness index. In Ireland many costs and price levels are considerably higher than those of its main competitors. Policy makers must decide on which factors are really crucial and which constraints are the most binding.

Policies to improve competitiveness have become a crucial constituent of national economic management. Ireland's current policy objectives have focused on creating an environment that encourages:

1. the growth of export-oriented firms, especially Irish-owned firms;
2. the retention and attraction of foreign direct investment in knowledge-based sectors such as electronics, pharmaceuticals, biotechnology, and software;
3. the development of linkages between existing and new greenfield firms;
4. continued investment in productivity improvements through automation, training, and research and development, and changing firms' behaviour;
5. the balanced locational distribution of economic activity.

While room for maneuver is to a significant extent circumscribed by EU obligations, small European countries have nevertheless found ample scope for forging new national policy initiatives.[6] Domestic authorities have responsibility for the provision of physical infrastructure, education and training, R&D policy, the structure of taxation, and many other aspects incorporated in the broad definition of competitiveness. The NCC's 2006 Competitiveness Report recommends (warning of dangers to competitiveness arising from the rapid growth of non-labour costs of doing business in Ireland) for the removal of restrictions and greater competition in these sectors as a way of controlling costs, action that is well within the remit of the government of a member state. It recommends better monitoring of public investment infrastructure projects and continued investment in education and research and a long list of specific measures to address these objectives.

The Irish economy continues to enjoy a relatively high place in the global competitiveness rankings in recent years—11th place in the IMD league, 21st place in the World Economic Forum's index, 7th out of 29 OECD countries in the Confederation of Danish Industry's comprehensive Global Benchmark Report 2006. Its success in this last ranking was mainly due to high productivity performance (the report drew on productivity data that did not take account of the dismal productivity statistics for 2005 and 2006) and an exceptionally high share of high-quality exports. The Danish report notes that the proportion of upmarket exports in total Irish exports has risen from 40 per cent in 1993 to 70 per cent in 2004.[7] This statistic may flatter Irish exports to some extent but there is no doubt that Irish policy has been informed by a belief that a major part of the production at the lower end of the price hierarchy will unavoidably move to low-wage countries in eastern Europe and Asia and that the future lies in the development of new unique products at the top end of the quality scale. In this respect, once again Ireland is not unique. Many countries are currently targeting the top end of the price hierarchy and are resorting to similar policy mixes to the Irish: use of advanced technology, better design and branding, better-quality material inputs. Staying ahead of the competition requires continuing emphasis on innovation and productivity.

Foreign Direct Investment (FDI) as a Driver of Change

The linkage between the new policy consensus, the pursuit of competitiveness, and FDI activity is extremely close. Foreign direct investment (FDI) has increased worldwide and it has become a potent measure of success in globalizing countries, the flag bearer of economic development and higher living standards and widely welcomed as such. In a reversal of historical trend, vocal criticism of FDI has given way to uncritical approval, at least in relation to FDI in the manufacturing and traded services sectors. If FDI was once viewed with excessive suspicion, the danger now is the opposite one of exaggerated expectations of its potential contribution to the host country.[8] In the case of Ireland the concerns now raised relate to the ability to retain FDI in the face of increasingly attractive low-cost locations in eastern Europe and elsewhere and the allied problem of persuading indigenous business to respond to the changed investment climate. Current strategy aims to foster a competitive business-friendly environment, through enhanced opportunities for research and technology absorption and through provision of a base of complementary enterprises that can benefit from networking in a single location.

Multinationals strive to make strategic investment decisions on the optimum location for different parts of their value chain. Recent research confirms that the share of FDI that is driven less by the prospect of securing supplies of cheap labour and materials is diminishing, although certainly this still remains an important consideration. For many investing firms, factors such as good governance, stable economic environment, sophisticated IT and physical infrastructure, a skilled and well-motivated workforce, protection of intellectual property, and access to growing markets are vitally important. Multinationals seek markets and efficient production locations, as much as cheap sources of labor supply. This reliance on a multifactor assessment increases as we move up the value chain.[9]

Host governments have a similar task on hand. They too search for a strategic approach to the new opportunities. Their challenge is to devise a strategy for attracting the type of foreign investment that will yield maximum positive spillovers for their economy. Strategic investments are sought that will generate net externalities in terms of innovation, capital investment, skilled job creation, and high value added activities. Inward R&D intensive investment can be particularly important in enabling the host country to integrate advantageously in global value chains by upgrading their innovation systems. In this instance, the potential effects are both direct (e.g. increased expenditure on R&D, high-quality employment, more market-oriented innovation) and indirect (market access and knowledge spillovers).[10]

A striking consequence of the new policy environment and the new consensus pillars has been the increasing range of activities that have become internationally mobile. Some of these are strategically important. Host countries such as Ireland, which have recently reached high standards of economic development, find that they have to attract new FDI activities such as R&D centres, location of regional headquarters, value added activities in financial sector (brokerage, investment banking, and portfolio management), shared services and contact centers, customer support operations, technological support, and business services. These activities account for as much as a quarter of total FDI activity. The remaining three-quarters are less intensively courted, and in some cases may not be particularly welcomed, because the economic benefits of FDI tend to be fully 'appropriated' by the foreign investor, leaving few positive spillover benefits for the host country and in some instance a net negative. Much FDI in the retailing and property sectors falls into this category.

Spillover Effects of Investment

Initially cost–benefit analysis focused on jobs directly and indirectly created by FDI subsidiaries. As unemployment has fallen, however, attention has shifted to the role of FDI in upgrading domestic labor skills and managerial expertise. The reasons for this are twofold. First, by raising productivity, the use of better-educated labor and the enhancement of skills insulates the affiliate from direct competition with low-cost suppliers. Second, a key economic benefit of enhancing managerial skills is that the managers working in multinational subsidiaries can use these skills to promote new projects and higher value added activities in the company that will anchor the multinational to an Irish location and ensure its continuance. A further positive spillover occurs where managers leave their positions in the multinational subsidiary in order to set up their own businesses locally. In this way, multinationals can perform a critical role in acting as *entrepreneurial nurseries*. A typical pattern is to establish enterprises supplying components to the multi-national plant, often done with the encouragement of their former employer.

Further positive externalities arise when additional jobs are generated by the multinational affiliate through backward and forward linkages. Barry suggests a 'ballpark estimate' of around 100 service sector jobs and 10 indigenous manu-facturing jobs created via backward linkages per every 100 employees at work in multinational subsidiaries in Ireland.[11] This is a fairly typical result, especially in countries where FDI is predominantly export oriented and 'crowding-out' of competing domestic enterprises is less of a problem. It represents a 'win-win' outcome and explains why local business organizations and trade unions are usually so supportive of this type of foreign investment inflow.

Positive spillovers explain why host countries court multinationals so assidu-ously. Are they *too* intensively courted? This question has been prompted by the provision by EU states of increasingly large tax and other fiscal incentives to multinationals. Since 'greenfield' FDI inflows in particular are sensitive to the rate of corporate and personal taxes, member states of the EU have lowered their tax rates in order to gain a larger share of global greenfield FDI. The perceived erosion of the EU-wide tax revenues has prompted the European Union to seek a degree of harmonization of the corporate profits tax base across the member states. Some see this as a prelude to harmonization of tax rates.

23

Understand your Situation

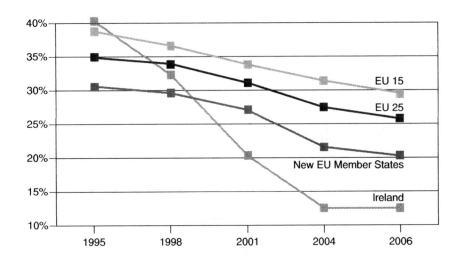

Fig. 1.2 Top standard tax rate on corporate income, 1995–2006

Source: Forfás (2006) *Annual Competitiveness Report*, i: *Benchmarking Ireland's Performance.*

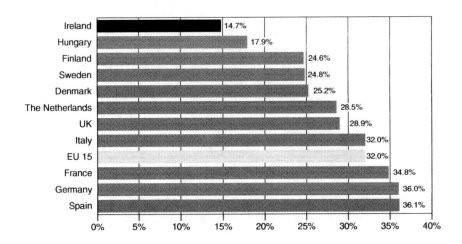

Fig. 1.3 Effective average tax rate on companies, 2005

Source: Forfás (2006) *Annual Competitiveness Report*, i: *Benchmarking Ireland's Performance*; Michael Overesh (2005) 'The Effective Tax Burden of Companies in Europe; *CESifo DICE Report* 4: 56–63.

As Figures 1.2 and 1.3 demonstrate, Irish standard and effective rates of corporate tax are indeed significantly lower than the EU-15 average. A key fiscal incentive in the Republic is the 12.5 per cent tax rate for all corporate income from 2003 and the Brussels-approved 'grandparenting' of the 10 per cent rate up to 2010 for all companies already in operation. Defenders of the low tax system argue that the market for FDI should be allowed to reach its own equilibrium, each country providing its own differentiated package of tax and infrastructure to incoming investors. The case for tax harmonization has validity only where countries are symmetric, in the sense that they offer equal attractions to an incoming investor. Foreign investors desire good physical infrastructure, a well-educated workforce, and a pleasant working environment as well as lower taxes. To some extent there is a trade-off between corporate tax rates and infrastructure. Core European countries continue to have different relative competitive advantages in terms of infrastructure, national innovations systems, proximity to major markets, and so on.

Frank Barry argues that any attempt to harmonize taxes would have seriously adverse consequences for low-tax countries such as Ireland, which have built up a strong FDI presence and which are highly dependent on continuing inflows of FDI to fuel economic growth. If the EU were to push ahead with tax harmonization, he argues, FDI would fall and the country would be forced to rely on its own domestic industry resources:

> Only 10 percent of indigenous manufacturing employment is in high-tech sectors, compared with 56 percent of jobs in the foreign sector. Indigenous manufacturing firms export less than one third of their output, which is quite low by EU standards, and are heavily concentrated on the UK market, making them vulnerable to currency fluctuations. They spend little on R&D and the sector has a poor record in developing patentable processes or inventions . . . If Ireland's foreign industry were to disappear precipitously, much of the economic progress made over the boom period could well disappear along with it.[12]

We argue below that the conventional narrative of a dynamic foreign sector contrasting with a moribund indigenous sector needs to be updated. The picture of a uniformly dynamic FDI sector has also to be modified. Several sectors in the stock of FDI have become uncompetitive and the relocation of multinational subsidiaries to low-cost countries has become an increasingly common phenomenon. In turn, this has prompted radical change in policy towards FDI.

While FDI continues to be actively sought, more emphasis is being placed on securing the right type of investment and there is more intense emphasis on building up linkages between the multinational subsidiaries, third-level institutions, and Irish-owned firms with the aim of strengthening domestic know-how and research capabilities. The new state aid rules governing R&D also offer incentives or bonuses for collaboration between companies and universities, following a long tradition of proactive state involvement to deal with market failures as a complement to new consensus policies.

Understand your Situation

Finally, while Irish policy has been preoccupied with inward flows of FDI for good historical reasons, the past decade has seen a major spontaneous upsurge in outward FDI flows. In 2004 and 2005, outward direct investment flows exceeded Ireland's inward flows by €23 billion and €36 billion respectively. Figures in UNCTAD *World Investment Report 2006* show that Ireland's outward FDI stock was 59 per cent of GDP in 2005 compared with only 35 per cent in Spain and a EU average of 41 per cent. The inward FDI stock (106 per cent of GDP) remains much larger than the outward stock, but outward FDI is growing rapidly. An indicator of the extent of this change is the fact that in 2006 affiliates of Irish companies in the USA employed as many as US affiliates employed in Ireland. Outward FDI has played an important role in the survival, growth, and prosperity of several of Ireland's major domestic companies in manufacturing and services.[13]

The new perspective on foreign direct investment flows, inward and outward, is both radical and comprehensive. It places in context the fact that, contrary to general impression, the *net* addition of jobs attributable to foreign multinationals in the Irish economy has been extremely modest in recent years. New jobs have been generated in Ireland by multinationals at about the same rate as they are being lost through rationalization of the Irish affiliates, closures, and relocations to lower-cost locations.

As Table 1.1 shows, the number employed in foreign-owned industry is no higher now than it was in 1999 and a significant decline has been suffered since the dotcom collapse in 2001. However, the quality of the resultant stock of FDI has been much improved. Labor productivity in the modern manufacturing sector (i.e. the overseas sector) has increased annually by 9.4 per cent in the decade to 2005, compared with 4.5 per cent in the indigenous sector.[14] This reflects the cumulative effect of more selective policies to inward FDI that are less focused on securing jobs on the ground, and more concentrated on the quality of jobs. The effectiveness of existing and future policies in encouraging the current stock of foreign companies to increase and/or to diversify investments into higher value added activities as well as in targeting new FDI in these areas will be a critical factor in sustaining Ireland's prosperity.

TABLE 1.1 Employment in industry and traded services, 1996–2005

	1996	1997	1998	1999	2000	2001	2002	2003	2004	2005
Overall total	246,356	262,335	276,806	293,420	317,173	313,681	304,821	296,507	295,493	298,372
Irish-owned	125,611	131,510	136,552	143,326	151,712	152,966	150,030	147,426	146,414	147,683
Foreign-owned	120,745	130,825	140,254	150,094	165,461	160,715	154,791	149,081	149,079	150,689

Source: Forfás Employment Survey 2005.

26

Realignment of Indigenous Industry: 'Strategic Churn' and Future Growth

Structural change in the Irish indigenous economy has received relatively little academic analysis.[15] This neglect is explained partly by the predominance of the foreign multinationals in terms of exports and productivity growth. Another factor is that the relatively static aggregate employment figures for indigenous industry have masked the radical transformation of the indigenous enterprise base that has taken place over the past decade. Declining sectors have experienced a fall-off in employment and sales, but this has been offset by job creation and export sales in new and diversifying companies operating in growing sectors, such as high-tech manufacturing and internationally traded services. This 'strategic churn' has resulted in a minimal net gain in aggregate employment (Table 1.2).

Employment in Irish-owned industry has increased by only 22,000 or 18 per cent since 1996. During this period, there were cumulative job gains of 150,000 and job losses of 124,000 illustrating the high turnover of jobs within the overall enterprise base. The 'churn' is clearly evident from figures of the percentage change in employment by sector (Table 1.3). Traditional sectors have continued to decline as they succumbed to international competition from low-cost economies. Between 1995 and 2005, employment in the Clothing, Footwear, and Leather sector fell by 71 per cent, Textiles by 53 per cent, Paper, Print, and Packaging declined by 22 per cent. The sharp decline in these sectors was offset by rapid growth in employment in internationally traded services, up 199 per cent to 21,961 in 2005, while sustained performance was achieved in sectors where Ireland has traditionally traded strongly, including food and advanced engineering. Although both of these sectors are classified as low-technology intensive, their ability to invest heavily in automation and R&D and to identify new market opportunities has ensured increased productivity and sustained performance. The substitution of new jobs in higher-value, more productive

TABLE 1.2 Full-time employment in agency-supported Irish-owned industry, 1996–2005

Year	1996	1997	1998	1999	2000	2001	2002	2003	2004	2005
Employment	125,611	131,510	136,552	143,326	151,712	152,966	150,030	147,426	146,414	147,683
Gains		13,168	14,258	14,614	17,494	19,851	15,379	14,841	13,681	13,594	13,835
Losses		−8,105	−8,359	−9,572	−10,720	−11,465	−14,125	−17,777	−16,285	−14,606	−12,566

Source: Forfás Employment Survey 2005 (revised). Data excludes County Enterprise Board client companies, i.e. manufacturing and traded services employing fewer than 10 employees.

TABLE 1.3 Employment change in Irish manufacturing, 1995–2005

NACE code/sector	% change in employment 1995–2005
Food products, beverages, and tobacco	14%
International services	199%
Basic and fabricated metal products	24%
Other sectors	74%
Other non-metallic mineral products	7%
Pulp paper and paper products; publishing and printing	−22%
Other manufacturing	10%
Machinery and equipment	1%
Wood and wood products	28%
Rubber and plastic products	−4%
Chemicals and chemical products	20%
Medical and precision instruments	104%
Electrical machinery and apparatus	−12%
Financial services	284%
Clothing, footwear, and leather	−71%
Textiles and textile products	−53%
Transport equipment	−2%
Electronic equipment	−15%
Office machinery and computers	1%

Source: FAS Employment Survey 2005 (revised). Data excludes County Enterprise client companies.

sectors for employment in the lower-value end of the economy is central to ensuring a sound indigenous base.

In addition to churning, we also need to take account of the productivity and indirect employment effects of expansion of Irish firms in overseas locations. Outward direct investment (ODI) strategies have led to the rapid growth of international traded services and manufacturing activities. Some of these activities are designed to facilitate increased exports from the Irish economy; others reflect emerging business models leading to investments in offshored elements of the value chain in more cost-efficient locations such as eastern Europe and China. It is easy to point to examples of Irish firms that have engaged in outward FDI strategies and have as a result become significant players in the global market (Riverdeep, Kingspan, CRH, Kerry Group, GlenDimplex, and Glanbia). Irish statistics do not fully reflect the international business development performance of either of these cohorts, adding to a misconception of an underdeveloped indigenous enterprise base. This misconception is further compounded by inappropriate comparisons between the performance of Irish SMEs and the rest of industry in Ireland, the latter being heavily influenced by affiliates of foreign multinationals.

Start-ups as an Indicator of Indigenous Realignment

Creating new employment opportunities through the support of export-oriented start-ups continues to be a central pillar of the national enterprise development agenda. Further evidence of the structural realignment within the indigenous enterprise base is revealed in the increasing number of High Potential Start-Up (HPSU) companies. This growth is attributable to strategic investments in education, research and development, and early-stage financing instruments while linkages from FDI activity in the economy and the impact of increased wealth on the national culture of entrepreneurship have also played an influential role.[16]

The increased focus on stimulating and encouraging HPSUs, combined with improved project building, increased availability of early-stage funding, and a strong emphasis on innovation and management teams, has yielded some significant results. A survey carried out by Enterprise Ireland showed a fourfold increase in the number of HPSUs between 1995 and 2005 (Figure 1.4).[17] A high proportion of these new enterprises are found in the software and international services sector, up from 10 per cent of all start-ups during 1989–93 to 63 per cent during 1999–2004. Industrial Products, which includes medical devices and life-sciences companies, also experienced strong growth. The firms in these sectors are competitive internationally; and levels and growth in productivity and value added per employee are extremely high.

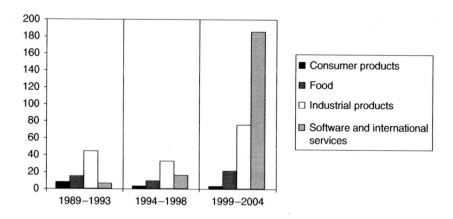

Fig. 1.4 Number of HPSU by sector, 1989–2004

Source: J. Barry and G. O' Brien (2004) *Review of Enterprise Ireland High Potential Start-up Companies.* Dublin: Enterprise Ireland.
Note: 1989–July 2004.

Understand your Situation

We can derive further insight into the main drivers of the emerging companies by examining the source or background of the entrepreneurs establishing HPSUs. Between 1999 and 2005, a total of 410 HPSU projects were supported by Enterprise Ireland. The entrepreneurs who started those businesses came from four main sources: indigenous businesses, MNCs, third-level institutions, and serial entrepreneurs (defined as an individual who has successfully started more than one business).

Special interest attaches to the spillover of entrepreneurs from Ireland's multinational subsidiaries. From an enterprise development perspective, this constitutes an important indirect economic benefit of the FDI strategy. Table 1.4 shows that 69 per cent of HPSUs between 1999 and 2005 have been started by industry-experienced entrepreneurs, i.e. individuals leaving existing employment to start new businesses. Initially most of these spin-outs emerged from MNC operations. However in recent years some Irish companies have spun out new enterprises as a result of managers and staff leaving to set up their own business or by the establishment of complementary subsidiary activities.

The assumption that *industry begets industry* holds true in the case of Ireland. The strategic clustering of companies (medical devices in Galway, financial services in Dublin, pharmaceuticals in Cork, and ICT in Limerick) also facilitated the growth of locally supplied support services and spin-out operations in and around a core base of multinationals and indigenous companies. Technology transfer, world-class manufacturing processes, and management development absorption have allowed Irish start-ups and established companies to develop the capabilities that are required to increase productivity and operate within the international marketplace. The favorable business environment and general economic prosperity are also attracting an increasing number of Irish expatriates to start technology companies in Ireland. It is hard to estimate how many exactly due to time lags that occur between returning to Ireland and actually starting a new business. Enterprise Ireland began recording this source

TABLE 1.4 Source of high-potential start-ups, 1999–2005

Source	'99	'00	'01	'02	'03	'04	'05	Total
Indigenous	7	26	17	12	32	26	33	153
MNC	18	15	21	22	12	22	19	129
Third level	0	2	5	8	12	5	9	41
Serial entrepreneurs	11	12	10	6	5	8	14	66
Miscellaneous	5	2	4	6	0	4	0	21
Totals	41	57	57	54	61	65	75	410

Source: Enterprise Ireland Database.

in 2003 and since then eighteen expatriate entrepreneurs have established HPSUs, a small number in absolute terms but with potential to increase.

Provision of Venture Capital to New Enterprise

Venture capital is a crucial component in the scaling of enterprises that have the ability to gain significant market presence as a result of a new innovative product or service. The Irish government has initiated several schemes to this end: the Business Expansion Scheme (BES), seed capital schemes, and more direct supports in the form of state equity investment in research and development projects at the level of the company, commercialization stage, and at exploratory research stage. However one of the most significant financing developments in the past ten years has been the development of an Irish venture capital industry.

The first Seed and Venture Capital Programme (1994–9) provided a state contribution of €66 million to act as leverage for further private sector equity capital. The objectives of the programme were:

- to provide equity and seed capital to SMEs, particularly those in the knowledge economy;
- develop the seed and VC market in Ireland;
- encourage private sector participation in seed and venture funds;
- develop seed and venture fund management skills within Ireland.

A second programme was funded under the 2000–6 National Development Plan. A study of the impact of VC-supported companies shows that 82 per cent of recipients were in ICT and healthcare and only 18 per cent in non-tech sectors.[18] The high-tech companies, as one would expect, were highly export oriented and spent a relatively high proportion of their sales revenue on R&D.

Productivity: A Priority for Sustainable Indigenous Development

Irish development agencies are responsible for formulating and administering programs to increase firm-level productivity. These programs include grant-based schemes such as the Enterprise Ireland Research Technology and Innovation (RTI) Scheme designed to stimulate R&D activity in existing enterprises (in order to generate new products and services or improved operational processes) and the Productivity Improvement Fund (PIF) that aims to stimulate companies to undertake investments in upgrading equipment, technology acquisition, and training projects to improve operational efficiency and become more competitive in their respective markets.

Industry Employment in Context: The Story behind the Story

The focus of this and the previous section of this chapter has been on industry and traded services. These activities are widely regarded as crucial to the long-run success of the economy. However, it is important to place their contribution in context of the entire economy. Total employment in the Irish economy rose from 1.2 million in 1994 to over 2 million in 2006, a rise of over 66 per cent (Table 1.5). This rise of over 800,000 contrasts with the increase in over 50,000 employed in manufacturing and internationally traded services during the same period (Table 1.1). We can allow for a multiplier effect that generated an estimated further 50,000 jobs down the line, and also concede that the 300,000 persons currently employed in Irish manufacturing and traded services are considerably more productive than their counterparts a decade earlier and that this too has indirect employment effects (say 100,000). Deducting 200,000 from 800,000 leaves we are left with a balance of 600,000 jobs unaccounted for, generated outside the manufacturing and internationally traded sectors, and largely beyond the purview of targeted public policy. How were these jobs generated?

This question still awaits a fully researched answer. Lack of *domestic* investment to link with and capitalize upon the inflows of FDI had for long been Ireland's weak point. Something changed in the 1990s in this respect. Spurred on by the industrial agencies and by the improved economic prospects, Irish-owned

T ABLE 1.5 Employment in the Irish economy, 1994–2006 (000s)

Economic sector (NACE Rev. 1)	1994	1998	2005	2006
Agriculture, forestry, and fishing	146.9	136.0	113.7	114.5
Other production industries	252.1	302.4	294.2	288.5
Construction	91.5	126.1	242.2	262.7
Wholesale and retail trade	169.1	211.1	266.9	284.4
Hotels and restaurants	68.4	97.8	111.0	116.3
Transport, storage, and communication	55.9	87.0	118.2	120.7
Financial and other business services	114.3	171.1	257.1	267.3
Public administration and defensce	66.4	70.9	98.2	105.1
Education	181	93.3	123.1	135.6
Health		113.9	188.0	201.2
Other services	74.4	84.5	116.4	120.6
Total in employment	1,220.6	1,494.0	1,929.2	2,017.0
Total unemployed		126.4	85.6	91.4
Total labour force		1,620.4	2,014.8	2,018.3

Source: CSO database. ILO definitions.

companies in the manufacturing sector started to grow instead of contracting and increased their workforce by 22,000. As already stated, productivity of that workforce rose rapidly (4.5 per cent p.a. 1995–2005), and with it real earnings and purchasing power. The development of the International Financial Services Centre (IFSC) in Dublin was another major landmark. With over 10,000 people now at work in IFSC activities, the IFSC has turned out to be an important employer and a source of significant tax revenue. In 2000, IFSC companies contributed about one-third of all receipts from corporation profits tax, equivalent to 0.5 per cent of GDP.

Arguably the big story—the story behind the standard Celtic Tiger story—is the growth in the marketed services sector, comprising a diverse array of activities, some exotic and high tech, others quite commonplace, ranging from construction to entertainment, from health services to travel and tourism. The latter are not headline catching but the fact remains that they happened to account for the vast bulk of the explosion in employment during the past decade and more.[19] Included in this category is Ireland's overseas property industry, some of it highly commercialized and other parts of it organized by self-employed entrepreneurs, enthusiastic exemplars of the new consensus regime. To date, this industry has generated substantial income and capital gains for those involved. Its precise extent and consequences have so far been relatively undocumented and under-researched. Some would hold that these marketed service activities are essentially endogenous, i.e. the consequence of the catalytic role spearheaded by the traded sector. We doubt if this is a wholly satisfactory explanation for several reasons. First, the introduction of a more vigorous competition policy opened up a wave of new business opportunities in sectors such as travel, tourism, communication, and financial services. Second, the lower corporate tax policies, originally intended for the exclusive use of the traded sector, were extended to the entire economy in response to complaints about their discriminatory impact on trade. This had major beneficial and probably unanticipated knock-on effects on a wide range of service industries, which in turn were further strengthened by the transformation to a low personal income tax regime during the 1990s and extending to the present. The new policy package also led to vastly improved access to capital for the self-employed entrepreneurs whose business propositions would have been given scant attention when the financial sector was protected and relatively insulated from outside pressures. However we leave a full discussion of these issues for a further paper.

Conclusions

The new consensus policy framework has helped significantly to create the Celtic Tiger. However, the Irish policy package has been differentiated by a strong emphasis on state activism in industrial development, discussed extensively in this chapter. While endorsing openness and market forces, the benefits of globalization have been sought through deepening and upgrading inward FDI and providing strong incentives to productivity and exports of indigenous firms. The government is actively involved in the pay bargaining process, in income distribution, and in the provision of state services. This chapter has examined the myriad ways in which this new policy regime and the move towards globalization are impacting both on the type of business activities being undertaken in Ireland and on the strategies that companies and policy makers will need to adopt in order to ensure continued growth and expansion in future.

Thus, in order to benefit from new consensus policies, a country must attain a high level of competitiveness. Much effort has been devoted to analysing how this competitiveness can be sustained and improved. It is essential that business and government are jointly involved in this process and companies must play their part in communicating the need for competitiveness to employees, customers, and government.

Does Ireland currently have a competitiveness problem? In one sense the answer must be no. The country has been one of the fastest growing in Europe, with low unemployment and strong fiscal parameters. This chapter has emphasized, however, that the comparative advantages and the policy initiatives that brought so much prosperity to Ireland in the past can no longer be relied upon to guarantee future growth. As we have seen, some policies have already been refocused—targeting and encouragement of more sophisticated and cost-resilient FDI activities, an increased commitment to indigenous sectors as drivers of future growth, and a heightened focus on measures that can achieve much needed productivity gains in the face of rising labour costs. In the case of foreign-owned industry the challenge is to deepen the linkages with the domestic economy and to move upwards on the value chain. All countries nowadays have ambitions to become a knowledge economy. The Irish authorities have no intention of being left behind in this race. Resources are being pushed into innovation at unprecedented levels. This change in landscape opens us huge opportunities for foreign and domestic investors and entrepreneurs.

Ireland's success in attracting FDI has been rightly acclaimed. The indigenous manufacturing and traded services sector industry has also played a strategically important role in the process. We have argued that the aggregate figure for net employment gains in this sector masks a major structural change from lower-to higher-productivity activities ('churning'). Considerable amounts of government money have been spent on developing indigenous high-potential start-ups and on providing a stronger R&D capacity and more seed and venture capital to Irish business. The results of this ambitious policy will need time to be realized. We show that there are some encouraging developments that augur well for the future growth of this sector.

Finally, we drew attention to the expansion of employment in non-government marketed service. This category includes financial services, construction- and property-related activities, and a myriad of personal and retail services. Some of these activities have expanded into uncharted areas, such as the development of Irish-owned multinational sandwich and fast food chains, international property development, and low-cost airlines. Further research is needed to discover to what extent growth in employment in these activities was the endogenous consequence of growth in the traded sector and to what extent it is the consequence of good overall policy making associated with the new consensus.

Notes

1. These ideas are further developed in Dermot McAleese (2004) *Economics for Business: Competition, Macro-stability and Globalisation.* 3rd edn. London: Financial Times/ Prentice Hall.
2. An extensive discussion of Ireland's globalization experience can be found in Michael J. O'Sullivan (2006) *Ireland and the Global Question.* Cork: Cork University Press and John O'Hagan (2005) *Economy of Ireland: National and Sectoral Policy Issues.* Dublin: Gill & Macmillan.
3. The reduction in tax rates has benefited new entrepreneurs and the already rich to a much greater extent than the average income earner. *'From San Francisco to Shanghai, Switzerland to Singapore, the Merely Rich are Becoming Super Rich,'* noted *The Economist,* 19 August 2006. Ireland could have been added to the list. CEOs have done particularly well out of the new policy regime. In the USA in 2004, the ratio of CEO compensation to that of the average production worker was 431 : 1; in 1982, it was 42 : 1. A similar pattern is evident in studies of remuneration of executives in top UK firms. Figures from the United States show that average income of the poorest 20% of American households grew by only a cumulative 5 percentage points during the period 1979 and 2003, while the income of the richest 1% of the population grew by 111%.
4. This widely adopted definition is a virtual paraphrase of that set out by the US President's Commission on Industrial Competitiveness in 1985. Big economies are prone to worry about their competitiveness as well as small countries.
5. The countries are: Denmark, Finland, France, Germany, Hungary, Ireland, Italy, Korea, the Netherlands, New Zealand, Poland, Spain, Switzerland, USA, UK.
6. Paradoxically as policy objectives have become more ambitious, the scope for independent economic policy to achieve these objectives has become more constrained. Thus monetary policy is determined by the ECB in Frankfurt, not by the Central Bank of Ireland. Fiscal policy of EU countries is constrained by the terms of the revised Stability and Growth Pact. EU policies agreed in Brussels have significantly eroded national discretion in areas such as competition policy, state aids,

taxation, agricultural support, and foreign trade. Hence it is important for any small country to deploy what discretionary power it possesses with maximum effectiveness. In Ireland, as in other countries, a major effort has been put into this project through setting up think tanks and special groups involving the social partners and academics to recommend policy initiatives. The report of the Enterprise Strategy Group (2004) *Ahead of the Curve: Ireland's Place in the Global Economy.* Dublin: Forfás, would be a typical example of this type of exercise.

7. Upmarket products are defined as groups of goods capable of earning a price that is at least 15% above the level of corresponding goods in the exports of the other EU-15 countries (Confederation of Danish Industry (Dansk Industri) (2006) *Global Benchmark Report 2006: Ready for Globalisation?* Copenhagen.

8. The impact of FDI, however, varies by sector: FDI in natural resources has different effects from FDI in manufacturing, Likewise, there is a difference between economic effects of export-oriented FDI and domestic market-oriented FDI.

9. A. T. Kearney has recently compressed all these factors into a single FDI Confidence Index. China, India, and the United States stood at the top of this index in December 2005. Ireland does not appear to have been included but our guess is that it would score highly in such a ranking.

10. UNCTAD *World Investment Report 2005* shows that R&D offshoring has increased in recent years to about 15% of total R&D expenditure in 2003 (up from10% a decade earlier). R&D is no longer a strictly central activity but an activity that builds upon global innovation networks. For a discussion of these issues see D. Audretsch (2000) 'Knowledge, Globalisation and Regions: An Economist's Perspective,' in J. Dunning (ed.), *Regions, Globalisation and the Knowledge Based Economy.* Oxford: Oxford University Press; R. Narula and A. Zanfei (2004) 'Globalisation of Innovation: The Role of the multinational enterprises,' in J. Fagerer et al., *Handbook of Innovation.* Oxford: Oxford University Press.

11. See Frank Barry (2004) 'Export Platform FDI: The Irish Experience,' *EIB Papers*, 2; Frank Barry and Colm Kearney (2006) 'MNEs and Industrial Structure in Host Countries: A Portfolio Analysis of Irish Manufacturing,' *Journal of International Business Studies*, 37 (3); F. Ruane and A. Ugur (2005) 'Export Platform FDI and Dualistic Development,' *Transnational Corporations.* A comprehensive overview is provided in F. Ruane and A. Ugur (2005) 'Trade and FDI in Manufacturing and Services,' in C. Newman and J. O'Hagan, *Economy of Ireland: National and Sectoral Policy Issues.* Dublin: Gill and Macmillan.

12. Barry, 'Export Platform FDI.'

13. Mary Everett draws attention to the misconception that outward direct investment (ODI) is a negative factor for the economy and goes on to argue for a broader assessment of its economic significance. As companies become very large in their home market, they can access overseas markets through supplying from their home base or, alternatively, setting up operations abroad. ODI to lower-cost locations allows Irish multinationals to access low-cost locations and/or skills, technologies, and patents, which may not be available locally. The Irish economy

also benefits, as she points out, from profit repatriation to resident Irish multi-national parents. Mary Everett (2006) 'Foreign Direct Investment: An Analysis of its Significance,' *Central Bank of Ireland Quarterly Bulletin*, 4: 105.

14. These figures are taken from J. Sexton (2007) 'Trends in Output, Employment and Productivity in Ireland 1995–2005,' in C. Aylward and R. O'Toole (eds.), *Perspectives on Irish Productivity.* Dublin: Forfás.

15. An important exception is P. P. Walsh and C. Whelan (2000) 'The Importance of Structural Change in Industry for Growth,' *Journal of the Statistical and Social Inquiry Society of Ireland*, 29.

16. Under the current support system in Ireland, a start-up is classified as an HPSU if it satisfies the following criteria: (1) plans to operate in either the manufacturing sector or in an internationally traded service sector in an export-led environment, (2) proposed product or service is technologically advanced, (3) likely to achieve significant growth within three years (i.e. sales above €1 m and employment of ten or more), (4) projected sales have a heavy export element, and (5) the business is Irish owned and located in Ireland.

17. Enterprise Ireland was established in 1998 as a result of the Culliton Report recommendation to merge a number of agencies responsible for supporting indigenous industry into one organization that could provide 'holistic' support to businesses. Any reference to Enterprise Ireland includes these previous agencies.

18. Irish Venture Capital Association (2005) *Impact of VC on the Irish Economy.* Forfás.

19. An example of an extensive new 'industry' that has developed unexpectedly from under our noses, without any state assistance whatsoever, is investment in foreign property. This investment has been led by Irish property developers, but numerous individuals of modest means, spread all through Ireland, who would not necessarily have pretensions to be described as entrepreneurs, have also participated. The appetite for property (at home and abroad) has been whetted by lucrative returns to date. One could argue this is as valid and valuable a way of earning income and adding to Ireland's GNP as investment in manufacturing or agriculture.

2 From Customer Understanding to Strategy Innovation: Practical Tools to Establish Competitive Positioning

Cliff Bowman and Richard Schoenberg

Introduction

This chapter is concerned with strategy development at the business unit level. It sets out to provide practical techniques that executives can use to understand their current competitive positioning and the strategy options that may be available to them. This includes both incremental developments of existing competitive strategies and the opportunities for more radical strategy innovations. Our emphasis is on explaining available strategy development techniques and how they might be used in practice, rather than on making further theoretical contributions to the topic.

The critical strategic question at the business level is how the firm can gain and sustain competitive advantage. The chapter begins by emphasizing the importance of understanding the target customer and what their needs are. This approach allows competitive positioning to be seen in terms of two fundamental business-winning criteria—how customers perceive the products/services they are being offered and the prices they are being charged. The resulting positioning map, or customer matrix, then serves as a powerful tool to identify the future strategic moves that are open to the business, again in terms of the fundamental business-winning criteria of perceived use value and price. We outline some of the common options available for improving competitive position and discuss the conditions under which each is likely to be successful. The approach is an extension of traditional 'positioning' views of strategy development, but importantly takes a demand-side rather than supply-side perspective.

Recently there has been much discussion of strategy innovation, the creation of new business models that challenge the existing industry logic and aim to change 'the rules of the game.' Many of the developments in strategy innovation have also emphasized the importance of taking a customer-centered approach. In the second part of the chapter we outline some of the techniques available to assist with strategy innovation and show how they can be used to complement the positioning approach to formulate innovative competitive strategies. In particular we focus on how executives might identify opportunities to radically reconfigure the use value offered to customers and/or the price at which their products can be sold. Some have argued that the recent weight attached to strategy innovation represents a revolution in strategic thinking. The treatment we present reflects our view that strategy innovation is most usefully seen as an evolution of conventional approaches to strategy formulation.

Understanding Customer Value: PUV Charts

Ultimately competitive strategy is about winning business. To win a customer's business the firm must offer a package perceived to be superior to alternative offerings, to offer more 'value for money.' Value for money is a subjective judgement the customer makes when they assess the use values on offer in the products or services, and the prices charged, which they then compare with alternative providers. The 'value for money' judgement they make is the difference between what they would be *prepared* to pay for the product, less the price charged. This is what an economist calls *consumer surplus*; so another way of describing 'value for money' is consumer surplus. We make a sale when we offer more consumer surplus than a competitor. Superior consumer surplus can come about in two ways:

- The use values or utility of our product are superior to competitors;
- The use values we offer are equivalent to competing offers but the price we charge is lower.

We explain later how these two dimensions can be used to explore competitive positioning and the implications of pursuing alternative competitive strategies. However, first it is necessary to understand the dimensions of use value that customers seek from our product or service—what is 'valuable' in the eyes of the customer? This question can only be answered by trying to understand how customers make purchase decisions. The process of constructing a Perceived Use Value chart can help to develop such insight. An example PUV chart is shown in Figure 2.1. It refers to a 40-year-old male seeking a new executive saloon car. The horizontal axis shows the dimensions of use value that are perceived as important by the focal customer. In this case our customer is seeking styling (he wants to look the part), performance, brand strength, engineering strength (he needs reliability), and build quality (he plans to keep the car for some time). The figures in brackets are the relative importance, or weighting, that the customer attaches to each dimension. The vertical axis shows the customer's perception as to how well each competitor's product delivers against the desired dimensions of use value. Figure 2.1 is drawn such that the three competitor products, R, S, and T, have been ranked by the customer relative to our firm's product (car Q), which appears as the baseline. Experience has shown that benchmarking in this way against the firm's own product aids the process of rating competing products along each dimension. Alternatively, the vertical axis can be an absolute percentage rating scale (as used in some of our later examples).

A PUV chart is constructed from the perspective of an individual customer. For example, we would all have slightly different perceptions of the same collection of saloon cars portrayed in Figure 2.1. What we would be looking for in terms of perceived use value, or utility, from the purchase of a car would be different from one customer to the next. How we individually assess alternative products will also vary. This means that in trying to understand customer behaviour we must be prepared to recognize that there may be important but subtle differences between potential customers. In practice, of course, it is unlikely to be feasible to develop a separate chart for every individual customer. However it may be possible to focus on groups of

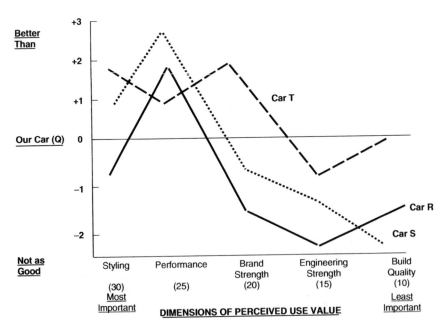

Fig. 2.1 Dimensions of PUV chart

Note: (30) weighting of PV dimensions.

customers who share similar perceptions of use value—i.e. alternative segments of demand. A series of charts constructed for different segments can highlight the relative attributes of the firm's own product and how these are valued by different types of customer. The result can serve as an accessible graphical decision aid as to which customer group to target and which dimensions of PUV to emphasize in any marketing campaign.

The critical feature of a PUV chart is the list of dimensions of use value perceived as important by the focal customer; the horizontal axis in Figure 2.1. The process of constructing the chart serves as a catalyst for a debate about what it is that the customer *really* values. In many cases the management team may undertake the exercise themselves as an initial step, relying on *their* perceptions of customers and their needs. However, it can be dangerous to rely on internal company perceptions because these are often shaped by the firm's own corporate culture and the dominant industry logic. The management team may, as a group, share a set of assumptions about customers and their needs which may not actually reflect the customers' true perceptions. This can be a particular problem in industries where executives have a strong 'technical' background. They are excited and impressed by the technical features of their products, and they assume that the customer values these features in the same way. Furthermore, customers may make purchase decisions on criteria that may not appear to be 'objective' or 'rational.' Indeed, in some cases customers may not be willing, or readily able, to explain their decisions. For example, in addition to the 'rational' dimensions of use value shown in Figure 2.1, further in-depth customer interviews revealed a set of 'emotional' car-buying criteria, with high weights attached to factors such as the ability to impress friends and colleagues and the reinforcement of executive status.

The only way to get fully reliable information on customers' perceptions is to engage in a dialogue with them. This can be done through focus groups, professionally conducted, that move beneath the obvious and tap into the underlying perceptions and motivations of customers. Alternatively, it is possible to glean valuable information through routine interactions. Where the organization has regular contacts with customers, these can be used unobtrusively to build up a picture of their perceptions of your performance and their views of competitors. This is especially appropriate in business-to-business selling. Note that the contact points for this intelligence may be at quite 'low' levels of the organization. This suggests some implications for how the process of formulating a competitive strategy should be managed. For example, the process may well need to include staff involved in operations, sales, and service activities, because the required information may be at these levels, not with the senior executives.

The Customer Matrix and Competitive Positioning

We began this chapter by arguing that competitive strategy is about winning business, which, in turn, requires a firm to either offer higher use value to customers than competitors, or offer the same use value but at a lower price. The 'customer matrix' uses the dimensions of perceived use value and perceived price to analyze competitive positioning and explore potential competitive moves. It provides a highly practical analysis because it frames the discussion of competitive strategy in terms of the two dimensions which define how business is won in the customers' eyes—perceived use value and price. The deliberate separation of these two components of 'value for money' assists us in analyzing competitive strategy.

The customer matrix is derived from the perceptions that customers have of the products/services being offered to them and the prices that they are being charged. The vertical axis is 'Perceived Use Value' (or PUV) and refers to the value perceived by the buyer in purchasing and using the product or the service. The position of competing products on this axis is derived from the construction of a PUV chart. This requires some simple arithmetic. For each product, its rating on each dimension of PUV is multiplied by the weighting for that dimension. These are then summed to produce an overall PUV score for each competing product. The horizontal axis is Perceived Price. Perceived price refers to the elements of price that the customer is concerned with. For example, in purchasing a heating system for a house the customer may be not only concerned with the initial cost of the installation, e.g. the price of the

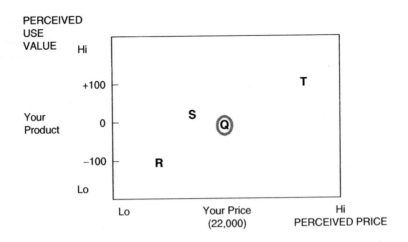

Fig. 2.2 Customer matrix

boiler, radiators, and installation, but she may also be interested in the running costs of the system over the years, like fuel costs, maintenance, etc.

Figure 2.2 shows the customer matrix generated for our 40-year-old male saloon car buyer. The position of the four competing products on the vertical axis is derived from the Figure 2.1 PUV chart. Our customer's perception of the price of each car is shown on the horizontal axis. This takes into account our customer's perception of the relative insurance and running costs as well as the initial purchase price. The resulting customer matrix provides a graphical representation of the competitive positions of our firm's product, car Q, as well as those of its three competitors, cars R, S, and T. The matrix offers insight into the firm's current competitive position. It can serve to open debate into issues such as: Who is our closest competitor? Why are we winning or losing business relative to them? Are new entrants a possibility? If so where might they try to position themselves? In this instance our main competitor is likely to be car S, which is offering higher levels of PUV for the target customer but at a lower price. Thus we would expect to lose market share relative to car S. Note also that products R, Q, and T are lying on a 'value for money' curve; that is, each offers the consumer equal value for money, as the PUV obtained rises in a curve-linear relationship to the perceived price. A value for money curve can be identified in many markets and where all the products lie on the curve the competitive situation can be relatively stable. Here car S is positioned north of the value for money curve and offers the customer superior PUV for the price.

The customer matrix also serves to highlight the strategy options available to a firm. To illustrate this let us turn to the more generic example shown in Figure 2.3,

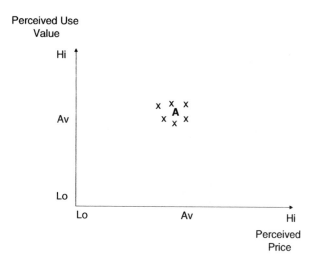

Fig. 2.3 Customer matrix for commodity-type market

Understand your Situation

where the 'Xs' represent the positions of products in the matrix. As far as the customer here is concerned all the firms are offering more or less equivalent products, and are charging very similar prices. This situation can be found in an increasing number of industries, not just those that are supplying obvious 'commodity' products like gasoline or car insurance. If firm A is facing the situation depicted in Figure 2.3 what are the options available for improving its competitive position? The firm could cut price by moving westward in the matrix, or it could raise the perceived use value of the products or services it offers (moving northwards), or indeed do both at the same time, a move north-west. These basic competitive strategies will now be explored.

Cutting Price

Here the firm moves *west* in the customer matrix, offering the same perceived use value as the competition, but at a lower price (see Figure 2.4). Such a move should lead to firm A gaining share. This move may not only increase sales for firm A; it may expand the market as a whole, if new consumers are attracted by the lower prices. However, other firms are likely to respond to the move by cutting prices to match firm A to preserve their share of the market, or they may even undercut firm A. Other things being equal, the net result of the competitors moving west with firm A is to reduce average price and profitability in the industry.

Competitors can imitate firm A's price-cutting strategy very rapidly, overnight if necessary. How then can firm A hope to gain an enduring advantage from competing on price? In order to achieve a sustainable advantage, firm A must be able to continually drive down prices and be able to sustain lower

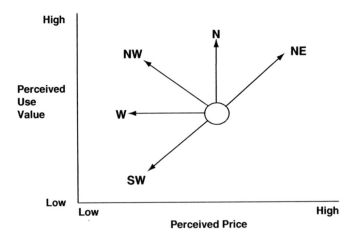

Fig. 2.4 Competitive strategy options

prices for a longer period than its competitors. This can only be achieved if firm A has either the lowest costs in the industry, or if the firm is able to sustain losses for extended periods, through subsidies from another part of the corporation, or from a government. If a firm is not the lowest-cost producer then the competitor that *is* lowest cost can always cut prices further, or sustain low prices for longer than firm A. So, if a firm chooses to compete on price it needs to have lower costs than its competitors. This involves exploiting all sources of cost reduction that do not affect perceived use value, e.g. economies of scale, learning from experience, 'right first time' quality, just-in-time manufacturing.

Adding Perceived Use Value

The second basic strategy indicated in the customer matrix is the move *north*: gaining advantage through adding more perceived use value for the same price as the competitors' offerings. The starting point for this strategy must be the target customer, and the target customer's perceptions of value. In order to effect this move north, rather than it resulting from luck, or trial and error, we must be clear who our target customers are. We must then have a thorough understanding of the target customer's needs, and how that customer evaluates different product offerings.

The customer uses various criteria to evaluate the extent to which a particular product can deliver a particular dimension of PUV. For example, how is 'performance' in a car evaluated? For some customers acceleration is critical, which may be assessed by inspecting the 0–60 mph statistics; for others it is top speed that counts. More interestingly, how is 'build quality' assessed? The customer may make inferences about build quality by interpreting the sound the car door makes when it is closed. Build quality might also be assessed by inspecting the alignment of body panels, or the paint finish. These may actually be very poor indicators, or poor proxy measures of build quality. However, as customer perceptions are paramount, it is essential that the firm understand what criteria the customer does use in making these evaluations, even if the customer is 'wrong.'

By systematically exploring customer needs and perceptions through market research and by continually listening to customers, firms can discover what is valued in their products and services and what could be added to them to improve perceived use value.

Let us return to Figure 2.1, where our firm's product is compared against the three closest rival cars. It appears that our firm's car (product Q) is seen to be inferior to the competition on the really important dimensions, but it performs well on the less valued dimensions. If our firm is to move north in the customer matrix then we either have to significantly shift the consumers' perceptions of our car's performance and styling, through changing the product, or maybe through changing perceptions through better advertising. A more ambitious strategy might be to try to shift consumers' perceptions of the dimensions of use value. For example, it may be possible to persuade the target customer that engineering strength is more important than styling. Either way, unless our firm improves its position relative to the competition on these dimensions of perceived use value it will lag behind its competitors such as car S. If we remain in a weaker PUV position we may find ourselves forced to cut price to try to preserve sales.

As with the price-cutting strategy, the key issue facing a firm pursuing a strategy of adding perceived use value is the ease with which competitors can match its move north. As a firm moves north by increasing perceived use value ahead of its competitors, it should be rewarded with an increased share of the market. Over time, it is likely that competitors will be able to imitate the move north by either acquiring or developing the required assets, and, as they follow the innovator northwards, the *average* level of perceived use value in the market is ratcheted upwards.

Thus in most industries the minimum acceptable standards of PUV are being continuously shifted upwards as competitive moves become imitated: 'order-winning' features become 'order-qualifying' features. For instance, anti-lock brakes and air bags are features of cars that were once order winning, which are now required just to be a player. Thus, the issue of sustainability of competitive advantage needs to be considered against this backdrop of continual northward shifts in the competitive arena. What can the innovator do once the competition has caught up? There are two basic options: keep moving north by staying one jump ahead of the competition through innovation, or move west through a cut in price.

But we argued earlier that, in order to compete on *price*, the firm needs to be the lowest-cost producer in the market. So, can you move north by adding perceived use value, and simultaneously achieve the lowest-cost position? If the move north increases market share, and if these share increases are translated into lower unit costs, through developing scale and pursuing experience-based savings, then there is no reason why the move north could not result in a low relative cost position.

Furthermore, if you *really* understand what it is that customers perceive as value in your products or services, you can confidently strip out everything that does not feed through to perceived use value. There is no point in offering a range of costly options, if this is not really what customers want. Of course, if you are not confident about what customers' needs are and how they evaluate alternative products then, to play safe, the tendency is to leave everything in the product, because you are not sure which parts of the total package are the valued features. Value innovation analysis, discussed later, can offer important insights here.

Other Competitive Moves

If the firm offers higher perceived use value, but demands a price premium for this added value, then this moves the firm's product position to the *north-east* in the matrix (Figure 2.4). The success of this strategy depends upon the existence of a group of buyers who are prepared to pay higher prices for the added perceived value. It also depends upon the ease with which the added perceived use value can be imitated. If it can readily be imitated by competitors then the price premium may be rapidly competed away. One other point to note with this move to the north-east is that it may well be shifting the firm's product into a new segment, where customers have different dimensions of use value, and where they may perceive the firm to be competing with different competitors. Moving into this unfamiliar ground can prove to be risky.

Moving *south-west* by cutting price *and* perceived use value is a diagonal move, which may well shift the firm into a new market segment. For example, if a car manufacturer located in the middle ground of the car industry (e.g. Ford) took this route it would be moving to a downmarket position. Whereas Ford's competitors might have been Toyota, Nissan, General Motors, and Daimler Chrysler, they would now find themselves being compared by potential customers with less prestigious, low-price, manufacturers. This may be a viable shift as long as the relative cost position of Ford enabled them to operate profitably against these low-price competitors.

The only direction that is guaranteed to deliver an increased share is a move *north-west*, adding value *and* cutting price. The firm must be the lowest-cost producer, and it must be able to move faster than the competitors to sustain its relative position. Typically, however, a competitive firm will move north initially by adding value, then when competitors imitate the added value the firm shifts west by cutting price. The share advantage gained through moving north may well enable the firm to become the low-cost producer through the achievement of scale and experience economies, making the price-cutting strategy feasible. So the north-west position is reached by moving north, then west.

Movements in the customer matrix are determined by changes in customer perceptions of price and perceived use value. Shifts of particular products in the matrix can occur even when the producing firm does nothing. If a competitor is able to move its product north by adding PUV then this has the effect of pushing other competitors' products *south* in the eyes of the customer. Products can be repositioned through changes in customer tastes and preferences, which can alter the dimensions of PUV seen to be important by the customer. This may result in products well endowed with the preferred dimensions of PUV moving further north.

Strategy Innovation

There has been much interest in recent years in strategy innovation, the creation of new business models that challenge the existing industry logic and aim to change 'the rules of the game.' Well-known examples of strategy innovation include Ryanair, the low-cost airline, which successfully challenged the high-service–high-cost formula of the European airline industry to become one of the fastest-growing carriers. Similarly, Direct Line Insurance transformed the UK insurance industry by offering direct underwriting via a telephone call, thereby cutting out the traditional insurance broker and reducing the established cost structure of the industry by 25–40 per cent. In the world of fashion retailing the Spanish firm Zara challenged more mature rivals by applying just-in-time techniques to enable it to bring catwalk fashions to its stores within fifteen days of their design. Over the past decade it has grown turnover tenfold yet maintains one of the highest profit margins in the industry.

Each of these companies has successfully created a new business model which has 'changed the rules of the game' within their industry. As Gary Hamel puts it, 'Strategy innovation is the capacity to re-conceive the existing industry model in ways that create new value for customers, wrong-foot competitors, and produce new wealth for all stakeholders.'[1]

Looked at in another way, each of the above examples of strategy innovation can be seen as a path-finding move on the customer matrix. Each redefined the accepted norms of PUV and/or price and forced competitors to re-evaluate their previous strategies. Ryanair and other low-cost airlines pioneered direct booking over the internet with 24/7 availability. This has added an important new dimension of PUV to customers, which traditional competitors have had to recognize. Zara's ability to bring constantly changing fashions into their stores has led to customers attaching more weight to this dimension of PUV, with a new awareness that they do not need to be limited to spring and autumn collection changes. More generally, moving north based on an understanding of current customer perceptions of use value is unlikely to be successful if a strategic innovator emerges that changes consumers' desires and expectations of the product's utility. Strategy innovations may also introduce radically different cost structures and, in turn, customer expectations of price. Again, Ryanair provides a leading example. Their low-cost business model allowed pan-European flights to be offered for tens rather than hundreds of pounds. Traditional airlines who had previously been attempting a move west on the customer matrix would have found their strategy comprehensively outpaced.

The Importance of Considering Strategy Innovation

The possibility of strategy innovation occurring in your own product market clearly warrants consideration when formulating competitive strategy. First, it may highlight an opportunity for strategy innovation that your business can exploit. Second, it provokes awareness of how others may attempt to change the rules of the game within your industry. It is notable that all three of the above examples occurred in industries that would have been described as mature (airlines, insurance, and fashion retailing). Yet in each case these mature industries have been transformed in potentially unforeseen ways by firms that were relatively new entrants into the industry.

Recent research into strategy innovation has provided a number of techniques to aid the identification of innovative strategies. Many of these developments have also emphasized the importance of taking a customer-centered approach and therefore provide a useful complement to the analyses discussed earlier in this chapter. In the sections that follow we outline two techniques that can offer insights into how we might identify opportunities to radically reconfigure the use value offered to customers and/or the price at which our products can be sold.

The techniques are particularly applicable to product markets characterized by widespread competitive imitation and a consequent lack of product differentiation. These 'near commodity' type markets are typified by the form of PUV chart shown in Figure 2.5, where customers perceive very little difference between individual

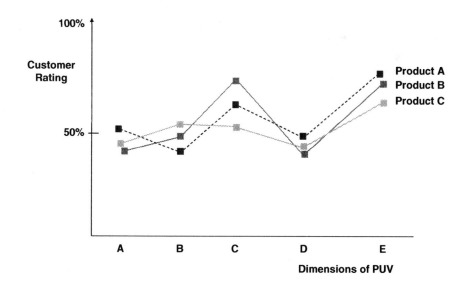

Fig. 2.5 PUV chart for market suffering strategic convergence

product offerings and purchase decisions become based solely on price. It is a paradox of today's business environment that while some companies are pursuing innovative strategies that redefine their industries, the majority of companies are pursuing strategies that are becoming ever closer to those of their competitors. The danger with such strategic convergence is that it is invariably accompanied by declining profit margins over time as pricing pressures take their toll. Attempts to compensate through cost-based advantages are frequently also subject to rapid imitation, possibly fueled by consultants selling the same best-practice 'solutions' across an industry. Strategy innovation potentially offers a way to escape from the head-to-head competition that strategic convergence inevitably leads to.

The Identification of Innovative Competitive Strategies

Value Innovation Analysis

The first technique builds on the PUV charts introduced earlier. A PUV chart shows the dimensions of use value that customers currently seek and how well the present product offerings match up to these. A 'value innovation' analysis, as proposed by Chan Kim and Renee Mauborgne,[2] considers whether there are opportunities to reconfigure the overall value proposition offered to customers, for example by exploiting key trade-offs which may exist between dimensions of use value.

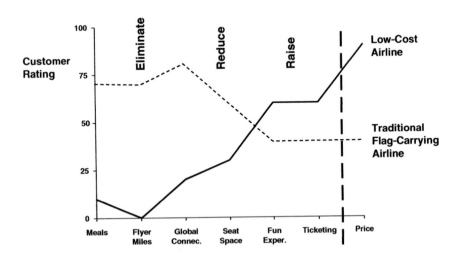

Fig. 2.6 Value innovation analysis for the European airline industry

Note: The product features and ratings are illustrative only.

Figure 2.6 shows an example of this type of analysis applied to the European air travel industry, illustrating how the low-cost airlines such as Ryanair and easyJet reconfigured the established industry value proposition of high service to one that emphasized convenience and low price.[3] In comparison to a typical flag-carrying airline operating on the same route, meal service and frequent flyer programs have been eliminated. Seat space and opportunities for connecting flights have been reduced. These eliminations and reductions contribute to a cost structure that allows prices to be reduced substantially against the industry norm (in Figure 2.6 giving a higher customer *rating* of price). Further, the creation of ticketless travel and 24/7 booking availability has met latent customer needs in terms of reservation convenience. The power of this alternative value curve and its associated business model has been evidenced by the rapid development of the low-cost airlines.

In general, the first step in any value innovation analysis is to construct a PUV chart of the product market as it currently stands. For this particular analysis it is useful to include price as a separate dimension, to give a complete pictorial representation of the value proposition as perceived by the customer.[4] Further, in near commodity markets where each competitor shares an almost identical PUV profile, it can be useful also to simplify the chart by representing the existing product offerings by a single 'industry-norm' profile.

Once the existing PUV plot is complete the technique involves posing four questions:[5]

- What dimensions of PUV might be eliminated that the industry has taken for granted?
- What dimensions of PUV might be reduced well below the industry standard?
- What dimensions of PUV might be raised well beyond the industry standard?
- What dimensions of PUV should be created that the industry has never offered?

These four simple questions can be a potent source of ideas for strategy innovation. The elimination and reduction of over-specified product features can drive cost reductions, promoting a move west on the customer matrix. Likewise the raising and creation of desired product features equates to a move north on the customer matrix and the prospect of stronger consumer demand. In combination the process may point the way to new business models which allow a strong move north-west on the matrix (Figure 2.7). In practice, however, we frequently see strategic innovators choosing to adopt either a predominantly westerly positioning or a predominantly northerly one. Where the new positioning is based on low price, as in the low-cost airline example, any PUV enhancement can be used to boost sales volumes. Similarly, where the

Understand your Situation

innovator moves north through the offer of significantly higher PUV, any cost reductions can be taken as increased profit margins. In many cases the move west or north is sufficiently marked that it also takes the innovator into a new customer segment, creating demand from a new group of customers for whom the reconfigured PUV has particular appeal.

An example of how PUV can be reconfigured to provide enhanced use value to a new customer segment is provided by Harley-Davidson motorcycles.[6] Figure 2.8 shows what a value innovation analysis conducted back in the

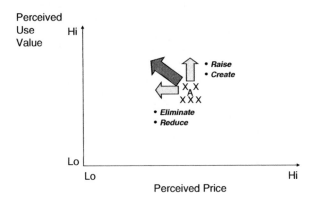

Fig. 2.7 Value innovation and moves on the customer matrix

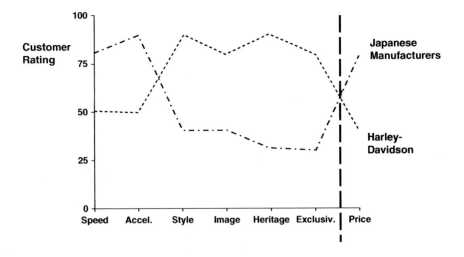

Fig. 2.8 Value innovation analysis for motorcycles (early 1980s)

Note: The product features and ratings illustrative only.

early 1980s might have looked like. At the time Harley-Davidson was close to bankruptcy, producing motorcycles that were based on designs originally dating from the 1950s and 1960s. The industry was dominated by Japanese manufacturers who offered affordable machines with high performance in terms of top speed and acceleration. The typical purchasers were young males seeking low-cost but high-performance transport.

However, Harley-Davidson's management recognized that their products offered more than pure function. Harley-Davidson motorcycles scored highly on more emotional attributes such as heritage, style, and exclusivity. The company correctly identified that these dimensions of use value potentially had stronger appeal to maturing young professionals, who sought a 'hobby experience,' rather than the industry's traditional customers. The company began a marketing and product development strategy which emphasized these dimensions to this new type of motorcycle rider. Product development sought to enhance the perceptions of style, heritage, and exclusivity through the maintenance of classic styling, the selective reintroduction of nostalgic features, in some cases down to white wall tyres and vintage paint schemes, and careful packaging of modern technological improvements. Further, Harley-Davidson created new complementary use values through the formation of the Harley Owners Group, which promoted the hobby aspect with factory-sponsored events and social activities. The average age and income of their customers has risen steadily reflecting the new target market and the success of the reconfigured value proposition is witnessed by profit margins that are amongst the highest in the automotive industry. Harley-Davidson's share price has grown at an annual compound rate of over 30 per cent during the twenty-year period since 1986.

Thinking beyond Traditional Industry Boundaries

A second, and related, technique to consider opportunities for strategy innovation involves actively challenging the accepted industry logic.[7] Most industries have a standard definition of what their product is, which tends to be held in common by all the players. The motorcycle industry manufactures motorcycles, the airline industry provides travel on an airplane, soap manufacturers produce soap. Thinking beyond the traditional industry boundaries, often deeply embedded as the assumed limits to the firm's activities, may expose opportunities for strategy innovation.

An inspection of substitute and complementary industries can provide insights into how the PUV of an existing product or service may be reconfigured. Consider domestic airlines, which have substitutes in the form of rail or coach travel. Airlines have the advantages of speed and perhaps exclusivity, but at a high price. Rail and coach are slow, but enjoy easy ticketing with no need for prior booking and are less expensive. Companies such as easyJet and Ryanair have innovated by combining the key benefits of these two substitute industries—they aim to offer inexpensive airline travel as easy to use as the coach. To catalyze such thinking it is often illuminating to construct a PUV chart showing your own product/service alongside the profiles of its substitutes. What attributes do consumers value in the alternative products? Can these be combined in a new offering?

Similarly, consideration of the products and services which complement your own offering can highlight opportunities. For example, the purchase of an automobile is complemented by insurance, ongoing maintenance, and frequently a finance package. Originally supplied by separate providers, motor manufacturers have recognized that they can provide additional value for their customers by packaging all of these complementary activities into a single offering. The key question to ask is: are there complementary services that can be rolled in to give their customer a more total solution? The concept of the Customer Activity Cycle, developed by Sandra Vandermerwe,[8] is a powerful aid to develop an appreciation of the customer's complete experience. What is the pre-purchase, purchase, and post-purchase sequence of activity? How can value be provided to the customer over the total activity cycle? Can more complete solutions be developed over and above the current industry product?

Finally, it can be enlightening to look critically at who the industry has conventionally seen as its customer. The insurance industry traditionally saw brokers as their immediate customers. Direct Line was able to change the established rules of the game by selling directly to the final consumer, eliminating the intermediary. Not only did this substantially reduce costs, it also facilitated higher levels of service and gained ownership of the customer relationship. In other instances the customer that pays for the product may not be the customer who actually uses it (e.g. business services in many large organizations are frequently paid for centrally but used locally). Each customer group may have different criteria in making their product choice—they may value different dimensions of PUV—which may present opportunities for targeting customers who lie outside the conventional industry definition.

Summary and Conclusion

This chapter has outlined some practical techniques that executives can use to understand their current competitive positioning and the strategy options that may be available to their businesses. We began by arguing that competitive strategy is about winning further business. This, in turn, requires an understanding of value from the customer's perspective. We introduced the perceived use value chart as a tool that helps develop insights into customer-defined value and how customers perceive the products competing for their cash. The customer matrix builds on these insights and serves as a powerful graphic representation of competitive positioning, defined in terms of the two primary business-winning criteria—perceived price and perceived use value. Once constructed, we illustrated how the customer matrix allows the management team to explore the implications of pursuing alternative competitive strategies.

The recent literature on strategy innovation has offered a rich discussion of novel and innovative competitive strategies. We examined two techniques derived from this literature that can aid the identification of innovative competitive strategies, which can be particularly relevant in markets that are suffering from commoditization and strategic convergence. Both value innovation analysis and an active challenging of existing industry boundaries can direct attention at how the overall value proposition offered to customers might be reconfigured. The techniques can point to novel competitive strategies which offer enhanced use value and/or lower price, frequently to a new customer segment.

The real power in all of the tools outlined lies in their focus on the customer. In our experience their application forces a management team to engage in a debate as to what the customer *really* values in their product or service and how these perceptions might vary across different customer groups. This demand-side perspective offers an extremely valuable contribution to strategic thinking, in that it helps the top team to develop a shared understanding of how further business might be won, and invariably raises important questions about the firm's products and markets. Very often it also demonstrates forcibly to the management team that they lack reliable and comprehensive information about their target customers and their competitors. This typically stimulates a quest for better market research, which, if undertaken sensitively, can itself serve as a positive process aspect, visibly reinforcing the message to customers that the business is concerned with meeting their needs.

Finally, we believe these techniques are powerful not only because of the analytical insight they provide, but also because their application helps executives develop a *belief* in the competitive strategy of their business. This is important since having a clear belief in the direction of the business makes the executives' life easier as it builds confidence in decision making. Armed with a clear and widely shared view of the desired competitive positioning of the business, day-to-day decisions can be made with more confidence at all levels of the organization.

Notes

1. G. Hamel (1998) 'Strategy Innovation and the Quest for Value,' *Sloan Management Review*, 39 (4): 8.
2. C. Kim and R. Mauborgne (2005) *Blue Ocean Stategy.* Cambridge, Mass.: Harvard Business School Press; C. Kim and R. Mauborgne (1997) 'Value Innovation: The Strategic Logic of High Growth,' *Harvard Business Review*, Jan.–Feb.: 102–12.
3. See N. Kumar and B. Rogers (2000) 'easyJet: The Web's Favorite Airline,' *European Case Clearing House.*
4. Recall that in our earlier discussion, and in the customer matrix, price is separated out as an independent dimension. This is to recognize its importance in determining overall value for money in the customer's eyes, which makes it one of the fundamental variables available to win further business.
5. Adapted from Kim and Mauborgne, 'Value Innovation: The Strategic Logic of High Growth,' 107.
6. See R. Schoenberg (2003) 'Harley-Davidson Motorcycles,' *European Case Clearing House.*
7. See C. Kim and R. Mauborgne (1999) 'Creating New Market Space,' *Harvard Business Review*, Jan.–Feb.: 83–93; S. Vandermerwe (1996) 'New Competitive Spaces: Jointly Investing in New Customer Logic,' *Columbia Journal of World Business*, Winter: 81–101; G. Hamel and C. K. Prahalad (1994) 'Competing for the Future,' *Harvard Business Review*, July–Aug.: 122–8.
8. S. Vandermerwe (1993) 'Jumping into the Customer's Activity Cycle,' *Columbia Journal of World Business*, Summer: 47–65.

Further Reading

Bowman, C. (1998) *Strategy in Practice.* Englewood Cliffs, NJ: Prentice Hall Europe.
—— and Faulkner, D. (1997) *Competitive and Corporate Strategy.* London: Irwin.
Hamel, G. (2000) *Leading the Revolution.* Boston: Harvard Business School Press.
Kim, C., and Mauborgne, R. (2005) *Blue Ocean Stategy: How to Create Uncontested Market Space and Make the Competition Irrelevant.* Boston: Harvard Business School Press.
Markides, C. (1999) *All the Right Moves: A Guide to Crafting Breakthrough Strategy.* Boston: Harvard Business School Press.
Vandermerwe, S. (2001) *Customer Capitalism: Increasing Returns in New Market Spaces.* London: Whurr Publishers.

3 And the Winner Takes it All? Necessary Conditions and Entry Strategies in Winner-Take-All Market

Rita Gunther McGrath

Introduction: The Fascinating Problem of the Winner-Take-All Market

The lure of being the dominant player in a winner-take-all market has led many a strategist to throw caution (and money) to the winds. Boo.com, Excite!, ValueAmerica.com, the Citibank point-of-sale venture, Iridium, and WebVan are but a selection of disastrous strategies aimed at securing a dominant position.

What could the executives involved have been thinking? Clearly, they believed that the markets they sought to enter were winner-take-all markets, in which the leading player captures a dominant share of profits. They also clearly believed that entering aggressively on a large scale would generate valuable first-mover advantages. Unfortunately, it is easy to attribute winner-take-all characteristics to any new market, when in reality there are specific conditions that are essential for a winner-take-all environment to emerge.

This chapter explores ideas relevant to the identification of winner-take-all markets and the strategies firms might use to compete in them. I will make two main arguments: First, that strategic choices made by firms shape the extent to which a market for innovation is winner-take-all. Secondly, that the most rewarding entry strategy (although never knowable in advance) is likely to be heavily dependent on the evolutionary stage of the category.[1]

Characteristics of Winner-Take-All Markets

A useful point of departure is with the theory of natural monopoly, which has a rich history that goes back as far as English common law and the regulation of ferries, wharves, and printing presses.[2] A natural monopoly is said to exist when average costs decline with additional production, meaning that it is less expensive for total demand to be met by one party, rather than by many parties making duplicative initial investments.

Governments have frequently decided that it is better for a regulator to assign monopoly rights in such markets, because otherwise there will be wasteful duplication of effort, under-investment (because firms cannot guarantee a return on their often substantial start-up costs), and higher prices (because no single player is maximizing efficiencies).[3] Such arguments underlie government-regulated limits on competition, such as the enforcement of patent protection for pharmaceuticals.

The historical arguments in support of regulating natural monopolies have largely fallen out of favor. Deregulation has changed the nature of competition in industries such as commercial aviation, telecommunications, and even the provision of gas and electricity. Innovation, rather than price-based competition, and competitive strategy, rather than government regulation, are expected to determine which companies will be fortunate enough to enjoy a dominant position.

I will focus on three characteristics that winner-take-all markets appear to have in common: (1) a change in the basis of competition in a category; (2) the potential for customer lock-in; and (3) the potential for competitor lock-out. As we shall see, strategic choices influence the extent to which these conditions exist.

A Change in the Basis of Competition

A change in the basis of competition sparks the process of a new winner-take-all market's emergence. For a company to dominate in this new space, the change must idiosyncratically favor their capabilities.[4]

One mechanism for domination is for companies to offer radically improved performance on some performance dimension that is already known to customers and which matters to them. This can reflect either improvements in efficiency or the addition of new benefits. For instance, AMD is using low power consumption to compete against Intel's chip designs in an era in which increased energy costs are of growing concern. On the differentiation side, shifts might take the form of adding positive attributes and reducing or eliminating negatives. Motorola's highly successful, super-thin flip phone the RAZR took advantage of the insight that many customers liked the flip-phone format, but disliked the bulky shape of the phones when folded. The innovation? Using 'thin' as the new basis of competition in mobile handsets.

Even more disruptive changes occur when innovations spark a shift in the criteria that customers use to compare alternative solutions. This often happens when (as Christensen says) existing providers 'overshoot,' meaning that they have satisfied as much demand as customers can use for a particular functionality.[5] Once this occurs, demands change. Thus, customers that once bought laptops on the basis of microprocessor speed now look for all kinds of other functions, such as portability, battery life, ruggedness, or weight. Intel, oriented around faster and faster chips, was forced to respond with wrenching changes involving the addition of lines of slower processes, and added functionality such as built-in wireless capability.

Entire product categories can be created when companies change customers' perceptions of price and value. Coin-converting firm Coinstar has built a high-growth business by converting loose change—a service that conventional banks give away for free! By locating its coin-conversion machines in supermarkets, Coinstar has successfully persuaded significant numbers of customers that it is worth nearly 9 per cent of a transaction to convert coins to other forms of currency by using its machines. As a banker recently told me, 'we would never have thought customers would pay to have spare change converted.'

The point of changing the basis of competition from a strategic perspective is to create problems for competitors while clearing a competitive space in which one's own capabilities are clearly superior. Thus, one set of strategic choices concerns the extent to which a new entrant (or an expanding incumbent) changes the basis of competition.

Although this is a good start, changing the basis for competition alone does not create a winner-take-all situation; indeed, all too often introducing a new basis of competition simply encourages massive amounts of new entry.[6] For a winner-take-all market to be possible and profitable, the presence of customer lock-in and competitor lock-out is essential.

Customer Lock-In

Customer lock-in gives winner-take-all market dynamics their particularly urgent flavor—enter too slowly, or with too little aggressiveness, and the installed base of locked-in customers will grow slowly, giving others the opportunity to gain the lead. The major dilemma is that the investments required to establish a significant installed base are massive, and fly in the face of the logic of parsimony that is most appropriate for small and new businesses. In effect, you are betting huge sums on the small chance of massive success, with a very high probability of negative outcomes. It's crucial therefore to think hard about how you might get customers locked in and how much investment it will take to achieve critical mass.

One compelling source of customer lock-in stems from the benefits each customer gains when other customers buy. This is the 'network externality' effect, which means that the value of an offering increases as more users are added to the network of people using it. Thus, fax machines are more valuable to the extent that more people own faxes, and so on. Network externalities are powerful and often non-linear in their effects. This prompts many companies to allocate enormous resources to seed the creation of a network of users, or exploit the fact that such a network exists, often without any demonstrated business model.

This kind of thing was *de rigueur* in the heady days of the internet bubble. Excite@Home, for instance, paid $780 million to acquire the free online card shop www.Bluemountainarts.com, just to get hold of its base of millions of regular subscribers, only to sell it back to its founders for a pittance after entering bankruptcy. News Corp's recent $580 million acquisition of the popular social networking site Myspace is a further example.

Access to a network of users is particularly powerful for businesses in which renewing content, setting prices, allowing customers to co-create content, or trading dynamically can be envisioned—all of which are strategic choices of business model made by the firm.

Google's advertising model, in which advertisers pay to place ads on sites featuring selected keywords, takes advantage of lock-in in three ways. Website owners become locked in because they have registered and earn money every time a visitor clicks on an ad. They are motivated to stay with Google because as the network of advertisers grows, the price per click-through can increase. Advertisers are motivated to do business with Google because it has access to the largest number of websites and searches. And visitors to websites become locked in because Google offers the most comprehensive access to search results targeted toward their interests, which are priced dynamically.

Switching costs can also lock customers in. Once an initial investment in learning, training, building a relationship, or in capital has been made, customers will be reluctant to repeat the process with a new provider. Idiosyncratic learning, transaction-specific programming, capital investments, and even simple familiarity and comfort level all create switching costs. The higher the switching cost, the more the customer is locked in.

So powerful are switching costs as a deterrent to open competition that sometimes regulators demand that companies ease them. Recent legislation regarding mobile phone number portability, for instance, seeks to make it easier for phone customers to switch carriers. Switching costs do not require network externalities, but are powerfully enhanced when the two are combined.

Customer lock-in can also occur when a company has figured out how to capture proprietary control over a trigger point in the customers' experience. Activities such as becoming aware of a solution, searching for alternatives, purchasing, and making payments all are points at which proprietary lock-in can be created.[7] Some of the more interesting competitive contests occur when a player that has enjoyed proprietary control comes up against other players determined to wrest it away.

The United States real estate market offers an interesting example—for decades, brokers kept information about available properties for sale in an area to themselves. Because the 'search' trigger for customers depends upon access to this information, buyers were forced to use brokers (and to pay a 6 per cent commission on their property purchases). Today, brokers' fees are predictably under attack.[8] Who is benefiting? New, internet-savvy brokers prepared to accept smaller commissions but also to do far less for the buyers because buyers have done most of their research online.

Sometimes, lock-in occurs as a consequence of leveraging product portfolios and complementary assets. Microsoft, for instance, has been extensively challenged in the courts for possible unfair competitive behavior because it sought to lock users accustomed to its operating system into using its web browser, Explorer, and its office productivity software. In contrast to competitors without such complementary offerings, Microsoft could leverage its existing ties to customers and the fact that its operating system profits could more than make up for the fact that it gave the browser away for free.

Lock-in is at its most powerful when several of these elements can be combined. Online markets and auctions, for example, create switching costs and also take advantage of network externalities. More buyers will go to a shopping site such as eBay because that is where more sellers are likely to be, and the resulting transactions are likely to be economically superior to those on another website. Adding such elements as dynamic pricing, searching, connecting, or otherwise creating an interactive element to the offering further locks customers in.

No discussion about customer lock-in would be complete without acknowledging that it is usually temporary. Qualcomm, for instance, has enjoyed significant lock-in from cellular equipment manufacturers with its CDMA chips. Its dominance in this market was so complete that disgruntled customers actually filed anti-trust complaints in European courts. Sprint, one of its key customers, has now decided to award construction of its next-generation Wimax network (at a price of $3 billion) to a technology that Intel is backing. Indeed, Sprint is partnering not only with Intel but also with Motorola and Samsung to create the new network. The result? According to Monica Paolini, a wireless technology expert, 'It looks like there's not going to be any single company dominating'.[9] It is worth noting that this outcome is a function of strategic decisions made by Sprint, rather than an intrinsic quality of the market itself.

Lock-in can erode when competing alternatives create compelling benefits for customers who do switch. America On-Line, which in its heyday spent millions to recruit customers to its dial-up service, is grappling with the emergence of large-scale broadband networks which make dial-up irrelevant to increasing numbers of its customers. It has recently abandoned all attempts to preserve its position in that business and has now announced that customers will be able to access all the services they used to pay for, for free, with its 'bring your own broadband' offer.

So, you've been able to conceive of a way of tilting the competitive dynamics in a category you seek to enter, and have got some way of creating customer lock-in. Still not enough to dominate a winner-take-all market, unless you also have mechanisms that will keep competitors at bay. This brings us to what I will call competitor lock-out.

Competitor Lock-Out

The classic manner in which monopolists dominate markets harks back to the legal definition of 'natural' monopolies. When confronted with a heavy fixed cost to enter a category with small marginal costs to expand it, early movers can do a great deal to deter subsequent entry by competitors. The simplest thing, of course, is to lower prices beyond actual costs, on the assumption that increasing volumes and learning curve effects will eventually lead the cost–price curves to cross and generate profitability.

Such a strategy can be highly risky if competitors are tenacious. It can become the business equivalent of a war of attrition. In this case, both companies invest heavily to generate a larger installed base than the other, investments which can go on for years without generating a payback. In the UK, the British Satellite Broadcasting network and News Corp's Sky TV were locked in such a battle, which ended only when the two agreed to merge. In the USA today, profitless satellite radio providers XM Radio and Sirius are losing millions for their investors while each tries to gain a critical mass of subscribers.

Alliances are often central to competitive lock-out. Sun Microsystems, for instance, created a mutually beneficial ecosystem, in which its partners benefit while those allied with other providers are locked out.[10] To the extent that your product or service is essential to the success of partners, they will be less likely to adopt a competing alternative.

Co-production or complementarity with customers can also lock competitors out. A co-produced or co-evolutionary category reduces the incentive of a customer to switch partners and start over. For instance, when a customer establishes a 'group' on Yahoo's portal, it becomes difficult for other providers that also offer group functionality to make much headway, since the customer has made investments that are idiosyncratic to the group location on Yahoo. When Harley-Davidson owners or Lego customers find their ideas incorporated into next-generation product designs, it becomes difficult for competitors to match the quality of the relationships established.

There may also be occasions in which competitor lock-out occurs because there simply isn't time, money, energy, or physical space to work with more than one provider. This is sometimes called 'pre-emption of scarce assets'. Back to Coinstar—once one coin changer is on-site at a grocery store, there isn't much point for either the store owner or customers to spring for a second one. In many traditional industries, owning a particular location or dominating a distribution route provides protection.

Lock-out can also be a deliberate government policy. Protecting favored competitors is often a bone of contention in globalizing industries, in which governments seek to give their domestic competitors some advantages, while firms operating internationally would obviously prefer as few barriers to competition as possible. Table 3.1 provides a summary of the argument so far.

What can we conclude? I will argue that absent a reconfiguration of the competitive standard in the industry, customer lock-in, and competitor lock-out, a winner-take-all strategy is not a realistic ambition. If you believe, however, that you might have the ability to create a model which combines these elements, the next question is how to go about entering a new category. In order to consider options for doing this, it's useful to have a framework which might suggest where the next competitive advantage in a category will emerge.

TABLE 3.1 Necessary conditions for the formation of a winner-take-all market

Changed basis of competition	Customer lock-in	Competitor lock-out
Radically improved performance on known competitive dimensions	Large installed base of other customers (network externalities)	Leverage high fixed cost, low-variable cost structure
		Lock key alliance or licensing partners into your 'ecosystem'
Change in criteria used to evaluate alternatives	Dynamic interactions with customer-specific value (pricing, payment, etc.)	
Change customers' perceptions of price versus value		Engage in co-production with customers
	High customer switching costs	
		Pre-empt a scarce resource or asset
	Proprietary access to customer purchasing trigger	
		Government regulations
	Leverage customer access with complementary assets	

Contested Terrain and the Seesaw of Industry Evolution

Christensen and colleagues observe that as industries evolve, profitability predictably shifts from one type of player to another in a systematic way.[11] Table 3.2 illustrates an adaptation of their central idea.

In phase I, the driver for success is offering a product or service that reframes the dimensions of performance expected. Because the category is new, much is unknown. To provide a solution at all requires coordination, the actual value of

TABLE 3.2 The seesaw of industry evolution

Phase	I Changed basis for competition	II Horizontalization	III Bullets to the combatants
Source of differentiation	A new category of offering which meets a new type of demand or which reframes competitive criteria	Leading providers overshoot or a public standard is established; Customers defect to solutions that are cheaper, simpler, or more flexible	Most solutions commoditized; only advantages lie in areas where solutions are 'not good enough' (to cite Christensen)
Standards and platforms	Entering player attempts to build on proprietary standards and platforms	Interfaces and platforms are increasingly standardized; new services are built on top of these standards	Interfaces, platforms, and networks standardized
Advantages tend to go to...	Fully integrated players who can manage unpredictable interdependencies between components or services	Partners in an ecosystem that can combine their outputs to create a solution; leaders can emerge through adroit use of licensing, alliances, positioning or proprietary complements	Service providers compete on operational excellence and supreme efficiency; product providers differentiate on functionality within modular architectures
Current example	Apple's integration of its iPod player with its iTunes software with licensing and resale rights from content companies Sprint/Nextel seeking to build a Wimax network	Mobile telephone operators working with hardware providers to create networks of interdependent coverage	Google using the standard interfaces of the web, browsers, and online content to add value by proprietary algorithms
Winner-take-all strategy?	Own the standard and keep it proprietary	Dominate a platform or component standard necessary to other players	Help customers compete or conserve more effectively than they could if they didn't buy from you

the solution isn't really known, and most of the time the aspirations of companies seeking to triumph are dashed. There is even evidence that for a category to enter phase I, many prior companies must fail along the way.[12]

Successful survivors manage the interdependencies necessary to create a complete solution for customers; if they win, they can deploy the winner-take-all strategy of being the sole source provider for that particular solution. Palm with the first successful Personal Digital Assistant, pharmaceutical companies with a proprietary drug, mainframe computer companies with proprietary hardware, software, and middleware, and most recently Apple's fully integrated approach to the digital music business are examples.

Phase I may be skipped entirely, usually through the establishment of common standards by a governmental or regulatory body. Thus, there never was a purely proprietary producer of FAX equipment or a single provider of GSM-based mobile communications, because a standard architecture was established, allowing competitors to tie their products to that common platform. Although growth in the resulting markets was substantial, it is worth noting that there was no dominant, winner-take-all player. In a 1988 article reviewing the history of facsimile machines, for instance, thirteen companies were listed as among the 'major players in the US Market.'[13]

In the rare cases in which a firm succeeds at dominating a phase I category, pressures on their competitive advantage will be substantial. Citibank, for instance, was the first bank in the greater New York area to offer automatic teller machine (ATM) capability to its customers. Its 'The Citi never sleeps' campaign proved so successful that its rivals banded together to form the MAC network, agreeing to make their machines interoperable. Citi machines worked only for Citibank customers; the Mac machines worked for everyone who belonged to a member bank, offsetting Citi's advantage. Today, ATM access is simply expected on the part of customers and offers no particular advantage.

Which brings us to phase II. In phase II, common standards have either been dictated or have emerged, allowing many players to participate in the category in some way. Enormous growth often accompanies a transition to phase II. Partnerships, alliances, licensing, and intellectual property are enormously important, as the goal is to establish one's own technology as the standard used by others.[14] The dominant player in phase I can have an advantage in converting their wholly integrated, proprietary solution to become a phase II platform. The tricky thing here is that becoming a platform often requires the leading player to invite competition in: through licensing, for example. To sustain a leading position, platform leaders also need to make sure that appropriate complementary innovations are introduced.[15]

Even relatively durable advantages in a phase II context, however, will come under pressure in competitive markets. As core layers and functionalities become commoditized (in Christensen's language, they are 'good enough' for most purposes) competitive advantage moves yet again to the sub-component manufacturers or service providers who can use their unique capabilities to extract superior margins. With physical goods, this often occurs at the component supply level—Qualcomm's dominance of CDMA chip manufacturing for cellular phones is an example. With service goods, dominance often occurs through the deployment of world-class process capabilities. Dell Computer and Wal-Mart come to mind as examples here.

A disruption by a new phase I-oriented player, or the introduction of a different regulatory or technological regime, can return pivotal activities to a phase I mode.

Strategic Choices in the Winner-Take-All Game

We have so far laid out the necessary ingredients that contribute to a market having a winner-take-all flavor: a change in the basis for competition, customer lock-in, and competitor lock-out. We have also suggested that firms will enjoy different strategies for success, depending upon which phase of development a particular category is in.

For an integrated, phase I player to succeed in dominating a category, the ability to offer a complete solution that is a quantum improvement over previous solutions is essential. Witness the many failed companies seeking to enter the PDA market without having cracked the problem of the user interface, battery life, or route to market. The rewards can be sweet, but early entry with a complete solution is key, and the differentiation offered to selected sets of customers is crucial.

Hill provides an excellent overview of the practices technology-oriented firms have used to establish their offerings as standards.[16] The delicate balancing act of players in phase II is between exploiting proprietary advantages (which almost always limits the size of the market accessed) and giving away sources of possible competitive differentiation, thus doing damage to your own ability to achieve competitive lock-out.

In phase III, advantage stems from the ability to deploy unique capabilities targeted at the remaining competitive problems in the segment. Phase III players take advantage of commoditization. When most offerings are 'good enough' as Christensen says, differentiation can come from the development of sub-components that are not good enough or from providing commodity products and services exceptionally well or with exceptionally low cost. Dell Computer benefited from the commoditization of computer hardware; and Wal-Mart benefits from the proliferation of competition among its suppliers. In neither case, however, are their markets winner-take-all. This can be explained because they lack the critical components of customer lock-in and competitor lock-out. Contrast their situation with that of Amazon.com, which has successfully pursued retail markets but has added lock-in and lock-out to its business mix.

The key point is that the nature of the winner-take-all situation created is different in each instance.

Conclusion

The most glorious successes and the most dramatic failures in business have been associated with the pursuit of a dominant position in a winner-take-all market. In this chapter, I have suggested that a competitive space will not be a winner-take-all category without a changed basis for competition: customer lock-in and competitor lock-out. Further, that company strategies will tend to shape whether these conditions will emerge.

Gaining the lead in such markets will further depend upon where the greatest value is being created. In new areas, a new solution and a provider that can deliver it completely have the strongest chances. When non-proprietary standards are beginning to emerge and the market horizontalizes, those players who are most adept at establishing their technologies as standards for one or another layer of the solution have a chance to win. And when a market has settled on key standards and many activities are commoditized, providers of services solutions and component technologies are often at an advantage. Making the transition from one category to the next is often difficult; as the competitive logic for winning in each is different.

Assuming that you have the appetite to engage in winner-take-all competition, how would one put the insights in this chapter to work? I think three sets of analyses might prove useful. The first is to examine existing winner-take-all markets in phases I and II and determine whether there is any opportunity to undermine the lock-in and lock-out conditions that could allow your company to grasp a part of that market. The second is to consider the opportunities you have before you and consider whether you could spark the formation of a winner-take-all category based on capabilities that are unique to your firm. The third is to use the ideas as guidance for the alliances, partnerships, licensing agreements, or other forms of cooperation you may wish to undertake with other companies.

The key assumptions to test are those that might cause you to mis-classify a more conventional competitive market as winner-take-all; or a winner-take-all market as one which you can enter later on.

Notes

I am indebted to Alex Gounares, who suggested that sometimes strategic choices made by firms can influence the extent to which a market becomes more or less winner-take-all.

1. G. Moore (2005) *Dealing with Darwin: How Great Companies Innovate at Every Phase of their Evolution.* New York: Portfolio (Penguin Books).
2. A. Bamzai (2004) 'The Wasteful Duplication Thesis in Natural Monopoly Regulation,' *University of Chicago Law Review,* 71 (4): 1525–74.
3. A. Kahn (1971) *The Economics of Regulation: Principles and Institutions.* New York: John Wiley.
4. M. B. Lieberman and D. B. Montgomery (1998) 'First-Mover (Dis)Advantages: Retrospective and Link with the Resource-Based View,' *Strategic Management Journal,* 19: 1111–25.
5. C. Christensen, M. Raynor, and M. Verlinden (2001) 'Skate to Where the Money will Be,' *Harvard Business Review,* 79 (10): 72–81.
6. W. A. Sahlman and H. Stevenson (1985) 'Capital Market Myopia,' *Journal of Business Venturing,* 1: 7–30.
7. I. C. MacMillan and R. G. McGrath (1996) 'Discover your Products' Hidden Potential,' *Harvard Business Review,* 74 (3): 58–68.
8. D. Darlin (2006) 'The Last Stand of the 6-Percenters?,' *New York Times,* 1 (4).
9. A. Sharma and D. Clark (2006) 'Air Superiority: Two Technology Giants Clash in Battle for Wireless Internet: Intel, Qualcomm Want to Say How Wide Array of Devices Will Connect to the Web; For Users, Still More Choices,' *Wall Street Journal,* 24 Aug.
10. R. Garud and A. Kumaraswamy (1993) 'Changing Competitive Dynamics in Network Industries: An Exploration of Sun Microsystems' Open Systems Strategy,' *Strategic Management Journal,* 14 (5): 351–69.
11. Christensen, Raynor, and Verlinden, 'Skate to Where the Money will Be,' C. M. Christensen, S. D. Anthony, and E. A. Roth (2004) *Seeing What's Next? Using the Theories of Innovation to Predict Industry Change.* Boston: Harvard Business School Press.
12. A. M. Knott and H. E. Posen (2005) 'Is Failure Good?,' *Strategic Management Journal,* 26(7): 617–43.
13. J. A. Pirani (1988) 'Redefining the Facsimile Market,' *Telecommunications,* 22 (3): 92–100.
14. C. W. L. Hill (1997) 'Establishing a Standard: Competitive Strategy and Technological Standards in Winner-Take-All Industries,' *Academy of Management Executive,* 11 (2): 7–25.
15. A. Gawer and M. A. Cusumano (2002) *Platform Leadership: How Intel, Microsoft, and Cisco Drive Industry Innovation.* Boston: Harvard Business School Press.
16. Hill, 'Establishing a Standard.'

4 Understanding the Financial Footprint of Strategy

William C. Lawler

Financial analysis is often taught as a separate discipline. In reality, however, financial results are directly related to the strategic plan of the firm. Every strategy has a financial footprint. When a management team is formulating a strategy, it is at the same time creating the financial model for shareholder wealth creation. It is imperative that every manager understands this relationship since financial outcomes are the result of strategic plans. In this chapter, financial analysis will be discussed in this context.

Today's business environment can be simplified as follows. On one hand, there are operating managers at three levels of responsibility. At the highest, top management has the responsibility to scan the horizon and identify business opportunities that are consistent with the firm's capabilities. One cannot pick up the *Financial Times*, the *Asian Business Journal*, or the *Wall Street Journal* without seeing comments from these managers touting these opportunities. At the next level there are those managers who then craft business plans to take advantage of these opportunities given the competitive environment. And then there are those managers who have the responsibility of implementing and monitoring said plans. On the other hand, there is another set of managers whose responsibilities are more financial in nature. They are the fund managers, the insurance company investment managers, and other like financial managers who have the fiduciary responsibility to create returns on the capital under their control. Their job is to do the required research to build an investment portfolio appropriate for the risk profiles of their investors. The foundation of this business environment is one basic financial ratio—Return on Invested Capital (ROIC). For the latter set of managers to commit their capital, the former set have to offer strategic opportunities that meet return on capital requirements.

Understand your Situation

Return on invested capital is defined as profit divided by invested capital but it is much more informative to break this into two components:[1]

$$ROIC = Profit/Invested\ Capital = Profit/Sales \times Sales/Invested\ Capital\ or$$

$$= Profit\ Margin \times Asset\ Turnover.$$

If queried about their profitability, most managers worldwide would answer with the first component: My profit was €500,000 last period or my profit margin was 10 per cent. What is wrong with this? If two managers competing in the same market space both made €500,000 last period, would they be equally as profitable? To answer this correctly one would have to know the investment base that was employed to generate this profit. If one manager needed €5,000,000 to earn this amount and the other only half that, the latter would be more profitable since the ROIC would be 20% (€500,000/€2,500,000) as compared to 10% (€500,000/€5,000,000). Although not always obvious, the proper measure of profitability is ROIC.

To illustrate, in Boston, on the East Coast of the USA, there is a men's store called Joseph's. It is located in an imposing granite building on a rather large lot on Newbury Street, the most expensive retail area of the city. The interior is as plush as the exterior. One cannot find a suit for under $1,000 and the profit margins are, no doubt, equally as high. To compare, just outside Boston, in a much less impressive retail area is a cinder block building with linoleum flooring where another well-known men's shop, Sym's, resides. A good-quality suit here sells for about $300. At first glance, one might think that Joseph's is more profitable than Sym's but logic tells us differently. If this were the case investors focused on the men's clothing industry would invest in Joseph's yet both establishments seem to attract investment. A more in-depth analysis would focus on the second component, asset turnover. Although Joseph's has the higher profit margin, their comparatively higher required investment due to their location gives them a lower turnover as compared to Sym's.[2] The result is that both are likely comparable in profitability (ROIC) although they employ very different strategies for competing in this industry. This results in very different financial footprints. To summarize, Joseph's drives their profitability by focusing on the profit margin while Sym's is more an asset turn business.

Regardless of where one is in the world, or in what industry, a careful analysis will show that competitors' underlying business models are either margin driven or more focused on asset turn. Very few firms have been able to excel at both in the long run.[3] From a generic strategy point of view, if a firm is successful at differentiating itself, buyers will pay a premium which is evidenced by a higher profit margin.[4] But differentiation strategies are difficult to sustain. As industries tend to commoditize over time due to consolidation or the lowering of entry barriers, there is a necessary shift toward business models driven more by the second component of ROIC, asset turnover.[5]

Rather than remain at a conceptual level, it is best to develop this discussion around a concrete example. The fifteen-year history of Compaq Computer from PC market entry in 1982 to its move to the enterprise computing space in 1996 provides an excellent example of the relationship between strategic positioning and financial results.

Market Entry and Growth Years: 1982 to 1989

Market Entry Strategy

While top management at the leading information technology firms such as IBM and Digital Equipment Company dismissed the early-stage development of the personal computer (PC) as a minor occurrence and subsequently focused only limited resources on the commercial PC sector, Rod Canion, at the time an executive in the semiconductor group at Texas Instruments, correctly forecasted this to be a major market opportunity. Unfortunately, although one could readily source components such as microprocessors, disk drives, and operating systems from any number of suppliers to build a PC, entry barriers to this evolving market related more to the established market leader IBM—brand, access to corporate IT purchasing agents, and service offerings. No corporate buyer would risk purchasing PCs from a firm without a history of success when IBM machines were readily available. In addition, few investors were interested in supporting such a high-risk market entry venture. Canion did not give up, however, and managed to identify a niche market with unmet needs—portable PCs. Field technicians, consultants, and the like needed computing capability in a portable form factor. In 1982 with venture capital backing, Canion formed Compaq Computer Company and brought the first portable computer to market.[6] Compaq's long-term target was always the desktop commercial PC market so in the early years all strategic investments focused on this goal. Since all components were readily available as were third-party value added resellers (VARs) such as MicroAge for sales and service, early investment focused primarily on two areas—marketing, and assembly and test. Compaq's name was carefully chosen and the marketing communications built on this. The first five letters—Compa—represented 'Compatibility,' a key factor in the purchase decision. Since most software application developers were interested in the size of the segment they wrote applications for and IBM was the undisputed market leader, the majority of applications ran on this system. Compatibility with the IBM operating system was crucial. The last letter—Q—stood for 'Quality' since Compaq knew it had to associate its name (i.e. brand) with this key attribute. Not only did Compaq claim this attribute it also invested heavily in the test function to ensure that its machines were both durable and reliable. Compaq's early strategy was successful and corporate purchasing agents, although at first very reluctant to buy from Compaq, did acknowledge its two key attributes—compatibility and quality.

In 1985 IBM made a crucial decision that allowed Compaq to become a major competitor in the commercial desktop PC market. Intel, one of the many microprocessor companies competing in that space, was bringing to market its 32-bit 80386 microprocessor, reputed to be the fastest. IBM, finally recognizing that this market was a real opportunity, had begun to develop its own P/S2 proprietary system and was reluctant to adopt the 80386. Compaq approached Intel with the offer of building a desktop PC around this new chip design. Although Compaq did not have a strong brand in the desktop segment, Intel, recognizing the crucial time-to-market factor, accepted and the Compaq DeskPro386 was introduced in late 1986. The marketing message now hyped a new key attribute—speed. Although IBM did eventually build a PC around the 386 chip, Compaq had a nine-month window where it had the fastest micro-processor and, with focused marketing communications, branded itself as the technology leader in the commercial desktop PC market. Within three years it was competing with IBM for global market share lead.

Market share leadership had many advantages but a vital one was scale. At the upstream portion of the value system, volume sourcing of components gave Compaq the power to negotiate more favorable pricing and downstream it had a like advantage with VARs such as MicroAge and distributors like Ingram. By the late 1980s, Compaq was exercising this power. A focused financial analysis reveals the impact of these strategic moves.

Financial Analysis

Component One: Profit Margin

As discussed above, ROIC has two components: profit margin and asset turnover. To compute the first requires a detailed analysis of the income statement for Compaq. The purpose of an income statement is to match the revenues for a period of time to those expenses incurred in the same period[7] in order to generate the revenues. Although corporations format their income statement in many different ways the most informative is shown in Table 4.1. At first it can be confusing since there are many different measures of profit for Compaq—gross profit, operating profit, profit before taxes, and net profit. Which is the appropriate one to use for the computation of the first component of ROIC—profit/sales?

TABLE 4.1 Compaq Corporation consolidated income statements, 1985–1989 (millions)

	1985		1986		1987		1988		1989	
Net sales	$504	100.0%	$625	100.0%	$1,224	100.0%	$2,066	100.0%	$2,876	100.0%
Cost of sales	326	64.7%	361	57.7%	717	58.6%	1,233	59.7%	1,715	59.6%
Gross profit	178	35.3%	265	42.3%	507	41.4%	832	40.3%	1,161	40.4%
Operating expenses:										
R&D	16	3.2%	27	4.3%	47	3.8%	75	3.6%	132	4.6%
Selling, general, and admin.	110	21.8%	152	24.3%	226	18.5%	397	19.2%	539	18.7%
Total operating expenses	126	25.0%	179	28.6%	273	22.3%	472	22.9%	671	23.3%
Operating profit—primary activities	52	10.4%	86	13.7%	234	19.1%	360	17.4%	490	17.0%
Income from strategic investments	0	0.0%	−2	−0.3%	5	0.4%	17	0.8%	27	1.0%
Operating profit—total	52	10.4%	84	13.5%	239	19.5%	377	18.3%	517	18.0%
Financing and other items	−8	−1.7%	−9	−1.4%	−10	−0.8%	−3	−0.1%	−19	−0.7%
Profit before taxes	44	8.7%	75	12.0%	229	18.7%	375	18.1%	498	17.3%
Provision for income taxes	17	3.4%	32	5.1%	93	7.6%	119	5.8%	165	5.7%
Net profit	27	5.3%	43	6.9%	136	11.1%	255	12.4%	333	11.6%

Year-over-year percentage change

	1986	1987	1988	1989
Sales	24.1%	95.8%	68.7%	39.2%
Cost of sales	10.7%	98.9%	71.9%	39.1%
R&D	66.3%	77.1%	58.9%	77.0%
S,G&A	38.3%	48.6%	75.8%	35.6%
Operating income	64.6%	172.1%	54.1%	36.0%

Understand your Situation

Gross profit is defined as net sales[8] less cost of sales where cost of sales is the total of manufacturing cost plus any required transportation and installation costs. These are the costs that can be related to the product and are often referred to as product costs. Since Compaq is selling PCs, which requires minimal transportation and installation, cost of sales reflects the cost to source the components, assemble, and test a PC. This measure is extremely informative especially when expressed as a percentage (often called gross margin). From the exhibit, Compaq's gross margin jumped seven percentage points (35.3 per cent to 42.3 per cent) in 1986 and then fell back a bit to hold constant at about 40 per cent through 1989. To what can this be attributed? From the discussion above, Compaq introduced the DeskPro386 in late 1986 but started the marketing of technology leadership earlier in the year. By differentiating itself in this manner, the financial data indicates that buyers seemed willing to pay a premium and Compaq, even after IBM brought its 386 PC to market in 1987, was able to sustain this. In general, the gross profit % (i.e. gross margin) can be used as a crude tool to identify the degree to which firms are able to differentiate themselves in a given market thereby capturing a price premium—as a general rule, above 30 per cent indicates some degree of differentiation and below that indicates a more commoditized offering.[9] Highly differentiated firms such as Cisco in the telecommunications sector enjoy gross margins approaching 70 per cent while those selling commodities such as grocers are closer to 15 per cent.

To arrive at operating profit, research & development (R&D) and selling, general, and administrative expenses (S, G, & A) are deducted from gross profit. Unlike cost of sales, which are related to the product, these are more an expense that is incurred each period and are often called period costs. In analyzing R&D, this is a good example why the relative percentage rather than the absolute value should be the focal point. The dollar amount of R&D has increased by about 70 per cent each period, which seems large, but the percentage as a function of sales has held relatively constant at just under 4 per cent. The percentage was higher in 1986 (4.3%) but this was due to Compaq developing the DeskPro386, and 1989 was also higher, which might be attributed to the slowing of growth lessening the scale factor (note the year-over-year percentage change in sales for 1989). Converting the absolute amounts on the income statement to percentages relative to sales is called common size analysis and is used throughout the financial community to identify trends. The pattern of selling, general, and administrative expense percentage tells a like story. It increases in 1986 due to the promotion of the DeskPro386 and then seems to steady state just below 19 per cent. The net result is an operating profit that increases markedly[10] in 1986 due to the promotion of the new product, peaks in 1987 at 19.1 per cent, and then falls back slightly to just over 17 per cent, most likely due to competitors bringing like technology to market. For Compaq during this time period there are two measures of operating profit. 'Primary activities' encompasses all the strategic decisions made by Compaq in running the PC activities while 'Total' expands this definition to take into account third-party activities that would be considered strategic. Like many companies, Compaq was making strategic investments in joint ventures and alliances at this time. By 1987 these investments were yielding positive results and in 1989 they contributed another 1 per cent to overall operating profit.

Financing and other items is a total of interest on debt financing and any ancillary income such as investment of excess cash in non-strategic areas such as government securities. In the early years the negative amounts reflect mostly interest on debt, but as Compaq generated profits this debt was paid down and non-strategic investment made such that by 1988 this total was now positive. As a result profit before taxes is greater than operating profit for the final two years of the period under analysis. The last expense item is provision for income taxes which then yields the final measure of profit, net profit.

Since we started by saying that the purpose of the income statement was matching, how well does the income statement match expenses to revenues? Cost of sales is a good match since the revenue reflects what a product was sold for and the cost of sales reflects what it cost to manufacture and deliver that product. Selling, general, and administrative expense is also a good match since it reflects what the cost was to market and sell the good. Research and development, however, is more a problem since the revenue related to this expense is not recognized until some time in the future. The income statement is not perfect and in industries with long development cycles such as pharmaceuticals this can lead to misstatement of the earning of a firm. For Compaq, with development cycles of twelve to eighteen months, this is probably not a serious flaw.

To return to the question that started this section: Which is the proper measure of profit to use in the profit margin calculation for a strategic analysis of a firm? It should be clear from this discussion that the operating profit—total not net profit is the correct choice since this represents the results of the strategic investments made in the primary activity of the firm. Interest expense is the result of a financing choice; had Compaq chosen to finance its assets solely with equity capital, interest expense would have decreased but operating profit—total would have not changed. Likewise, income from investments in government bonds is not the primary activity of Compaq. Investors are motivated by the recurring earnings that result from the primary activities of Compaq, not temporary non-strategic investments. Finally, taxes are often the result of location in favorable tax locales rather than primary activity. As a result, for the period under review Compaq's first component is:

	1985	1986	1987	1988	1989
Profit margin	10.4%	13.5%	19.5%	18.3%	18.0%

Understand your Situation

Component Two: Asset Turnover

The second component in the ROIC calculation, asset turnover, requires an in-depth analysis of the balance sheet. Whereas the income statement shows the results over a period of time, the balance sheet is as of a point in time. Table 4.2 shows the balance of asset, liability, and stockholders' equity accounts at year end, 31 December. There is some logic to this format. First, note that total assets must be equal to the total of liabilities and stockholders' equity for any given year. For instance, in 1988 Compaq has a total of $1.59 billion in assets and this must be equal to those that have financed these assets—$0.775 billion from creditors ($0.48 billion in short-term debt and another $0.296 billion in long-term)[11] and $0.815 billion from shareholders ($0.341 billion in original investment in stock and another $0.474 billion of earnings that belong to stockholders but have been retained in the business for reinvestment). What many users do not understand is that the amounts are not current values, they are the value at the time the asset was acquired. In some industries where assets turn over quickly this may not matter, but in those industries where assets are more long term (e.g. real estate) the balance sheet may show valuations that are materially different from current value. Lastly, valuation is based upon primary use and not resale value. The value of a building represents the estimated future cash flows from the use for which the building was acquired, not what it could be sold for in the current market.

As with the 'profit' factor in the first component of ROIC, the 'invested capital' factor in the denominator of the second component—sales/invested capital—has to be defined precisely. Asset investments are directly related to the strategy of a firm. They can be classified into two categories: infrastructure and operating cycle investments. Infrastructure investments reflect the R&D facilities, the manufacturing plant and equipment, the logistics network, and the sales, marketing, and administrative offices. Since the ultimate purpose of an investment is to generate sales consistent with a given strategy, turnover ratios (i.e. sales/average type of investment) are used to evaluate these investments. These ratios are compiled over time to assess improvement of the strategic investment in generating revenues and are also compared to competitors to appraise the effectiveness of various strategic investment scenarios. For 1989 the Infrastructure turnover ratio for Compaq can be computed as follows (please refer to Table 4.2 data):

Property, plant and equipment, net	($429 + $705)/2 =	$ 567
Strategic investments, and other	($46 + $72)/2 =	59
Total infrastructure investment		$ 626
Infrastructure turnover	$2,876/$626 =	4.6

Note, to calculate the ratio we need the <u>average</u> infrastructure investment not the year end; so end-of-year 1988 (which is beginning-year 1989) and end-of-year 1989 are averaged to get a better estimate of the 1989 infrastructure investment necessary to generate the $2,876 million in sales. For companies in high-growth stages not using averages can seriously understate the turnover ratio since assets are typically at their largest at end of year in anticipation of higher sales in the next period. The 4.6 figure is interpreted as follows: for every 4.6 dollars of revenue one dollar in infrastructure investment was required in 1989. By itself this ratio is meaningless and only has meaning if put into context. For the full period the infrastructure turnovers are as follows:

	1985	1986	1987	1988	1989
Infrastructure turnover	8.8	6.6	7.2	5.9	4.6

Now this ratio takes on some meaning. It seems that Compaq's ability to generate revenues with its strategic infrastructure investments has weakened. This is a good example of the use of ratio analysis. The causal factor is still unknown but the analysis has moved the investigator from pages of financial data to focused questions. What is clear is that additional research should be focused on answering this question: Have pricing pressures from other competitors entering with like technology weakened revenues to this extent or have more recent investments been not as effective? Comparative competitor ratios would also be helpful in this analysis.

TABLE 4.2 Compaq Corporation consolidated balance sheets, 1985–1989 (millions)

	1985		1986		1987		1988		1989	
Assets										
Current assets:										
Cash and cash equivalents	$ 77	25%	$ 57	15%	$ 132	15%	$ 281	18%	$ 161	8%
Accounts receivable, net	76	24%	116	31%	255	28%	428	27%	530	25%
Inventories	76	24%	81	21%	276	31%	387	24%	559	27%
Other	11	3%	5	1%	18	2%	18	1%	62	3%
Total current assets	240	77%	260	69%	681	76%	1,115	70%	1,312	63%
Property, plant and equipment, net	67	21%	102	27%	192	21%	429	27%	705	34%
Strategic investments and other	6	2%	16	4%	28	3%	46	3%	72	3%
Total assets	$312	100%	$378	100%	$901	100%	$1,590	100%	$2,090	100%

(Continued)

TABLE 4.2 *(Continued)*

	1985		1986		1987		1988		1989	
Liabilities and stockholders' equity										
Current liabilities:										
Notes payable	$ —	0%	$ —	0%	$ —	0%	$ —	0%	$ 30	1%
Accounts payable	53	17%	64	17%	200	22%	239	15%	254	12%
Accrued and other liabilities	22	7%	43	11%	116	13%	218	14%	259	12%
Income taxes	10	3%	12	3%	26	3%	23	1%	20	1%
Total current liabilities	84	27%	119	31%	343	38%	480	30%	563	27%
Long-term debt	90	29%	73	19%	149	17%	275	17%	274	13%
Deferred taxes	1	0%	3	1%	10	1%	21	1%	81	4%
Total liabilities	175	56%	194	51%	501	56%	775	49%	919	44%
Stockholders' equity:										
Common stock	97	31%	101	27%	181	20%	341	21%	364	17%
Retained earnings	40	13%	82	22%	219	24%	474	30%	807	39%
Total stockholders' equity	137	44%	183	49%	400	44%	815	51%	1,172	56%
Total liabilities and stockholders' equity	$312	100%	$378	100%	$901	100%	$1,590	100%	$2,090	100%

While most managers understand infrastructure investment since it is so visible, the second category of asset investment, operating cycle, is often overlooked. As Figure 4.1 shows, the operating cycle begins with procurement of components, which are then transformed into finished goods and sold. The accounts receivable period begins once the item sold arrives at the customer (where there may be an installation if the VAR has to add any specialty items) and cash then is collected to end the cycle. Both inventory and accounts receivable have to be financed so there is a required investment in this cycle. Some of the investment is provided by third parties such as component vendors, subcontractors if either assembly or logistics and installation are outsourced, and advance payments from customers, but the remainder must be financed by Compaq. For 1989, the operating cycle turnover ratio would be calculated as follows using Table 4.2 data:

Accounts receivable, net	($428 + $530)/2 =	$ 479
Inventories	($387 + $559)/2 =	$ 473
Other	($16 + $62)/2 =	$ 40
less third-party financing		
Accounts payable - suppliers	($239 + $254)/2 =	$ (246)
Accrued liabilities - third party	($218 + $259)/2 =	$ (239)
Income taxes	($23 + $20)/2 =	$ (22)
Total operating cycle investment		$ 486
Operating cycle turnover	$2,876/$486 =	5.9

The logic of this analysis is parallel to the infrastructure turnover ratio calculation above. Since balance sheet data is being used, end-of-year 1988 and 1989 data are averaged. The analysis reveals that Compaq had to invest $486 million to finance the 1989 operating cycle yielding a turnover ratio of 5.9. This metric becomes more meaningful when comparative numbers for the whole period are compared:

	1985	1986	1987	1988	1989
Operating cycle turnover	5.7	7.7	8.4	7.4	5.9

The pattern seems to repeat itself. Compaq was most effective in 1987 with one dollar of operating cycle investment supporting $8.40 of sales but by 1989 the same dollar was supporting only $5.90.

Since the operating cycle turnover ratio has many pieces, a more in-depth analysis can be done on its major elements—inventory, accounts receivable, and accounts payable.[12] Because some of these are not directly related to sales, rather than turnover ratios the focus shifts to the time it takes for each component to complete its respective portion of the operating cycle. To illustrate, for 1989 Compaq sold $1.715 billion of inventory for the year (from 1989 cost of sales in the income statement) or $4.7 million of inventory per day ($1.715 billion/365 days). The average inventory for the year was $473 million (from the balance sheet, end-of-year 1988—$387 million—plus end-of-year 1989—$559 million—divided by 2). This reveals Compaq had on average 101 days of inventory on hand for the year ($473 average inventory divided by $4.7 million of inventory sold per day). Stated a bit differently, the procurement and transformation to sales portion of the operating cycle took 101 days. The

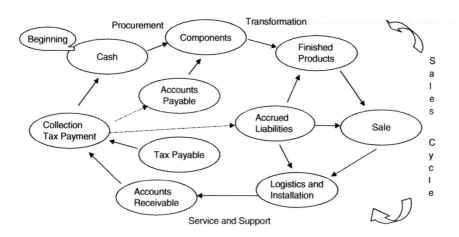

Fig. 4.1 The operating cycle

Understand your Situation

sales to collection can be analyzed in the same manner. For 1989 Compaq had $2.876 billion of sales which yields an average of $7.88 million per day. Average accounts receivable for the year was $479.3 million (the average of 1988 and 1989 balances from the balance sheet) which yields an average time of 61 days ($479.3/$7.88) for the collection period. In summary, for 1989 it took Compaq 101 days to procure and transform the components into finished goods and then sell them and another 61 days to collect on these sales for a total of 162 days in the operating cycle.[13]

Does Compaq have to finance all of this investment? The answer is 'No' since both vendors and other third parties provide some financing.[14] The average accounts payable to vendors for component purchases for 1989 was $246.3 million (computed from the balance sheet as above) and since Compaq sells $4.7 million of inventory per day this represents 52 days of inventory financing provided by vendors ($246.3/$4.7). The trend over the period in question is as follows:

	1985	1986	1987	1988	1989
A/R days	55	56	55	60	61
Inventory days	90	79	91	98	101
Account payables days	58	59	67	65	52

Interestingly, the deterioration in the operating cycle turnover is not related to any one item but is more due to decline in all of them. From 1985 to 1989, accounts receivable take an additional 6 days to collect (and thus have to be financed for these additional days), inventory takes 11 days longer in the cycle, and use of vendors for financing has decreased by 6 days.

It is now time to summarize this analysis of the second component of ROIC, asset turnover. From the above data for Compaq in 1989 the asset turnover can be calculated as follows:

Infrastructure investment:			
Property, plant and equipment, net	($429 + $705)/2 =	$	567
Strategic investments and other	($46 + $72)/2 =		59
Total infrastructure investment		$	626
Operating cycle investment:			
Accounts receivable, net	($428 + $530)/2 =	$	479
Inventories	($387 + $559)/2 =	$	473
Other	($16 + $62)/2 =	$	40
less third-party financing			
Accounts payable – suppliers	($239 + $254)/2 =	$	(246)
Accrued liabilities – third party	($218 + $259)/2 =	$	(239)
Income taxes	($23 + $20)/2 =	$	(22)
Total operating cycle investment		$	485
Total invested capital		$	1,111
Asset turnover	$2,876/$1,111		2.59

For the period under review the asset turnovers are as follows:

	1985	1986	1987	1988	1989
Asset turnover	3.46	3.55	3.90	3.29	2.59

This is not surprising since the above analysis revealed that both the infrastructure and operating cycle investment effectiveness in generating sales had deteriorated over this time period. The next section points out the impact on profitability.

ROIC Calculation

The above financial analysis discussion has been rather long and detailed but the results are always worth this effort. For Compaq over the 1985 to 1989 time period, a period where it attained a large degree of market power, the ROIC can now be calculated as follows:

	1985	1986	1987	1988	1989
ROIC	35.8%	47.8%	76.1%	60.1%	46.5%
$\wedge$					
Asset turnover	3.46	3.55	3.90	3.29	2.59
$\times$					
Profit margin	10.4%	13.5%	19.5%	18.3%	18.0%

Combining the strategic discussion with the financial results, it is clear that Compaq has created substantial shareholder value with its aggressive Desk-Pro386 entry. By 1987, only one year and a few months after the new product introduction, profitability has more than doubled (ROIC increasing from 35.8 per cent to 76.1 per cent) mostly due to the increase in the profit margin.[15] A very impressive result. The ensuing two years, however, are a bit worrisome since profitability fell to 46.5 per cent, a 40 per cent relative decline. The majority of this is due to the asset turnover decline—had this stayed constant at 3.90 ROIC in 1989 would have been 70.2 per cent (3.90 × 18.0 per cent). What has caused this? Was it due to the extreme growth over this period and the inadequacy of legacy systems to maintain control? Or might it have been due to lack of management attention with too much on the income numbers and not enough on the balance sheet? These are questions that investors should have been asking in 1989.

Competitor Moves and Countermoves: 1990 to 1991

Intel's Scenario Analysis

As Compaq started to exercise its new-found market power in renegotiating contracts with both suppliers and resellers, the structural aspects of the industry began to change. The balance of power between Compaq and its suppliers and buyers shifted in Compaq's favor. Most accepted this as simply the evolution of the commercial PC industry but one supplier, Intel, did a more thorough analysis. In the late 1980s, it ran a scenario analysis. The first was to do nothing which ceded control of the industry to dominant PC firms such as Compaq. The future of this scenario was bleak since Compaq, with its large market share, would allocate microprocessor sourcing across many suppliers. Compaq clearly understood that with careful allocation of its volume across a selected group of microprocessor suppliers it could be assured that each would have sufficient revenues to do the required R&D to stay competitive, but, more importantly, be also assured that no one could become dominant. With this scenario, Intel's profitability would be controlled to a large extent by Compaq. Intel management chose a different scenario—an aggressive branding campaign targeted at differentiating its microprocessor as the fastest and most reliable. This was a 'Bet the company' move but Intel management felt it had no better long-term alternatives. In later years, managers from Compaq, Intel, and other firms in this industry all agreed that, although Intel's microprocessor at the time was one of the top choices, it had no insurmountable advantage. Regardless, with aggressive marketing Intel attempted to create pull for its product through the perception of undisputed market leadership. Understanding the competitive logic of the move, Compaq immediately ended all sourcing agreements with Intel and shifted its substantial demand to key Intel rivals.[16] Unfortunately for Compaq, Microsoft joined with Intel and the Wintel alliance was created with Microsoft optimizing its operating system to Intel's chip architecture and vise versa. By mid-1990 embedded Wintel technology was becoming more important to buyers than the PC maker's name. Although Canion and his management team had not given up the fight, Compaq was forced to resume sourcing chips from Intel.

Financial Consequences

Component One: Profit Margin

As expected, this shift in power within the industry had a dramatic impact on Compaq. Table 4.3 reveals that in 1991 sales declined for the first time ever, gross margin had dropped over three points as its differentiation advantage began to erode and both R&D and selling, general, and administrative expenses had increased as Compaq attempted to fight back.[17] Total operating profit fell by 45 per cent (18 per cent to 9.8 per cent).

Component Two: Asset Turnover

Asset turnover also moved in the wrong direction. Using the same methodology as above with data from Table 4.4, the ratio continued to fall, dropping below 2 by 1991.

TABLE 4.3 Compaq Corporation consolidated income statements, 1989–1991 (millions)

	1989		1990		1991	
Net sales	$2,876	100.0%	$3,599	100.0%	$3,271	100.0%
Cost of sales	1,715	59.6%	2,058	57.2%	2,053	62.8%
Gross profit	1,161	40.4%	1,541	42.8%	1,218	37.2%
Operating expenses:						
Research, development and engineering	132	4.6%	186	5.2%	197	6.0%
Selling, general and administrative	539	18.7%	706	19.6%	722	22.1%
Total operating expenses	671	23.3%	892	24.8%	919	28.1%
Operating Profit—Total	490	17.0%	649	18.0%	299	9.1%
Income from Strategic Investments	27	1.0%	64	1.8%	20	0.6%
Operating Profit—Total	517	18.0%	713	19.8%	319	9.8%
Financing and other	−19	−0.7%	−42	−1.2%	−145	−4.4%
Profit before taxes	498	17.3%	671	18.6%	174	5.3%
Provision for income taxes	165	5.7%	216	6.0%	43	1.3%
Net profit	333	11.6%	455	12.6%	131	4.0%
Year-over-year Percentage Change						
Sales	39.2%		25.1%		−9.1%	
Cost of sales	39.1%		20.0%		−0.2%	
R&D	77.0%		31.1%		2.3%	
S,G&A	35.6%		40.2%		6.1%	
Operating income	36.0%		32.6%		−53.9%	

Infrastructure investment:
Property, plant and equipment, net	($892 + $884)/2 =	$	888
Strategic investments, and other	($136 + $160)/2 =		148
Total infrastructure investment		$	1,036
Operating cycle Investment:			
Accounts receivable, net	($627 + $624)/2 =	$	626
Inventories	($544 + $437)/2 =	$	491
Other	($83 + $269)/2 =	$	176
less third-party financing			
Accounts payable – suppliers	($292 + $196)/2 =	$	(244)
Accrued liabilities – third party	($351 + $442)/2 =	$	(397)
Total operating cycle investment		$	652
Total invested capital		$	1,688
Asset turnover	$3,271/$1,668 =		1.94

Understand your Situation

The trend for the three-year period shows a steady decline not only in asset turnover but in each of the components.

	1989	1990	1991
Infrastructure turnover	4.59	3.99	3.16
Operating cycle turnover	5.92	5.86	5.02
Asset turnover	2.59	2.37	1.94

Unmistakably the major issue is that infrastructure investment is generating much less sales revenue while the operating cycle investment seems to be declining at a lesser rate. In fact, a detailed analysis of the operating cycle

TABLE 4.4 Compaq Corporation consolidated balance sheets, 1989–1991 (millions)

	1989		1990		1991	
Assets						
Current assets:						
Cash and cash equivalents	$ 161	7.7%	$ 435	16.0%	$ 452	16.0%
Accounts receivable, net	530	25.4%	627	23.1%	624	22.1%
Inventories	559	26.7%	544	20.0%	437	15.5%
Other	62	3.0%	83	3.1%	269	9.5%
Total current assets	1,312	62.8%	1,689	62.2%	1,782	63.1%
Property, plant and equipment, net	705	33.7%	892	32.8%	884	31.3%
Strategic investments, and other	72	3.5%	136	5.0%	160	5.7%
Total assets	$2,090	100.0%	$2,717	100.0%	$2,826	100.0%
Liabilities and stockholders' equity						
Current liabilities:						
Notes payable	$ 30	1.4%	$ —	0.0%	$ —	0.0%
Accounts payable	254	12.1%	292	10.7%	$ 196	6.9%
Accrued and other	259	12.4%	351	12.9%	442	15.6%
Income taxes	20	1.0%	—	0.0%	—	0.0%
Total current liabilities	563	27.0%	643	23.7%	638	22.6%
Long-term debt	274	13.1%	75	2.8%	74	2.6%
Deferred taxes	81	3.9%	141	5.2%	184	6.5%
Other	—	0.0%	—	0.0%	—	0.0%
Total liabilities	919	44.0%	859	31.6%	896	31.7%
Stockholders' equity:						
Common stock	364	17.4%	596	21.9%	537	19.0%
Retained earnings	807	38.6%	1,262	46.4%	1,393	49.3%
Total stockholders' equity	1,172	56.0%	1,858	68.4%	1,930	68.3%
Total liabilities and stockholders' equity	$2,090	100.0%	$2,717	100.0%	$2,826	100.0%

ratio reveals that the main problem is with accounts receivable collections. Inventory actually moved faster through the system (by 14 days which is substantial) but this may be due to offering better terms to suppliers (note that Compaq is paying its suppliers 9 days sooner by 1991).

	1989	1990	1991
A/R days	61	59	70
Inventory days	101	98	87
Account payables days	52	48	43

ROIC Summary for 1989–1991

Intel's bold move—and Microsoft's quick recognition of the opportunity—has had a major impact on Compaq's profitability. While 1990 was still a very profitable year, by 1991 the full impact of this shift in power is evident in the financial footprint. Over this two-year period, profit margin dropped by 45 per cent (18.0 to 9.8 per cent) and asset turnover by another 25 per cent resulting in an overall drop in profitability of just under 60 per cent (46.5 to 18.9 per cent).

	1989	1990	1991
ROIC	46.5%	47.0%	18.9%
^			
Asset turnover	2.59	2.37	1.94
×			
Profit margin	18.0%	19.8%	9.8%

Compaq's Reaction 1991–1996

In late 1991 Compaq's board called a special meeting asking Canion and his team to address this issue. He argued that the battle was not over and outlined a plan to gradually become more cost focused but not to totally give up on technology leadership. The board also invited Eckhard Pfeiffer, the chief operating officer, to make a presentation. His was much different and called for an immediate change in strategic direction. Because the Wintel alliance made it virtually impossible to sustain a differentiated strategic position, Pfeiffer focused his presentation on competing in the industry using a cost leadership strategy. He presented a bold plan to slash expenses in order to recover some operating profit but concentrated much of the presentation on leaning out the organization to drive the second component of ROIC. After a long and contentious board discussion, Pfeiffer was brought in to replace Canion, the founder of the company.

Financial Results

Table 4.5 shows the impact of Pfeiffer's plan on the profit margin over the first five years. As he had predicted the Wintel alliance strategy commoditized PCs and the gross margins for Compaq reflect this. By 1996, they had fallen to 23 per cent! However, by slashing both R&D and S,G, & A expenses the new management team was able to stabilize operating profit at approximately 10 per cent. Note that in the first year of the new management, 1992, sales increased by 25.3 per cent while both R&D and S,G, & A *decreased* respectively 3.2 per cent and 12.2 per cent (refer to the year-over-year percentage changes section). This was repeated to a lesser extent in 1993.

The impact on the asset turnover was more dramatic. Pfeiffer without a doubt had leaned out the organizational infrastructure investment, increasing the effectiveness of this category in generating sales more than fourfold (from 3.16 to 13.68). Accepting the fact that Compaq could not continue to differentiate itself, R&D facilities were downsized as was any further investment in marketing and sales facilities. While the operating cycle investment changed minimally over the first four years, the upswing in this ratio in 1996 can be traced to better inventory management. This was due to new reseller programs that were introduced and will be discussed in the final section. The results of the analysis of the data in Table 4.6 in the format developed previously are as follows:[18]

	1991	1992	1993	1994	1995	1996
Infrastructure turnover	3.16	4.39	8.89	12.07	12.84	13.68
Operating cycle turnover	5.02	4.84	5.94	5.31	5.11	8.18
Asset turnover	1.94	2.30	3.56	3.69	3.65	5.12

Operating cycle detail:

A/R days	70	72	60	62	67	64
Inventory days	87	80	65	70	67	43
Account payables days	43	45	38	34	36	44

The overall impact on ROIC proved that Pfeiffer's logic was sound. While profit margins had remained relatively stable at about 10 per cent, overall profitability increased almost threefold (18.9 per cent to 53.0 per cent) under his first five years due to a much leaner organization driving the second component of ROIC.

	1991	1992	1993	1994	1995	1996
ROIC	18.9%	19.0%	34.3%	43.0%	31.8%	53.0%
^						
Asset turnover	1.94	2.30	3.56	3.69	3.65	5.12
×						
Profit margin	9.8%	8.2%	9.6%	11.7%	8.7%	10.4%

TABLE 4.5 Compaq Corporation consolidated income statements, 1991–1996 (millions)

	1991		1992		1993		1994		1995		1996	
Net sales	$3,271	100.0%	$4,100	100.0%	$7,191	100.0%	$10,866	100.0%	$14,755	100.0%	$18,109	100.0%
Cost of sales	2,053	62.8%	2,905	70.9%	5,493	76.4%	8,139	74.9%	11,367	77.0%	13,913	76.8%
Gross profit	1,218	37.2%	1,195	29.1%	1,698	23.6%	2,727	25.1%	3,388	23.0%	4,196	23.2%
Operating expenses:												
Research, development, and engineering	197	6.0%	173	4.2%	169	2.4%	226	2.1%	270	1.8%	407	2.2%
Selling, general, and administrative	722	22.1%	699	17.0%	837	11.6%	1,235	11.4%	1,835	12.4%	1,913	10.6%
Total operating expenses	919	28.1%	872	21.3%	1,006	14.0%	1,461	13.4%	2,105	14.3%	2,320	12.8%
Operating profit—total	299	9.1%	323	7.9%	692	9.6%	1,266	11.7%	1,283	8.7%	1,876	10.4%
Income from strategic investments	20	0.6%	15	0.4%	0	0.0%	0	0.0%	0	0.0%	0	0.0%
Operating profit—total	319	9.8%	338	8.2%	692	9.6%	1,266	11.7%	1,283	8.7%	1,876	10.4%
Financing and other	−145	−4.4%	−28	−0.7%	−76	−1.1%	−94	−0.9%	−95	−0.6%	−1	0.0%
Profit before taxes	174	5.3%	310	7.6%	616	8.6%	1,172	10.8%	1,188	8.1%	1,875	10.4%
Provision for income taxes	43	1.3%	97	2.4%	154	2.1%	305	2.8%	399	2.7%	563	3.1%
Net profit	131	4.0%	213	5.2%	462	6.4%	867	8.0%	789	5.3%	1,312	7.2%
Year-over-year Percentage change:												
Sales	−9.1%		25.3%		75.4%		51.1%		35.8%		22.7%	
Cost of sales	−0.2%		41.5%		89.1%		48.2%		39.7%		22.4%	
R&D	2.3%		−3.2%		19.7%		47.6%		48.6%		4.3%	
S, G, & A	6.1%		−12.2%		−2.3%		33.7%		19.5%		50.7%	
Operating income	−53.9%		8.0%		114.2%		82.9%		1.3%		46.2%	

TABLE 4.6 Compaq Corporation consolidated balance sheets, 1991–1996 (millions)

Assets	1991		1992		1993		1994		1995		1996	
Current assets:												
Cash and cash equivalents	$ 452	16.0%	$ 357	11.4%	$ 627	15.4%	$ 471	7.6%	$ 745	9.5%	$ 3,993	37.9%
Accounts receivable, net	624	22.1%	987	31.4%	1,377	33.7%	2,287	37.1%	3,141	40.2%	3,168	30.1%
Inventories	437	15.5%	834	26.5%	1,123	27.5%	2,005	32.5%	2,156	27.6%	1,152	10.9%
Other	269	9.5%	140	4.5%	164	4.0%	395	6.4%	485	6.2%	856	8.1%
Total current assets	1,782	63.1%	2,318	73.8%	3,291	80.6%	5,158	83.7%	6,527	83.5%	9,169	87.1%
Property, plant and equipment, net	884	31.3%	808	25.7%	779	19.1%	944	15.3%	1,110	14.2%	1,172	11.1%
Strategic investments and other	160	5.7%	16	0.5%	14	0.3%	64	1.0%	181	2.3%	185	1.8%
Total assets	$ 2,826	100.0%	$ 3,142	100.0%	$ 4,084	100.0%	$ 6,166	100.0%	$ 7,818	100.0%	$ 10,526	100.0%
Liabilities and stockholders' equity												
Current liabilities:												
Notes payable	$ —	0.0%	$ —	0.0%	$ —	0.0%	$ —	0.0%	$ —	0.0%	$ —	0.0%
Accounts payable	$ 196	6.9%	$ 516	16.4%	$ 637	15.6%	$ 888	14.4%	$ 1,379	17.6%	$ 1,962	18.6%
Accrued and other	442	15.6%	444	14.1%	607	14.9%	1,125	18.2%	1,301	16.6%	1,890	18.0%
Income taxes	—	0.0%	—	0.0%	—	0.0%	—	0.0%	—	0.0%	—	0.0%
Total current liabilities	638	22.6%	960	30.6%	1,244	30.5%	2,013	32.6%	2,680	34.3%	3,852	36.6%
Long-term debt	74	2.6%	—	0.0%	—	0.0%	300	4.9%	300	3.8%	300	2.9%
Deferred taxes	184	6.5%	176	5.6%	186	4.6%	179	2.9%	224	2.9%	230	2.2%
Other	—	0.0%	—	0.0%	—	0.0%	—	0.0%	—	0.0%	—	0.0%
Total liabilities	896	31.7%	1,136	36.2%	1,430	35.0%	2,492	40.4%	3,204	41.0%	4,382	41.6%
Stockholders' equity:												
Common stock	537	19.0%	400	12.7%	586	14.3%	739	12.0%	890	11.4%	1,107	10.5%
Retained earnings	1,393	49.3%	1,606	51.1%	2,068	50.6%	2,935	47.6%	3,724	47.6%	5,037	47.9%
Total stockholders' equity	1,930	68.3%	2,006	63.8%	2,654	65.0%	3,674	59.6%	4,614	59.0%	6,144	58.4%
Total liabilities and stockholders' equity	$ 2,826	100.0%	$ 3,142	100.0%	$4,084	100.0%	$6,166	100.0%	$7,818	100.0%	$10,526	100.0%

Dell

Dell Positioning Strategy

In 1982 Michael Dell started customizing PCs for technically literate customers while still an undergraduate at the University of Texas. Within two years his business became so large that he dropped out of college and started Dell Computer. Whereas Compaq targeted the total commercial market and, hence, had to offer service since at that time PCs were not that reliable, Dell was able to deal directly with the technically literate segment it targeted. Service was not a critical need to those that understood PCs. This had a profound impact on the underlying business models of the two future competitors. Compaq, as discussed above, relied on a large, complex reseller network to sell and, more importantly at first, to provide service. It assembled PCs based upon aggregated forecasts of these resellers, which were often wrong. To supply these resellers Compaq had to build a large global distribution infrastructure. Dell, on the other hand, by targeting the technically literate niche[19] did not have to rely on resellers. It dealt directly with the end customer, used the distribution infrastructure of Federal Express or UPS rather then building its own, and provided the minimal support necessary over the phone. This allowed Dell to build to order (BTO) rather than building to a forecast (BTF). No machine was assembled until an order was received directly from a customer. The end result was that a PC built by Dell moved through the operating cycle much quicker.

By the early 1990s, the needs of the commercial PC market changed. Most commercial organizations now had internal IT support groups that could service PCs, the technology was far more reliable, and most users were experienced enough to not require the level of service once demanded. The value of the service offering diminished, and companies became more price conscious. Reseller relationships became less important and companies were willing to deal directly. Dell's initial niche market customer value proposition now aligned with the overall commercial PC market. Dell and Compaq began to compete for the same corporate customers.

In 1992 Dell's sales more than doubled and 1993 demand again was on the increase but Dell imploded. Its legacy systems were unable to handle the demand and there were questions as to whether Dell's direct model was scalable. Michael Dell brought in Morton Topfer from Motorola as vice chairman with the mandate to correct the problem. Topfer, in turn, brought in seasoned supply chain executives. They knew that Dell's customer value proposition—customized PCs—had an advantage over all other competitors and were determined to make it work. The financial analysis below shows their results.

Financial Footprint of Dell

From Table 4.7, Dell's common size measures are not that much different from Compaq but the absolute numbers are interesting. In 1991 Dell was about one-quarter the size of Compaq with an operating profit 24 per cent less than Compaq (7.5 per cent as compared to Compaq's 9.8 per cent). By 1996 Dell had moved closer to Compaq in revenue but was still substantially small than Compaq (41 per cent of revenue) but operating profit % was now 87 per cent of Compaq's. But Dell's year-over-year growth in sales was substantially better than Compaq in the final two years. Dell was gaining momentum in the market at the expense of Compaq. In addition, Dell's growth now seemed to be under control. Sales grew at 52 per cent in 1995 and expenses matched this rate resulting in a comparable growth in overall operating profit. In 1996, due to a somewhat lower relative growth in cost of sales and S, G, & A, operating profit increased at almost twice sales. Dell's model had proved scalable.

An analysis of the balance sheet paints an even more interesting picture. Using the same approach as before, the asset turnover and the underlying details highlight the advantages of Dell's business model. Without the distribution infrastructure needed to support a complex reseller network, by 1996 Dell supported $35.50 in sales with every dollar of infrastructure investment. Although Pfeiffer had increased Compaq's infrastructure turn fourfold over the past five years, it still pales in comparison to Dell (13.7 vs. 35.5). The operating cycle turnover comparison is no better. Since Compaq had a reseller between itself and the end customer while Dell dealt directly, Compaq had to wait much longer to collect on what was shipped to the resellers (64 days vs. 38). And while Pfeiffer had worked to optimize inventory days in Compaq's BTF model it was no match for Dell's BTO system (43 days vs. 20). Both enjoyed the same amount of financing from vendors so, in the end, the number of days in the operating cycle that Compaq must finance was about 63 days (64 + 43 − 44) while Dell's was less than one-quarter that (38 + 20 − 45 = 13 days). Although there is much variability in these metrics since Topfer took over, if the 1996 numbers are sustainable the supply chain group has proved its worth.

	1991	1992	1993	1994	1995	1996
Infrastructure turnover	23.5	16.6	17.1	29.2	33.6	35.5
Operating cycle turnover	9.6	10.7	17.1	29.2	18.8	142.4
Asset turnover	6.8	6.5	8.5	12.0	12.1	28.4
A/R days	36	39	44	42	44	38
Inventory days	66	58	38	24	31	20
Account payables days	40	43	51	50	39	45

TABLE 4.7 Dell Corporation consolidated income statements, 1991–1996 (millions)

	1991		1992		1993		1994		1995		1996	
Total sales	$890	100.0%	$2,014	100.0%	$2,873	100.0%	$3,475	100.0%	$5,296	100.0%	$7,759	100.0%
Total cost of sales	608	68.3%	1,565	77.7%	2,440	84.9%	2,737	78.8%	4,229	79.9%	6,093	78.5%
Gross profit	282	31.7%	449	22.3%	433	15.1%	738	21.2%	1,067	20.1%	1,666	21.5%
Operating expenses:												
Research and development costs	33	3.7%	42	2.1%	49	1.7%	65	1.9%	95	1.8%	126	1.6%
Selling, general and administrative expense	182	20.5%	268	13.3%	423	14.7%	424	12.2%	595	11.2%	826	10.6%
Total operating expenses	215	24.2%	310	15.4%	472	16.4%	489	14.1%	690	13.0%	952	12.3%
Operating profit—primary	67	7.5%	139	6.9%	(39)	−1.4%	249	7.2%	377	7.1%	714	9.2%
Income from strategic investments	0	0.0%	0	0.0%	0	0.0%	0	0.0%	0	0.0%	0	0.0%
Operating profit—total	67	7.5%	139	6.9%	(39)	−1.4%	249	7.2%	377	7.1%	714	9.2%
Other income/(expense), net	—	0.0%	—	0.0%	—	0.0%	(36)	−1.0%	6	0.1%	33	0.4%
Profit before taxes	67	7.5%	139	6.9%	(39)	−1.4%	213	6.1%	383	7.2%	747	9.6%
Provision for income taxes	16	1.8%	38	1.9%	(3)	−0.1%	64	1.8%	111	2.1%	216	2.8%
Net profit	$ 51	5.7%	$ 102	5.0%	$ (36)	−1.3%	$ 149	4.3%	$ 272	5.1%	$ 531	6.8%
Year-over-year percentage Increase												
Sales			126.3%		42.7%		21.0%		46.5%			
Cost of sales			157.4%		56.0%		12.2%		44.1%			
R&D			28.1%		15.6%		32.7%		32.6%			
S, G, & A			47.1%		57.8%		0.2%		38.8%			
Operating income			108.1%		−128.1%		−738.5%		89.4%			

TABLE 4.8 Dell Corporation consolidated balance sheets, 1991–1996 (millions)

	1991		1992		1993		1994		1995		1996	
Assets												
Current assets:												
Cash and cash equivalents	$ 132	35.6%	$ 95	10.3%	$ 337	29.6%	$ 527	33.1%	$ 646	30.1%	$ 1,352	45.2%
Accounts receivable	120	32.3%	374	40.3%	411	36.0%	538	33.8%	726	33.8%	903	30.2%
Inventories	35	9.4%	303	32.7%	220	19.3%	293	18.4%	429	20.0%	251	8.4%
Other current assets	26	7.0%	80	8.7%	80	7.0%	112	7.0%	156	7.3%	241	8.1%
Total current assets	313	84.4%	853	92.0%	1,048	91.9%	1,470	92.2%	1,957	91.1%	2,747	91.8%
Property, plant and equipment, less accumulated depreciation	49	13.2%	70	7.6%	87	7.6%	117	7.3%	179	8.3%	235	7.9%
Intangible and other assets	9	2.4%	4	0.4%	5	0.5%	7	0.4%	12	0.6%	11	0.4%
Total assets	$371	100.0%	$927	100.0%	$1,140	100.0%	$1,594	100.0%	$2,148	100.0%	$2,993	100.0%
Liabilities and stockholders' equity												
Current liabilities:												
Accounts payable	$ 95	25.6%	$295	31.8%	$ 283	24.8%	$ 448	28.1%	$ 466	21.7%	$1,040	34.7%
Income taxes payable	—	0.0%	27	2.9%	18	1.5%	25	1.6%	—	0.0%	—	0.0%
Accrued liabilities	58	15.6%	171	18.5%	238	20.8%	279	17.5%	473	22.0%	618	20.6%
Total current liabilities	153	41.2%	494	53.3%	538	47.2%	752	47.2%	939	43.7%	1,658	55.4%
Long-term debt	—	0.0%	48	5.2%	100	8.8%	113	7.1%	113	5.3%	18	0.6%
Deferred income taxes	—	0.0%	16	1.7%	31	2.8%	77	4.8%	123	5.7%	232	7.8%
Total liabilities	153	41.2%	558	60.2%	669	58.7%	942	59.1%	1,175	54.7%	1,908	63.7%
Stockholders' equity:												
Common stock	55	14.8%	178	19.2%	320	28.1%	358	22.5%	436	20.3%	474	15.8%
Retained earnings	163	43.9%	191	20.6%	151	13.2%	308	19.3%	570	26.5%	647	21.6%
Treasury stock (at cost)	—	0.0%	—	0.0%	—	0.0%	(14)	−0.9%	(33)	−1.5%	(36)	−1.2%
Total stockholders' equity	218	58.8%	369	39.8%	471	41.3%	652	40.9%	973	45.3%	1,085	36.3%
Total liabilities and stockholders' equity	$371	100.0%	927	100.0%	$1,140	100.0%	$1,594	100.0%	$2,148	100.0%	$2,993	100.0%

Bringing the two components together in the ROIC summary for Dell puts Pfeiffer's accomplishments into perspective. Although admirable, they may have been for naught. What if Dell can sustain this performance?

	1991	1992	1993	1994	1995	1996
ROIC ∧	51.0%	44.7%	−11.6%	73.7%	87.2%	261.5%
Asset turnover ×	6.8	6.5	8.5	12.0	12.1	28.4
Profit margin	7.5%	6.9%	−1.4%	6.1%	7.2%	9.2%

The Future

Sustainable Competitive Advantage

Compaq was not caught unawares. In 1993 it built a direct-ship warehouse in Houston but was not able to emulate Dell's model. First, it created channel conflict and the major resellers immediately demanded that Compaq not compete with them. Since these resellers controlled the customer relationships and the customers had minimal switching costs Compaq negotiated. It tried to build a quasi-direct-ship model where partially assembled PCs were shipped to resellers who would then 'customize' them. It did not work. In addition, Compaq found that a BTO system required very different IT and logistics support from its BTF model. Its embedded systems, although very sophisticated, could not support such a model. Eighteen months later the warehouse was dismantled. Both Hewlett-Packard and IBM tried similar strategies with the same results. Sustainable competitive advantage is often defined as doing something different that others cannot imitate. Dell had achieved this.

The Board Rooms

Assume that the comparative 1996 ROICs for Dell and Compaq as shown below are circulated for board discussion at Dell.[20] What actions would follow? It should be obvious that Dell would become more aggressive in pricing. Even at a razor-thin 1 per cent profit margin Dell could achieve a 28 per cent ROIC, which after tax would be sufficient to satisfy investors.[21]

	Dell	Compaq
ROIC ∧	261.5%	53.0%
Asset turnover ×	28.4	5.12
Profit margin	9.2%	10.4%

Understand your Situation

Now assume that the comparative 1996 ROICs for Dell and Compaq are circulated for board discussion at Compaq. It had already tried to imitate Dell and failed. The board was aware that Dell was becoming more aggressive in pricing and understood the logic (i.e. since PCs were now undifferentiated Compaq would be forced to match Dell's price and at a 1 per cent profit margin Compaq would earn about 5 per cent ROIC, which would not satisfy investors). In retrospect, the purchase of Digital and the move by Compaq into the enterprise space should not have been a surprise.

The Compaq board made the correct move even if the long-run results were not optimum. In 1997 Dell's model became so efficient that it required no invested capital to support it. As shown below, vendor and third-party financing were sufficient to finance the operating cycle and the needed infrastructure. What is the ROIC of a company that requires no invested capital to run its business model? How does one compete against such a firm?

Infrastructure investment:			
Property, plant and equipment, net	$ 432.5		
Strategic investments and other	14.5		
Total infrastructure investment	$ 447.0		
Operating cycle investment:			
Accounts receivable, net	$ 1,790.0	A/R days	35
Inventories	253.0	Inventory days	9
Other less third-party financing	570.0		
Accounts payable — suppliers	$ (2,020.0)	Account payables days	51
Accrued liabilities — third party	(1,176.0)		
Income taxes	0		
Total operating cycle investment	$ (583.0)		
Total invested capital	(136.0)		
Asset turnover	Undefined		

To Close

In today's business world best-in-class companies like Dell are able to manage their business models with optimized investment. Jeff Immelt, CEO of GE, gained early recognition when he was able to covert the jet engine division's operating cycle to solely third-party financed. Wal-Mart requires all vendors to be electronically linked via an intranet such that real-time granular sales data can be used to lean out inventory in the entire system. Strategy and financial planning are now done at the extended enterprise—e.g. Wal-Mart and its third-party affiliates—rather than at firm level. Companies like Dell and Wal-Mart map their whole value system and manage it such that both infrastructure and operating cycle investments are minimized. Gone are the days of redundancy.

Why should Dell build a distribution infrastructure when there are companies such as UPS willing to provide the service with a high level of efficiency? Why should Cisco build infrastructure to assemble and test low-end switches and routers when there are highly efficient third-party sub cons willing to provide this service? Cisco employs a product lifecycle planning model to focus its investment where it can gain the highest overall return. ROIC is a rather simple calculation but a very powerful business model.

Notes

1. The finance literature focuses more on return on equity investment (ROE) than on return on invested capital (ROIC). The latter ratio defines investment as both equity and debt while the former focuses on the equity factor only. The role of a finance manager within a firm is to attain the proper mix of debt and equity funds. Operational managers responsible for strategy formulation and implementation are only concerned with proper investment of funds and not how the funds were raised—either through equity or debt. As a result, ROIC is the proper financial measure when doing strategic analysis.
2. Many managers would argue that 'if you can't make it on margin you make it on volume.' This is half true—to be precise, it is volume in relation to the investment necessary to drive this volume or asset turnover.
3. Microsoft is one that has been successful at maximizing both factors. In fact, it has been so successful that it is constantly under regulatory scrutiny.
4. The formal definition of a successful differentiation strategy is that the value created in the eyes of the customer is greater than the cost to differentiate. This price premium, by definition, would be evidenced by a higher profit margin for a successful differentiation strategy.
5. While the term 'product' is used throughout this chapter this by no means excludes service organizations. Whether the product is either tangible or intangible in nature, the discussion in this chapter will apply.
6. Compaq's first product was the size of a small suitcase and weighted just under 30 pounds but it was both portable and reliable.
7. Note that these expenses can be actual expenses such as a sales commission or estimated such as a depreciation expense where the purchase price of a capital asset (e.g. a building) is allocated over its projected useful life.
8. Net sales is defined as total sales less any returns or allowances.
9. This general rule does not hold true for software companies since their only cost of sales is estimated warranty expenses and capital-intensive industries such as semiconductor manufacturers where gross margin is more a factor of capacity usage.
10. Although three percentage points may not seem that significant when looking at it in relative terms, from 10.4% to 13.7% is greater than a 30% increase.
11. Rounding errors in this data may cause small differences in totals.

12. Cash is ignored in this strategic analysis. It is an investment yet to be made and, as such, had no impact on the operating results for the period under investigation. For firms with large cash holding, this approach requires that the firm be split into two: a holding company with liquid assets and an operating company where the above analysis would be appropriate. For year-end 2005, Microsoft held $37.8 billion of its $70.8 billion in total assets in cash and that was after paying $36 billion in dividends in 2005.

13. This is often referred to in the business press as the cash-to-cash cycle.

14. Accrued liabilities from third parties are not analyzed separately because this component is made up of many items—unpaid wages of the workforce, customer advances, outsourced services, and the like.

15. Had the profit margin remained constant the increase in the asset turnover would have resulted in an ROIC of only 40.6% (10.4% × 3.90).

16. By 1989 many microprocessor companies had comparable 32-bit chips.

17. Some of the percentage increase also can be attributed to the overall decrease in sales in 1991 since many of the operating expenses were fixed rather than variable.

18. Calculations will not be shown for the rest of this chapter. The date is given as are the final results and the reader is encouraged to check these by doing the required analysis as demonstrated in prior sections.

19. In the mid-1980s, this clearly was a niche market since few IT support groups in large corporations even supported PCs.

20. As shown in this chapter the analysis to develop these is not difficult and the data is readily available.

21. Assuming a 40% tax rate would yield about a 17% after-tax return—28% less (40%) 28% = 17%.

5   HR Dreams: Where Human Resource Management is Headed to Deliver Value

Dave Ulrich

My psychologist wife has taught me that to understand our past, we can read our journals. To understand our present, we need to look honestly and seriously in a mirror. And, to understand our future, we need to examine our dreams. Dream analysis has two parts. One part focuses on our daytime dreams which symbolize our hopes and aspirations and define where we want to go. For organization leaders this focus implies having a vision, mission, or purpose statement that sets a direction for where their organization is headed. The other part of dream analysis examines the subconscious elements of our night-time dreams. These dreams often deal with the implicit challenges we face and give our mind a way to ponder what challenges we face and how we might deal with them through our dreams. So by analyzing our night-time dreams we can begin to accomplish our daytime visions.

The same logic may be applied to the HR profession. We can look to our past in textbooks and articles; we can grasp our present by looking in the mirror of what we do; but we create our future by examining our dreams. These dreams are rooted in the challenges of businesses today and how HR professionals should respond. They also highlight the hopes and aspirations of HR professionals. This essay begins with a brief overview of the context of business, then suggests an overarching vision for our future, reports ten challenges that we must address, and concludes with implications for both the structure of the HR organization and the personal requirements for HR professionals.

Context of Business

In conference after conference focused on 'the world of business' similar themes surface. Technology has increased access, accessibility, visibility, and connection.

Understand your Situation

The connected world is smaller, changing rapidly, and has more open information. Customers have become increasingly segmented and persnickety. Investors have become increasingly attuned to and actively concerned about not only financial results, but intangibles. Employees represent increasingly diverse demographic backgrounds including not only race and gender, but personal preferences, global or cultural backgrounds, and orientation to work. Competitors come from both traditional large global players and increasingly smaller innovators. And all of these themes occur in the context of global business where what happens in one corner of the world affects business throughout the world.

Many spend enormous amounts of time specifying these trends and their implications on business. Most of these trends are outside the control of any one individual or any one company. They occur in both predictable and unpredictable ways. They affect all aspects of business from how to fund a firm to how to position the firm in customer minds and how to engineer and deliver products. They also affect human resources. HR's legacy was to monitor terms and conditions of work through industrial relations, then to design systems and practices that shape how people are treated in an organization based on a theory of personnel administration. With this orientation, HR professionals had little reason to be more than casual observers of business trends. Now, the HR profession is being asked to help businesses compete and to do so, HR must not only observe, but understand and adapt to these business trends.

A Vision for HR's Future

Some write about why they 'hate' HR, because essentially it does not respond to the opportunities of today's business challenges. It is probably more useful to figure out how to adapt HR so that it can adapt to and thrive in the business context facing most companies. Thinking about how HR can and should respond to these business challenges evokes a number of new demands on HR. In seminars, I often stipulate the changing business conditions HR professionals must master, then ask participants to identify what HR should focus on to respond to these conditions. The lists often include:

- *Talent*: getting and keeping good talent;
- *Change*: making sure that organizations change and adapt;
- *Governance*: building governance processes that ensure confidence;
- *Intangibles*: identifying and delivering intangible value to investors;
- *Leadership*: ensuring the next generation of leadership within a company;
- *Execution*: making sure that strategies are delivered as planned;
- *Globalization*: adapting HR practices to a worldwide setting;
- *Performance management*: driving performance and results throughout the company;

- *Communication*: learning to share information with those inside and outside the company;
- *HR transformation*: figuring out how to transform the HR function from a traditional administrative service to more strategic.

These and other demands redefine what HR professionals should pay attention to, how HR practices should be designed, and the focus of HR functions or departments. As we reflected on these types of demands, we concluded that there is an underlying theme, that of creating value. In changing times, HR professionals, practices, and functions address these demands to create value.

Value is defined by the receiver more than the giver, so a focus on value means that HR must identify the receivers of HR services and prescribe what they receive from insightful HR work. These receivers and the value they receive include:

- Employees who receive value from their contributions at work. This value may be framed in terms of an employee value proposition where employees who contribute to their organization's success receive value from their organization. This value may come in the form of a vision that gives the employee meaning or purpose, opportunities to learn and grow, impact by doing work that has meaning, community by being part of a team of like-minded and committed individuals and working for a respected leader, flexibility in terms and conditions of work. These dimensions of the employee value proposition may be enhanced by HR.

- Customers who receive the products or services that lead them to purchase more from the target organization. Customer value may be assessed by tracking customer share, or the percentage of a customer's total revenue spent with the target firm. Organizations build customer share by connecting strategy, products, services, management practices, and value with target customers.

- Investors who receive confidence in a firm's sustainable performance. Increasingly, a firm's financial results (profits, earnings) explain about 50 per cent of a firm's market value with the other half being determined by what is called intangibles. Intangibles represent confidence investors have in a firm's future and sustainable earnings. They might include predictability of results, clarity of strategy, core functional competence (marketing, manufacturing, technology), and key organization capabilities (speed, culture, accountability, leadership, talent).

- Line managers who receive the tools and processes to make sure that espoused strategies happen.

Understand your Situation

As HR focuses on the creation of value, these four stakeholders become critical to HR's success. They determine how well HR practices, professionals, and departments are making wise investments.

Ten Challenges, Principles, and Practices

A value focus for HR raises new challenges and opportunities. The challenges are things that HR professionals should understand and help manage to create value; the opportunities are the tools and techniques to help overcome these challenges. Most of the challenges come from research on what is known about how organizations can compete in dramatically changing markets. Below are some of the principles HR professionals should master, how these principles affect organization capabilities, and what HR professionals should know and do to turn the principles into practices (see summary in Table 5.1)

TABLE 5.1 Ten principles and capabilities HR professionals should master to create value

Principle: We are good at ...	Capability An organization is known for and successful if ...	HR professionals should be able to ...
Talent: Assuring competent and committed people	It attracts, motivates, retains, and engages competent employees	• Do talent audit of what is and what is necessary • Build an employee value proposition that engages talented employees
Speed: Making important changes happen fast	It is able to change and change quickly to align with customer needs	• Build and enact a disciplined change process • Assimilate change into a new identity
Shared mindset: Turning customer reputation and identity into employee actions	It is able to build a culture that reflects customer expectations and turns them into employee actions	• Perform a cultural audit • Make customer reputation real to employees
Accountability: Implementing disciplines that result in high performance	It is able to meet commitments and do what it says it will do	• Build and implement a disciplined performance management system • Follow up to ensure consequences
Collaboration: Working across boundaries to ensure leverage and efficiency	It is able to make the whole more than the sum of the parts	• Increase efficiency through productivity improvement efforts • Increase leverage by sharing ideas, people, products, services

Learning: Generating and generalizing ideas with impact	It is able to generate new ideas and then generalize those ideas across boundaries	• Generate new ideas by experimenting, acquiring skills, continuous improvement, benchmarking • Generalize ideas across boundaries
Leadership brand: Embedding leaders throughout the organization who embody the leadership brand	It is able to identify a leadership brand that connects customer reputation and employee behaviors	• Ensure that leaders demonstrate the leadership code • Prepare a statement of leadership brand and invest in it
Innovation: Doing something new in both content and process	It is able to innovate and create new ways to do things	• Establish an innovation protocol that helps shape new ideas • Install a spirit of innovation among all employees
Strategic clarity: Articulating and sharing a point of view about the future	It is able to envision a future state and ensure that employees and practices are aligned to it	• Establish a process to ensure strategic clarity • Align organization actions to make the strategy happen
Efficiency: Managing the costs of operation	It is able to work to reduce costs	• Increase productivity • Manage processes efficiently • Allocate resources on key projects

Talent: We are Good at Attracting, Motivating, and Retaining Competent and Committed People

Assuring talent means going beyond the platitudes such as 'people are our most important asset' and 'strategy follows people' and investing time and resources to secure superior talent. Employees must be both competent and committed. Competent employees have the skills for today's and tomorrow's business requirements. Committed employees deploy those skills regularly and predictably. HR professionals may assess the extent to which their organization regularly attracts and keeps top talent and the extent to which that talent is productive and focused. Assuring competent employees comes as organizations buy (bring in new talent), build (develop existing talent), borrow (access thought leaders through alliances or partnerships), bounce (remove poor talent), and bind (keep the best talent).

Competence of employees may be tracked by assessing the percentage of employees who have the skills to do their job today and in the future, by benchmarking current employees against competitors (it is good that employees are targeted by search firms because it suggests a reservoir of talented employees), and by productivity measures that track employee output per unit of employee input. One firm invited investors to visit and ask any employee any question about the firm's strategy, product, or financial position. This test of business literacy impressed investors who were able to determine first hand the competence of employees. Assuring commitment comes when leaders build an employee value proposition that ensures that employees who contribute more will in turn receive more of what matters most to them. HR professionals may track commitment through retention of the top employees (we often suggest that the most strategic human resource decision a company can make is to place its worst performer in a competitor), by employee attitude surveys done frequently as pulse checks, and by direct observation as executives can intuitively sense the engagement level of employees. HR professionals who build both competent and committed employees ensure a flow of talent that helps the organization perform well over time.

Speed: We are Good at Making Important Changes Happen Fast

Gaining speed goes beyond change to fast change. Speed means that the organization has an ability to identify and move quickly into new markets, new products, new employee contracts, and new business processes. Leaders embed this capability into the organization by being focused on making decisions rigorously, by implementing change processes throughout their organization, by removing bureaucratic barriers to change, and by eliminating change viruses. Changing the capacity to change takes time because the laws of entropy keep change from happening, but when large firms act like small nimble firms, they master the speed capability.

Speed may be tracked in a variety of ways, all involving time. Time may be tracked from concept to commercialization of an idea, from changeover of an assembly line to a new product, from collecting customer data through market research to making changes in customer relations, from proposing an administrative change to fully implementing that change. Just as increasing inventory turns show physical assets are well used; saving time demonstrates both financial savings in terms of labor productivity, but also increased enthusiasm and responsiveness to opportunities.

Shared Mindset: We are Good at Ensuring that Customers and Employees have Positive Images of and Experiences with our Organization

Gaining a shared mindset, or firm brand identity, becomes a vital capability. Many firms have moved from individual product brands to firm brands. The Marriott name on a hotel adds value because it gives the traveler confidence in the product. Being affiliated with the Olympics brand is worth millions to companies who want to be associated with the positive image of the Olympics tradition. HR professionals may help identify and shape their shared mindset, or firm brand, by building a consensus among their management team of what they want the firm to be 'known for' by its best customers in the future. Once a consensus is reached on this identity, they may invest in a series of actions to make the identity real to both customers and employees.

Shared mindset may be measured with a simple exercise. Ask your team to answer the question: What are the top three things we want to be known for by our best customers in the future? Collect the responses to this query and measure the degree of consensus as the percentage of responses that fall into the most common three categories. We have done this exercise hundreds of times, often to find a shared mindset in the 50–60 per cent range. Leading firms score in the 80–90 per cent range because they have a clear sense of what they want to be known for by customers. The next step in the exercise is to invite key customers to answer the same question. They will monitor the extent to which the internal and external mindsets are shared and be the ultimate determinant of the value of the culture.

Accountability: We are Good at the Disciplines that Result in High Performance

Some firms have developed accountability habits. It is just not acceptable to miss goals. Performance accountability becomes a firm capability when employees realize that they must meet their performance expectations. Accountability comes when strategies translate into measurable standards of performance, then when rewards are linked to the meeting or missing of standards. When there is a line of sight between rewards, appraisals, and strategies, accountability is more likely to follow. When an HR professional designs an employee's performance appraisal form, it should reflect the strategy the employee is attempting to accomplish and what specific actions the employee should take to help accomplish the strategy. Rewards, both financial and non-financial, then reinforce the strategy and enable the employee to receive clear and definitive feedback on his performance.

Accountability can be monitored. By looking at a performance appraisal form, can you derive the strategy of the business? Are the items measured on the appraisal indicative of the strategy? What percentage of employees receive an appraisal each year? How much variance is there in compensation based on employee performance? Some firms have a pay for performance philosophy, but their annual increases range from 3.5 to 4.5 per cent. They claim an accountability culture, but they are not. What percentage of employees feel they have received a helpful feedback session in the past year?

Collaboration: We are Good at Working across Boundaries to Ensure both Efficiency and Leverage

The whole needs to be greater than the sum of the parts. Some organizations have more value broken up than held together. These organizations do not understand collaboration as a capability. Collaboration may come when the combined organization gains efficiencies of operation through shared services, technology, or economies of scale. Collaboration may also come when the combined organization accomplishes more together than it could separately through learning and sharing ideas across boundaries, allocating resources to key areas, and creating strategies that leverage products and customers. HR professionals build collaboration by seeking both efficiencies and leverage throughout the organization.

Collaboration may be tracked for both the institution and team levels. Institutionally, you may determine your break-up value and compare it with your current market value. If the break-up value is 25 per cent more than the current market value of the assets (rule of thumb), collaboration is not occurring the way it should. Within the organization, collaboration may be tracked by monitoring the flow of talent and ideas across boundaries. Are people moving from one area to another? Are ideas or practices in one part of the firm being done in another part of the firm? Finally, collaboration may be measured by cost savings in administrative costs through shared services. For example, shared services have been found to produce 15–25 per cent cost savings in employee administrative costs. The average large firm spends about $1,600 per employee per year in administration, thus you can calculate the probable cost savings of shared services: ($1,600 *0.2 (cost savings) * number of employees).

Learning: We are Good at Generating and Generalizing Ideas with Impact

Generating new ideas comes from benchmarking (seeing what others have done and adapting it), experimentation (trying new things to see if and how they work), competence acquisition (hiring or developing people with new skills and ideas), and continuous improvement (improving on what was done through suggestion systems and process analysis). Generalizing ideas means that the ideas move across a boundary of time (from one leader to the next), space (from one geography to another), or division (from one business unit to another). Sharing ideas across boundaries may be done through leveraging, technology, creating communities of practice, or moving people. HR professionals who encourage individual and team learning can also create organization learning through these practices.

Tracking learning may come at individual or organization levels. For individuals learning means letting go of old practices and adapting new ones. You may ask employees 'what is the half life of knowledge in your current job? When is 50 per cent of what you know how to do out of date?' This question explores the extent to which employees are focused on generating and generalizing new ideas for their work. Learning within the organization shows up in continuous improvement. Are we getting better at production? Marketing? Customer service? Employee engagement? By establishing baselines and tracking results, learning becomes a part of the organization improvement effort.

Leadership: We are Good at Embedding Leaders throughout the Organization who Deliver the Right Results in the Right Way—Who Carry our Leadership Brand

Some organizations produce leaders. These organizations generally have a leadership brand, or clear statement, of what leaders should know, be, and do. A leadership brand exists when the leaders from top to bottom of an organization have a unique identity. These leaders are identifiable. They are focused. They possess attributes of success and deliver results. HR professionals have the responsibility to produce the next generation of leaders by helping establish the leadership brand, assessing the gaps in the present leadership against this brand, then investing in future leaders.

Leadership brand may be tracked by monitoring the pool of future leaders. How many back-ups do we have in place for our top 100 employees? In one company, this figure dropped from about 3 : 1 (three qualified back-ups for each of the top 100) to about 0.7 : 1 (less than one back-up). This company discerned that the downsizing had impaired the leadership bench to a serious level.

Customer connection: We are Good at Building Enduring Relationships of Trust with Targeted Customers

Many firms have discovered through customer value analysis that 20 per cent of customers account for 80 per cent of business performance. These target customers become absolutely critical for a firm to compete and win. Creating customer connectivity may originate in a variety of practices. It may originate in databases that identify and track each individual customer preference. Customer connectivity may also come from dedicated account teams who build long-term relationships with targeted accounts. Customer connection may also come from involving a customer in the firm's HR practices. To leverage such opportunities, many firms are including customers in staffing, training, compensation, and communication practices. The net result of these activities is customer intimacy and the resultant sales. Customer connectivity may also be enhanced when large proportions of the employee population have meaningful exposure to or interaction with external customers. All of these result in an information and mindset convergence between employees and customers.

Customer connectivity and service may be tracked through share of targeted customer rather than market share. This means that you identify your key accounts, then track the share of those key accounts over time. In addition, regular customer service scores may offer insight on how well the customer perceives your connectivity.

Innovation: We are Good at Doing Something New in Both Content and Process

Innovation focuses on share of opportunity by creating the future rather than relying on past successes. Innovation matters because it fosters growth. It excites employees by focusing on what can be, anticipates customer requests and delights customers with what they did not expect, and builds confidence with investors by creating intangible value. HR professionals who focus on innovation constantly ask: What's next? This is asked in all domains of their business. Innovative product offerings include revolutionary new products or product extensions (that is, added features, performance, or functionality). Business strategy innovation changes how the enterprise makes money (as with the current emphasis on services), where the enterprise does business (opening up new geographies), how the enterprise goes to market (via new channels), how the customers experience the firm (its brand identity), or how the firm serves customers (as when eBay discovered it could grow by helping customers sell things to each other). Administrative innovation occurs when new processes are introduced in finance, IT, marketing, HR, manufacturing, or other staff systems.

Innovation may be tracked through a vitality index such as revenues (or profits) from products or services created in the last three years. Innovation may also be monitored through the introduction and deployment of new processes in the organization.

Strategic Unity: We are Good at Articulating and Sharing a Strategic Point of View

More organizations have strategies than accomplish them. Often this comes about because there is not a unity of shared understanding of the desired strategy. Three agendas go into creating strategic unity. An intellectual agenda assures that employees from top to bottom share both what the strategy is and why it is important. This agenda is delivered through simple messages repeated constantly. A behavioral agenda assures that the ideas in strategy shape how employees behave. This comes less by telling employees what to do and more by asking employees what they will do given the strategy. By allowing employees to define their behaviors relative to strategy, they become committed to it. A process agenda ensures that the organization's processes (e.g. budgeting, hiring, decision making) align with strategy. These processes may be re-engineered to ensure that they create unity. When all three agendas are in place, strategic unity likely follows.

Tracking strategic unity comes when employees have strategic literacy as evidenced from a common answer to the question, 'what is the strategy of this business which sets us apart from competitors and helps us win with customers?' The behavioral agenda for strategic unity is measured by asking employees what percentage of the time they felt they were doing work that facilitated the strategy and by asking them if their suggestions for improvement were heard and acted on.

Efficiency: We are Good at Managing Costs of Operation

In competitive markets, managing costs efficiently increases flexibility. HR professionals may reduce costs through process, people, and projects. Process improvements come through kaizen or other productivity improvement efforts that reduce variance, remove steps in getting work done, reduce inventories and work space, and assure a flow of products and services. People improvements come from doing more with less through technology, teams, and more efficient processes. Project investments come from managing capital spending to allocate money wisely for future investments. HR professionals who only pay attention to costs and ignore growth fail because you cannot save your way to prosperity; but HR professionals who avoid costs and efficiency improvements will not likely have the opportunity to grow the top line.

Tracking efficiency may be the easiest of all. Measuring costs of good sold, inventories, direct and indirect labor, and capital employed may all be tracked from the balance sheet and income statement.

Clearly, these are not the only capabilities that HR professionals working with leaders may instill into an organization. But, they are indicative of the types of capabilities that make intangible tangible. They delight customers, they engage employees, they establish reputations among investors, and they provide long-term sustainable value.

Two Implications for HR

HR Structure

The business context sets the agenda, the HR vision of value focuses on the outcome, and the ten principles define the capabilities HR professionals can and should create. To create these capabilities and deliver value, HR departments and functions are evolving how they deliver HR. Increasingly, HR departments are being split in half, one half focusing on HR transactions and operations, the other on HR transformation and strategic work. Both parts add value, the transaction work ensuring efficiency, costs, and error-free work; the transformation work enabling strategies to be executed.

HR transactions must be done to ensure that employees' administrative concerns are treated quickly and accurately. But they should also be done to minimize costs while maintaining quality. The production of administrative efficiency comes through establishment of service centers where HR work is consolidated, through e-HR where employees become self-reliant and connected through technology, and through outsourcing HR to a service provider who can ensure consistency and efficiency. This mix of processes helps streamline and reduce the cost of HR operations. It also reduces the number of people who work in HR by automating, standardizing, and re-engineering HR processes.

HR transformation means investing in HR practices that help make strategy happen by accomplishing the ten capabilities discussed above. These capabilities become the outcomes of HR practices, the deliverables of HR. To build sustained value, HR professionals must work as a unified team. Embedded HR professionals may be called generalists, partners, relationship managers, or business-based HR. Regardless of title, they are assigned to work with organization units (business, geography, or functional unit). Their task is to participate in the strategic planning process and to ensure that strategies happen through organization capabilities. They sit on the management team of their unit; they do organization audits; they set organization priorities; and they source HR expertise from centers of expertise. They are measured by the extent to which they can help make strategies happen.

HR professionals in centers of expertise are known for their technical acumen and are known as specialists in delivering key capabilities. They are current in their specialty area but are also able to tailor and adapt ideas to the requirements of the business units. They contract their knowledge to the embedded HR professionals to help solve problems. They create menus of choices for how to deliver state of the art HR. They share knowledge from one unit to another. They also represent some of the corporate initiatives sponsored by the executives. They are measured by the application of innovative HR practices throughout the company and the extent to which the company shares experiences across units.

HR professionals at corporate level have responsibility for HR philosophies that permeate the entire organization. They represent the firm to external stakeholders (regulators, investors, communities) and need to help establish a corporate brand or reputation. They also help senior executives select HR initiatives that will permeate the entire organization. They work with boards to ensure effective governance and with senior executive leaders as coaches and team facilitators.

The combination of these factors ensures that the human resource management organization operates as a unified team that creates value through transformation.

HR professionals

HR professionals have evolved in recent years. From just doing administrative processes, they are increasingly being asked to help create value and contribute to business success. We have identified three dimensions to describe these changes: what HR professionals do (actions), why they do it (roles), and how they do it (competencies).

We have talked about actions HR professionals may undertake to deliver value. With business leaders, they can coach by providing candid feedback and feed-forward. As coaches, they help leaders align their intent with their behaviors. With strategists, they can become architects of the organization required for the future. As architects, they create blueprints for delivering critical capabilities. With business teams, they facilitate the process of change and implementation. As facilitators, they are attuned to the process of change and the dynamics of large-scale system change. Within HR, they are gifted at delivering and doing what they promise. As deliverers, they accomplish results by building HR plans and delivering HR practices. These four actions give HR professionals specific guidelines on what they should do to deliver value.

HR roles focus on the identity and reputation of HR professionals. In previous years, we have talked about four roles for HR professionals: employee champion, administrative expert, strategic partner, and change agent. Because of the business context we presented, the value HR should create, and the ten capabilities HR professionals can build, these roles have morphed. Employee champion is so important it can be divided into the employee advocate who cares about employee requirements today and human capital developer who cares about building for tomorrow's employees. Administrative expert has shifted to functional expertise since it requires detailed knowledge of HR theory and research. Strategic partner and change merge, since without change, strategy does not happen. And we envision HR professionals as leaders who embody the leadership brand and communicate it throughout their organization by word and by policy. These five roles, employee advocate, human capital developer, functional expert, strategic partner, and leader, become the roles that HR professionals should play to add value.

HR competencies focus on the knowledge and skills required to make sure that actions occur in the right way. We have pursued research since 1988 on the required competencies of HR professionals. Our data set is now over 30,000 individuals and suggests five domains for HR competencies. We have identified five domains that HR professionals must master to be seen as competent. Strategic contribution refers to an HR professional's ability to make strategy and change happen by encouraging customer input to decision making. Personal credibility refers to the HR professional's ability to build relationships of trust with business leaders. Knowing the business ensures that HR professionals can discuss strategic, marketing, operational, and financial issues with clarity. Mastering HR practices ensures that HR professionals know the theory and research of HR and can adapt this knowledge to their specific organization requirements. Learning to leverage HR technology will help HR professionals demonstrate the technological literacy that business requires.

As HR professionals master the actions, play the roles, and demonstrate the competencies, they become valued contributors to their organizations.

Conclusions

We end where we began. The business world is changing. It requires that HR professionals contribute by creating value. This value is created when HR professionals master the ten proposed principles and can turn that knowledge into a set of organization capabilities. HR professionals are more able to do this value added work when the function is accurately structured and when HR professionals act, play roles, and demonstrate the right competencies.

This roadmap is a daydream for HR. It lays out where HR can and should be headed. And, like a night dream, it lays out challenges ahead and how HR can respond to those challenges. Night dreams that alert us to our deeper and hidden concerns can be turned into successful daydreams by doing the things talked about in this chapter.

6   Services, Counsel, and Values: Managing Strategically in the Public Sector

J. A. Murray

Introduction

Public management is in the throes of great change. In some countries, it is even undergoing a form of reinvention as hoped for since the early 1990s.[1] Much of this change is bound up with innovation in the way public services are delivered, managed, and accounted for. New structures and processes abound and there is widespread borrowing from private sector practice. However, the pace and scope of change often leaves senior management—even the committed champions of change—at a loss for guidance in pursuing new waves of change or in managing the consequences of those recently implemented. Their concerns have much in common with private sector managers in industries and companies beset by revolution and restructuring: how to understand what is happening in the environment while having to respond and decide immediately; how to take action without new models of new realities; how to cope with unexpected and unintended consequences of actions already taken; how to stay in command of such rapid evolution and provide the leadership that others seek anxiously; how to manage strategically rather than tactically when context is poorly understood, options are many and ill specified, and leadership is more important than ever before.

In this chapter I will address some of these concerns by discussing the core and unchanging strategic responsibilities of the senior public manager; the context in which the interpretation of these responsibilities is being recast, and by suggesting some of the strategic management challenges and dilemmas that arise.[2]

Public Managers Managing Strategically

Popular discussion of public management most commonly focuses on the *ability to deliver services.* For most citizens, that is what the apparatus of state does. It is a feature of daily life, experienced through the delivery of traditional core activities of justice, education, health, and defense but also through the provision of a vast array of public services and transfers ranging from the weather forecast to renewing motor tax or the collection of refuse. The difficulty for public service providers and managers is that for many of these services their provision earns no plaudits, but delay, breakdown, inefficiency, or high cost stirs immediate wrath. As with so-called organizational 'hygiene' factors, meeting these needs makes no one particularly satisfied—it merely prevents us, as citizens, from becoming dissatisfied.[3] There are no thanks, but there is instant complaint.

Behind this most public face of strategic management responsibility lies another equally important aspect, but one experienced in a very restricted forum: in the market for *advice and wise counsel,* particularly at the interface of the political and administrative systems. While the capacity to deliver public services exists in the realm of mass, if not universal, experience the delivery of advice inhabits a restricted domain occupied by those who must make decisions central to a country's well-being and those appointed to provide them with counsel that is well judged, independent, evidence based, and timely. This aspect of public strategic management is traditionally held and nurtured by the Mandarinate—the most senior public managers—and shaped through formal learning, considerable experience, socialization into a value system, and by a particular system of appointment and succession planning. To state the obvious, the delivery of public services ultimately depends on the quality of policy decisions. No amount of capacity to deliver services efficiently will make the wrong service a good one. Yet how the capacity to provide wise counsel is shaped remains unclear. Policy emerges from an unstable brew of political-administrative interaction, analysis, evidence, judgement, expediency, and incident.

And finally, but most fundamental, is the capacity to act in a *value-based, value-driven* manner. The civil and public service is not a value-free, amoral, social mechanism of delivery. Its legitimacy and the security of civil society rest in its capacity to preserve and assert its independence, to never fail in its commitment to probity and in its skill in 'speaking truth to power.' If that capacity is lost, political advisers, consultants, outsourcers, and assorted charlatans and sorcerers quickly begin to drive the strategic management process; 'spin' drives government and the legitimacy of state and government is readily undermined.

So, we have three vital dimensions of strategic public management: the delivery of public services, observable by all citizens as a feature of daily life; the provision of effective advice to the politicians who decide policy, observed by few and reliant on fewer still; and capacity to deploy and renew basic values of good public management, lying beneath the surface of action but fundamental to good government. Each aspect is beset by pressing challenges and their resolution will come only by struggling with a variety of paradoxes and dilemmas.

The Evolving Context of Strategic Public Management

Constant Themes

It seems obvious that effective strategic management should always be a central concern of public managers. Without the capacity to make good decisions and to implement them well, ineffective government is the best expectation one might have; the worst expectation is a failed state. The stewardship of strategic management capacity is therefore a central responsibility. In a normative sense, every senior public manager must devote effort, as a priority, to understanding, building, and deploying the capacity to manage strategically. This does not change although it may be more and less difficult at different times.

This is not an easy task. It often demands concentrated effort to allocate time towards assessing future needs and to shaping the capacity to respond, implement, and learn, especially when more immediate and tactical pressures demand response often driven by the political process, impatient citizens, and media seeking another problem and to fix the blame, not the problem. In the context of public management, capacity is predominantly concerned with people—with understanding the future's demands on knowledge and intellectual assets; with acquiring, developing and sharing human capital. Given a background of classical brueaucracy and the ideal of the generalist civil servant, such thinking runs against the grain of some deeply embedded assumptions and practice. It may also conflict with practice in the selection and development of leaders who must take on the mantle of stewardship without a great deal of tailored preparation. Some of those newly arrived in leadership positions may not fully recognize the responsibility. Some may consider it someone else's responsibility.

However, these are unchanging demands, many shared with colleagues in the private and voluntary sectors. There is always a struggle to manage strategically when the pressures and immediate rewards of managing tactically are so great. The contemporary context generates some unique pressures that are best seen from the perspective of public demand and from patterns in international evolution.

The New Themes

From the 'demand side,' citizens and politicians are far more demanding than was formerly the case with regard to performance. They expect 'performance' where formerly they placed more emphasis on process and presence: to be there and to act in a rule-based manner was, often enough, acceptable. Now, they demand that capacity to decide, design, and implement be immediately available and results delivered. They expect these results to match the best international standards. They expect the apparatus of government to be responsive, and to deliver performance in a manner that is fast, flexible, efficient, and innovative—but also well considered, cost effective, compliant with demanding governance and accountability requirements, and true to values of an independent public service. If there are deep-rooted conflicts between some of these imperatives, it is seen as the job of public managers to get on with it and resolve such conflicts as arise—without compromising the desiderata. Management, as most senior managers discover, deals in paradox and dilemma; public management a little more so than private.

General expectations are increasingly set by reference to the private sector and increasingly to the standards of global corporations of which so many citizens are employees, customers, or avid readers of promotional descriptions. In this context, the citizen is consumer, setting commercial standards and expecting choice to solve problems of poor performance. This is the essence of the notion of the 'performing state.'[4] Citizens and their public representatives expect high performance, calibrated in relation to private sector corporate standards, and, when faced with underperforming monopoly state providers, see radical reform or competition and choice as the 'obvious' remedies.

Audience democracy[5] adds to these pressures by pushing the related debate and decision making into a very public arena whose landscape is significantly determined by media, interest groups, and pundits. In an audience democracy the political decision maker is drawn into a more public and 'instant' process of deliberation and decision that may leave the pace and content of traditional political and administrative processes floundering or bypassed. In a more traditional democracy, debate and consideration by a deliberative parliamentary-type mechanism supported by a reflective civil service providing considered advice created a buffer zone between public demand, government decision, and state action. The buffer provided time for thought, analysis, debate, and resolution. It dampened overreaction and consequent overcompensation. In an audience democracy this buffer disappears as public demand and political decision making meet and react more instantly on a stage choreographed by media, special interest groups, and political 'spin.' It is a stage on which the communication media also assume the mantle of monitoring implementation on behalf of 'the public.' At its worst, 'gotcha' journalism and weak political leadership can suppress almost all deliberative process and leave the apparatus of state swinging in the wind from one episode of policy making and implementation to the next. Anecdote-based policy overwhelms evidence-based policy; strategic management is driven out by tactical reaction; public management degenerates into an old-fashioned shambles as managers rush from one minor crisis to the next. This is an extreme scenario, but one of which we nonetheless catch glimpses internationally.

Do these changing circumstances demand a 'new' approach to strategic public management? The question is not easy to answer objectively as the data on state performance is so difficult to generate and to correlate with public management practice. In terms of general international discourse one would say yes, in light of the general sense of frustration that is voiced about the perceived performance of the state and the frequent attribution of poor performance to various aspects of state incapacity 'to get the job done.' This critical commentary is commonplace among citizens, politicians, and media commentators. However, it must be acknowledged that the absence of some level of such commentary would be extraordinary—and indeed perhaps impossible in a democracy—since one person's reason for satisfaction with the state may be another's cause for complaint: my successful planning application may create a disgruntled neighbor. Demand for healthcare is infinite, so any limits will be rejected by some. An efficient tax regime or prison service is unlikely to win plaudits from its best 'customers.' It is of the essence of the state's duty to regulate conflict. It cannot be popular with everyone, all the time. There is not such simple optimizing rule as satisfy customers, at a profit.

Surveys of attitude provide one thread of evidence as to generalized perceptions and satisfaction. International comparative data provides another means of calibrating performance on a relative basis. One might consider the incidence of public inquiries, tribunals, commissions of investigation, special reports, or international agency complaints and fines, as an indicator of the incidence of failure, insofar as they investigate the malfunctioning of public service organizations. With considerable variation across countries, many surveys show general confidence in public institutions on a downward course, along with many other traditional institutions. Various public statistics on public outputs and outcomes indicate mixed results across countries and no clear correlation between the quantity of input (normally money, sometimes personnel or capital) and the level of output, never mind the quality of output or outcome.

Other evidence that provides international comparisons[6] is limited and provided principally by World Bank, European Central Bank, the Global and World Competitiveness Reports, and the Cultural Planning Office of the Netherlands. Such reports, especially the annual competitiveness reports, stress measures of public sector performance that are believed to relate to economic and business prowess. Most measures of public output or process efficiency reveal considerable room for improvement—better health, education, justice, or social inclusion achievements. But these are calibrated against constantly moving standards and their interpretation is often that things could be much better rather than that they are shamefully broken.

The argument, rather, hinges not as much on failure and crisis as media and critics suggest but rather on the widespread demand within countries and the public service itself for improved, and in some cases transformed, capacity to perform to increasingly high expectations. It hinges on a sense of needing enhanced capacity for an uncertain future in which past successes do not guarantee continuing success. And on a more negative note, it turns on the failures recorded in various inquiries, commissions, and reports on the way in which public affairs have sometimes been mismanaged.

The Evolving Themes

These growing demands, located in the desire for a 'performing state' and increasingly embedded in an audience democracy where anecdote-based policy threatens to overwhelm evidence-based policy, have emerged against a backdrop of clearly evolving patterns in public management over the past two decades. One is the changed legitimacy of private sector management practice and the other is the international diffusion of new public management practice and ideas.

The perceived status of private sector management practice grew very significantly in the past several decades among public sector managers and politicians. Managerial practice in large private sector firms became increasingly visible and accessible through research, publication, business schools, and international consultancy. A new generation of European firms grew into substantial national enterprises and subsequently into multinational companies of scale and staying power. Their management was professional and assumed role model status for a new generation of politicians who were increasingly likely to ask of the public service 'why can't you be more like the private sector?' or, no doubt more irritatingly for the civil servant, 'if only you would behave like the private sector we wouldn't be in this mess.' For many civil servants interaction with the private sector prompted similar thoughts. The result was that the receptivity of the political-administrative system to models and methods from private sector management practice changed quite radically—from 'that has nothing to do with us,' or even 'that would be abhorrent to us,' to an attitude of open-minded learning and borrowing. In consequence, a flow of ideas and theory from the management disciplines became possible and joined the international flow of 'new public management' ideas. Sectoral thinking (public, private, voluntary) receded as a conceptual foundation, replaced by concepts of process and activity-based organization which reveal underlying commonality with variation shaped by different contexts.

International civil service reform is a second important thread in the fabric of contemporary public strategic management. The experience of most OECD member countries forms part of a pattern of international scope, centered originally on the impact of reforms emerging from Westminster-based administrations, America, and other European administrations as well as those in Asia and in many emerging economies. Strategic management practice is interwoven with this international pattern.

By the early 1990s reform was 'in the air.' Reform in the UK, New Zealand, Australia, and the United States was a matter of frequent coverage in popular media as well as discussion in political and administrative circles. Two politicians with far-reaching impact—Thatcher and Reagan—came to power in part on the back of tax revolts and disillusion with 'big government.' Active membership of the European community and of organizations such as OECD had brought public managers and politicians into contact with a European, Antipodean, and American brew of early reform movements. Senior and middle-ranking managers increasingly found themselves active members of an international network of peers interested in reform.

An active international diffusion process concerning reform existed and continues, mediated by individual agents of change and by institutional actors. Champions of change found they had new international fora—conferences, research groupings, journals, and books where ideas could be tested and experience shared. Consultancy firms discovered a new and profitable growth market in transferring and translating private sector practice and technique to public sector application. This engagement provided channels through which the ideas and experience of international reform and the ideas of the 'new public management' flowed freely between nations.

These ideas and their diffusion were not uniform in content or timing. Each country carries its unique traditions of public management. International patterns, new ideas, and evolving practice intermingle with each country's history to produce new variations. Pollitt and Bouckaert's[7] comparative study of public management reform distinguished between Anglo-Saxon countries (Australia, Canada, New Zealand, UK) which they believe 'are much more open to the "performance-driven," market-favouring ideas of the NPM (new public management) than others;'[8] countries of a *Rechtsstaat* tradition, interested in reform but resistant to NPM ideas (Germany, France); and a north-western European group (Finland, the Netherlands, Sweden) with 'a general disposition towards consensual, often meso-corporatist styles of governance.'[9] When they examined the different paths taken by public management reform processes in the countries studied, they concluded that there is neither random variety nor a convergent pattern in what has happened. As few countries share either common starting positions or common aspirations about end states, it is little wonder that there are no identical reform paths from the present to the future. However, they do suggest that there are patterns or clusters among countries reflecting how each has pursued reform.

A conservative policy of *maintaining* the status quo by trying to improve structure and practice is used to characterize Germany and the EU. A group of *modernizers*, who cleave to a belief in a large role for the state in civil society while demanding fundamental change in the way the administrative apparatus is managed, is seen as including Canada, France, the Netherlands, and Sweden. Their reforms center on results-oriented budgeting, evaluation, a new approach to human resource management, decentralization and devolution, and strategic planning. A third cluster consists of those they call the *marketizers*, whose approach is to introduce competition and market mechanisms on the widest possible scale to all former activities of the public sector. Here they position Australia, New Zealand, and the UK with occasional appearances from Finland and Sweden. Finally they identified a cluster of *minimalists*, for whom only the ultimate core functions of the public sector should be retained when everything possible has been privatized and outsourced. They found no permanent members of this last cluster but occasional temporary residence and rhetorical bluster among the UK, New Zealand, Australia, and the USA. Pollitt and Bouckaert regard this overall four-part pattern as 'rough and approximate,'[10] because of variation in political and administrative approaches through time and variations in socio-economic circumstances.

Matters of *substance* (the 'what' of reform) are measured by Pollitt and Bouckaert in terms of financial, personnel, organizational, and performance measurement reforms. Matters of *process* (the 'how' of reform) are measured in terms of the balance of top-down/bottom-up decision making, legal structures, and organizational process.

In personnel management, while a unitary service has not been breached, the international pattern of reform lies in a search for greater flexibility, responsiveness, results orientation, and appropriately skilled civil servants. The shift in promotional criteria from seniority and qualification to results and responsiveness was clearly present.

Turning to the 'how' of reform, to its process, three aspects were noted: the balance of top-down/bottom-up process; the use of new organizations and structures; and the aggressiveness of reform action (ranging from a 'forge ahead' to a 'tiptoe' approach).[11] By and large, the more 'purist' NPM countries have followed a pattern of top-down implementation, the extensive use of new organizations, and an aggressively rapid pace.

In another commentary on international patterns in the first wave of reform of public management, Schick[12] finds some virtually universal themes and ideas as well as some generally contested ideas. The common themes include comprehensive rather than piecemeal reform, reform that is not confined to specific administrative processes, devolution-based reform, incentive-rather than rule-driven reform, and reform focused on operations and service delivery. The common ideas include being goal driven and measured, empowering managers, devolved authority and accountability, and being output and outcome focused.

Schick also isolates a set of ideas that are contested in the reform process—within and between countries. These include the appropriate extent of citizen choice, the outsourcing of services, the adoption of private sector models, and the separation of service delivery from policy. A common theme of all reform movements has been to urge government to concentrate on quality in its 'steering' activity and to leave 'rowing' to others where possible.[13]

In summarizing the fortunes of reform movements internationally, Schick notes a number of features.[14] He notes that the process takes considerable time; that the regular institutionalization of change is an essential process in order to make it possible to move on to each next phase, an important reminder of the possibility of regression and relapse at any time. High aspirations and brave beginnings are not enough. Those managing change must also attend to the detail of embedding new ways in the structures, systems, and culture of the organization.

An increasing interpenetration of private sector strategic management practice and the increasing convergence of the basic commitments and concepts associated with change and renewal in public and private sectors characterizes established international patterns of evolving practice. The current pressures demanding performance, speed, and responsiveness are also felt in common although their impact in the public management domain is generally more complex, more fraught with intrinsic goal conflict and managerial dilemma, and more difficult to manage in the absence of singular and unambiguous performance measures.

Challenges and Dilemmas

Returning to the three central management responsibilities—service delivery, wise counsel, and the stewardship of values—we will now consider how each is shaped by evolving practice and contemporary pressure and identify three particular challenges to managers in each area.

Service Delivery

The challenges here are, above all, the provision of high-quality efficient service; the management of scope and public sector boundaries; and management of the linkage to the concept of the 'competing nation.'

The provision of high-quality efficient service delivery is quite simple to declare as a goal. The challenge lies in its delivery. At the heart of the modern reform movement in public management lay a simple shift in voter preference. Emerging from the post-war period of growth in state activity and welfare provision, voters began to resist the associated tax burden, to interrogate the 'value for money' of services received and to reject 'big government.' This position became progressively more acute and more divorced from ideological debate. The demand is now for excellence in service benchmarked against private sector standards but without any willingness to pay extra. The familiar pattern in private sector competitive markets of consumers demanding 'more for less' is translated into the public domain. Citizens have become consumers in this sense. The consequence is the need for public services to be managed in much the same way as commercial services. Securing efficiencies demands the 'industrialization' of service provision, largely based in the engine of information and computing technology and on associated organizational and skill changes. Simultaneously, access, transparency, speed, and customization of service are required to meet quality expectations. And the requirement is how to do all this within an unchanging tax burden—how to re-engineer the system, invest in new technology and skills, and configure new services but lower the cost per unit of service delivered.

It seems clear that this challenge and associated dilemma cannot be met simply by adaptation of existing organizational arrangements. A central breakthrough in private sector practice when faced with similar dilemmas in the 1990s was to reconceive the organizational apparatus as a bundle of activities linked through processes that could be unbundled and realigned in new ways in governance and spatial terms. Realignment of governance meant that hierarchy and ownership was not the only answer to large organizational undertakings. Once the component activities could be identified, described, and routinized, they could be undertaken by 'anyone,' and outsourcing and network organization was born. With the rapid advance of globalization and the liberalization of trade regulations, these activities could then be redistributed spatially across the globe. The central question for the organization became which activities to hold within its own ownership and which to outsource or engage network partners to undertake. At the heart of this strategic design challenge lie decisions about the scope of the firm and the boundaries of the organization.

The same challenges now arise in a most urgent form for public management. Where they have arisen before they were most often dealt with as questions of ideology and political philosophy. Now they are also questions of management and organization design and sit squarely in the management arena. So the old questions must be revisited, but from a fresh and urgent perspective: what are the 'pure' public services that cannot be provided other than through the public sector? Of the rest, how should their component activities be redesigned and allocated among various providers in the private, voluntary, and public sectors with the goal of providing the citizen with maximum quality, efficiency, and responsiveness? The challenge is immense in relation to the existing knowledge base, the need to design network and outsourcing arrangements that comply with public sector standards and accountability, and the nature of the industrial relations environment. But the potential gains are great too, in terms of efficiency, responsiveness, and speed and the relative ease of introducing competition. An even greater gain may be the freedom for public management to concentrate on its core responsibilities, unburdened by the need for operational service provision.

Finally there is a challenge to manage service provision in a manner that relates positively to national competitiveness. The interplay of government institutions, regulation, and public services with national competitiveness is receiving increasing attention. Annual country competitiveness reports draw attention to the popular perception of this interdependency with their stress on government performance, public infrastructure, and public service provision as essential components of collective competitiveness. These considerations effectively introduce market forces and considerations to public service management at second hand: public services influence the cost and quality of firms' products and these have to compete in a global market. Competitiveness in that global market is partially determined by the variations in public service provision at nation level. In this way, the management of planning permission and regulation for the construction of new business premises becomes a component in national competitiveness as do the provision, cost, and quality of infrastructural services and legal, intellectual property, and personal freedom factors. The consequent managerial challenge is complex. The public manager must address the strategic implications of delivering value for money services in a resource-constrained environment; of delivering these services through various governance arrangements across the public, voluntary, and private sectors; and of calculating the national competitiveness effect of the various options and combinations. Effective service delivery becomes a multi-level challenge of local, national, and international scope.

Wise Counsel

Here we encounter some very different challenges and dilemmas. No amount of excellence in service delivery will compensate for poor policy decisions. Poor policy decisions unrelated to substantial service provision may have even more disastrous impact: decisions on foreign policy, on international negotiations and agreements, on security, on human rights, on justice and law reform, on educational philosophy deeply affect the fortunes and well-being of a nation. The list is extensive and does not require over-elaboration to make the point. Such decisions are substantially forged at the interface between senior politicians holding departmental or sectoral briefs and their senior civil servants. Sometimes they are honed at cabinet table or presidential office, particularly where they have whole-of-government implications, stand at the centre of electoral policy, or are at the eye of a political storm.

Three central challenges for senior public managers are how to acquire and develop the skills that underpin the ability to provide good advice; how to provide advice while cleaving to the professional imperative to 'speak truth to power;' and how to construct the interface between policy decisions and implementation.

How the necessary skill is developed is an age-old and as yet unresolved question. Machiavelli wrote his advice to the Prince but not his advice to his successor. One of the founders of Harvard Business School's educational philosophy wrote on the subject of 'why wisdom can't be told' in relation to the formation of senior managers. Yet is is precisely this poorly defined skill that is at the heart of status and prestige among senior public managers. The tradition of the 'generalist' civil servant was one dimension in the shaping of the skill. Civil servants through extended service in a variety of functions and departments absorbed a very varied set of experiences that prepared them for the inherent variety and surprise that drive so much of the policy advice requirement. Along with lifelong service, it also armed them with an extended informal network that channeled information, influence, and power in a flexible and responsive manner. In some systems earlier educational formation was believed to be pivotal: 'Enarchs' in France, firsts in history or classics from Oxbridge, Ivy League background, or other forms of educational elitism. The vital factor in these cases may not have been so much the education itself but the common formation providing the elite with inbuilt networks pre-dating public management careers, shorthand means of communication, and shared values.

Undoubtedly, mentoring and championing has also played a significant role as high potential was identified and careers guided in many informal ways long before there was discussion of succession planning and career development. So the roots of the ability to provide wise counsel stretch back into early educational experience and forward into the accumulation of breadth and depth of general management experience in public management. But the ability also has a unique personal dimension—the capacity to be a counselor at the most senior level in a nation's affairs but not to overstep the line into being a decision maker on policy and to accept the responsibility for implementation of decisions, even when they run counter to what would have been one's personal choice. This is an unusual and scarce personal quality. Dilemmas abound in its deployment: how to give advice even-handedly when one may have a preferred option; how to be intimately involved in decision making but retain an impartial independence; how to be satisfied with giving advice when the ability to make the decision is equally present; how to hold mastery of a complex policy issue but act in support of political decision makers who may be less knowledgeable and driven by political necessity as well as analytical optima; how to 'speak truth to power' when it is unpalatable yet retain trust and the role of expert counselor.

Acquiring and developing the relevant skills and exercising them effectively have always been pressing challenges but they have become more urgent in a period when the traditional patterns of formation cease to hold. The role of educational elites appears to be lessening as educational access and achievement diversifies, as a public sector career-for-life lessens as a commonplace, as public management ceases to be a preferred career for the best and the brightest, as increasing numbers of specialists are recruited to focused and professional roles, as departments hoard talent more aggressively rather than support periodic redeployment to broaden experience, as systems open up to mid-career recruitment from other sectors. All of these factors wash away the foundations of a learning-by-doing approach to development and a lengthy process of apprenticeship and selection. They undermine a predominantly tacit approach to development and selection. When this happens, tacit processes and knowledge must be converted to explicit to allow for codification and transmission in shorter time periods. And as happens with all professions, knowledge and its acquisition becomes a more formal, continuing, and active process. The 'professionalization' of senior public management becomes a strategic priority for the public service. One of the inherent dilemmas universally encountered in such periods of transition is driven by the fear engendered in some members of the 'old order' as their mysterious skill base is rendered explicit. The dilemma is whether to defend the poorly understood tradition which has made them, or to push for professionalization: 'if I pursue the latter, do I make myself redundant, do I lose the power of priesthood, do I stand naked like the emperor with no clothes if too much is made known and knowable?'

Finally, we have the challenge of constructing the interface between policy decisions and their implementation. Because the policy interface role is of such high status it is not unusual for the consequences of decision to be seen as anticlimactic—'mere management' in the eyes of some; work for the less intellectually gifted and perhaps just a little boring. A study of Canadian civil servants noted that some felt that the system 'emphasises good policy outcomes while paying insufficient attention to good management.'[15] Recruits from outside the service 'frequently noted that they were in the midst of intelligent, cultured and well-read intellectuals. But this also meant that sometimes the debate seemed to be too academic—without sufficient link to the practical consequences.'[16] There is a dangerous fault line here between the world of policy and that of implementation. Private sector practice teetered on the same line in the days of strategic planning when planners and strategists occupied the lofty heights of corporate headquarters, produced plans for approval by the chief executive's office and for implementation by 'management.' That particular set of practices collapsed early in the 1980s with the construction of strategic management as a discipline emphasizing the unitary nature of strategy and implementation and the imperative of having line managers strategizing and of having strategists managing in the line. However, there is considerable evidence that the old illusion is still maintained in public sector practice. Initial rounds of capability reviews in the UK documented a startling paradox. A cross-departmental comparison of reviews in 2006 showed three of the top five ranked capability elements related to strategy while three of the bottom five elements related to delivery.[17] In public management practice it still seems possible to construe strategy as abstract, unsullied by the messiness of execution. Yet this may be precisely the root of the problems with delivery, of the infamous implementation deficit that characterizes so many public management systems. If the Mandarinate divorces thinking from doing, strategy from implementation, a systemic fault is created. The challenge—intellectually as much as practically—is for senior management who provide vital advice to see that advice in terms of implementation consequences and, in turn, to derive as much satisfaction from policy implementation as from involvement in its formulation.

Stewardship of Values

Underlying public service values are generally agreed on in Western democracies and I will concentrate on these. Their central themes are probity, nonpartisan independence, equity in treatment of the citizen, and the fearless provision of independent advice. These commitments have generally been protected by significant security of job tenure and by various unions and staff associations. In turbulent times, clear values that are strongly held are one of the few unchanging guidance mechanisms that provide a means of navigation through poorly understood and rapidly changing circumstances. They remain unambiguous when many other points of reference become unclear.

Values also underpin the institution of government and are central to the legitimacy of the state. If legitimacy is threatened, the state is threatened. If legitimacy is lost, the state is lost. There are too many dramatic examples of the consequences of such loss for any country whose institutions of state are perceived as legitimate to risk their failure. It is well to remember that loss of legitimacy can be piecemeal but cancerous in its spread. An inequitable and mismanaged tax system invites citizens to subvert it. Inequity in the provision of public services presents the state as partisan and invites alienation and the decay of civil society. Obscure, opaque, convoluted management-by-rules invites subversion, bypassing, special relationships, or preferred treatment and lurches towards petty corruption. Pulling even a small thread in the fabric of public service values risks unraveling the entire garment of good government. Stewardship of values is at the heart of the strategic management mandate.

The three particular challenges that relate to values are stewardship of their continued institutionalization; the differentiation and development of values; and their interpretation and reinforcement through leadership behaviour.

The stewardship of values has much to do with their organizational institutionalization. Schein argues that organizational culture has three levels: behavior of the organization's members; values to which people attribute their behavior—although stated and operating values may prove different; and assumptions and beliefs which grow from values into the realm of the 'taken for granted' where they are scarcely noticed in any conscious manner but nevertheless drive behavior powerfully because they guide 'the way we do things here.'[18] The task of institutionalizing and reinforcing values therefore operates at all three levels and demands vigilance as well as action at all three. As government systems move, by demand in the arena of public service delivery, to a more consumer-based model, behaviors, values, and assumptions also shift. Being 'client centered' and 'customer oriented' demands new behaviors and values in action. They are forged in some degree of contest with older behaviors and values. By and large these emergent values will be appropriate to the new world of public service delivery but danger also lurks in this process of emergence. Consumer values of 'you get what you pay for' or 'you get what you can afford' can, for example, be destructive of essential values of equity of access and provision. Values are therefore constantly in the making and demand 'management' to ensure that bedrock values are not damaged while appropriate new values become, in due course, part of the taken for granted. Senior public managers face the challenge of guiding the preservation and evolution of a value system that will ultimately anchor their system's legitimacy. They face the challenge that doing this may often create dilemmas for them such as arise when values reduce efficiency (as equity of access often does) or when decisions must be made about delivery systems that span public, private, and voluntary sectors that have different and even conflicting values.

The process of values differentiating and developing has been noted above as a necessary and natural aspect of the evolution of the public sector and its management. Both processes are the consequences of change and this presents two further challenges—that of engendering the process when oftentimes faced with resistance and that of managing the process 'safely' once change is set in progress. Civil service systems are notoriously self-reinforcing, closed to much of the outside world by traditional patterns of early recruitment, long periods of socialization, and career-long service. Some would argue that they are almost hermetically sealed in a social sense; that they are 'closed systems' acting in a largely self-referenced manner. Such systems will have difficulty in recognizing their own underlying features because behaviors and values are significantly guided by unrecognized assumptions and the invisible power of the 'taken for granted.' Change in this context is particularly difficult if it confronts the deep and the unspoken principle. So managing the emergence of new values will never be easy and may involve difficult and sensitive engagement with culture at a systemic level. By contrast, the safe passage to the establishment of new or modified values may also be fraught. New values relating to efficiency, or to engagement in the provision of advice in the volatile forge of an audience democracy, require high degrees of self-awareness and self-reflection if they are to stay constant to unchanging values such as equity and independence.

It is perhaps stating the obvious to assert that a central leadership role for the senior public manager is to give life to values through personal behavior, through stating their values and consistently applying them in daily activity, and through visiting publicly the value assumptions and the taken for granted. While these desiderata sound uncomplicated they are difficult to practice as any reflective senior executive will confirm. Values are ultimately what are seen in action, in the cut and thrust of debate, in the making of trivial and major decisions, in the elaboration of options and the framing of advice. Because life in general, and public management in particular, are complex and messy undertakings, the line of progress from value basis to action is seldom uncomplicated. Values are therefore interpreted through continuous testing and significant conflict and struggle. Public managers must be self-conscious of this struggle which they play out in front of their organizations on a continuous basis and through which they provide the leadership that shapes how values remain constant, how they evolve, and how they emerge.

In Conclusion

The world of public management is replete with change and challenge in a manner that has not been experienced in Western democracies for several generations. The challenges have few easy solutions and are more likely to present the manager with dilemmas and paradoxes. The core tasks of delivering public services, providing wise counsel to political decision makers, and securing the foundation stone of public service values remain constant in nature but are in flux in interpretation and expression.

The context of the stategic public management job shapes practice in powerful ways, while some basics of the senior management task remain unaltered. New demands from citizens and politicians create the fabric of the performing state where the central expectation is to get things done, now. Combined with the effect of audience democracy, this generates a demand for public service that is better, cheaper, faster, compliant, accountable, and transparent. Ideas spill over from private sector practice, sometimes well adapted, sometimes unthinkingly imitated. The diffusion of new public management practices has spread inexorably but with different impact depending on the history and character of each country's public service traditions. Some ideas and principles have achieved almost universal acceptance, at least in concept; others are contested. Each country and its public servants must therefore configure their own response to challenges that are general as well as those particular to any one administration.

Delivering services requires simultaneous advances in efficiency and quality; a rethink of the boundaries and scope of the state; and a new engagement with the causal relations between public service and regulation and national competitiveness. The crafting of effective advice presents major challenges in terms of understanding the nature of the skills involved, their formation, and their adaptation to new circumstances. The maintenance of the independence on which the provision of good advice must rest requires special effort in a faster, more transparent, and potentially less reflective policy context. And a serious concern remains about the connection of policy, strategy, and implementation with the senior public manager standing on the dangerous fault line. Values and their expression through action ultimately secure the safety and legitimacy of the state and civil society. The challenge of stewardship in a rapidly evolving system is considerable. Just as many inertial forces act against the evolution of the value system, so too the rapid pace of change in behaviour brings dangers of inappropriate change that may become institutionalized without full awareness. Not surprisingly, this places a pressing leadership responsibility on public managers at all levels to manage the value system actively and to act out values in an exemplary fashion.

Notes

1. D. Osborne and T. Gaebler (1992) *Reinventing Government*. New York: Addison Wesley.
2. Some of the arguments pursued in this chapter are also developed in J. A. Murray (2007) 'Building Capacity,' paper to the IPA National Conference, Dublin, 31 May,

and J. A. Murray (2001) *Reflections on the SMI: The Strategic Management Initiative.* Policy Institute, Trinity College Dublin, University of Dublin, Nov.

3. F. Hertzberg (1968) 'One More Time: How do you Motivate Employees?,' *Harvard Business Review* (Jan.–Feb.): 53–62.

4. A. Schick (1999) 'Opportunity, Strategy, and Tactics in Reforming Public Management,' in *Government of the Future: Getting from Here to There*, PUMA (99) 4. Paris: OECD.

5. B. Manin (1997) *The Principles of Representative Government.* Cambridge: Cambridge University Press.

6. S. van de Walle (2006) 'The State of the World's Bureaucracies', *Journal of Comparative Policy Analysis*, 8 (4): 437–48.

7. C. Pollitt and G. Bouckaert (2000) *Public Management Reform: A Comparative Analysis.* Oxford: Oxford University Press.

8. Ibid. 60.

9. Ibid. 61.

10. Ibid. 94.

11. Ibid. 90.

12. Schick, 'Opportunity, Strategy, and Tactics.'

13. Osborne and Gaebler, *Reinventing Government.*

14. Schick, 'Opportunity, Strategy & Tactics.'

15. Larson P. and D. Zussman (2006) 'Canadian Federal Public Service: The View from Recent Executive Recruits', *Optimum Online: The Journal of Public Sector Management*, 36 (4).

16. Ibid. 3.

17. Cabinet Office, PMDU (2007) 'Capability Reviews Tranche 3: Findings and Common Themes. Civil Service—Strengths and Challenges', Mar.: 21, http://www.civilservice.gov.uk/reform/capability_reviews/publications/pdf/Tranch_3_summary.pdf

18. E. Schein (2004) *Organisational Culture & Leadership: A Dynamic View.* San Francisco: Jossey-Bass.

Part II

Develop your Options

7 The Rising Costs of Offering Valueless Propositions in a Connected World

Seán Meehan and Willem Smit

Introduction

Today companies find themselves in environments in which rapid changes in communications technology as well as globalization of markets are creating communities of customers and prospects rather than a multitude of isolated customers. To the executive, the promise of a Connected World is obvious: easy real-time reach of vast audiences, well-informed knowledgeable customers, and almost costless mass customization of products and services. Less obvious are the perils: rising feelings of customers being 'over-communicated,' increasingly volatile and less predictable future demand, and a growing customer rage toughen the conditions in which many companies operate. Faced with opportunities and inherently risky environment, CEOs and marketing managers are advised to operate on two different levels: building the right organization and making the right strategic decisions.

On the organizational level, a concern of CEOs is to assure that their company is genuinely customer focused. Thus they are advised to enhance the customer-oriented values and norms, and put an organization structure in place that promotes the development and sharing of customer knowledge and skills across business functions.[1]

On the strategic decision-making level, CEOs' marketing decisions are *ideally* guided by the customer vantage point, an 'outside-in' external perspective.[2] Practically, they are advised to advocate the (targeted) customer's interests in the company decision making, particularly relating to (1) development and maintenance of the company's value propositions to their customers, and (2) the financial accountability of marketing their value propositions.[3]

In the last few years, it was the 'financial accountability of marketing' that dominated the marketing debate in many executive suites—is our marketing budget justified? What is the pay-off on advertising and sales promotion? And the return of the investment in customer relationship management (CRM) programs? Companies are able to assess the financial return on either particular marketing expenditures,[4] or marketing strategies in general,[5] and this has given them a better idea which marketing activities build shareholder value.[6]

Marketing metrics are great and measurement has advanced markedly, however our concern is that they may mis-estimate the return on marketing, and customer profitability in a connected world; particularly if the issue is regarded in isolation from the other aspect in marketing strategy decision making: advocating the customer's interests in the value proposition offering, and its delivery. Value propositions become value*less* propositions, when at least one of the three prerequisites for a good and profitable marketing strategy is not met:

1. When a firm cannot start and maintain a dialogue with profitable customers.
2. When a firm does not succeed in offering the right products and/or services.
3. When a firm fails to deliver the value proposition well.

If this is the case, a firm incurs higher costs from developing and offering propositions valueless in the eyes of its (targeted) customers and consequently that may end up in harmful customer sentiments like annoyance, dissatisfaction, and even anger. Our argument is that, unless firms first have minimized these costs of valueless propositions, they can hardly optimize their return on marketing. Moreover, we believe that due to structural changes in customer behaviors the costs of failing one of these three prerequisites are getting higher and higher. These days, across industries, marketing managers and their organizations deal with 'Connected Customers' which increases the likelihood and severity of aiming wrong value propositions at the wrong target groups. Longitudinal research in the airline industry has given the empirical evidence that customer complaints even negatively impact a company's stock returns.[7] In a more and more connected world, any company's mistake in the value proposition delivery is very likely to become more costly through the amplified detrimental effects of negative word of mouth.

In line with the notion of marketing metrics and with a basic accountants' principle of 'different costs for different purposes,'[8] we will enumerate the different costs coming from offering valueless propositions to connected customers. And we will outline why these costs are rising.

Table 7.1 provides the organizing framework for this chapter. It lists the three prerequisites for a successful marketing strategy. First, a firm needs to start a dialogue with the right (profitable and well-networked) customers. Second, to keep this dialogue going, it is crucial to offer the right and competitive value

TABLE 7.1 Prerequisites for successful marketing strategy, connected customer trends, costs of valueless propositions, new network tactics

Prerequisites for a successful marketing strategy[a]	Connected customer dual-trends		Costs of valueless propositions	New network tactics to reduce costs of valueless propositions
	Mainstream	Undercurrent		
Starting and maintaining a dialogue with the right customers	More connections of customers with businesses with the growth in number and reach of different channels	⟷ Rising feelings of 'being over-communicated'	• A firm reaches the wrong (unprofitable) customers • A firm tries to target the right customers but isunable to reach them because of the unwillingness to build relationships	• Assessing a customer's lifetime value[b], and their network relationships • Stimulating permission to build relationship with customer[c]
Offering the right value proposition	More connections of customers with information providers leading to more knowledgeable and well-informed customers	⟷ Increasing difficulty in predicting future customer needs and wants	• A firm makes the wrong value proposition.	• Developing customer knowledge[d] • Engaging in immersion[e] • Mobilizing network of firm relationships to share customer information[f]
Delivering the value proposition in the right way	More connections with other customers and more engagement in customizing products and services	⟷ Growing customer assertiveness	• A firm makes the right value proposition but fails in the execution.	• Pursuing effective management of customer complaints[g] • Rewarding positive word of mouth[h]

[a]Derived from Derek F. Abell (1980) *Defining the Business: The Starting Point of Strategic Planning*. Englewood Cliffs, NJ: Prentice-Hall, from Abell's components of a product-market-technology combination, stipulating: (1) which customers, (2) which products and services, and (3) which technologies.

[b]Werner J. Reinartz and V. Kumar (2000) 'On the Profitability of Long-Life Customers in a Noncontractual Setting: An Empirical Investigation and Implications for Marketing,' *Journal of Marketing*, 64 (Oct.), 17–35; Rajkumar Venkatesan and V. Kumar (2004) 'A Customer Lifetime Value Framework for Customer Selection and Resource Allocation Strategy,' *Journal of Marketing*, 68 (Oct.), 106–25.

[c]Seth Godin (1999) *Permission Marketing: Turning Strangers into Friends and Friends into Customers*. New York: Simon & Schuster.

[d]Ashwin W. Joshi and Sanjay Sharma (2004) 'Customer Knowledge Development: Antecedents and Impact on New Product Development Performance,' *Journal of Marketing*, 68 (Oct.), 47–59.

[e]Patrick T. Barwise and Seán Meehan (2004) *Simply Better: Winning and Keeping Customers by Delivering What Matters Most*. Boston: Harvard Business School Press.

[f]Willem Smit, Gerrit H. van Bruggen, and Berend Wierenga (2007) 'The Nature and Antecedents of Information Sharing in Marketing Channels,' *IMD Working Paper*.

[g]Christian Homburg and Andreas Fürst (2005) 'How Organizational Complaint Handling Drives Customer Loyalty: An Analysis of the Mechanistic and the Organic Approach,' *Journal of Marketing*, 69 (3): 95–114.

[h]Fred Reichheld (2006) 'A Satisfied Customer Isn't Enough,' *Harvard Business Review* (excerpt from 'The Ultimate Question: Driving Profits and True Growth'); note that Reichheld's claim of the Net Promotor score 'is the best predictor of growth' is currently under debate. Analysis published by Keiningham, Timothy L., Bruce Cool, Tor Wallin Andreassen, and Lerzan Aksoy (2007); 'A Longitudinal Examination of Net Promoter and Firm Revenue Growth', *Journal of Marketing*, 71 (July), 39–51 could not replicate his assertions regarding the 'clear superiority' of the Net Promotor Score compared to other measures, like customer satisfaction ratings.

proposition to its customers. And finally, it should deliver the value proposition flawlessly.

In the next paragraphs we will explain how mainstream trends of a connected world provide opportunities to meet these prerequisites more easily and better. For instance, customers are more connected these days, and there are thus more different and efficient ways to reach them. Yet, there is also another important side to the story. Coinciding with these positive opportunities, there are a number of undercurrents for which we would like give a word of caution. These undercurrents could make it harder for a firm to meet the prerequisites of a successful marketing strategy. If the undercurrents are dealt with inappropriately, these might cause connected customers to be annoyed, dissatisfied, and even angry.

Finally, we will propose new network tactics to counter these undercurrents and thus ensure value propositions are in fact valuable.

The Trends and Undercurrents of the Connected Customer

In their most recent biannual survey of the primary concerns of the marketing fraternity, the members of the Marketing Science Institute (MSI) identified understanding 'the Connected Customer' as a significant concern.[9] More and more firms now see an environment in which rapid changes in information communication technology as well as in the globalization of markets are creating communities of customers and prospects rather than a multitude of isolated customers and they realize this calls for significant re-evaluation of current approaches.

Customers are now more connected to:

- their suppliers and competitors;
- third-party information providers; and
- each other.

In the first place, today's business customers as well as consumers are increasingly connected to their suppliers and other firms, via traditional mass marketing, augmented with one-to-one marketing and many-to-many marketing techniques. Firms ever more benefit from the modern (digital) communication links to start and maintain dialogues with their customers. We will give an overview of the opportunities firms have in participating in the mainstream of growing number and reach of different channels. But at the same time, we outline the dangers of the underlying undercurrent. Then, we will suggest tactics in dealing with these developments.

In the second place, customers are more and more connected to third-party information providers, through a variety of product review and price comparison services. This created transparency in the marketplace increases the relevance of customer satisfaction and can provide better insight into 'best value' to customers. This trend gives firms a better insight into customer needs and competitive offers. Thus it increases competition and continuously challenges the offerings firms make. It heightens the importance of making the right value proposition. We will discuss this main trend and undercurrent, followed by tactics for firms to avoid making the wrong value proposition.

Customers are not only more connected to firms and third-party information providers, but also connected to each other—via mobile telephony, the internet, and countless special-interest groups that cross national borders. These intense inter-customer links increase the speed and the power of group and social-network effects on individual behaviors; word-of-mouth effects are stronger and make it more important for firms not to fail in the delivery of the value proposition. We will talk about the main trend of customization and co-creation with customers, but also about the undercurrent of rising expectations and growing customer assertiveness.

As a result of having so many and different connections, today's customers are better informed, but they also leave a more visible 'evidence trail' for companies, in the form of vastly improved CRM databases. For example, European grocer Tesco combines their loyalty card data on what customers were buying at Tesco with survey research on what customers were not buying. Tesco found that, in some of their store formats, young mothers bought fewer baby products in their stores because they trusted pharmacies more. So, Tesco launched BabyClub to provide expert advice and targeted coupons. Its share of baby products sales in the UK grew from 16 per cent in 2000 to 24 per cent in 2003.

Naturally, this digital era with rich new sources of customer data creates an opportunity for improved marketing decision making, which can fuel profitable growth, but if firms really want to benefit from these three main trends of the 'connected customer,' they should consider first the rising feelings of customers of being 'over-communicated,' and that this increases difficulties in predicting future customer needs and wants, and results eventually in a growing customer assertiveness.

Customer–Firm Connections: Many Channels and Limited Customer Attention

The first main trend is that today's customers are more connected to their suppliers and other firms than ever before. In a world where firms increasingly rely on developing and treasuring their skills and knowledge, cultivating relationships with customers provides the basis for their competitive advantage. They involve customers as co-creators and co-producers of value.[10] Firms' investments in CRM have 'experienced explosive growth over the last decade.'[11]

The popularity of CRM took off in the last decade because more intensive competition made companies focus defensively on retaining customers and de-emphasise customer acquisition-related marketing expenditures and activities. That is not the only reason for more continuous relationships between customer and firms. Co-creation with customers is eminent in the services industries which generally direct offerings to the end users (telephone, utilities, banking, etc.),[12] and also in business-to-business relationships, where most companies began to institute key account, national account, and global account management processes and programs to consolidate and increase share of each account's business to fewer suppliers preferably resulting in a sole source relationship. Manufacturers have integrated their supply chain partners into their own operations in order to lower inventories, reduce transaction costs, and increase cooperation.[13]

Many firms attempt to engage their customers through loyalty cards or reward programs. For instance, many supermarkets have issued loyalty cards to their shoppers;[14] in the United States, more than 80 per cent of all households have at least one supermarket loyalty card, and in France this is even 90 per cent. In addition, many households are members of multiple loyalty programs simultaneously.[15]

Managing customer relationships and their respective networks has become more critical to stimulate customer loyalty, cooperation, and positive word of mouth. Fifteen years of academic research supports the view that stronger customer–firm relationships lead to a better performance.[16]

To support their strategy for good customer relationship management, many firms have responded to the fragmentation in media consumption by expanding the number of channels through which customers can be reached.[17] Since advertising products and services through traditional mass media is getting less effective, firms increasingly turn to using one-to-one and many-to-many interactive techniques to get a dialogue with customers. For instance, traditional product brand companies that sell through indirect channels have been pursuing a multi-channel strategy. They are setting up websites with functionalities to facilitate information and entertainment to connect individual consumers for their marketing campaigns. Sara Lee's subsidiary producing and selling coffee and tea products, Douwe Egberts, announces and promotes its new products through its website (www.de.nl) encouraging product trial by sweepstakes.

Yet, we believe that the growth in stronger and more customer–firm relationships is reaching some sort of maturity. There are clear signs of customer fatigue in relationship-building efforts by firms. More people are trying to avoid marketing messages. Some actively block receiving messages. Others obstruct relationship-building efforts by either refusing to disclose or even falsifying their personal information.

Contacting customers as a direct response to increased media fragmentation has intensified the fight for customer attention. In addition to the traditional ways to contact customers directly—postal mail, fixed phones, fax machines—the number of (digital) portals has increased with mobile phones, email, instant messaging, picture messaging, RSS-feeds. The problem in getting customer attention is that many marketing messages reaching customers are considered uninteresting or even annoying. A good example is email spam: in June 2006, the global ratio of spam in email traffic from new and unknown bad sources was 64.8 per cent (1 in 1.54), an increase from 54 per cent in September 2003, up from 18 per cent in April 2002.[18] Research indicates spammers are increasingly turning to new media such as mobile text messaging, web-based instant messaging, weblogs, and social networking communities such as Myspace. com, to bypass email-based anti-spam measures and more effectively target recipients based on their age, location, and other characteristics.

Bombardment with many uninteresting and irrelevant messages causes a sense of information overload, and not surprisingly many customers are beginning to feel over-communicated.[19] Subsequently they can become increasingly marketing resistant. The growing annoyance is leading to deliberate and unintended avoidance of marketing communication messages. Avoidance is bound to grow when classic TV channels are replaced by an 'on-demand' world in which viewers choose what to watch, when (and even where) to watch it, in terms of the ability to pause, rewind, and fast-forward.

From passive forms of resistance, some customers have gone to more active forms of resisting marketing messages. Force-fed marketing tactics are proving less and less successful. The first is blocking phone contact or email. Moreover, more and more people use the options to protect their telephone and internet privacy: caller ID on the phone, voice mail, answering machines, non-published, non-listed numbers, and Do Not Call (DNC) registries. DNC registries prohibit telemarketers and other companies to call cold-canvas in most circumstances. In the USA, from 2003 86 million have contacted the National Do Not Call Registry to have their numbers registered. Since 1999, 12.8 million UK consumers and businesses have registered their fixed line, mobile phone, and fax numbers at the Telephone Preference Service (TPS). Among other European countries, Ireland and the Netherlands also have DNC registries; respectively, the National Directory Database and the InfoFilter.

The prime reason for registering at Do Not Call directories is that consumers do not want to receive sales calls (94 per cent).[20] The menace of 'silent calls' is the second reason. People receiving silent calls believe they are either being targeted by burglars, or, even worse, think that they are being stalked. In a recent case in the UK, the Office of Communications (OFCOM), the independent regulator, upheld a complaint brought by the UK Direct Marketing Association (DMA) against a telemarketing firm which in a four-month period made over 26 million marketing calls. Of these, 1.5 million were silent calls, which the OFCOM said amounted to a persistent misuse of an electronic communications network under the Communications Act 2003. For marketers, however, these DNC lists and the public's concern for privacy require fundamental changes to the way they conduct business.

Privacy concerns drive the second active form of customers' resistance to firms' attempts to get in touch. There is an increase in the refusal to disclose personal information. A study among UK shoppers shows that people are very selective in giving out their personal information to marketing organizations.[21] They have no problem in giving details on their hobbies and interests, but they are more reluctant to pass on more sensitive information like finances and health. There is even a propensity to falsify specific details of the personal information. The reason people give for falsifying personal information is their concern about data protection. They are worried that their information might be passed to third parties leading to the receipt of even more unwanted marketing communications.

Our advice is to run with the main trend, but to be sensitive to the countervailing undercurrents of a growing fatigue of relationship building: being over-communicated, ignoring marketing messages, blocking access, and falsifying information. The undercurrent of 'being over-communicated' complicates starting and maintaining a dialogue with customers, and it thus increases the costs for firms of getting it right. We suggest two network tactics: (1) being even more selective in reaching the customers, and more critically, (2) gaining permission to start relationship building with customers.

The first network tactic concerns the selection of target customers. The effect of the greater connectivity is that customers have the possibility to communicate more easily with firms. The more communicative customers are not necessarily the profitable ones. Since company attention is a scarce resource too, this raises the importance of assessing the profitability of customers: Customer Lifetime Value (CLV).[22] Figure 7.1 offers a classification of the five costly mistakes companies make in their efforts to reach their target customers. Companies should better avoid contact with 'opportunity seekers' (a known term in the direct marketing industry), and reduce plain waste in putting energy in trying to communicate to customers and prospects who are not profitable and do not want to communicate with the firm. Companies should try to engage in a dialogue with customers and prospects who are profitable but do not receive attention yet.

After defining a better selection of which customer and prospects to target, it is crucial to overcome the growing difficulties in reaching (and acquiring new) over-communicated customers. That is especially the case with the 'unwilling patients.' Since these customers have become more resistant to marketing and more selective in the relationships they wish to build, it takes more skill to start a customer dialogue. One effective tactic is to gain permission from customers to communicate with them.[23] Instead of collecting email addresses and spamming,

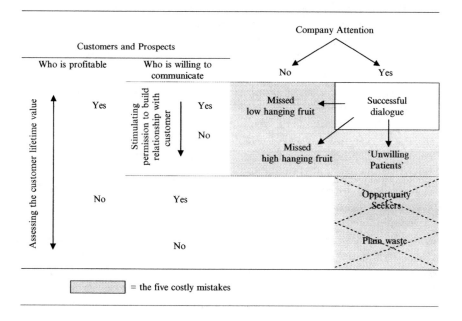

Fig. 7.1 Minimizing costs in reaching the right customers

or buying a database and mailing them, it is crucial to find ways to ask customers/ prospects for permission to have a piece of their attention. That means opt-in email rather than unsolicited commercial email, and using techniques such as customer segmentation and direct email marketing to send appropriate—and possibly even welcome—messages. A good illustration of such a permission tactic is Mercedes in the USA. Before Mercedes, for instance, introduced its sports utility vehicle (SUV) into the US market in 1998, it had gained permission from prospects. With help from its dealer network, it had sent personal letters to a selected group of existing Mercedes drivers to involve them in the actual design of the car. Based on the replies, they sent additional customized follow-up surveys to each responding prospect. So, during the development time of the car, the company had gained permission to stay in touch with them.

Customer-Information Provider Connections: More Transparency Versus Unpredictable Future Demand

The second main trend is more and stronger customer connections to third-party information providers. With a larger variety of product review and price comparison services, customers have gotten more visibility on what is available in the marketplace. In developing value propositions, companies also are helped by this increased transparency in the market. First, customers now have access to information about a company and its products from a multitude of sources: ConsumerReports.org (USA), Which.org (UK), Consumer Association (Ireland), and Consumentenbond (the Netherlands), for third-party information, Amazon's customer reviews,[24] and eBay's seller rating. Second, customers can find competing products more easily. Search engines, comparison sites, and online reviews all enable customers to find the best products at the lowest price. Not only for buying products and services online, but also for purchases offline, the internet has become an important source of information. Think of new car buyers visiting on average seven different websites, such as Autobytel and Edmunds, and spending on average five hours researching vehicle models, features, and options online.[25]

Paradoxically, the trend of better-informed customers leading to more market transparency does not make consumer demand more predictable. On the contrary, the shortening of product lifecycles,[26] high failure rate in new products,[27] increased frequency of unexplainable hypes, fragmentation of media, greater than before variety-seeking behaviors, decreasing brand loyalty, and increased price elasticity have made it more difficult to predict future customer needs and wants for a longer period. These developments end up in the costs of offering propositions that are not valuable to customers.

Network tactics to reduce these costs of valueless propositions concern adopting innovative ways of getting customer insight. In the first place, firms can change their own tactics to collect market information. In the second place, firms can put their network of relationships to work.

First, a firms' own tactics to stay attuned to connected customers' wishes, since the traditional market segmentation, like demographics and socio-economic variables, is considered 'old hat.' We advise them to focus on 'customer knowledge development' and 'immersion' to minimize the likelihood of developing the wrong value propositions. Particularly in the pre-launch phase of new product development, customer knowledge development is more and more useful. It is the process of developing an understanding of customer new product preferences that unfolds through the iteration of probing and learning activities.[28] Examples are probing activities, which include the deployment of new product ideas, concepts, and prototypes among target customers, and learning activities, which entail the analysis of customer feedback and the development of subsequent probes on the analysis.

In addition to this gathering of pre-launch intelligence, firms keep themselves better updated about the actual reality of their product's user's daily routines with 'immersion.' Immersion is 'asking the customer directly.' Not important is the amount of time spent in direct face-to-face contact with customers, 18 per cent of the time of best-performing firms, versus 15 per cent of the time of worst-performing firms.[29] It is about the nature of these contacts: less socializing but more 'getting down to business and getting to know how their company is performing relative to its promises and the customer's expectations.' They also persistently asked their customers how they could do better. Many companies, like Procter & Gamble, find it important to add qualitative observations by customers. Among retailers and apparel makers, a common tool today is the closet check: going into homes and looking in the closets and drawers to see what people wear.

Another network tactic to minimize the development of wrong value propositions and increase the insight on customers is to mobilize channel partners to collaborate on the basis on sharing information.[30] Often data sets and market information of channel partners are complementary. Especially when the relationships between firms are highly interdependent there is sufficient common interest to disclose more strategic market information. Supermarket chain Carrefour and manufacturer Colgate exchanged their market information in order to optimize the performance of the oral care category in French hypermarkets. Their collaboration increased sales by 16 per cent.[31]

Businesses where transactions are facilitated and information is sought over the internet should team up with internet partners. Car dealers generate quality leads through the use of search engine marketing (SEM). SEM enhances dealer website visibility by using one of two marketing methods: search engine optimization and paid/sponsored clicks. Currently, 75 per cent of dealers who use SEM subscribe to search engine optimization, which improves search rankings without having to pay for clicks (also known as organic searches). Additionally, 57 per cent of dealers who subscribe to SEM use paid/sponsorship clicks (Google, Yahoo!, MSN). While only 33 per cent of dealers currently use search engine marketing, more than 80 per cent of those dealers believe it improves website visitation, as it takes vehicle shoppers directly to the dealer website as opposed to shopping through an online buying service. Visitation to dealer websites has the added benefit of increasing visibility of the service and parts department to potential buyers.[32]

Customer–Customer Connections: Customer Involvement Versus Assertiveness

The third main trend is the increase in connections among customers. We see a reinforcing cycle of wider access to broadband, more social computing, and rising experience (see Figure 7.2), which makes the customer–customer influences stronger and stronger. With wider access to broadband, people 'snack,' conveniently look for more information, also about products and firms.

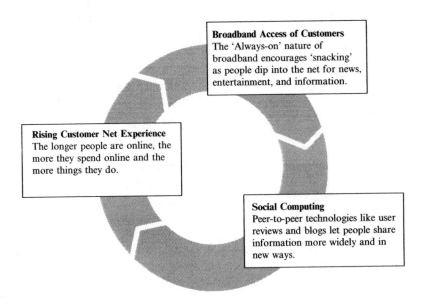

Fig. 7.2 Broadband access, social computing, and experience are changing net users' online behavior

Source: Adapted from Forrester Research, Inc. (2006) 'Social Computing's Impact on Financial Services: How Social Computing will Erode Financial Brands and What To Do about It' (June 22).

Broadband also makes it easier to share their customer experiences with each other in many different and novel ways. And this will subsequently build the collective net experience of customers.

In delivering many value propositions, companies ask the participation of customers. Customer engagement is meant to help customization of products and services.[33] Among many firms, mi-Adidas[34] and Dell allow their customers to design their own products. Now a certain degree of customization has become the standard, the customers' expectations have risen, and subsequently it gets more difficult for firms to meet customers' requirements satisfactory with their offerings. Whilst companies have expanded opportunities to reach customers and simultaneously the possibilities to be reached by them, the facilitating technologies have also raised customers' communication expectations that their calls and emails must be answered ASAP and 24 / 7. They do not want to be sent to voicemail or 'email jail.' In addition to the higher communication expectations, we see an undercurrent that complicates getting customers' attention: the emergence of customer rage.

Customer rage is one of the signs that most companies have difficulties in dealing with the increase in customer assertiveness. Several studies in the USA, UK, and Germany show that customers are increasingly dissatisfied with products and services they acquire. In the USA, 39 per cent of customers have experienced problems with any of the products or services bought. Of these unsatisfied customers, 70 per cent were very or even extremely upset with how companies reacted to their problems.[35]

Research on word-of-mouth effects provides plenty of evidence that a satisfied customer may tell some people about his experience with a company, but a dissatisfied one will tell anyone who will listen. In a networked environment with connected customers, not meeting customers' expectations is getting more and more harmful: via mobile telephony, the internet, and countless special-interest groups and virtual communities,[36] bad customer experiences and complaints are rapidly and powerfully shared among a larger group of people. Social network effects of negative word-of-mouth are accelerated by the new electronic links. So, more prospective customers find out if a company has mistreated former customers.[37]

This cycle and undercurrent of electronically wired opinion leadership and word-of-mouth communication accelerates the spreading of growing customer assertiveness. Customers have become more critical and assertive. Mistakes by a firm in delivering the value proposition are quickly shared with others.[38] A recent example is Dell's burning batteries. The market leader in customized PCs recalled 22,000 notebook computer batteries in December last year, but got beat up in the press and consumer blogs after the picture of the exploding laptop at a conference in Osaka, Japan, surfaced on the internet in June. It was mainly Jeff Jarvis's BuzzMachine blog which seems to have become the place where Dell bashing can be done by a group of people who feel they have been treated poorly by the computer leader (http://www.buzzmachine.com/ ?tag=dell).

Another well-known anecdote of 'company bashing' is Jeremy Cooperstock, who created the website Untied.com after an unprofessional response by United Airlines to his complaint letter. Since Untied.com started collecting complaints in October 1998, he has received approximately 9,500 letters from people who have been treated with disdain by the airline company. All of these letters were posted on his website.

We advise two network tactics to minimize the negative effects of poor value proposition delivery. First, like so many marketing strategy books, we advise effective management of customer complaints. From research we know that service recovery increases the customer's satisfaction[39] (sometimes even higher then pre-failure levels[40]).

Only complaint management can undo the negative effects from negative word of mouth. A possible tactic is to reward customers who actively promote

143

the company among friends. It may well be smart to make a distinction between 'promoters' and 'detractors.'[41] Quantifying the value of a promoter or a detractor helps to put a value to word of mouth. A next step in assessing the lifetime value of a customer can be to correct it for the value in attracting (or detracting) other prospects/customers.

Conclusion

All firms are dealing with a new reality called the connected world. The newest communication technologies and the connected customers give companies opportunities to engage in a dialogue with current and new customers, to be better informed about market development in *real time*, and to involve customers to mass-customize their value propositions.

Yet, each development to more and stronger connections between firms and customers also has an undercurrent. These undercurrents may increase the costs of valueless propositions. Targeting audiences that do not want to build a relationship, developing the wrong value proposition, and delivering it poorly, all lead to rising feelings of 'being over-communicated,' increasing difficulty in predicting future demand, and growing customer dissatisfaction, rage, disbelief, doubt, anger, and skepticism. These realities have become a major part of marketing managers' everyday practices. Companies can no longer afford to ignore raised customer power. We lay out possible strategies by which companies can react. The first strategy is to improve dialogue with the right customers by assessment of customer lifetime value and permission marketing. The second strategy is to improve offering the right value proposition by customer development programs and immersion strategies. The third strategy is to reduce negative network effects of poor value proposition delivery by excellent complaint management and by rewarding customers with positive word of mouth.

Notes

1. See the stream of literature on market orientation: John C. Narver and Stanley F. Slater (1990) 'The Effect of a Market Orientation on Business Profitability,' *Journal of Marketing*, 54 (Oct.): 20–5; Ajay K. Kohli and Bernard J. Jaworski (1990) 'Market Orientation: The Construct, Research Propositions, and Managerial Implications,' *Journal of Marketing*, 54 (Apr.): 1–17; Rohit Deshpandé, John U. Farley, and Frederick E. Webster Jr. (1993) 'Corporate Culture, Customer Orientation, and Innovativeness,' *Journal of Marketing*, 57 (Jan.): 23–37; Seán Meehan, Patrick Barwise, Mark

Vandenbosch, and Willem Smit (2007) 'The Impact of Organizational Values on the Effectiveness of Market-Oriented Behaviors,' *MSI Reports*, Issue 3, 07–116.

2. George S. Day (1994) 'The Capabilities of Market-Driven Organizations,' *Journal of Marketing*, 58 (Dec.): 37–52.

3. Following Christine Moorman and Ronald Rust (1999) 'The Role of Marketing,' *Journal of Marketing*, 63 (Special Issue): 180–97, we focus on the critical roles that marketing plays in connecting elements of the firm to its customers: (1) value proposition development and delivery (product and service delivery) and (2) financial accountability.

4. Paul D. Berger, Ruth N. Bolton, Douglas Bowman, Elten Brigs, V. Kumar, A. Parasuraman, and Creed Terry (2002) 'Marketing Actions and the Value of Customer Assets: A Framework for Customer Asset Management,' *Journal of Service Research*, 5 (1): 39–54.

5. For an excellent review of critical issues involved in adopting marketing metrics, see Tim Ambler (2000) *Marketing and the Bottom Line: The New Metrics of Corporate Wealth*. London: Financial Times/Prentice Hall.

6. The 'chain of marketing productivity,' as outlined by Roland T. Rust, Tim Ambler, Gregory S. Carpenter, V. Kumar, and Rajendra K. Srivastava (2004) 'Measuring Marketing Productivity: Current Knowledge and Future Directions,' *Journal of Marketing*, 68 (4): 76–89, identifies the marketing assets and understanding the contribution to the firm's shareholder value thereof. Other metrics are the effects of marketing investments on customer perception improvements, on customer attraction and increased retention, on increased Customer Lifetime Value (CLV), and subsequent increase in customer equity (Roland T. Rust, Katherine N. Lemon, and Valarie Zeitháml (2004) 'Return on Marketing: Using Customer Equity to Focus Marketing Strategy', *Journal of Marketing*, 68 (1): 109–27). Comparing the increase in customer equity to another investment gives CEOs the base for evaluating the different investments options.

7. Xueming Luo (2007) 'Consumer Negative Voice and Firm-Idiosyncratic Stock Returns,' *Journal of Marketing*, 71 (July): 75–88.

8. The principle 'Different costs for different purposes' means that costs that are relevant in one decision situation are not necessarily relevant in another. In each decision situation any manager (and a marketing manager too) must examine the data at hand and isolate the relevant costs. In this case, the costs of valueless propositions are defined as the sacrifices made—intentionally or unintentionally—(measured by the resources given up and by missed out revenues), to build a strong and profitable customer relationship.

9. Founded in 1961, the Marketing Science Institute is a consortium of companies and marketing academics. It aims to bridge the gap between marketing science theory and business practice. Its membership consists of over 70 corporations with researchers from over 100 universities worldwide. Every two years, the MSI publishes research priorities. The MSI 2006–2008 Research Priorities are the result of a three-step process of focused discussions at Trustees' Meetings and MSI conferences, an

open-ended survey of MSI member company trustees, and a quantitative survey sent to all MSI member company trustees. The response was obtained from more than 140 managers (covering 87% of their member companies).

10. Stephen L. Vargo and Robert F. Lusch (2004) 'Evolving to a New Dominant Logic for Marketing,' *Journal of Marketing*, 68 (1): 1–17.

11. Raji Srinivasan and Christine Moorman (2005) 'Strategic Firm Commitments and Rewards for Customer Relationship Management in Online Retailing,' *Journal of Marketing*, 69 (Oct.): 193–200.

12. Bill Karakostas, Dimitris Kardaras, and Eleutherios Papathanassiou (2005) 'The State of CRM Adoption by the Financial Services in the UK: An Empirical Investigation,' *Information & Management*, 42 (Sept.): 853–63.

13. Markham T. Frohlich and Roy Westbrook (2001): 'Arcs of Integration: An International Study of Supply Chain Strategies,' *Journal of Operations Management*, 19 (2): 185–200; Markham T. Frohlich and Roy Westbrook (2002) 'Demand Chain Management in Manufacturing and Services: Web-Based Integration, Drivers and Performance,' *Journal of Operations Management*, 20 (6): 729–45.

14. Jorna Leenheer and Tammo H. A. Bijmolt (2003) 'Adoption and Effectiveness of Loyalty Programs: The Retailer's Perspective,' *MSI Report No. 03–124*, Cambridge, Mass.; Cristina Ziliani and Silvia Bellini (2004) 'From Loyalty Cards to Micromarketing Strategies: Where is Europe's Retail Industry Heading?,' *Journal of Targeting, Measurement & Analysis for Marketing*, 12 (3): 281–9.

15. AC Nielsen (2002), 'Consumer Insight 2002.'

16. Robert W. Palmatier, Rajiv P. Dant, Dhruv Grewal, and Kenneth R. Evans (2006) 'Factors Influencing the Effectiveness of Relationship Marketing: A Meta-analysis,' *Journal of Marketing*, 70 (Oct.): 136–53.

17. T. P. Barwise and A. Styler (2003) 'MET Report: Marketing Expenditure Trends 2001–04'. London Business School, Dec.

18. Press Release MessageLabs, 1 Sept. 2006.

19. Anonymous (2006) 'Where Television Advertising Fits in the New Media Ecology,' *Marketing Week*, 32 (4 May).

20. Hal Varian, Fredrik Wallenberg, and Glenn Woroch (2005) 'The Demographics of the Do-Not-Call List', *IEEE Security and Privacy*, (1): 34–9.

21. Gary S. Robertshaw and Norman E. Marr (2006) 'The Implications of Incomplete and Spurious Personal Information Disclosures for Direct Marketing Practice,' *Database Marketing & Customer Strategy Management*, 13 (3): 186–97.

22. Werner J. Reinartz and V. Kumar (2000) 'On the Profitability of Long-Life Customers in a Noncontractual Setting: An Empirical Investigation and Implications for Marketing,' *Journal of Marketing*, 64 (Oct.): 17–35.

23. Seth Godin (1999) *Permission Marketing: Turning Strangers into Friends and Friends into Customers*. New York: Simon & Schuster.

24. Judith A. Chevalier and Dina Mayzlin (2006) 'The Effect of Word of Mouth on Sales: Online Book Reviews,' *JMR Journal of Marketing Research*, 43 (3): 345–54.

25. J. D. Power and Associates (2006) 'New Antoshopper Study: Shoppers Increasingly Turn to Manufacturer and Dealer Web Sites to Research New Vehicles', 10 October.

26. Peter N. Golder and Gerard J. Tellis (2004) 'Growing, Growing, Gone: Cascades, Diffusion, and Turning Points in the Product Life Cycle,' *Marketing Science*, 23 (2): 207–18. Abbie Griffin (1997) 'The Effect of Project and Process Characteristics on Product Development Cycle Time,' *Journal of Marketing Research*, 34 (1): 24–35.

27. Greg A. Stevens and James Burley (2003), 'Piloting the Rocket of Radical Innovation,' *Research Technology Management*, 46 (2): 16–26.

28. Gary S. Lynn, Joseph G. Morone, and Albert S. Paulson (1996) 'Marketing and Discontinuous Innovation: The Probe and Learn Process,' *California Management Review*, 38 (3): 8–37; Ashwin W. Joshi and Sanjay Sharma (2004) 'Customer Knowledge Development: Antecedents and Impact on New Product Development Performance,' *Journal of Marketing*, 68 (Oct.): 47–59.

29. Seán Meehan, (1997) 'Market Orientation: Values, Behaviors, and Performance.' Ph.D. dissertation, University of London.

30. Willem Smit, Gerrit H. van Bruggen, and Berend Wierenga (2007) 'The Nature and Antecedents of Information Sharing in Marketing Channels,' *IMD Working Paper*.

31. Anita Greenwood, and Sebastin Levy (2004) 'Brushing up the Oral Care Category,' ECR Europe Conference, Brussels.

32. JD Power and Associates press release, 12 Sept. 2006.

33. Jerry Wind and Arvind Rangaswamy (2001) 'Customerization: The Next Revolution in Mass Customization,' *Journal of Interactive Marketing*, 15 (1): 13–32.

34. Ralph W. Seifert (2002) 'The "mi adidas" Mass Customization Initiative,' IMD case 6–0249 159.

35. Customer Care Alliance (2005) '2005 National Customer Rage Study' (2 Nov.), presentation by Scott M. Broetzmann and Marc Grainer.

36. Arthur Armstrong and John Hagel III (1996) 'The Real Value of ON-LINE Communities,' *Harvard Business Review*, 74 (3): 134–41. Robert V. Kozinets (2002) 'The Field behind the Screen: Using Netnography for Marketing Research in Online Communities,' *Journal of Marketing Research*, 39 (1): 61–72; Kristine de Valck, (2005) 'Virtual Communities of Consumption: Networks of Consumer Knowledge and Companionship' Ph.D. thesis, Erasmus University Rotterdam.

37. Patrali Chatterjee (2001) 'Online Reviews: Do Consumers Use Them?; in M. C. Gilly and J. Myers-Levy (eds.), *ACR 2001 Proceedings*. Association for Consumer Research, 129–34.

38. Ainsworth Anthony Bailey (2004) 'Thiscompanysucks.com: The Use of the Internet in Negative Consumer-to-Consumer Articulations,' *Journal of Marketing Communications*, 10 (3): 169–82.

39. Stephen S. Tax, Stephen W. Brown, and Murali Chandrashekaran (1998) 'Customer Evaluations of Service Complaint Experiences: Implications for Relationship Marketing,' *Journal of Marketing*, 62 (2): 60–76. Amy L. Smith, Ruth N. Bolton, and

Develop your Options

Janet Wagner (1999) 'A Model of Customer Satisfaction with Service Encounters Involving Failure and Recovery,' *Journal of Marketing Research*, 36 (Aug.): 356–73.

40. Amy L. Smith and Ruth N. Bolton (1998) 'An Experimental Investigation of Customer Reactions to Service Failure and Recovery Encounters: Paradox or Peril,' *Journal of Service Research*, 1 (1): 5–17.

41. Fred Reichheld (2006) 'A Satisfied Customer Isn't Enough,' *Harvard Business Review* (excerpt from 'The Ultimate Question: Driving Profits and True Growth'). Note that Reichheld's claim that the Net Promotor core 'is the best predictor of growth' is currently under debate. Analysis published by Timothy L. Keiningham, Bruce Cooil, Tor Wallin Andreassen, and Lerzan Aksoy (2007) 'A Longitudinal Examination of Net Promoter and Firm Revenue Growth,' *Journal of Marketing*, 71 (July): 39–51 could not replicate his assertions regarding the 'clear superiority' of the Net Promoter Score compared to other measures, like customer satisfaction ratings.

8 Managing the Evolving Global Production Network

Kasra Ferdows

Managing the global production network is becoming more complex. The critical issue is no longer where to produce a *product* but where to perform individual production *tasks*. A decade ago, a toy maker might have moved the production of its toy robot to China; today, if it has moved with the times, it is more likely to have its plastic body produced in Malaysia, speakers in Korea, motors for legs in Taiwan, voice recognition software in the USA, assembly in China, and finishing, inspection, packing, and storage for worldwide distribution in Dubai.

Coordinating all this is not easy. Some companies make a mess out of it and turn their global production into a function that hinders their agility and performance; others turn it into a formidable advantage.

There are no simple explanations for the differences between the two groups. You find both types in the same industry. Seemingly similar production networks—similar in their global spread of factories, degree of outsourcing, and logistics systems—work well in one company but not another. Delve deeper, and you find that the production networks in most companies are results of a series of incremental decisions through the years, each justified by convincing arguments and extensive cost analysis. So there must be something in the *cumulative* effect of these decisions—not the individual ones. The answer must lie in the differences in higher-level strategies in these companies.

But what are these higher-level strategies for crafting the firm's global production network? My objective in this chapter is to answer this question. Specifically, I propose a framework for clarifying the strategic options for directing the evolution of these networks. It is based on clinical analysis of four companies and examples from a few more. The rich literature in management of multinational enterprises–in particular, the network theory (e.g. Ghoshal and Bartlett),[1] evolutionary theory (e.g. Kogut and Zander),[2] learning organization (e.g. Hedlund),[3] and knowledge transfer (e.g. Grant),[4] all of which view the multinational organization as a web of inter- and intra-firm relationships—provide the conceptual foundation of this framework. A common theme among these theories is that multinational organizations can benefit greatly from transferring resources and competencies developed in different locations within their company, Another conceptual foundation behind this framework is from the literature in industrial networks (e.g. Karlsson)[5] and manufacturing networks (e.g. Shi and Gregory).[6] This literature, among other things, focuses on how advances in information and communication technologies and increased pace of globalization have made it easier for firms to access the capabilities of other firms.

I should add at the outset that what I present in this chapter is only one out of many steps in this long road. There are many issues in managing a global production network that are not addressed here. Still, I hope this framework is a useful tool for senior managers who wish to clarify the direction for the evolution of their company's global production networks.

Models of Production Networks

There are two seemingly irreconcilable models for building production networks. One advocates staying footloose—that is, continuing searching the world for a better factory inside or outside the company and moving production there as soon you find one; the other advocates developing deep roots—making long-term commitment to each production site and giving it the resources to reach its full potential.

Both models have their own logic. Those in search of more agility in an increasingly uncertain and volatile world usually argue for more footloose networks; and those who want more stability to develop unique production capabilities, ironically to cope with the same uncertain and volatile world, argue for more rooted networks. The first group wants to leverage capabilities of others and conserve own resources for other functions like design and marketing; the second group wants to use own production and supply chain capabilities as a competitive weapon.

Companies often move unwittingly towards one of these models, especially the footloose model. They make incremental decisions without fully appreciating their cumulative and unintended consequences. There are always impressive cost–benefit calculations and presentations to support each decision, but, paradoxically, often the more elaborate these presentations, the more likely they are to take the attention away from the big picture and the long-term strategy.

It is not unusual to see companies in the same industry moving in opposite directions. While Philips, the giant Dutch electronic company, announces its intention to sell or close one-third of its 150 factories worldwide, its competitor, Samsung, continues to pour billions into its factories. Of course both companies are convinced they are right: Philips sees decreasing importance for owning its production, Samsung more. 'If we get out of manufacturing, we will lose,' says Samsung's CEO and vice chairman, Yun Jong Yong.

Box 8.1 Simplify and Expand the Pool of Good Suppliers: IKEA's Successful Footloose Manufacturing Network

With a network of 1,300 suppliers in 53 countries, IKEA, a Swedish furniture company with €14.8 billion sales in 2005 and growing at 15% annually, works overtime to find the right manufacturer for its 9,500 products. Simplicity, a tenet of Swedish design, helps keep costs down. IKEA's 12 full-time designers in Almhult, Sweden, along with 80 freelancers, work hand in hand with the in-house production team to identify the least costly suppliers with appropriate capabilities.

This is a trial-and-error process and the search never stops. IKEA uses its 46 trading offices in 32 countries to look for new suppliers. Most are in Europe, but IKEA is adding suppliers from other regions, particularly Asia. In 2005, China, with 18% of all its purchases, tops the list, followed by Poland (12%), Sweden (9%), Italy (7%), and Germany (6%).

Although IKEA is constantly adding new suppliers, it still builds close working relationships with its existing ones. It helps them in many ways, ranging from securing raw materials to coping with political and economic upheavals. For example, after the fall of the Berlin Wall, it set up a new company, Swedwood, to participate in the privatization of its suppliers in eastern Europe. Today Swedwood has evolved into an IKEA supplier with advanced production facilities of its own in nine countries, mainly in eastern Europe.

IKEA's suppliers are an integral part of its unique and clever system. IKEA designs its products in standard modules and procures similar pieces used in different products from the same suppliers—for example, flat table tops and bookcase shelves are bundled together and ordered from one supplier and the legs, columns, and other cylindrical wooden pieces from another. Then, in its own warehouses, IKEA sorts out the different boxes by models, and since the customer does the final assembly, it sells the pieces in the very boxes that come from suppliers.

It's a brilliant use of footloose manufacturing. IKEA simplifies what it needs from factories, hence has many potential bidders and gets competitive prices, *and* does not reveal design of its new products to its widespread and leak-prone supply network. That it then sells its bulky products in stackable, easy to transport 'flat pack' boxes that allow customers to carry them home without a truck and pay less because they do the assembly themselves makes the system even more brilliant.

Both models can be successful. IKEA has succeeded with the footloose model (see Box 8.1) and Intel with the rooted model (see Box 8.2).

The problem arises when a company adopts a model by default. In particular, those that end up with a footloose network—and there seem to be more of them in recent years—often get there not by a deliberate strategic choice but through a series of ad hoc decisions. They may shift production from one of their factories to another halfway around the world to shave off production costs; they may decide to use contract manufacturers to fill a temporary gap in the production capacity or launch a new product quickly when there is as yet no internal production capability; they may see an opportunity to reduce production costs, avoid investment in manufacturing, and show a quick improvement in return on capital employed if they outsource production. Perhaps they have no other option: their production volume is too small to justify building a devoted factory or they simply don't have enough resources to add production capacity.

Each of these decisions may be justified in isolation. However, together they can put the company on a slippery slope that pushes it further towards the footloose model. And the process is often irreversible.

Box 8.2 Between the Laws of Rock and Moore: Intel's Rooted Manufacturing Network

Intel has had to cope with not only the familiar Moore's Law, but also with the less familiar Rock's Law. Gordon Moore, an Intel co-founder, back in 1965 predicted that the number of transistors on a microprocessor would double every 24 months. Arthur Rock, Intel's first chairman, predicted that the cost of tools required to manufacture semiconductors would double every four years. Both have been right in the last forty years.

Any company facing such compelling 'laws' would perhaps be weary of investing in manufacturing. And if it did, you would expect to see it close old factories and open new ones frequently. But not Intel. Intel has been the largest investor in plant and equipment in the industry over the last decade, and instead of closing its 'old' plants, it continues to 'retrofit' and keep them up to date. Results: a network of 15 viable manufacturing sites, 6 in the USA and 9 outside the USA.

This is a *deep*-rooted manufacturing network. Each of these factories has received substantial capital investments every year and from time to time a large infusion of funds (sometimes billions of dollars) for major upgrades. The factory in Penang (Malaysia), for example, received substantial investments in 1988 (when it was opened), 1994, and 1997; the Irish plant in Leixlip in 1993, 1994, and 2004; the Costa Rican plant in 1997 and 1999; and so on. The same pattern is observed in the US plants: $2 billion in 2002 in the New Mexico plant to upgrade its equipment, $345 million in 2005 to upgrade the plants in Colorado and Massachusetts, etc. Clearly, once Intel chooses a manufacturing site, it puts a deep stake into the grounds with the intention of staying for the long run. It gives the factory the requisite resources, new knowledge, and training to survive and succeed.

While other companies faced with pale versions of the Moore's and Rock's Laws are turning away from investment in manufacturing and adopting a more footloose model, Intel continues to boost its deep-rooted manufacturing network. It demonstrates that, contrary to the popular view, manufacturing can be a critical competitive weapon especially when products and processes change quickly.

Smart companies watch the evolution of their manufacturing networks carefully. They may choose to become more footloose, more rooted, or build a judicious combination of the two networks with clear demarcation lines. But whatever they do, they do with a clear long-term strategy. They avoid the potential perils of moving unwittingly towards footloose manufacturing.

Attractions of Footloose Production

Several trends are making footloose production more attractive these days.

Increasing Incentive to Outsource Production

Contract manufacturers are competing more fiercely than ever to convince the original equipment manufacturers (OEMs) give up manufacturing. Consider the cellphone industry: Hon Hai, Flextronics, Compal Communications, BenQ Corp, and Arima Communication, five giant contract manufacturers, made over a third of the 800 million handsets sold in 2005. They offer lower production costs, partly because they can benefit from economies of scale and moving down the learning curve quickly, and partly because they accept small profit margins. They compete intensely for the OEM business and some of them have suffered losses in recent years.

Others, besides contract manufacturers, also want to take over more production tasks for the OEMs. FedEx, UPS, DHL, Ryder, Maersk, and other so-called 'third-party logistics providers' (3PLs) are expanding their services for the OEMs. They are managing OEMs' raw materials and finished goods stocks, packing, shipping, and even doing some of their light manufacturing. Suppliers, too, are doing more: they are managing the inventory of their products in the customers' factories (through so called 'vendor-managed inventory' schemes), and making more complete subassemblies.

Meanwhile, shorter product lifecycles, faster-changing technologies, more uncertainty about the future, and generally more market volatility are convincing senior managers that investment in manufacturing is becoming more risky. So they're more open to offers by contract manufacturers, suppliers, or 3PLs.

Increasing Incentive to Move Production

Even when an OEM is not outsourcing its manufacturing, it is under increasing pressure to move production to low-cost locations. There are always places with lower wages, lower taxes, more generous government subsidies, and access to cheaper raw materials. According to one estimate, foreign companies opened 60,000 factories in China alone between 2000 and 2003. Other countries in South East Asia, eastern Europe, and many other regions are also receiving record levels of manufacturing investments.

This massive movement of production is destabilizing the manufacturing networks in many companies. The threat of moving production to lower-cost locations has placed a heavier burden on existing factories to justify their new investments, production quotas, product allocations, and, ultimately, existence. This burden often leads to a race to cut production costs, and, ironically, more incentives to move production to lower-cost locations. These companies edge further towards the footloose model.

Hidden Costs of Footloose Production

Footloose production has four significant hidden costs:

Atrophy of Expertise

Production know-how is not static. Like everything else, those who do more of something learn to do it better, and if they really focus on improving their method systematically, they develop deep expertise. The incremental improvements in production know-how are usually in tacit form, embedded in the skilled employees in the factory. It is not easy to transfer tacit knowledge. An OEM that invests little in manufacturing and frequently shifts production between its factories would not only slow down the process of developing new tacit know-how, but after a while would lose whatever expertise it might have had.

And that would also harm its design capabilities. Toyota designs better cars partly because of its deep knowledge of manufacturing.

Hurting Morale

Imagine you're working in a factory at Hewlett-Packard, Motorola, Nokia, or Xerox and you hear that production of some of your core products has just been given to Solectron, a contract manufacturer recently acquired by Flextronics, a bigger contract manufacturer. The next rumor is impending lay-offs. How would that affect your productivity?

The adverse effects are real, but hard to quantify and rarely included in the analysis of outsourcing decisions.

Even frequent shifting of production between a company's own factories, in the hope of reaping a quick benefit, hurts morale. It creates an atmosphere of uncertainty and instability that persuades the most valuable employees to leave (thereby accelerating the atrophy of the company's production expertise) and makes those who remain feel less secure and motivated.

Commoditizing the Product

Contract manufacturers have a strong incentive to use common components, subassemblies, modules, or even finished products. They put subtle but enticing pressure on the OEMs to use more standard modules and assembly processes. In doing so, they accelerate the process of turning the product into a commodity, resulting in smaller profit margins for the OEMs.

The PC market is a good example. As more and more PCs are made by contract manufacturers, what was once a highly differentiated market has become a cut-throat commodity market. The thinner margins of commodity products put more pressure on the PC companies to cut production costs and more motivation to use contract manufacturers and standard components. The same thing is happening to low-end mobile phone handsets, digital cameras, and many other products.

Helping Competitors

Up to 2004, BenQ Corp., a Taiwanese contract manufacturer, used to design and manufacture mobile phones for Motorola. Then it began selling phones in the treasured China market under its own brand name. Motorola abruptly cancelled its order, with costly short-term problems for both BenQ (which had lost 20 per cent of its order book overnight) and Motorola (which had to find a new production source for those models immediately). But Motorola also faced a long-term problem: it had fostered a new and potentially formidable competitor. In June 2005, BenQ acquired Siemens Mobile Devices (the world's fourth largest handset maker) and since then it has expanded its market in Europe and elsewhere.

Other contract manufacturers—like Flextronics, Solectron, HTC, Quanta, Premier Imaging, and Compal–are also moving into a potential collision course with the OEMs. Many contract manufacturers are adding more services, from product design to managing the entire supply chain, starting from procuring raw materials to delivering the finished goods to end users. They are getting bigger and more knowledgeable. Even if they don't enter the market with their own brands, they can help other companies that compete with their OEM customers. After all, they are in the business of solving manufacturing, design, and supply chain problems for more than one company.

While the electronic sector, with cellphones, laptops, high-definition TVs, MP3 players, digital cameras, and other products, is further down this road, other sectors are not far behind. Household appliances, toys, pharmaceuticals, automotive components, furniture, textiles, and other sectors are also moving further towards the footloose model and, in the process, creating third-party entities that can help their rivals or potentially become their direct competitors.

Clarifying the Long-Term Options

We need a systematic approach to cut through the complexity of all these trade-offs and see when footloose manufacturing can fit the long-term strategy, when it can hinder it, and when it must be watched very carefully. I suggest a simple framework as a starting point. The framework is based on two fundamental attributes of the product: uniqueness of its design and exclusivity of its production process. See Figure 8.1.

In a nutshell, moving towards a footloose model is appropriate only when the product is turning into a commodity and the processes used for its production and delivery are becoming more standardized and widely available. In any other case this move can create long-term problems.

Develop your Options

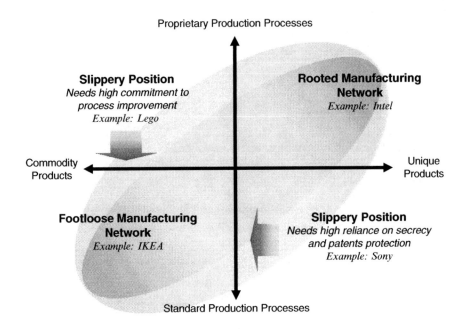

Fig. 8.1 When to be Footloose, when rooted

The logic is straightforward. The requisite know-how to produce a commodity product is usually highly codified and easy to transfer from one factory to another, inside or outside the company. Therefore, a footloose manufacturing network can work well. IKEA, for example, uses standard and widely available processes for production of its products. The products are simple assembly of easy to produce modules. Many suppliers around the globe have the required equipment and capability, and IKEA can pick and choose among them. (See Box 8.1.)

Can Intel, Toyota, or BMW copy IKEA's footloose manufacturing model? No—at least not for their core products. This is not just because they need more sophisticated suppliers who should be willing to make large dedicated investments, but more fundamentally, because they compete through producing unique products with proprietary production systems. They have distinctive capabilities in their factories, and since much of the accumulated know-how behind these capabilities is tacit, they cannot transfer them from one factory to another easily. They need the stability of the rooted manufacturing networks to succeed with such strategy.[7]

Most companies have products that fall somewhere between the extreme cases of IKEA and Intel. They have products that are somewhat unique and

156

production processes that are partly proprietary. Normally, that translates to operating close to the diagonal on this framework.

But they could also be off the diagonal. A digital camera, a toy, or a tennis racket with unique features that are produced by standard production methods from standard components are examples of situations that fall below the diagonal. The temptation to go for the footloose model (for example outsourcing production to contract manufacturers) is great in these situations. But that would accelerate commoditization of these products because it helps others learn about the specific components, suppliers, and methods needed to produce similar products. A firm that wants to operate in this zone (like Apple producing its iPods by an undisclosed contract manufacturer) must rely heavily on secrecy, exclusivity, heavy investment in patent protection, and aggressive pursuit of copycats. Otherwise it'll have to get into long-term and deep partnerships with a few carefully selected contract manufacturers, which in effect is akin to building a rooted manufacturing network.

Footloose manufacturing is even more dangerous for those that operate above the diagonal. Companies like Nucor and Chaparral that make commodity products (for example, steel rebars and profiles) with highly proprietary production processes operate in this zone. These companies have been successful, but to stay in this position, they must keep up their relentless pace of process improvement. That can be done only in a rooted production network. Instability and meager investment in factories would erode the foundation of such strategy.

Lego, the Danish toy maker, also has been operating in this zone until very recently. In an industry where footloose manufacturing is the norm, Lego maintained a rooted model for many years, producing about 20 billion units of its famous 'brick' (a small plastic cube) per year in its factories in Denmark, Switzerland, USA, and, recently, Czech Republic, its plastic moulds in Germany, and a facility for brick decoration and packaging in South Korea.

The temptation to move production of a seemingly simple product like the brick to lower-cost locations or outsource it altogether must have been unremitting, and Lego seems to have succumbed recently. In 2006, reversing its decades-long strategy, Lego outsourced production of 80 per cent of its products to Flextronics. The early results are not encouraging; Flextronics seems to have run into a number of quality and delivery problems and transfer of know-how has proved to be a much greater challenge than expected.

It's not difficult to see why. Lego competed, rather effectively for many years, by relying on its proprietary production know-how and continuous investment in its factories. Its superior production know-how (which ranges from technical matters in mould design, plastics, and precision assembly to managerial ones in scheduling, order fulfillment, die maintenance, and processes reliability) served Lego well for a long time in improving quality, enhancing product design capabilities, and keeping costs in control. Again, most of this know-how is in tacit form and very difficult to transfer to an outsider like a contract manufacturer, particularly when it seems to be the cause for a major lay-off. And there is a real risk of losing much of this know-how in a few years.

In short, operating in the zone above the diagonal demands high levels of unwavering commitment to developing proprietary production methods. Companies without such deep and lasting commitment are likely to find it hard to stay in this zone. New production methods inevitably leak outside and, to stay ahead, they must constantly invest in new capabilities. That is a hard sell when products are commodities and there are suppliers who, at least initially, are willing to accept a smaller margin to get the job. This is a zone with a very slippery slope towards footloose manufacturing.

Choosing the Right Mix

For an OEM that competes with highly differentiated products that can only be made by proprietary production methods, the choice is clear: it must develop a rooted model. Of course, it can still use contract manufacturers but only temporarily and for filling a short-term gap. And when it does, it should ensure that the ad hoc nature of the relationship is transparent to all parties, especially its own senior managers and those who work in its factories.

Firms that don't offer highly differentiated products have a choice. If, like IKEA, they don't want to compete on the basis of proprietary production processes, they can adopt a footloose model.[8] However, if they do, then, like Nucor and until recently Lego, they need to build a rooted manufacturing network.

Most other companies should consider a mix of the two models, but must be careful to use each model appropriately. Zara, the Spanish clothier with over 1,000 stores in 42 countries, shows how such a hybrid model can work. (See Box 8.3.)

Zara is on the forefront of 'fast fashion.' It uses a rooted network for the more complicated and time-sensitive products—like women's suits in seasonal colors—and a footloose model for the simpler and predictable items, like men's shirts in classic colors.

This policy looks logical and senior managers in many companies say that's what they do. But look closer and you find that most are doing the reverse: they send the difficult, unpredictable, complicated products to contract manufacturers and outside suppliers and keep the predictable, simpler products for their own factories. Perhaps the usual key performance indicators for factories—production costs, productivity, capacity unitization, return on assets, and so on—are to blame. Zara, on the other hand, is careful not to do that. Its senior

Box 8.3 Zara's Hybrid Model

Spanish clothier Zara has been a phenomenally successful company. The 2006 sales of its parent company, Inditex—two-thirds of which came from Zara—were €8.2 billion, 22% over 2005; net profits were €1.02 billion, 25% over 2005. This was on top of a great performance in 2005, when sales had grown by 21% and profits by 26%. And these have not been unusual years: from 1991 to 2003, essentially thanks to Zara, Inditex's sales grew more than twelve fold and net profits fourteen fold.

What is Zara's secret? Perhaps the most important one is its system of design, production, distribution, and retailing.[a] In an industry where orders must be given months in advance, Zara can take a new model from design through production and have it delivered to its 1,000 stores in 42 countries in a mere 15 days. Zara introduces around 13,000 new models per year, which with different sizes and colors translate into about 400,000 *new* stock-keeping units.

What kind of manufacturing network can support this relentless pace? Rivals, like Gap and H&M, with no production facilities, follow the footloose model. Zara, on the hand, sticks to a hybrid model: a rooted network of its own factories (eighteen of which are near its headquarters in La Coruña, in the north-west of Spain, two in Barcelona, one in Lithuania, with few joint ventures in other countries) for roughly half of its products and a footloose model of several hundred suppliers in Europe, North Africa, and Asia to produce the other half. (See Figure 8.2.)

The footloose model is for the simpler products with more predictable demand patterns, like sweaters in classic colors. Zara distributes these orders among multiple suppliers and continues to look for better sources. But it reserves the manufacture of the more complicated and time-sensitive products, like women's dresses in the latest seasonal colors, for its own factories.

These factories are tightly integrated into Zara's design and distribution systems. Zara can ramp up or down production of specific garments quickly and conveniently because it normally operates many of its factories for only a single shift. These highly automated factories can operate extra hours if need be to meet seasonal or unforeseen demands. Specialized by garment type, Zara's factories use sophisticated just-in-time systems developed in cooperation with Toyota that allow the company to customize its processes and exploit innovations.

Owning so many production assets is unusual in this industry, but they give Zara a level of control over schedules and capacities that, its senior managers argue, would be impossible to achieve if it were entirely dependent on outside suppliers, especially ones located on the other side of the world.

When Zara produces a garment in-house, it still uses local subcontractors for simple and labor-intensive steps of the production process, like sewing. But it treats them like an extension of its own enterprise. These are small workshops, each with only a few dozen employees, and Zara is their primary customer. Zara may add or drop the suppliers in its footloose model, but has built a long-term relationship with these subcontractors. They are an integral part of Zara's rooted manufacturing network.

Other companies also use footloose and rooted models side by side, but often not like Zara. Many expect their own factories to match the cost of outside suppliers, pushing them to keep simple and predictable products in-house and outsource the complicated and problematic ones— exactly the opposite of Zara. Such companies can easily slide into footloose manufacturing.

Zara's enviable accomplishment is in keeping these networks focused on different strategic targets: the footloose network on reducing production costs and filling temporary and seasonal capacity gaps, and the rooted network on developing unique production capabilities that support its fast-response supply chain system.

[a]For more details please see K. Ferdows, M. Lewis, and J. A. D. Machuca (2004) 'Rapid-Fire Fulfillment,' *Harvard Business Review*, Nov.

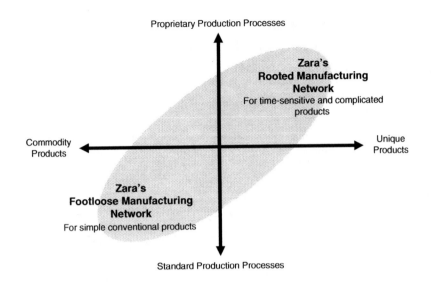

Fig. 8.2 Zara's judicious use of both models

managers realize that footloose and rooted models serve different strategic purposes and keep them separate. If Zara made its factories match the production cost of its suppliers, it would soon disrupt its well-functioning rooted model.

Avoiding the Slide

An abrupt move to footloose manufacturing can send a shock to the organization but at least it is visible and a conscious decision. The real danger of footloose manufacturing, as mentioned earlier, lies in the fact that it can creep up through a series of ad hoc decisions. A firm may slide into it without a deliberate or long-term strategy.

What are the danger signs? One of the early signs is when the company starts to move towards the commodity end of its market–relying more on competing on price than on other things like quick and reliable delivery, superior quality, opportunity for customization, or introducing products with more innovative engineering and design features. If the role of manufacturing is reduced to minimizing the direct production costs, it is hard to maintain a rooted model.

Another sign is when production of the new or more complicated products is outsourced. If it is not brought back into the company after a short period, alarm bells should sound.

Another, more worrisome, sign is when in addition to production, other functions like engineering, procurement, design, and distribution are also subcontracted out. The rapid transformation, currently under way, of contract manufacturers into so-called 'original design manufacturers' (ODMs) shows that this is a real threat. It can lead to untenable strategic positions. There are already examples where it is more appropriate to consider that it is the ODM that is outsourcing its marketing to the OEM than the OEM subcontracting its design, production, and distribution!

The most ominous sign is also the most subtle one. Decisions that shape the manufacturing network in a company, ultimately, reflect the prevailing *mindset* of its senior management. Those who move towards the footloose model, deep down, believe that proprietary capabilities in manufacturing are not significant sources of competitive advantage in their businesses; those moving towards the rooted model believe they are.

It is not easy to detect a mindset. But in the end, the best way to avoid the slippery slope of footloose manufacturing is to convince the senior management that manufacturing can be a formidable source of competitive advantage. If needed, like Zara, you can use a hybrid model: footloose to differentiate on cost and rooted on other dimensions. But make sure to draw clear lines around each and avoid putting them in direct competition with each other. Don't use the same performance indicators for the two networks.

Notes

1. S. Ghoshal and C. A. Bartlett (1990) 'The Multinational Corporation as an Interorganizational Network,' *Academy of Management Review,* 15: 603–25.
2. B. Kogut and U. Zander (1993) 'Knowledge of the Firm and the Evolutionary Theory of the Multinational Corporation,' *Journal of International Business Studies,* 24: 625–45.
3. G. Hedlund (1994) 'A Model of Knowledge Management and the N-form Corporation,' *Strategic Management Journal,* 15: 73–90.
4. R. M. Grant, (1996) 'Towards a Knowledge-Based Theory of the Firm,' *Strategic Management Journal,* 17: 109–22.
5. C. Karlsson (2003) 'The Development of Industrial Networks: Challenges to Operations Management in an Enterprise,' *International Journal of Operations and Production Management,* 19 (1): 44–61.
6. Y. Shi and M. Gregory (1998) 'International Manufacturing Networks: To Develop Global Competitive Capabilities,' *Journal of Operations Management,* 16 (2–3): 195–214.
7. K. Ferdows (1997) 'Making the Most of Foreign Factories,' *Harvard Business Review,* Sept.–Oct., for more details on how to plan and implement such strategies.

Develop your Options

8. For an excellent description of how to manage a footloose manufacturing network, see Joan Margetta (1998) 'Fast, Global, and Entrepreneurial: Supply Chain Management, Hong Kong Style,' *Harvard Business Review*, Sept.–Oct. The article describes how Li and Fung, a Hong Kong-based company that supplies apparel, toys, and other products to big retailers, successfully manages a highly footloose global manufacturing network.

9   From Lines to Loops: An Iterative Approach to Strategy

Donald Sull

In 1975, the Boston Consulting Group (BCG) analyzed how Honda captured nearly two-thirds of the US motorcycle market. The consultants' report painted a picture of senior executives in Japan systematically analyzing the US market, designing a strategy that leveraged Honda's domestic volume advantage to climb up the experience curve, drive down unit costs, and price aggressively to win share in the low end of the market. Indeed, Harvard and other business schools quickly excerpted the 368-page BCG report into shorter case studies that gained wide acceptance in strategy courses.[1] The resulting Honda A case has remained a best-seller ever since to teach the power of careful strategic planning, and illustrate the economic benefits of climbing up the experience curve.

In September 1982, Richard Pascale assembled the six executives who led Honda's entry into the US motorcycle industry.[2] The story they recounted—which was later summarized in an equally popular Honda B case—bore little resemblance to the account of rational planning implied by the BCG study. Honda entered the market, these executives recalled, without any strategy other than seeing whether they could sell something in the United States market. The team initially focused on selling Honda's large 250 cc and 305 cc bikes, in part because founder Sochiro Honda believed that their handlebars resembled the eyebrow of the Buddha—a powerful selling point in his view.

Only after the larger motorcycles experienced unexpected mechanical breakdowns did the team push the small 50 cc Supercub, despite their firm conviction that these were too small for Americans who aspired to oversized Harley-Davidsons. When the Supercub unexpectedly took off, they revised their assumptions of what would or wouldn't work in the US market and started aggressively marketing the smaller bike, adopting an advertising campaign designed by a college student with the tagline 'you meet the nicest people on a Honda.' Honda's success had little to do with foresight into the economics of experience curves, and everything to do with agility–moving forward, trying things, making mistakes, and adjusting on the fly.

The clear contrast between the accounts in the Honda A and B cases led Henry Mintzberg to declare the score 'learning 1, planning 0,' and argue for a view of strategy as emerging out of an ongoing process of trying things, learning from mistakes, and making mid-course corrections.[3] But the victory of Honda B has proven less decisive than Mintzberg's score suggests. Everyone recognizes that the lessons from the contrasting Honda stories are important, but it's unclear what to do with them. At the London Business School, for example, we teach the Honda A and B cases in the first week of the MBA program. The contrasting stories make a big impression, but at the end of class, the students struggle to reconcile the lessons of Honda B with their understanding of strategy.

The Honda A and B cases raise a fundamental question: How can managers formulate and execute strategy in markets that won't stand still? In an ideal world, managers could formulate a long-term strategy, methodically implement it, and then sustain the resulting competitive advantage. Reality, as the Honda B case illustrates, is rarely so straightforward. Technologies advance, regulations change, customers surprise you, macroeconomic variables and competitors deliberately stymie your initiatives. How can managers implement a strategy while maintaining the flexibility to roll with the punches? The first step, this chapter argues, is by fundamentally reconceptualizing the strategic process as an iterative loop rather than sequential series of activities.

From a Linear View of Strategy to the Strategy Loops

The first step is to abandon the view of strategy as a linear process, in which managers sequentially draft a strategy, implement the strategy, and then sustain their positional or resource advantage. This linear approach suffers from a fatal flaw: It hinders people from incorporating new information into action in three ways. First, the linear approach assumes that strategy formulation and execution are distinct activities that can be separated in practice. Many business schools implicitly endorse this notion by teaching strategy formulation and implementation as separate courses. This sequential view fails to capture critical information. Planners craft their strategy at the beginning of the process, precisely the point in time when they know the least about how events will unfold. In executing the strategy, a firm generates new information, such as competitive, customer, and regulatory response, that is critical to the strategy.

A linear view of strategy encourages leaders to escalate commitment to a failing course of action, even as evidence mounts that the original strategy was based on flawed assumptions.[4] The US escalation in Vietnam is the archetypical example. When this happens, leaders commit to their initial plan, assuming it is right. They thereafter stake their credibility on the plan being correct. When things go awry, they are unwilling to change their strategy to avoid admitting that they were wrong in the first place. Instead they often attribute failure to 'unexpected setbacks' which is simply another way of saying new information. Alternatively they blame disappointing results on poor execution without re-examining whether the initial assumptions incorporated in their plan were sound.

Finally, a linear approach ignores the importance of timing. Traditional strategic planning may help plan long-lead-time investments, but empirical research has found that the vast majority of important decisions are driven by shifts in the external environment rather than the formal planning process.[5] To the extent time enters into the linear view of strategy, it tends to take the form of raw speed, as firms sprint to beat rivals. But rushing to execute a flawed plan only ensures that a company arrives at the wrong place faster than its rivals—hardly a desirable outcome. Instead, managers need to notice and capture new information that might influence what to do and when to do it, including the possibility of delaying as well as accelerating specific actions in light of shifting circumstances.

Managers and academics have, of course, recognized the limitations of the linear approach to strategy and attempted to work around them. One approach is to identify key assumptions ex ante and then think exhaustively in the planning process to envision possible outcomes before implementing the strategy.[6] But managers cannot identify an exhaustive list of factors that will matter in the future, let alone predict their interactions or implications. Another approach is to accept the presence of uncertainty, make your best guess on an optimal strategy with the data at hand, implement the strategy, and hope for the best.[7] Although executives might try to mitigate risk by diversifying their lines of business, the fundamental logic reduces to a gamble where managers make their bets and hope for a good outcome.

The linear approach to strategy may work in predictable markets, but its inability to incorporate new information renders it useless in fast-changing markets that are constantly churning up new data. The limitations of the linear approach are too fundamental to patch, but rather require a fundamental reconceptualization of the strategy process as an iterative loop rather than a line. According to this view, which I call the strategy loop, every strategy is a work in progress that is subject to revision in light of new information that emerges over time. To capture and use this new information, the strategy loop entails four steps: making sense of a situation, making choices on what to do (and what not to do), making those things happen and making revisions based on new information. (See Figure 9.1.)

Develop your Options

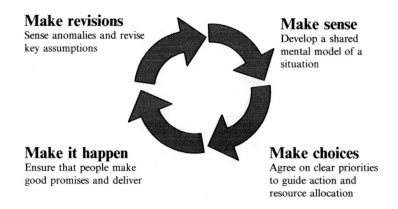

Make revisions
Sense anomalies and revise
key assumptions

Make sense
Develop a shared
mental model of a
situation

Make it happen
Ensure that people make
good promises and deliver

Make choices
Agree on clear priorities
to guide action and
resource allocation

Fig. 9.1 The strategy loop

These steps can be embedded within formal processes, such as strategic planning, budgeting, resource allocation, or performance management, but they should also be contained within the myriad informal conversations that fill out the typical manager's day. And these discussions should not be concentrated at the top of the company; they must also take place at every level of the organization. Strategy will remain stranded in the executive suites unless teams throughout the organization can effectively translate broad corporate objectives into concrete action by making sense of their local circumstances, making choices on how best to proceed, making things happen on the ground, and making revisions in light of recent events.

The fundamental advantage of strategy loops is their ability to incorporate new information and translate it into effective action. Indeed, an iterative approach to integrate strategy and execution appears in a variety of domains, including the military, entrepreneurship, software development, that demand action in the face of uncertainty. The application of loops in these domains illustrates how an iterative approach mitigates the limitations of the linear approach to strategy.

First, an iterative approach integrates strategy formulation and execution into a strategic yin and yang that cannot be separated. Consider software programming. Historically, software programmers followed a linear process (known as a waterfall approach) that separated development into two sequential steps of planning and execution. Programmers initially planned the product features based on users' needs at a point in time, and subsequently assigned the work to programmers to execute. The linear approach appears rational, but frequently produced features that users no longer wanted by the time the project was complete.[8] Too much changed between the initial product specification and ultimate delivery, including customer preferences, underlying technology, and competitive dynamics. To address these problems, software programmers have shifted to an iterative approach (often referred to as 'agile' programming), which breaks long projects into a series of shorter iterations.[9] Users and programmers meet, as often as once a month, to make sense of the shifting market conditions, and then reprioritize features for the next iteration of programming. The regular meetings tightly integrate strategy and execution, allowing the programmers and marketers to modify their product strategy based on new information produced in the course of execution.

Second, an iterative approach to strategy builds in explicit revision as new information emerges, thus mitigating the tendency to escalate commitment to a failed course of action. By staging investments in rounds, venture capitalists and entrepreneurs build in occasions to re-examine a start-up venture's strategy as new information arises. Based on these assessments, venture capitalists may decide to cut their losses and stop funding a venture, or alternatively they may use the new information to urge a revision of the business plan. Consider ONSET Ventures, a Menlo Park-based venture capital firm that specializes in helping raw start-ups, before the customer need, business model, or market have been articulated, let alone verified. Industry wide, only 20 per cent of these new ventures go on to further rounds of financing. Over the last twenty-two years, ONSET has backed more than one hundred start-ups, with over 80 per cent receiving further rounds of financing. Like all venture capital firms, ONSET doles out funding in stages, which allows the partners to re-evaluate the opportunity and business model in light of new information. ONSET partners insist upon revision, however, by instituting a simple rule to abstain from scaling a start-up until its business plan has been reformulated at least once, thereby mitigating the risk of escalating commitment to the initial strategy.

Finally, by breaking time into discrete chunks (defined by each iteration) and by building in an explicit step for revision, an iterative approach to strategy and execution increases the odds that managers will spot changes in context that open a window of opportunity and act before the window closes. Thus, the iterative approach enhances timing. Consider the example of aerial combat during the Korean War. For years military observers had puzzled over the results of air battles between Soviet MiG-15 and US F-86 Sabres during that conflict.[10] The Soviet MiG was the better plane on paper, as it climbed quicker, flew higher, and enjoyed dramatically superior firepower. Going into the Korean War, experts predicted a kill ratio of ten to one—that is ten Sabres would be lost for every enemy MiG shot down. As the war progressed, the kill ratios were indeed lopsided, but it was the Sabre pilots who enjoyed the ten-to-one kill ratio over their adversaries.

Fifteen years later, US Air Force Colonel John Boyd analyzed this surprising reversal of fortune, and discovered the Sabres had two advantages over the

MiG–a bubble canopy increased pilots' visibility relative to the MiG's small window, and full hydraulics enabled the Sabre to switch from one action to another more quickly than the MiGs, which were only partially hydraulic. Based on their advantages in observing the situation and shifting maneuvers South Korean pilots and their allies devised a strategy of quickly shifting from one maneuver to another during a dogfight. These frequent maneuvers created opportunities to strike, which the Sabre pilots would notice and seize more quickly. Boyd conceptualized air battles as taking place in loops, where the pilots cycled through steps of observing the situation, orienting themselves, deciding what to do, and acting. His critical insight was that combatants who consistently moved through this cycle (known as the OODA loop) enjoyed a material advantage in timing their strikes to seize fleeting opportunities.

Programmers, venture capitalists, and military leaders have all adopted an iterative approach to action under uncertainty. The strategy loop, which consists of discussions to make sense, make choices, make it happen, and make revisions, follows this iterative logic, but adapts it to the setting of large, complex organizations where discussions are the primary mechanism for coordinating activity.

Discussions through the Strategy Loop

Reconceptualizing strategy as an iterative loop is simple enough in theory, but extremely difficult to put into practice in large, complex organizations. Managers and employees must constantly update their understanding of a fluid situation, prioritize activities, and periodically revisit their assumptions. To make things happen, they must sell projects upwards and downwards, energize subordinates, monitor performance, and make mid-course corrections. And they must do these things in real time as new information enters the equation which forces people to rethink their understanding of the situation and the appropriate actions.

All these activities require ongoing discussions. Several studies find that managers spend between two-thirds and three-quarters of their time engaged in formal and informal discussions.[11] In large, complex organizations, conversations serve as the central mechanism to coordinate action in real time as the environment shifts.[12] These discussions can be embedded in formal processes, such as strategic planning, budgeting, resource allocation, or performance management, but also include the myriad informal conversations that fill out the typical manager's calendar, including chance encounters and water cooler chats.

In contrast to simple theories of decision making, these conversations are unstructured, messy, even haphazard in practice.[13] When making sense, a

---

Box 9.1 What are we Talking About?

It is not enough to understand the four types of discussions that make up the strategy loop. Leaders must also exercise judgement in deciding which discussion to have when and how to lead it most effectively. The following questions help them along the way:

- *What are we talking about?* This simple question often surfaces a disturbing lack of focus in discussions.
- *Are the right people in the room?* Discussions to make sense work best when different points of view are brought to bear, while making things happen requires that the people who will ultimately do the work—rather than their boss or colleague—are in the room.
- *Are we talking about the right thing right now?* Managers must make a call on what conversation is appropriate for the current situation. Are we jumping to choices before we have made sense of what is going on, for example, or are we revisiting assumptions when we should be getting things done?
- *Does the conversation have the right tone?* Leaders must understand what an effective discussion sounds like in each step. They should establish and maintain a spirit of open enquiry during discussions to make sense, for example, and promote respectful arguments during discussions to make choices.
- *Are we skipping key conversations?* Managers must ensure that they are having all the conversations they need. Execution-focused teams are particularly prone to ignore discussions to make sense and make revisions, while more strategic groups may love discussions about the market but omit critical discussions to ensure they deliver.

---

team can meander through several alternative interpretations of a situation before settling on one that best fits the data. Nor do the discussions march through the loop in lock step. A new product development team, for example, might begin by making sense of the opportunity, make initial choices, and then surface insights that cause them to revisit their initial sense making. Managers can enhance these discussions by understanding the four different types of discussions and maintain clarity on what a group is discussing at any point in time. If, in contrast, they give free rein to multiple simultaneous discussions, meetings all too often degenerate into a tower of Babel with people talking right past one another. To avoid this pitfall, managers should frequently ask themselves a simple question: are we trying to make sense, prioritize, make it happen, or revise assumptions? It is surprising how often the answer is confusion. Box 9.1 provides some questions to ask to help managers ensure they are discussing the right things at the right time.

These discussions are also distributed throughout the organization, rather than concentrated at the top of the house.[14] Discussions about resource allocation in large, multi-unit organizations, for example, typically unfold across levels in the hierarchy, with front-line employees spotting opportunities, middle managers selecting among potential investments the ones that they lend their credibility to, and senior executives using enterprise-wide criteria when screening proposals. The strategy loop does not apply only to corporate strategic planning. Indeed, it is most powerful when applied throughout the organization to teams charged with implementing the overarching corporate priorities. It is here that the rubber meets the road, and employees lower in the organization should go through the loop to make sense of what corporate objectives mean in their context, make choices on how to allocate their time and resources, make it happen in light of local circumstances, and finally make revisions based on what they have learned.

As environmental uncertainty increases, discussions become even more necessary to coordinate activity required to seize opportunities and manage risks that emerge out of a situation in flux. A 1990 survey, for example, found that nearly three-quarters of executives reported that they spent more time in formal meetings than they had five years earlier, and nearly half expected further increases in the frequency of formal meetings.[15]

Although they are critical to get things done and respond to changes in the environment, these conversations often bog down in an endless series of unproductive meetings where the usual suspects cover the same ground without making progress. Managers express frustration with interminable meetings where participants 'spin their wheels,' 'cover the same ground,' or 'talk in circles.' Not only are these meetings frustrating for participants, they can hinder execution.

The solution, however tempting it may sound, is not to eliminate meetings altogether. Rather, executives must increase the return on their investment in discussions. Here the strategy loop can help. The key insight of the framework is that executives can best enhance organizational effectiveness by mindfully managing discussions through an iterative loop of translating understanding into action and revising both understanding and actions in light of new information. They can do so by understanding the four distinct types of discussions— i.e., to make sense, make choices, make it happen, and make revisions. These conversations have a bearing on each other but each is characterized by separate objectives, pitfalls, and the actions to increase their effectiveness.

These steps in the strategy loop are simple to summarize, but difficult to put into practice. The path through the loop is strewn with pitfalls, stemming from bounds on our ability to process information, psychological biases that favor confirming what we already believe, social conventions to avoid conflict, the political interrelationships between interpretations and power, and the nearly ineluctable flow of inertia in human affairs.[16] For a summary of each stage in the strategy loop, see the exhibit entitled 'discussions through the strategy loop.'

Discussions to Make Sense

The first step of the strategy cycle consists of gathering raw data from different sources to identify patterns in complex, incomplete, conflicting, or ambiguous

Table 9.1 Discussions through the strategy loop

	Make sense	Make choices	Make things happen	Make revisions
Objective	Develop a shared mental model of a situation	Agree on clear priorities to guide action and resource allocation	Ensure that people make good promises and deliver	Sense anomalies and revise key assumptions
Archetype	Improvisational comedy	Agile programming		After-action review
Information support	Shared dashboard of real-time, granular data	Ongoing monitoring of 'hard' and 'soft' priorities	Monitor performance against promises	Variance reporting of key variables to spot anomalies
Required leadership traits	• *Coup d'œil* • Curiosity • Empathy to see other points of view	• Decisiveness • Enterprise perspective • Credibility to make the call	• Trustworthiness • Flexible tenacity • Ability to inspire others	• Intellectual humility • Respect for other viewpoints • Sensitivity to anomalies
Pitfalls	• Advocating pre-existing positions • Anchoring too quickly on one viewpoint • Bias for premature action	• Superficial agreement • Politicized prioritization • Priority proliferation • Searching for complete consensus	• Private promises • Passive agreement • Meaningless yes • Implicit agreements • What without why	• Blame game • Escalating commitment to failed course of action • Cognitive biases toward confirming evidence
Helpful tips	• Question assumptions • Interact frequently	• Explicit prioritization • Simple rules to prioritize	• Publicly monitor promises • Link promises to priorities	• Build in regular reviews • Bring in external reviewers
Killer questions	• What fresh data would convince us that our assessment is wrong?	• What will we stop doing?	• What did you promise to do? • What have you done? What is hindering you?	• What did we expect to happen versus what really happened? • Why the difference? • What should we change?

Note: Discussions at each stage in a strategy loop have different objectives, face different pitfalls, and require distinct management approaches to improve the quality of the conversation.

information. The objective of these conversations is to develop a shared mental model of a situation that helps people anticipate how the situation might unfold. There is no assumption that making sense results in accurate long-term predictions about the distant future. Rather the stage provides just enough clarity to proceed through one iteration of the strategy loop.

Develop your Options

In this step of the agility loop, the team leader should establish a tone of open enquiry rather than advocating a pre-existing view of what is going on. Uncertain markets inundate companies with information from multiple sources, and these data are typically incomplete, inconclusive, conflicting, ambiguous, and of questionable reliability. Teams are most likely to make sense of novel situations if they dig into the data with an open mind, and enquire what might be going on. In this step, advocacy of a preconceived interpretation can hinder effective sense making. Consider the Cuban Missile Crisis, for example.[17] While President John F. Kennedy was trying to make sense of the situation, his chief military advisers including General Curtis LeMay insisted that the Russian actions signaled hostile intent, based on their long-standing assumption that nuclear war with the Soviet Union was inevitable.

Research on effective decision making has found that groups in rapidly changing markets do best to avoid anchoring too quickly on a single view.[18] In novel situations, the best interpretation is rarely obvious and the obvious one is often wrong. Thus the discussion leader must ensure that participants feel safe to put forth alternative interpretations.[19] Kennedy's team might have settled on the 'obvious' interpretation that Nikita Khrushchev's intentions were hostile, but Llewellyn 'Tommy' Thompson, a former ambassador to the Soviet Union, argued that the Soviet leader probably felt backed into a corner and might accept a face-saving way to de-escalate the tensions—an interpretation that proved accurate. (This example also illustrates the benefit of empathy in making sense of an ambiguous situation. Thompson knew Khrushchev personally, which helped him to see the situation from Khrushchev's perspective rather than by viewing the Soviets as an abstract enemy.)

Instead of passively waiting for divergent views to emerge, leaders can actively stimulate them. President Kennedy required his advisers to generate different alternatives to a military strike, which made it safe for them to discuss the apparently 'soft' options of blockade and diplomatic negotiation—alternatives that ultimately prevailed, allowing the USA to avoid a nuclear war. A quick test of whether a team feels comfortable proposing alternative interpretations is to track the number of framings that were proposed and seriously discussed.

Conversations to make sense can, of course, derail in many ways. The team might cower before a powerful leader, lapse into 'group think,' or ignore the available data when forming conclusions. One warning sign is when some participants check out of the conversation altogether, perhaps because they believe the leader has already made a decision in a 'meeting before the meeting' and is just trying to obtain everyone's buy-in.

One of the most dangerous pitfalls occurs when a team follows the conventional wisdom and exhibits a 'bias for action.' This risk is particularly acute among managers who pride themselves on getting the job done. This happens when a team shortchanges the sense-making discussion and jumps right into a debate about what to do and how to do it. But if the conversation rushes too quickly through the messy thrashing around of sense making, managers risk diving into the details of implementation before they have explored alternatives or tested the fit between their interpretation and the situation. Leaders cannot simply ban action proposals, since take-charge managers tend to think in terms of plans of action. When such proposals arise, however, the leader can dig backward to unearth the assumptions that underlie the plan of action rather than push forward into details of implementation. They can ask, for example, 'If that is the solution, what is the problem?' or 'What fresh data would convince us that this is the wrong course of action?'[20]

Guiding discussions to make sense requires a distinct set of management traits. The first is 'coup d'œil,' or the ability to grasp the essence of a situation based on limited data. Coup d'œil is often compared to seeing only a few pieces of a jigsaw puzzle yet rapidly grasping what the overall picture must look like. Curiosity is another critical trait. Managers who remain curious remain open to new interpretations to explore unfamiliar ways of framing a situation. Curiosity also helps a team remain alert to signals from many different sources—an important skill since the critical piece of the puzzle often comes from an unexpected source. Robert Rubin, the former Treasury Secretary and co-managing director of Goldman Sachs, described how he would tackle any new situation, from evaluating a risk arbitrage deal to managing economic crises, by pulling out a yellow legal pad and writing down a long list of questions—a stark contrast to many managers who try to affirm their authority by asserting answers rather than asking questions.[21] Finally, it is not enough for leaders to tolerate dissent, they must actively foster it. Rubin had a variety of tactics to stimulate open debate as a meeting started moving toward a consensus, including arguing the opposite of what he believed to be the case to stimulate argumentation and appointing a devil's advocate to probe contrary views. Figure 9.1 summarizes some key differences between the four types of discussions.

Discussions to Make Choices

Conversations to make choices should result in a small set of clear priorities to focus resources and attention. Determining the right priorities is a critical function of management under any circumstances, but uncertain markets make it more difficult to do this effectively. The constant deluge of potential opportunities and threats leads firms to hedge their bets against every foreseeable contingency, thereby spreading their chips too thin and failing to execute on key initiatives. These conversations conclude when a group agrees on a set of priorities consistent with their interpretation of the situation, and sufficiently concrete to be understood by everyone required to execute.

Develop your Options

At their heart, these conversations are about making hard trade-offs. As a result, the leader should establish a tone of respectful argumentation, where team members can express valid disagreements that might otherwise simmer below the surface. Without active intervention to stimulate debate, these conversations easily drift towards superficial agreement with unresolved trade-offs lurking below the water line.[22] One way leaders can encourage discussions about trade-offs is by making it safe for team members to say 'no' to requests for their services or resources. In many organizations, people feel compelled to say yes to every request, to be helpful or to avoid looking like a jerk. But a well-thought-out no carries valuable information—it surfaces questions about the importance of the request relative to the organization's overall strategy and objectives, flags resource constraints, and highlights real trade-offs that are hard to resolve but dangerous to gloss over.

One way to make it easier to say no is to create a category to park initiatives that might be attractive in the future, but do not warrant resources immediately. Consider the Beta Group, an early-stage venture capital firm that applies cutting-edge technologies to novel applications, such as tiny rods—known as pixels—which capture energy on a golf club head that would normally dissipate, and channel it back to the ball to increase impact. When evaluating potential technologies, the Beta partners quickly triage them into one of three categories: the 'dumpster' for technologies with no promise; investment for those with high upside; and a 'refrigerator' for promising ideas whose time has yet to come. The refrigerator, which holds about four dozen opportunities at any one time, provides an alternative to a flat-out no without draining resources from immediate priorities.

Discussions to make choices frequently derail when participants add more priorities without increasing resources or taking other initiatives off the table, leading to a proliferation of priorities. In part, priority proliferation arises because managers follow the conventional wisdom and view their job as making decisions. When leaders make decisions, they tend to focus on a specific issue in isolation, decide what to do, and then quickly move to the specifics of implementation. This narrow focus on what to do and how to do it often ignores the existing portfolio of activities going on within the organization. As a result, decision makers fail to consider which current activities they should terminate to free the time, attention, and resources required for the new initiative. Over time, decision making generates a plethora of so-called 'priorities.' When priorities multiply into a laundry list of nice things to have, they lose their power to focus action and guide resource allocation.

A simple rule to manage priority proliferation is to cut an existing objective for every new one added. Managers can also minimize this pitfall by making the prioritization explicit and regular. Consider Extreme Programming, an iterative approach to software design where the customer begins the process by listing desired features on 3″ by 5″ index cards (known as 'story cards'), and then rank orders them based on their desirability. The technical team programs as many features as they can, given the resources available in an iteration. At the next iteration—typically a month later—the customer and programmers meet again to discuss any new information about the difficulty of programming or shifts in the marketplace that might alter the relative desirability of features. Based on these discussions they literally re-rank the index cards. British telecommunications leader BT is extending the discipline of monthly prioritization beyond software development through 'hothouses,' where the parties involved in a business initiative meet regularly to explicitly thrash through trade-offs. Discussions about conflicting priorities are not (and indeed should not be) easy, but by building in explicit prioritization, managers can introduce these difficult discussions early in the process and ensure they explicitly revisit priorities on a regular basis.

Another common pitfall in discussions to make choices occurs when the participants talk and talk around an issue, in the hopes of reaching perfect consensus. Achieving consensus is, of course, desirable to improve the quality of decision and build buy-in for a selected course of action, but it takes time. In fast-moving markets the cost of delay can outweigh the benefits of consensus. In her research on successful decision making in high-velocity environments, Kathleen Eisenhardt found that the most successful IT firms neither sought complete consensus, nor went to the other extreme of a dictatorial boss calling all the shots.[23] Instead, they followed a policy of 'qualified consensus,' where the top management team would seek consensus up to a certain point, and then invoke a set of pre-agreed rules to make a decision. The rules depended upon the team and the decision, but examples included the person with the most functional expertise decides, the person with the most passion selects, the team takes a vote, or the boss calls the shot. The precise form of the rules mattered less than having a clear way to qualify the consensus that everyone knew in advance and considered legitimate.

The central leadership quality to make choices is decisiveness. The Prussian military thinker Carl von Clausewitz wrote that great generals required only two traits—*coup d'œil* and the courage to make hard choices based on their understanding of the situation.[24] (He also noted that this combination of traits is rare.) The hardest choices are typically not what to do, but what not to do or what to stop doing. A second leadership trait is the ability to say no, typically providing a compelling rationale grounded in the overarching strategy and objectives of the organization. To help managers develop this trait, one French engineering company recently added the ability to say no as explicit criterion to evaluate managers' performance. Finally, managers need the credibility to make the hard calls and have them stick. The recent return of founders including Steve Jobs, Charles Schwab, and Michael Dell may stem in part from the credibility that they bring to the job, and their ability to bring people along even when they make very difficult decisions.

Discussions to Make it Happen

Execution is fairly straightforward when a single person calls the shots, like an entrepreneur single-handedly running a small business. But making it happen grows more difficult as the number of people cooperating increases. When many people are involved, execution requires people to work out what everyone needs to do, and also ensure that everyone is motivated to do their part. Making it happen can quickly grow very complicated in large, complex organizations. A simple mechanism—the promise—provides a powerful means to ensure that people understand what they need to do and deliver. Making it happen, to a large extent, hinges on the quality of promises made and the consistency with which they are honored.

Discussions to make it happen should solicit personal promises to actions aligned with agreed priorities. These conversations revolve around the promises that employees and managers make to each other to get things done.[25] These promises might take place within an existing process, such as budgeting or performance management, but the process is a means to elicit and manage good commitments, not an end in itself. A promise is a personal pledge a provider makes to satisfy the concerns of a customer within or outside an organization. Both 'customer' and 'provider' refer to roles, not individuals, and these roles can vary depending on the specific situation. A business unit head within a bank, for example, is a customer when requesting technology support from the CTO or soliciting a promise from a subordinate. But she is a provider when supplying products to another division or making a promise to the CEO.

People often equate a promise with a contract, and focus on the specific clauses of what the provider has committed to deliver. But the discussions that give rise to a promise are far more important than the terms of the deal. In leading these discussions, managers should set a tone of supportive discipline. These conversations are disciplined when managers demand explicit promises and hold people accountable for delivery, but supportive to the extent leaders help colleagues deliver on their promises. This support can take several forms, including providing additional resources, relief from other priorities, or political cover. When discussions for action decouple support from discipline, they typically lead providers to sandbag and spin their performance to avoid blame. In this step, managers must ensure that less powerful colleagues and subordinates feel safe to express their concerns about requests and can actively negotiate what they need before they feel comfortable making a promise.

The most effective discussions to make it happen share five fundamental characteristics: they are public; actively negotiated; voluntary; explicit; and linked to priorities. These discussions typically derail when leaders let any of these attributes slip. For instance, private-side deals—as opposed to public commitments—leave room for people to wriggle out of what they said they would do. Passive promises occur when people agree to do something without actively probing to understand what they are really signing up to. Providers often make passive promises, when they and the customer assume that a request is business as usual and requires little exploration. Coerced commitments arise when people feel compelled to say yes to every request—no matter how unrealistic or random—that comes from a more senior executive or manager from a more powerful unit. Vague commitments offer too much scope for interpretation of what constitutes execution, and make it hard to hold people accountable. Ad hoc commitments emerge when people make promises that are locally optimal, but poorly aligned with corporate priorities.

Scrum—another variant of agile software programming—exemplifies a process which elicits good promises from the programmers who are on the hook to develop the software. Scrum (which takes its name from the rugby huddle of the same name) has the programming team convene in the same place and time each day to publicly make and track their promises. Every workday the team members (typically less than ten) stand in a circle and answer the same three questions: What have you done since the last Scrum? What will you do between now and the next Scrum? What is getting in the way of meeting the goals? The public forum for making promises and monitoring delivery induces programmers to make good on their promises, since no one wants to let the team down or diminish their reputation for doing what they said. It also allows them to actively talk through what each is promising and ensure their promises are sufficiently explicit for colleagues to adjust their behaviour accordingly. Programmers volunteer for assignments to ensure they are voluntary, and the commitments are always linked back to the priorities set in monthly meetings with customers.

The most important leadership trait for making it happen is trustworthiness, or the leader's consistency in honoring his promises. A leader who holds subordinates to their commitments without keeping his own word will quickly earn a reputation as a tyrant. By making a promise, an executive takes on the responsibility for all the unexpected contingencies that could complicate execution, and overcoming these requires tenacity in the face of inevitable setbacks and obstacles. Tenacity does not, of course, mean doing the same thing over and over again and expecting different results. That, as Einstein pointed out, is the definition of insanity. Instead, the tenacity in achieving the end must include flexibility in means. Finally, a leader must inspire subordinates and colleagues to make aggressive promises, without coercing them to commit.

Inspiration is not the same as charisma. Indeed, one of the most effective ways to elicit ambitious promises is to link them explicitly to a mission that the provider agrees matters.

Discussions to Make Revisions

Managers must recognize emerging patterns to anticipate new opportunities and threats. But spotting new patterns also requires us to revise or even abandon our established mental models, and therein lies the rub. When our established patterns of thinking clash with changing circumstances, the existing mental models typically prevail. In the strategy loop, letting go of the old is as important as spotting the new. Managers must keep their mental models fluid and modify them in light of changes in the broader context, as a first step to adapting their organizations to these changes. Indeed, managers must remain open to the possibility of abandoning their established models altogether.

Conversations to make revisions treat action as experiments, analyse the findings, and use these lessons to revise assumptions, priorities, and promises. Leaders should initiate a conversation to make revisions after achieving a significant milestone in making things happen. These conversations add the most value after a prolonged period of heads-down execution, when team members have not yet paused to reflect on whether results have confirmed their original assessment of the situation. Shifts in contextual factors, such as regulatory changes or unexpected moves by competitors, almost always create a gap between initial assumptions and how things actually turn out. Since no plan survives contact with reality, it is critical to design in regular occasions to pause and reflect on what the team has learned.

Many managers skip these discussions. When things are working, teams tend to follow the principle that if it ain't broke, don't fix it. Moreover, many leaders believe that a bias for action requires them to fix their sights forward rather than gaze backward. Even failure, which should be a catalyst to revisit assumptions, often fails to spur revision. People fear that a conversation to understand why something failed will focus on parceling out blame rather than distilling lessons. On the rare occasions when these conversations do take place, they often derail when the team jumps ahead to making choices for the future before they have fully understood the past.

In principle, discussions to make revisions are simple: the team should discuss what they expected to happen and why; what actually happened; and what accounted for any gaps. Leaders can facilitate these discussions by explicitly framing assumptions as hypotheses and actions as experiments.[26] Even if they are clearly framed as retrospective opportunities to learn, these conversations remain delicate. People feel threatened by the prospect of having their actions scrutinized and criticized, and often personalize feedback as a negative reflection on their competence, judgment, or motivation. To avoid this, such conversations should maintain a tone of dispassionate analysis—think of the scientist in a lab coat evaluating results from an experiment. Leaders should take pains to avoid a judgemental tone or personal recriminations. The wrong tone is that of the tyrannical headmaster looking for excuses to chide the students.

The fear of blame is not the only obstacle to discussions for revision. Psychologists have documented a depressingly long list of factors that keep us locked in the cages of our established mental models. People tend to escalate commitment to a failed course of action (think Vietnam or Iraq) to justify their previous investments and avoid admitting that they were wrong. Ingrained cognitive biases lead us to fixate on data that confirms our expectations and ignore or downplay disconfirming information.

Given all these obstacles, leaders must go out of their way to build rigorous and frequent revision into strategy loops. By staging funding in rounds, for example, venture capitalists force the partners and entrepreneurs to re-examine the start-up's performance against plan and shifts in the context. And many venture capitalists view their most important role as protecting their own partners from falling in love with bad investments. In the partner room, these VCs engage in a hard-hitting and skeptical evaluation of one another's deals, often asking questions like 'if this company walked in the door today, would we invest?' and 'why shouldn't we cut our losses right now?' The partners of ONSET Ventures (the early stage VC mentioned in Box 9.1) go even further to foster revision. They explicitly assume that their portfolio companies will morph their business model at least once before scaling, and therefore select entrepreneurs to fund in large part on their ability to learn and adapt to shifting circumstances. To inject a distanced perspective, the ONSET partners invite in later-stage venture capitalists to evaluate the progress and prospects of their portfolio companies.

The fundamental leadership trait required for revision is intellectual humility—not the most common trait among executives. 'Some people,' Robert Rubin observed, 'seem more certain about everything than I am about anything.'[27] In an uncertain world, leaders must acknowledge that their mental models are simplified maps of complex terrain, and based on provisional knowledge subject to revision in light of new information. This recognition leads executives to actively seek out disconfirming information that highlights where their map is wrong. As a corollary to intellectual humility, executives must respect other points of view—not just because respect smoothes the road for implementation and is desirable in and of itself. Respect for other points of view increase the likelihood that a manager will hear and take on board alternative perspectives that might lead her to revise her own assumptions. Finally, managers should remain alert to anomalies—new information that surprises them or doesn't jibe with expectations. In an uncertain world, a manager's mental map can quickly become outdated. Anomalies provide clues as to where a mental map is wrong, and managers who discover and act on these clues can seize the initiative from rivals slower to explore where their assumptions fail to match reality. When managers observe an anomaly, they should investigate it first hand until they are satisfied they understand the source of the discrepancy.

Discussions—formal and informal, short and long, one on one and in groups—are the key mechanism to coordinate activity within large, complex organizations. Uncertain markets make these discussions more necessary and, at the same time, more difficult. Managers who master the four types of discussions that comprise the strategy loop are more likely to spot emerging opportunities, seize them, and make mid-course corrections than their less agile rivals.

Notes

1. The original study is publicly available in its entirety because it was commissioned and paid for by the Secretary of State for Industry. See Boston Consulting Group (1975) *Strategy Alternatives for the British Motorcycle Industry.* London: Her Majesty's Stationery Office.
2. Richard T. Pascale (1984) 'Perspectives on Strategy: The Real Story behind Honda's Success,' *California Management Review,* 26 (3): 47–72. Pascale's article sparked an ongoing discussion in the strategy field. For a summary of the debate, see Henry Mintzberg (1990) 'The Design School: Reconsidering the Basic Premises of Strategic Management,' *Strategic Management Journal,* 11 (6): 171–95, and H. I. Ansoff (1991) 'The Design School: Reconsidering the Basic Premises of Strategic Management,' *Strategic Management Journal,* 12 (6): 449–61, and various authors (1996) 'The "Honda Effect" Revisited,' *California Management Review,* 38 (4): 78–117.
3. Henry Mintzberg (1991) 'Learning 1, Planning 0,' *Strategic Management Journal,* 12 (6): 464–66.
4. For a review of the escalation of commitment literature, see J. Brockner (1992) 'The Escalation of Commitment to a Failing Course of Action: Toward Theoretical Progress,' *Academy of Management Review* 17 (1): 39–61.
5. Based on a comparative case study of the strategic planning process in eight of the ten largest oil and gas companies, Robert Grant found that few major decisions resulted from the formal strategic planning process. See Robert M. Grant (2003) 'Strategic Planning in a Turbulent Environment: Evidence from the Oil Majors,' *Strategic Management Journal,* 24 (6): 491–517. Another study of the impact of the formal planning process on 1,087 strategic decisions made by 129 Fortune 500 companies between 1982 and 1986 found that only global expansion decisions (and to a lesser degree divestment choices) were driven by the formal planning process. The timing of other decisions, including those involving technology,

acquisitions, capacity expansion, new products, strategic alliances, and organizational changes, were not influenced by the formal planning process but driven by external events. See Deepak K. Sinha (1990) 'The Contribution of Formal Planning to Decisions,' *Strategic Management Journal*, 11 (6): 479–92.

6. See P. Ghemawat (1991) *Commitment: The Dynamic of Strategy*. New York: Free Press. Ghemawat argues that strategy consists of making commitments or infrequent large changes in resources that have large and enduring effects on a company's future alternatives. The importance of these decisions implies that managers can and should clearly analyze their consequences long into the future. Ghemawat's argument hinges on the assumption that managers can identify what matters ex ante and can analyze the consequences of their actions, although he, of course, admits the presence of uncertainty.

7. See R. Amit and P. J. H. Schoemaker (1993) 'Strategic Assets and Organizational Rent,' *Strategic Management Journal*, 4: 33–46. Amit and Schoemaker acknowledge that their view offers little guidance to managers. See also M. E. Raynor (2007) *The Strategy Paradox: Why Committing to Success Leads to Failure (and What to Do about It)*. New York: Currency.

8. In 1995, the Department of Defense published a study that reviewed software projects costing the taxpayers over $35 billion. The study found that only 2% of the code was used as written, with the rest requiring either significant revision or going unused. The study found that nearly half of the software features fulfilled the requirements users specified in the design stage, but still went unused. But by the time the software was delivered, the customer wanted something different. See *Crosstalk*, a journal of defense software engineering, http://www.stsc.hill.af.-mil/Crosstalk/2002/04/leishman.html. A study of 400 projects over a fifteen-year period found that less than 5% of the code was regularly used; see D. Cohen, G. Larson, and B. Ware (2001) 'Improving Software Investment through Requirements Validation,' *IEEE 26th Software Engineering Workshop*. Alan MacCormack and colleagues have conducted extensive qualitative research comparing linear (referred to as waterfall) and agile programming approaches. See Alan MacCormack (2001) 'Product-Development Practices that Work,' *Sloan Management Review*, 42 (2): 75–85; and Alan MacCormack, Chris F. Kemerer, Michael A. Cusumano, and Bill Crandall (2003). 'Trade-offs between Productivity and Quality in Selecting Software Development Practices.' *IEEE Software*, 20, 5 (Sept.–Oct.): 78–85. Large-scale studies include M. Thomas (2001) 'IT Projects Sink or Swim,' *British Computer Society Review*. Another study attributed more than 80% of all software to detailed specifications that were frozen too early and left no room to adapt to shifting circumstances, see P. Clements and D. Parnas (1986) 'A Rational Design Process: How and Why to Fake it,' *IEEE Transactions on Software Engineering*, Feb.

9. For an excellent summary, see Jim Highsmith (2004) *Agile Project Management*. Boston: Pearson Education.

10. For information on Boyd see Robert Coram's readable 2002 biography *Boyd: The Fighter Pilot who Changed the Art of War*. New York: Back Bay Books and

Develop your Options

Grant T. Hammond (2004) *The Mind of War: John Boyd and American Security.* Washington, DC: Smithsonian Books.

11. The findings of several studies of how managers spend their time have shown with remarkable consistency that formal and informal conversations are by far the primary activity. See E. Brewer and J. W. C. Tomlinson (1964) 'The Manager's Working Day,' *Journal of Industrial Economics,* 12 (3): 191–7; Henry Mintzberg (1971) 'Managerial Work: Analysis from Observation,' *Management Science,* 18 (2): 97–110; and Lance B. Kurke and Howard Aldrich (1983) 'Mintzberg was Right! A Replication and Extension of *The Nature of Managerial Work,*' *Management Science,* 29 (8): 975–84.

12. The strategy loop approach bears a family resemblance to Karl Weick's sensemaking perspective. See Karl Weick (1995) *Sensemaking in Organizations.* Thousand Oaks, Calif.: Sage; and Karl E. Weick and Karlene H. Roberts (1993) 'Collective Mind in Organizations: Heedful Interrelating on Flight Decks,' *Administrative Science Quarterly,* 38 (3): 357–81; and the related stream of literature dealing with high-reliability organizations (HR), see Karlene H. Roberts (1990) 'Some Characteristics of High Reliability Organizations,' *Organizational Science,* 1 (2): 1–17. The strategy loop perspective shares with sense making and HRO the assumption that ongoing discussions represent the central mechanism organizational participants use to make sense of a constantly shifting environment. The strategy loop perspective, however, also incorporates discussions to prioritize and particularly to solicit and monitor performance promises.

13. See Henry Mintzberg, D. Raisinghani, and A. Theoret (1976) 'The Structure of "Unstructured" Decisions,' *Administrative Science Quarterly,* 21 (2): 246–75.

14. See Joseph L. Bower (1970) *Managing the Resource Allocation Process.* Boston: Harvard Business School Press; Robert Burgelman (1983) 'A Process Model of Internal Corporate Venturing in the Diversified Major Firm,' *Administrative Science Quarterly,* 28 (2): 223–44. For a comprehensive review of this stream of literature, see Joseph L. Bower and Clark Gilbert (eds.) (2006) *From Resource Allocation to Strategy.* New York: Oxford University Press.

15. Steven G. Rogelberg, Cliff Scott, and John Kello (2007) 'The Science and Fiction of Meetings,' *Sloan Management Review,* 48 (2): 18. The 1990 survey results are reported in P. M. Tobia and M. C. Becker (1990) 'Making the Most of Meeting Time,' *Training and Development Journal,* 44 (8): 34–8.

16. The following discussion draws on Donald N. Sull (2007) 'Closing the Gap between Strategy and Execution,' *Sloan Management Review,* Summer.

17. See Arthur Schlesinger, Jr. (1965) *A Thousand Days.* Boston: Houghton Mifflin and R. Kennedy (1969) *Thirteen Days: A Memoir of the Cuban Missile Crisis.* New York: W. W. Norton. For an excellent analysis of decision making by Kennedy's team, see Michael A. Roberto (2005) *Why Great Leaders Don't Take Yes for an Answer.* Upper Saddle River, NJ: Wharton School Publishing, ch. 2.

18. See K. M. Eisenhardt (1989) 'Making Fast Strategic Decisions in High-Velocity Environments,' *Academy of Management Journal,* 32: 543–76; and K. M. Eisenhardt

(1990) 'Speed and Strategic Choice: How Managers Accelerate Decision Making,' *California Management Review*, 32: 39–54.

19. See A. C. Edmondson (1999) 'Psychological Safety and Learning Behavior in Work Teams,' *Administrative Science Quarterly*, 44: 350–83; A. C. Edmondson (2003) 'Speaking up in the Operating Room: How Team Leaders Promote Learning in Interdisciplinary Action Teams,' *Journal of Management Studies*, 40: 1419–52. Edmondson's construct of psychological safety is critical throughout the strategy cycle, but it takes a slightly different form in each step. In making sense, for example, psychological safety ensures that participants feel safe to broach alternative interpretations of what is going on, while in making things happen providers should feel secure to negotiate what they need before they can make a binding performance promise.

20. This question is a slightly modified version of Professor Alexander's question described in Richard E. Neustadt and Ernest R. May (1988) *Thinking in Time: The Uses of History for Decision Makers*. New York: Free Press, 152–3.

21. See Robert E. Rubin and Jacob Weisberg (2003) *In an Uncertain World*. New York: Random House and Lisa Endlich (1999) *Goldman Sachs: The Culture of Success*. New York: Alfred A. Knopf.

22. For concrete suggestions on how to manage hot topics, see Amy C. Edmondson and Diana McLain Smith (2006) 'Too Hot to Handle: How to Manage Relationship Conflict,' *California Management Review*, 49 (1): 6–31.

23. See Eisenhardt, 'Making Fast Strategic Decisions in High-Velocity Environments.'

24. Carl von Clausewitz (2003) *Vom Kriege*. Berlin: Bildungsverlag Eins, first book, third chapter.

25. For an in-depth perspective on the promise-based view of the firm, see Donald N. Sull and Charles Spinosa (2007) 'Promise-Based Management: The Essence of Execution,' *Harvard Business Review*, Apr.: 78–86; and Donald N. Sull and Charles Spinosa (2005) 'Using Commitments to Manage across Units,' *Sloan Management Review*, 47 (1): 73–81.

26. For a thoughtful and practical guide to after-action reviews based on practices within the US Army, see David A. Garvin (2003) *Learning in Action: A Guide to Putting the Learning Organization to Work*. Boston: Harvard Business School Press, 106–16.

27. Rubin and Weisberg, *In an Uncertain World*, p.xii.

10   Opening up Strategic Space through Discontinuous Innovation

John Bessant

The Trouble with Innovation . . .

Back in the 1880s there was a thriving industry in the north-eastern United States in the lucrative business of selling ice. The business model was deceptively simple—work hard to cut chunks of ice out of the frozen northern wastes, wrap the harvest quickly, and ship it as quickly as possible to the warmer southern states—and increasingly overseas—where it could be used to preserve food. In its heyday this was a big industry—in 1886 the record harvest ran to 25 million tons—and it employed thousands of people in cutting, storing, and shipping the product. And it was an industry with strong commitment to innovation—developments in ice cutting, snow ploughs, insulation techniques, and logistics underpinned the industry's strong growth. The impact of these innovations was significant—they enabled, for example, an expansion of markets to far-flung locations like Hong Kong, Bombay, and Rio de Janeiro where, despite the distance and journey times, sufficient ice remained of cargoes originally loaded in ports like Boston to make the venture highly profitable.[1]

But at the same time as this highly efficient system was growing researchers like the young Carl von Linde were working in their laboratories on the emerging problems of refrigeration. It wasn't long before artificial ice making became a reality—Joseph Perkins had demonstrated that vaporizing and condensing a volatile liquid in a closed system would do the job and in doing so outlined the basic architecture which underpins today's refrigerators. In 1870 Linde published his research and by 1873 a patented commercial refrigeration system was on the market. In the years which followed the industry grew—in 1879 there were 35 plants and ten years later 222 making artificial ice. Effectively this development sounded the death knell for the ice-harvesting industry—although it took a long time to go under. For a while both industries grew alongside each other, learning and innovating along their different pathways and expanding the overall market for ice—for example, by feeding the growing urban demand to fill domestic 'ice boxes.' But inevitably the new technology took over as the old harvesting model reached the limits of what it could achieve in terms of technological efficiencies. Significantly most of the established ice harvesters were too locked in to the old model to make the transition and so went under—to be replaced by the new refrigeration industry dominated by new entrant firms.

Now let's wind the film forwards to the last part of the twentieth century and a very different industry—the computer disk drive business. Just like the ice industry before it, a thriving sector in which the voracious demands of the growing mini-computer industry for powerful machines for engineering, banking, and others meant there was a booming market for disk drive storage units. Around 120 players populated what had become an industry worth $18 bn in 1995—and like their ice predecessors, it was a richly innovative industry. Firms worked closely with their customers, understanding the particular needs and demands for more storage capacity, faster access times, smaller footprints, etc. But just like our ice industry, the virtuous circle was about to be broken—in this case not by a radical technological shift but by the emergence of a new market with very different needs and expectations. Whilst the emphasis in the mini-computer world was on high performance and the requirement for storage units correspondingly technologically sophisticated, the emerging market for personal computers had a very different shape. These were much less clever machines, capable of running much simpler software and with massively inferior performance—but at a price which a very different set of people could afford. Importantly although simpler they were capable of doing most of the basic tasks which a much wider market was interested in—simple arithmetical calculations, word processing, and basic graphics. As the market grew so the learning effects meant that these capabilities improved—but from a much lower cost base. The effect was, in the end, just like that of Linde on the ice industry—but from a different direction. Of the major manufacturers in the disk drive industry in the 1990s only a handful survived—and leadership in the new industry shifted to new entrant firms working with a very different model.[2]

These are not isolated examples but typical of a pattern in innovation. Think about the revolution in flying which the low-cost carriers have brought about. Here the challenge came via a new business model rather than technology—based on the premiss that if prices could be kept low a large new market could be opened up. In order to make low prices pay a number of problems needed solving—keeping load factors high, cutting administration costs, enabling rapid turnaround times at terminals—but once the model began to work it attracted not only new customers but increasingly established flyers who saw the advantages of lower prices.

What these—and many other examples—have in common is that they represent the challenge of *discontinuous* innovation. None of the industries was lacking in innovation or a commitment to further change. However, the ice harvesters, mini-computer disk companies, or the established airlines all carried on their innovation on a stage covered with a relatively predictable carpet. But shifts in technology, in new market emergence, or in new business models pulled this carpet out from under the firms—and created a new set of conditions on which a new game would be played out. The trouble is that under such conditions, it is the new players who tend to do better because they don't have to wrestle with learning new tricks and letting go of their old ones. This is why discontinuous changes can often be disruptive to established players. And why this makes learning to anticipate and deal with such conditions a key strategic challenge for established players—and a wonderfully rich opportunity for new entrepreneurial players.

The Challenge of Discontinuity

Innovation matters—of course. There can't be many organizations which don't recognize that unless they change their offerings (products/services) and the ways they create and deliver those offerings, they run the risk of being overtaken and even losing the race altogether. Innovation is what drives organic growth in a world where growing by acquiring becomes an increasingly expensive but risky game. And it offers ways of giving a competitive edge, of helping a business stand out from what is now a truly global set of hungry players. For all but a few economies endowed with cheap labour or access to low-cost energy or natural resources, the manufacturing game of low-cost competition is already lost—the only way out is up the knowledge ladder, competing on non-price factors like design, customization, and service. But to get and sustain an edge in this territory requires a serious commitment to innovation, to constant renewal of products, processes, and an increasing component of services. In the case of services with much lower barriers to entry and imitation the innovation challenge has long been one of staying ahead by constantly changing and updating what is on offer and the ways in which it can be offered.

So far, so obvious. But innovation involves a moving target—it's not enough simply to build a capability for organizing and managing the process and then leaving it to run. Firms get their edge by doing something different—but very quickly others spot what they are doing and imitate (and often improve on) it. And that applies not only to the particular innovations—changes in product,

Triggers / sources of discontinuity	Explanation	Problems posed	Examples (of good and bad experiences)
New market emerges	Most markets evolve through a process of growth, segmentation, etc. But at certain times completely new markets emerge which cannot be analyzed or predicted in advance or explored through using conventional market research/analytical techniques	Established players don't see it because they are focused on their existing markets May discount it as being too small or not representing their preferred target market—fringe/cranks dismissal Originators of new product may not see potential in new markets and may ignore them—e.g. text messaging	Disk drives, excavators, mini-mills Mobile phone/SMS where market which actually emerged was not the one expected or predicted by originators
New technology emerges	Step change takes place in product or process technology—may result from convergence and maturing of several streams (e.g. industrial automation, mobile phones) or as a result of a single breakthrough (e.g. LED as new white light source)	Don't see it because beyond the periphery of technology search environment Not an extension of current areas but completely new field or approach Tipping point may not be a single breakthrough but convergence and maturing of established technological streams, whose combined effect is underestimated Not invented here effect—new technology represents a different basis for delivering value—e.g. telephone vs. telegraphy	Ice harvesting to cold storage Valves to solid state electronics Photos to digital images Voice over internet protocol telephony Filament light bulbs to LED sources
New political rules emerge	Political conditions which shape the economic and social rules may shift dramatically—for example, the collapse of communism meant an alternative model—capitalist, competition—as opposed to central planning—and many ex-state firms couldn't adapt their ways of thinking	Old mindset about how business is done, rules of the game, etc. are challenged and established firms fail to understand or learn new rules	Centrally planned to market economy e.g. former Soviet Union Apartheid to post-apartheid South Africa Free trade/globalization results in dismantling protective tariff and other barriers and new competition basis emerges
Running out of road	Firms in mature industries may need to escape the constraints of diminishing space for product and process innovation and the	Current system is built around a particular trajectory and embedded in a steady state set of innovation routines which militate	*Encyclopaedia Britannica* finally running out of road as it is displaced by first CD-based, then

(Continued)

TABLE 10.1 (Continued)

Triggers/ sources of discontinuity	Explanation	Problems posed	Examples (of good and bad experiences)
	increasing competition of industry structures by either exit or by radical reorientation of their business	against widespread search or risk-taking experiments	online, and now open source encyclopedias like Wikipedia Sometimes the firms manage to break out and establish a new trajectory—e.g. Nokia from timber products to mobile phones or Preussag from metals and commodities to tourism.
Sea change in market sentiment or behavior	Public opinion or behaviour shifts slowly and then tips over into a new model—for example, the music industry is in the midst of a (technology-enabled) revolution in delivery systems from buying records, tapes, and CDs to direct download of tracks in MP3 and related formats. Long-standing issues of concern to a minority accumulate momentum (some-times through the action of pressure groups) and suddenly the system switches/ tips over—for example, social attitudes to smoking or health concerns about obesity levels and fast foods	Don't pick up on it or persist in alternative explanations—cognitive dissonance—until it may be too late Rules of the game suddenly shift and then new pattern gathers rapid momentum wrong-footing existing players working with old assumptions	Apple, Napster, Dell, Microsoft vs. traditional music industry McDonalds, Burger King, and obesity concerns Tobacco companies and smoking bans Oil/energy and others and global warming Opportunity for new energy sources like wind power where Danish firms have come to dominate
Deregulation/shifts in regulatory regime	Political and market pressures lead to shifts in the regulatory framework and enable the emergence of a new set of rules—e.g. liberalization, privatization, or deregulation	New rules of the game but old mindsets persist and existing player unable to move fast enough or see new opportunities opened up	Old monopoly positions in fields like telecommunications and energy were dismantled and new players/combinations of

		enterprises emerged. In particular, energy and bandwidth become increasingly viewed as commodities. Innovations include skills in trading and distribution - a factor behind the considerable success of Enron in the late 1990s as it emerged from a small gas pipeline business to becoming a major energy trade
Business model innovation	Established business models are challenged by a reframing, usually by a new entrant who redefines/reframes the problem and the consequent 'rules of the game'	New entrants see opportunity to deliver product/service via new business model and rewrite rules—existing players have at best to be fast followers	Aamzon.com in retailing Charles Schwab in share trading Southwest and other low-cost airlines Direct Line insurance
Unthinkable events	Unimagined and therefore not prepared for events which—sometimes literally—change the world and set up new rules of the game.	New rules may disempower existing players or render competencies unnecessary	9/11
Shifts in 'techno-economic paradigm'—systemic changes which impact whole sectors or even whole societies	Change takes place at system level, involving technology and market shifts. This involves the convergence of a number of trends which result in a 'paradigm shift' where the old order is replaced.	Hard to see where new paradigm begins until rules become established. Existing players tend to reinforce their commitment to old model, reinforced by 'sailing ship' effects	Industrial Revolution Mass production

process, or service—but also to the ways in which innovation is organized and managed. When Dell introduced its process innovations around orchestrating a network approach to supplying computers via a customized and agile approach it secured a strong market edge. But over time others have learned the tricks and Dell has had to elaborate, extend, and change its approach to stay ahead of an increasing number of imitators.

Organizations can and do learn to manage innovation—and we know quite a lot about how the process can be organized to deliver a continuous stream of product, process, and service innovations. It's about things like systematic market and technological search, strategic selection, careful project and risk management, and effective commercialization of innovative ideas. The trouble is that even a well-developed capability for what might be called 'steady state' conditions may not be enough when those rules change. The kinds of discontinuous shock described earlier can and do happen and can come from many different directions—Table 10.1 gives some examples.

Managing Innovation beyond the Steady State

Under these conditions established players often do badly—in part because the natural response is to press even harder on the pedal driving the existing ways of organizing and managing innovation. In the ice industry example the problem was not that the major players weren't interested in R&D—on the contrary they worked really hard at keeping a technological edge in insulation, harvesting, and other tools. But they were blindsided by technological changes coming from a different field altogether—and when they woke up to the threat posed by mechanical ice making their response was to work even harder at improving their own ice-harvesting and shipping technologies. It is here that the so-called 'sailing ship' effect can often be observed, in which a mature technology accelerates in its rate of improvement as a response to a competing new alternative—as was the case with the development of sailing ships in competition with newly emerging steamship technology.[3]

In similar fashion the problem for the firms in the disk drive industry wasn't that they didn't listen to customers but rather that they listened too well. They build a virtuous circle of demanding customers in their existing marketplace with whom they developed a stream of improvement innovations—continuously stretching their products and processes to do what they were doing better and better. The trouble was that they were getting close to the wrong customers—the discontinuity which got them into trouble was the emergence of a completely different set of users with very different needs and values.

It's easy to see why new entrants have an advantage when the game changes—they have no prior commitments or sunk costs, and they don't have a previously successful model for how they organize and manage innovation. But we should be careful here: not all established firms do badly when discontinuous conditions emerge, and not all new entrants do well. Indeed we know the mortality rate for new firms swarming around a new technological field is very high—we only hear about the successful players who manage to find their way through to the emergent successful dominant design—but there is often a trail of corpses left on the battlefield. The emerging field of voice over internet protocol telephony (VOIP) is clearly going to revolutionize telecommunications—but although we can see key new entrant players like Skype there were many others who saw the opportunities building out from peer-to-peer networking but weren't able to exploit the opportunity well enough and disappeared.

Not all technological revolutions do upset the established players. If they see the new developments early enough and pick up on their significance they can often strengthen their position. Two US researchers studied discontinuous technological shifts across a wide range of industries over an extended time period and noted that under some conditions major technological shifts could be 'competence destroying'—at which point new entrants would dominate the new industries enabled by radical technology.[4] But under other conditions the radical technologies were 'competence enhancing' and strengthened the hand of existing incumbents. This suggests that disruption is not always a 'changing of the guard' between existing incumbents and new entrants. We can see this playing out at present with the shift towards solid state lighting. Thomas Edison's bulb has been with us since 1886 so we shouldn't be surprised that, like the ice harvesters, there are limits to how much further it can go in terms of product or process improvement. But new developments in the field of light-emitting diodes mean that there is a new set of light sources which last twenty times as long as a light bulb and offer energy savings of 85 per cent—and that's at the start of their innovation careers. Needless to say this could pose a problem for established lighting firms like Siemens, Philips, or General Electric, especially since the original patents around such solid state devices were held by a small Japanese chemical company. But it is clear that a combination of licensing and R&D plus a commitment running into billions of dollars means that the major players will be able to exploit their experience, brands, distribution channels, and other assets to ensure this innovation is competence enhancing.

We also need to remember that successful exploitation of an idea isn't just about having the right idea at the right time for the market. Innovation depends on translating that potential—and sometimes a new technology whose market time has come isn't enough. In 1970 a team from the UK firm EMI exhibited a device at a Chicago medical show which offered an alternative to X-ray imaging based on computer-aided tomography (CAT). The idea caused a huge stir, prompting one commentator to call it 'the photocopier of the medical industry,' predicting that it would eventually be found in every hospital and clinic around the world. He was right—the body scanner has become a standard and vital piece of medical equipment around the world and represents a huge market. Its inventor, Godfrey Hounsfield, won a Nobel Prize for the original idea reflecting the breakthrough which CAT technology represented. Yet ten years after that launch, and despite having strong patent protection around the idea, EMI pulled out of the industry, leaving it to more successful imitators like General Electric and Siemens.

How does an established and otherwise smart firm manage to fail to exploit a radical innovation in a market which was ripe for such a technology? It's a question which has fascinated researchers for many years—and the general view is that the problem lay with what are called 'complementary assets.' EMI had a strong R&D capability but their manufacturing experience was essentially in high-volume consumer products like transistor radios, TV sets, and record players—not in the small-batch, high-tech project kind of production which making scanners required. Similarly their sales and marketing networks were geared around consumer electronics and a long way from the specialized world of radiographers, surgeons, and medical technicians. In essence there was nothing wrong with the technology itself, nor the market opportunity— but with the networks which they had in place to capture value from it and to preserve their competitive position. Other players in the industry had more appropriate 'complementary assets' and so they were able to take the competitive high ground despite being followers in the technology development stakes.

This has important implications for understanding the winners and losers in the discontinuous innovation game. As we've seen existing incumbents are often on the defensive when technologies shift or new markets emerge—but the spoils do not always go to the new entrants. One way of surviving the waves of radical change is to have in place complementary assets which can insulate a firm from the shocks of the change—at least for long enough to adapt to the new conditions. And the lack of these may stymie an otherwise well-placed new entrant to the field—as EMI found to their cost. Of course the reverse is also true: as Mary Tripsas points out in her detailed analysis of innovation patterns in the typesetting industry over many years, the big threat to existing players comes when there is a technological or market shift *and* a new set of complementary assets are needed to exploit the opportunity. The real problematic innovations are not the competence-destroying ones but those that are both competence destroying *and* complementary assets destroying.[5]

Effectively discontinuous innovation offers threats and opportunities for both new and established players. By changing the rules of the game it puts a premium on entrepreneurial behavior—being able to spot an emerging opportunity and exploit it. For new entrants it is the 'classic' entrepreneur's challenge of being able to manage the growth of a business from a bright but often high-risk idea—and doing it from a weak asset base. For established players the challenge is one of reinventing themselves to allow at least a part of the business to behave as if it were an entrepreneurial start-up—and of holding back the conservative forces of the mainstream organization to let this happen. In both cases there's a significant need for strategic leadership.

Innovation Capabilities for Different Innovation Space

So what kinds of capabilities do firms need to develop to be able to deal with both 'steady state' and discontinuous innovation? These represent two very different kinds of innovation space in which organizations have to operate. Type 1 is essentially one where the challenge is innovating within a relatively stable framework—the rules of the game are clear, the identity and nature of competitors is known, the sources of ideas and the relationships along which they flow (for example with customers or suppliers, universities, and others) are well established and the underlying requirement is essentially around 'doing what we do, but better.' This is not a trivial task but organizing and managing it tends to favor established players who have learned through experience how best to structure and operate the innovation process for this relatively steady state.

By contrast type 2 is a volatile, unpredictable, and essentially fluid state—on the edge of chaos. A new game is emerging—triggered by discontinuous shifts in markets, technologies, or external regulations—but quite what the rules are, or even the precise nature of the game, is not clear. They emerge over time as the fluid and turbulent state gradually gives way to a more stable set of conditions with a clear trajectory for future development.[6] A good example of this can be seen in the case of bicycles which went through an extended period of fluidity in design options before the dominant diamond frame emerged which has characterized the industry for the past century.

Table 10.2 contrasts the innovation management challenges posed by these two very different environments. Type 1 organizations are, not surprisingly, something which established players are good at creating and operating: geared to 'doing what we do better' and to repeating the innovation trick—structures and procedures to enable a steady stream of product, process, and service innovations. But type 2 organizations are much more like new entrants—agile and flexible, able to switch directions, to experiment around the emergent new rules of the game.

Working 'out of the box' in this way requires a new set of approaches to organizing and managing innovation—for example how the firm searches for

Develop your Options

weak signals about potential discontinuities, how it makes strategic choices in the face of high uncertainty, how it resources projects which lie far outside the mainstream of its innovation operations, etc. Established and well-proven routines for 'steady state' conditions may break down here—for example, an effective 'stage gate' system would find it difficult to deal with high-risk project proposals which lie at the fringes of the firm's envelope of experience.

The problem is further compounded by the networks of relationships the firm has with other firms. Typically, much of the basis of innovation lies at a system level involving networks of suppliers and partners configuring knowledge and other resources to create a new offering. Discontinuous innovation is often problematic because it may involve building and working with a significantly different set of partners from those the firm is accustomed to working with. Whereas 'strong ties'—close and consistent relationships with regular partners in a network—may be important in enabling a steady stream of continuous improvement innovations, evidence suggests that where firms are seeking to do something different they need to exploit much weaker ties across a very different population in order to gain access to new ideas and different sources of knowledge and expertise.[7]

The big question for established players is how they can develop some type 2 innovation management capabilities. One option is to set up their own version of new entrant firms, simply spinning off entities which they hope will be able to colonize and settle the new world of a type 2 environment. This is a low-risk option but also means that there may be little synergy or leverage across to and from the core business. Another option is to try and develop a parallel innovation management capability within the mainstream business—but in order to do this a number of new approaches will be needed.

In practice there are many options between these two poles, including setting up special units within an established business or managing more

TABLE 10.2 Different archetypes for steady state and discontinuous innovation

Type 1 Innovation organization	Type 2
Operates within mental framework based on clear and accepted set of rules of the game	No clear rules—these emerge over time High tolerance for ambiguity
Strategies path dependent	Path independent, emergent, probe and learn
Clear selection environment	Fuzzy, emergent selection environment
Selection and resource allocation linked to clear trajectories and criteria for fit	Risk taking, multiple parallel bets, tolerance of (fast) failure
Operating routines refined and stable	Operating patterns emergent and 'fuzzy'
Strong ties and knowledge flows along clear channels	Weak ties and peripheral vision important

'open innovation' operations which leverage the entrepreneurial strengths of smaller players. A number of large firms—for example, Microsoft, Intel Cisco Siemens, and GSK—have developed sophisticated 'fishing' strategies looking around for smaller smart players to buy or at least link up with to help them keep an edge.[8]

In the next section we look briefly at some of the approaches which firms are experimenting with to try and develop type 2 capabilities.

Developing New Innovation Capabilities

In order to develop capability to deal with discontinuous shifts, organizations need to experiment, imitate, adapt, and in other ways learn new patterns of entrepreneurial behavior. And they have to develop them to the point where

TABLE 10.3 Emergent 'good practice' model outline for discontinuous innovation

Key dimension in innovation model	Type 2 characteristics
Search—firms need to scan and search their environments (internal and external) to pick up and process signals about potential innovation. These could be needs of various kinds, or opportunities arising from research activities somewhere, or pressures to conform to legislation, or the behavior of competitors—but they represent the bundle of stimuli to which the organization must respond	Search at the periphery—pick up and amplify weak signals Use multiple and alternative perspectives Manage the idea generation process inside the firm—enable systematic and high involvement in innovation Develop an external scanning capability—scouts and hunters Use technological antennae to seek out potential new technologies Tune in to weak market signals—e.g. working with fringe users, early trend locations (such as chat rooms on internet) Develop future exploring capability—scenario and alternatives Explore at periphery of firm—subsidiaries, joint ventures, distributors as sources of innovation Bring in outside perspectives
Strategic selection—from this set of potential triggers for innovation firms need to choose what they will commit resources to doing. Even the best-resourced organization can't do everything, so the challenge lies in selecting those things which offer the best chance of developing a competitive edge.	Build pluralism into decision-making processes Create 'markets for judgement' Decentralize seed funding for new ideas- for example via internal venture funds or development budgets Build dual structures for innovation development and decision making Develop 'fuzzy front end' approaches

(Continued)

195

Develop your Options

Table 10.3 (*Continued*)

Key dimension in innovation model	Type 2 characteristics
Implementation—having chosen an option, organizations need to grow it from an idea through various stages of development to final launch—as a new product or service in the external marketplace or a new process or method within the organization. On the way they have to solve a host of problems (like where to get hold of the knowledge they need, how to find and integrate different groups of people with key skills, how to get the bugs and wrinkles out of the emerging innovation, how to steer the project against tight budgets of time and cost, etc.) and they have to do all this against a background of high uncertainty!	Build flexible project development organizations—emphasize probe and learn rather than predictive project planning Work actively with users on co-evolution of innovation Build parallel resource networks
Innovation strategy—innovation is about taking risks, about going into new and sometimes completely unexplored spaces. We don't want to gamble—simply changing things for their own sake or because the fancy takes us. No organization has resources to waste in that scattergun fashion—innovation needs a strategy. But equally we need to have a degree of courage and leadership, steering the organization away from what everyone else is doing or what we've always done and into new spaces.	Explore alternative future scenarios and consider parallel possibilities Identify strategic domains within which targeted hunting can take place Build capacity for ambiguity/multiple parallel strategies Actively explore 'how to destroy the business' to enable reframing
Innovative organization—firms need a structure and climate which enables people to deploy their creativity and share their knowledge to bring about change. It's easy to find prescriptions for innovative organizations which highlight the need to eliminate stifling bureaucracy, unhelpful structures, brick walls blocking communication, and other factors stopping good ideas getting through. But we must be careful not to fall into the chaos trap—not all innovation works in organic, loose, informal environments or 'skunk works'—and these types of organization can sometimes act against the interests of successful innovation. Too little order and structure may be as bad as too much.	Build a culture which supports and encourages diversity and curiosity-driven behavior. Set up appropriate incentive structures Enable complex knowledge flows
Proactive linkages—firms need to build bridges across boundaries inside the organization and to the many external agencies who can play a part in the innovation process—suppliers, customers, sources of finance, skilled resources and of knowledge, etc.	Develop non-committal exploratory supply relationships in addition to longer-term strategic alliances- 'strategic dalliances' Explore and develop parallel 'weak ties'

they are structured and embedded as a long-term capability, not just a one-off special project. In this section we list some of the emerging principles around which such learning can take place, structured according to a simple process model of innovation which involves five key dimensions.[9]

Table 10.3 distills some elements of the emerging 'good practice' model for discontinuous innovation management mapped onto this framework.

Some Examples of New Patterns of Innovation

In the following section we give some illustrative examples drawn from a continuing programme of research on this question.[10] They highlight the extensive nature of such experimentation around finding routines for dealing with discontinuous innovation.

Extending Peripheral Vision

Dealing with discontinuity requires the capacity to pick up early and weak signals about the emergence of discontinuities. So organizations need to try and enhance their 'peripheral vision,' carrying out (re)search activities into new and unexpected areas. But this is often difficult to justify not least because of the difficulty of deciding *where* to focus such alternative search activity. It is a little like the story of the drunk searching for his keys under the lamp-post because it is better illuminated. Clearly he needs to extend his search to the dark areas beyond—but how does he choose a particular direction in which to begin his search from 360 degrees of such darkness?

One approach is to increase both the number of antennae available to the organization, and the 'open innovation' strategies of firms like Procter & Gamble and IBM are designed to do this, often involving extensive use of the internet as a technological 'amplifier' for weak signals.[11]

Another approach uses the well-established principles of early involvement of active users[12] to configure a stakeholder network which contains both an early warning system and an innovation development capacity. Given that trends in the industry are likely to lead to some discontinuous innovation this offers then a mechanism for placing a wide number of bets and also identifying possible partners for future development activity.

This kind of approach is being explored by the British Broadcasting Corporation—a major producer of broadcast media now trying to deal with the discontinuous challenges of the new digital media environment. Attempting to second guess a massively complex world 'out there' from the standpoint of a small R&D group is clearly a non-starter. One alternative is to try to engage a rich variety of players in those emerging spaces via a series of 'open innovation' experiments. BBC Backstage is an example, trying to do with new media development what the open source community did with software development. The model is deceptively simple—developers are invited to make free use of various elements of the BBC's site (such as live news feeds, weather, TV listings, etc.) to integrate and shape innovative applications. The strapline is 'use our stuff to build your stuff'—and since the site was launched in May 2005 it has already attracted the interest of hundreds of software developers. Ben Metcalf, one of the program's founders, summed up the approach. 'Top line, we are looking to be seen promoting innovation and creativity on the Internet . . . if someone is doing something really innovative, we would like to . . . see if some of that value can be incorporated into the BBC's core propositions.'

New business models are often the result of emergence from within a group of different stakeholders—essentially the architects and the players of the new game. So another strategy is to get involved in exploring radically different approaches in order to be in early enough to pick up weak signals and in deeply enough to shape what emerges. For example, the Danish pharmaceutical firm Novo Nordisk is exploring a number of avenues in parallel with its 'steady state' pharmaceutical product development model. It is looking, for example, at future models which might involve a much higher level of care services wrapped around a core set of products for treating chronic diseases like diabetes. Its activities include working with health education programs in Tanzania, carrying out extensive psycho-social research on diabetes sufferers to establish actual needs and problems in diagnosis and treatment, and contributing to multi-stakeholder groups like the Oxford Health Alliance set up in 2003 with members drawn from an international set of academics, health professionals, government agencies, and private sector firms sharing a common goal—'to raise awareness among influencers and educate critical decision-makers so that the pressing case for preventative measures can advance, and we can begin to combat chronic disease.'

CEO Lars Rebien Sørensen doesn't underestimate the mindset change this represents: 'in moving from intervention to prevention—that's challenging the business model where the pharmaceuticals industry is deriving its revenues! . . . We believe that we can contribute to solving some major global health challenges—mainly diabetes—and at the same time create business opportunities for our company.'

Enhancing Signal-Processing Capacity

The difficulty is not simply one of picking up on a wide variety of signals. Organizations operate in a world in which they are bombarded by a stream of intonation which they need to filter and select from. They have typically evolved a sophisticated signal-processing capacity which only permits strategically relevant information to enter. The challenge in managing discontinuous innovation is to build a parallel capacity in which interesting but apparently 'off-message' signals can be processed into a form where they can be communicated to the rest of the organization.[13]

Coloplast—an award-winning Danish medical devices firm—has recognized this difficulty, drawing a parallel with an immune system which detects alien organisms and rejects them. In their sophisticated product development system they have a series of filters which effectively screen out at a very early stage any signals about innovation possibilities outside of a focused mainstream. As one interviewee put it, 'round here we don't have a product development funnel, we have a tube!' In an attempt to extend their capability to deal with discontinuous innovation they have set up a small team of technology and market 'scouts' whose task is not simply to pick up on potential weak signals but also to explore and process them into a form in which the rest of the organization can be made aware of them without the instant rejection they would normally receive. Building the 'business case lite' for such ideas requires a sophisticated understanding not only of the new possibilities but also the internal context (political as well as resources) into which they will be introduced. Much of the work of this team is around building coalitions of support for the new ideas before they are brought into the formal strategic planning process.

Developing Alterative Strategic Frames

A significant problem for existing incumbents in the face of discontinuous challenges appears to be a reluctance to reframe the underlying models of the business. The example of Polaroid is widely cited where the slow response to digital imaging as a completely new game rather than just a technological shift led to the company's downfall.[14] They aren't alone—as writers like Foster and Kaplan point out in many examples of firms which lose by being too heavily committed to defending a status quo.[15] The problem is compounded by the presence of many aspects of organizational life which reinforce old models—for example reward systems which favor working with established customers[16] or knowledge flows which underpin established product architectures.[17]

In order to escape this trap organizations seek to develop alternative ways of framing their activities. One route for this is to explore alternative scenarios for the future and to look at ways in which the current resource base could be reconfigured to provide an alternative but viable business model. For example, Shell has developed its long-established capabilities in scenario planning[18] into an approach called 'Gamechanger' in which detailed alternative future scenarios are developed and used to provide challenging reframing possibilities. In turn these help identify relevant domains within which 'targeted hunting,' for new opportunities, can take place. Such exploration provides a mechanism for pursuing several 'parallel future' development projects without compromising mainstream activities and helps maintain a tolerance for ambiguity suited to discontinuous conditions.

Such ventures do not always succeed, A specialist motor vehicle company carried through an extensive scenario-based review of its options but became increasingly concerned at the relative fragility of its current business model, Rather than extend the reframing process it chose to retreat and consolidate around the existing model and eventually sold off its future projects research operation.

Extending Resource Allocation Approaches

A significant problem around discontinuous innovation occurs when well-developed strategic resource allocation and review system are confronted with radical challenges.[19] Whilst such systems evolve as a robust way of managing a stream of projects under steady state innovation conditions they may not be suited to discontinuities. For this reason a number of organizations decentralize the funding process for high-risk/radical venturing and make use of various forms of corporate venturing approach.[20] These arrangements range from completely separate venture units to internal venture capital sources for which project owners can make bids. The intention—although not always the outcome—is to provide an alternative and parallel channel for exploring radical options and allocating at least early-stage funding.

Summary

The paradox of discontinuous innovation is that whilst it is very hard to see it coming (precisely because it is a step change, not more of the same), there is a certainty that it will happen! We just don't know when or where. So organizations can't afford to ignore it—if they are established players they risk losing their place at the table if they can't cope in a world where the underlying rules of the game have changed. And if they are entrepreneurs looking for opportunities the clean canvas on which the new rules can be written is a wonderful but rare chance.

History is full of examples where discontinuities—market, technology, business model, etc.—change the rules of the game and disrupt the existing world. When this happens there are winners and losers—winners who spot and exploit the emerging opportunities and losers who miss seeing (or reacting quickly enough) until it is too late to act. But it's not simply a matter of 'new entrants win, established players lose'—many of today's longest-established and successful businesses have developed the ability to grow and become stronger by being able to ride the waves of discontinuous change. The skill lies less in exploiting any particular discontinuity's characteristics than in the ability to spot it coming early and then make strategic decisions about dealing with it. Does it threaten or strengthen established competencies? Can we exploit it alone or do we need to explore ways of working with others—and if so, with whom? Do we need a different approach to defining and exploring this market—perhaps as a parallel or complementary activity to our mainstream? Can we balance the 'bread and butter' of steady state innovation with more radical exploration beyond our frontiers?

Whether a far-sighted newcomer or an established player ready to reinvent itself, dealing with discontinuity needs strong strategic leadership—committing resources to exploring far and outside the box, listening carefully to the messengers when they return from such exploration, and being prepared to think the unthinkable and reinvent the business on the back of what they say. Given that this may require confronting the anxieties and critical concerns of some very agitated stakeholders inside and outside the business such leadership may also involve more than a modicum of courage!

Notes

1. J. Utterback (1994) *Mastering the Dynamics of Innovation*. Boston: Harvard Business School Press.
2. C. Christensen (1997) *The Innovator's Dilemma*. Cambridge, Mass.: Harvard Business School Press.
3. S. Gilfillan (1935) *Inventing the Ship*. Chicago: Follett.
4. M. Tushman and P. Anderson (1987) 'Technological Discontinuities and Organizational Environments,' *Administrative Science Quarterly*, 31 (3): 439–65.
5. M. Tripsas (1997) 'Unraveling the Process of Creative Destruction: Complementary Assets and Incumbent Survival in the Typesetter Industry,' *Strategic Management Journal*, 18 (Summer): 119–42.
6. W. Abernathy and J. Utterback (1975) 'A Dynamic Model of Product and Process Innovation,' *Omega*, 3 (6): 639–56.
7. W. Phillips et al. (2006) 'Discontinuous Innovation and Supply Relationships: Strategic Dalliances,' *R&D Management*, 36 (4): 451–61.
8. C. Markides (1997) 'Strategic Innovation,' *Sloan Management Review*, Spring: 9–24; J. Birkinshaw and C. Gibson (2004) 'Building Ambidexterity into an Organization,' *Sloan Management Review*, 45 (4): 47–55.

Develop your Options

9. J. Tidd, J. Bessant, and K. Pavitt (2005) *Managing Innovation: Integrating Technological, Market and Organizational Change*. 3rd edn. Chichester: John Wiley & Son.
10. W. Phillips et al. (2006) 'Beyond the Steady State: Managing Discontinuous Product and Process Innovation,' *International Journal of Innovation Management*, 10 (2).
11. L. Huston (2004) 'Mining the Periphery for New Products,' *Long Range Planning*, 37: 191–6; J. Seely Brown (2004) 'Minding and Mining the Periphery,' *Long Range Planning*, 37: 143–51.
12. Brown, 'Minding and Mining the Periphery;' S. Thomke (2002) *Experimentation Matters*. Boston: Harvard Business School Press; E. Von Hippel (1988) *The Sources of Innovation*. Cambridge, Mass.: MIT Press; E. Von Hippel, S. Thomke, and M. Sonnack (1999) 'Creating Breakthroughs at 3 M,' *Harvard Business Review*, 77 (5): 47–55.
13. Brown, 'Minding and Mining the Periphery.'
14. M. Tripsas and G. Gavetti (2000) 'Capabilities, Cognition and Inertia: Evidence from Digital Imaging,' *Strategic Management Journal*, 21: 1147–61.
15. R. Foster and S. Kaplan (2002) *Creative Destruction*. Cambridge, Mass.: Harvard University Press.
16. Christenson, *The Innovator's Dilemma*.
17. R. Henderson and K. Clark (1990) Architectural Innovation: The Reconfiguration of Existing Product Technologies and the Failure of Established Firms,' *Administrative Science Quarterly*, 35: 9–30.
18. A. de Geus (1996) *The Living Company*. Boston: Harvard Business School Press.
19. R. Leifer et al. (2000) *Radical Innovation*. Boston: Harvard Business School Press.
20. W. Buckland, A. Hatcher, and J. Birkinshaw (2003) *Inventuring: Why Big Companies Must Think Small*. London: McGraw Hill Business.

11 How to Create the Industries of the Twenty-First Century

Costas Markides

Name a company that does not aspire to create a radical new market, enriching itself and its shareholders in the process. Identify a CEO who does not dream of being labeled a visionary for leading their organization into virgin territories, discovering in the process exciting new technologies, products, and markets. We all aspire to become a modern-day Christopher Columbus—the pioneer, the inventor, the adventurer that discovers the industries of the future.

Yet, as I will show in this chapter, *this is nothing more than misplaced hope for the majority of big established companies*! There are two reasons why I say this: first, big established companies *cannot* create radical new markets; second, big established companies should *not want* to create radical new markets.

I will explain why I make such a bold and controversial statement in this chapter. But don't take my word for it—all you have to do is to examine how the radical markets of the twentieth century were created to predict how those of the twenty-first century will come about. And there is one fact that the historical evidence points to: *radical* new markets are almost never created by big established firms.

Academic researchers have been studying radical, new-to-the-world markets for the last fifty years. As a result, we now know many things about these markets. For example, we know how they get created and by whom. We know who colonizes them and who makes money out of them. We even know how they will evolve and how they will die. Despite all this knowledge, most of the advice that academics and consultants have been giving companies on how to create radical new markets is wrong! It's as if the advice is given without reference to (or maybe in despite of) all the facts and realities of new markets.

In this chapter, I will explore the reasons why big established companies cannot and should not be in the business of creating radical new markets. I will then explore the implications of our analysis for big companies. I will argue that rather than attempting to create radical new markets, big established companies are better off if they position themselves to exploit the pioneering efforts of others.

Big Established Firms Cannot Create Radical New Markets

It is highly unlikely that a radical new market will be created by a big established firm. This is because the innovation process that creates radical new markets cannot be replicated inside the modern corporation.[1]

To understand why this is the case, there is one thing about radical innovations that we must never forget—these kinds of innovations are *disruptive* to both consumers and producers. They are disruptive to consumers because they introduce products and value propositions that disrupt in a major way prevailing consumer habits and behaviors—what on earth did our ancestors do in the evenings without television! They are disruptive to producers because the markets that they create undermine the competences and complementary assets on which existing competitors have built their success.

Consumers faced with new goods and services based on radical innovations have to learn about these new products—not only what they are, but how to use them and sometimes how to appreciate the benefits that they bring. Consumers must break habits, and change their purchasing and consumption patterns. Sometimes they must make costly investments in learning how to use the new product. Amongst other things, this can involve shouldering serious risks (*will my investment in this new product be wasted? what will this new product do, if it actually works that is?*). Taken together, these various obstacles to change are sometimes called 'switching costs' by economists and it is a complete no-brainer to observe that the switching costs associated with adopting an innovation are almost always higher for radical than for incremental innovations.

Much the same applies to producers. New radical innovations frequently follow the discovery or development of new technologies, and they often demand the development of new skills and new ways of doing business. These changes affect not only the producers of both the new and old products, but also many other firms that produce complementary goods or provide ancillary services. Such changes often reach upstream or downstream to transform supply chains, distribution channels, and delivery logistics. It is sometimes said that every product has its own infrastructure—its own particular value chain—and if that's the case, then it can be said that a new product based on a radical innovation would require the development of its own infrastructure. Therefore, as a new product displaces one or more established products, old infrastructures have to be destroyed and new ones built. Radical innovations also induce changes in the valuation of assets and skills and in patterns of behavior by producers, their suppliers, distributors, wholesalers, and retailers.

In short, radical innovations create new markets and destroy old ones. In a way, all of this helps to explain why radical innovations are so disruptive: they introduce noticeably big changes into our lives. No one likes change unless it is clear that it is for the better. But here lies the problem: for firms that have carefully built up businesses around existing products, new products are always a threat. They cannibalize existing activities and demand new (and sometimes rather risky) investments in doing new things (or in doing old things in new ways). These innovations also challenge consumers and force them to reconsider their behavior in ways that may expose them to considerable risk.

Furthermore, the way that producers and consumers typically evaluate these risks often creates further problems. It is in the nature of radical innovations that the new products and services that they introduce are new and unfamiliar. It is, therefore, often very difficult for anyone—producers and consumers alike—to assess just what the benefits are that they will bring. The costs of change, however, are far more immediate and are usually much easier for everyone to assess. Hence, when really new products or services come to market, they come with promises that are hard to evaluate and threats that usually seem to be much easier to see and to assess. Therefore, first reactions are not always positive. Under these circumstances, it is not at all obvious who would be seriously interested in championing new disruptive innovations.

This is an important point to appreciate, because it raises a very interesting puzzle: since radical innovations require major changes from both consumers and producers and since the benefits of change are hard to assess early on, *neither consumers nor producers would have an incentive to champion radical new markets*! Who, then, introduces radical new innovations in our lives?

Not Demand Driven but Supply Pushed

Perhaps not surprisingly, radical innovations that give rise to entirely new markets are rarely driven by demand or customer needs. Demand-driven innovations can, at best, only account for incremental innovations that develop and extend existing markets. Such innovations usually come in the form of either product extensions or process innovations and, valuable as they are, they cannot help us understand where new markets come from.

Radical new markets get created in a haphazard manner when a new technology gets *pushed* onto the market. This often seems to happen 'by accident'. What this really means is that even though the pace and direction of innovative activity follow the broad guideposts set out by the existing technology paradigms, new technologies often emerge without a clear end consumer or market need making it hard to understand why they have emerged when they have. It also means that even research projects that were motivated by a clear market need often end up producing unexpected outputs. Thus, movements along technological trajectories seem ordered only with the benefit of hindsight.

An Example: The TV Market

Consider the creation of the television market. Arguably, its ultimate founder was one Joseph May. He was an engineer who, while doing routine maintenance operations on a USA-to-UK undersea telegraph cable in 1872, noticed that the ability of a material called selenium to conduct electricity was affected by light. Photosensitivity like this makes it possible to use selenium to measure the intensity of light and to translate variations in colouring or shading in a picture into a pulsating electrical current.

Within a decade of May's fortuitous discovery, a leading learned journal had proclaimed that: 'the complete means of seeing by telegraphy has been known for some time by scientific men.' However, it took several further decades to make the step from this level of scientific understanding to the kind of broadcast television which keeps us glued to the screen for thirty hours a week. Although much of the technical work was done by obsessive, single-minded scientists and engineers like Philo Farnsworth and John Logie Baird, the great champion of television turned out to be the legendary head of RCA, David Sarnoff. He was a visionary whose interest in television was at least partly spurred by his fear of what it might do to RCA's commanding position in radio.

Notice that so far in the development of this new product, consumers have not even appeared as a driving force. On the other hand, one would not want to say that television came about wholly by accident. May's discovery was accidental but Farnsworth, Baird, and Sarnoff all knew what they were doing. What seems to have happened is that somehow, someone stumbled across an advance in knowledge that seemed likely to yield a new product. At this very early stage of recognition, the new product can hardly be described as anything more than a possibility—moving it forward might or might not result in something useful.

Anyone who has watched pharmaceutical firms screen for new chemical entities will recognize just what we are talking about here: the advance in knowledge yields no more than a set of possibilities which, after serious and systematic study, might just result in something useful. The fact that what initially looked like something which might help heart patients ends up as a miracle cure for erectile dyfunctionality is an equally familiar story—indeed, some say that it is part of the charm of the whole process that outcomes seem often to be wholly unrelated to what people thought they would find when the process started.

This kind of innovation process has a name—'supply push'—and it is an innovation process that emerges in a very wide variety of industries. In some cases, scientists and engineers will have a shrewd idea of just what the process is likely to produce. Well-informed lead users may also anticipate the outcome of further systematic study. However, in most cases the early discovery of new scientific knowledge is just a set of promises, a list of possibilities. This is, of course, why many disruptive innovations look like accidents: no one who is there at the birth of the new idea seems to know where it has come from or where it is likely to lead, something that is often true even in hindsight.

The Characteristics of Supply-Push Innovations

Supply-push innovation processes share certain characteristics. First, they are developed in a haphazard way *without a clear customer need driving them*. Second, they emerge out of the efforts of a *large number* of scientists working *independently* on seemingly *unrelated* research projects who devise the technology for their own uses. Third, they go through a *long gestation process* when nothing seems to happen until they suddenly explode onto the market. Now ask yourself: is this an innovation process that can be replicated in the R&D facility of a single firm?

When one reads stories like the development of television (or Post-it notes or Viagra or Aspartame or countless other inventions), one finds it very easy to think that new technologies typically emerge in a serendipitous fashion. This feeling becomes all the stronger when one watches scientists and engineers at work and sees just how often they fail to fully appreciate the significance of what they are doing and how often the breakthroughs that they achieve are propelled by what seems like no more than inspired guesswork at best or just plain 'good luck.' And yet, it is hard to believe that the development of scientific and engineering knowledge is wholly random, that there is no pattern to the nature of successive innovations in a particular sector or to the speed at which they follow each other.

In fact, supply-push innovations follow an ordered pattern that economists call a 'technological trajectory.' In essence this means that scientists around the world working on a particular area share certain beliefs and assumptions or paradigms. These paradigms set priorities, identify what the important problems are, establish acceptable methods for pursuing them, and condition expectations about what to expect from applying these methods to those priorities. This mental model, this sense of what one should do and what will happen if one does it, provides a guiding hand on the design and conduct of research projects that removes at least some of the serendipity from the whole process. While it is not always the case that one finds what one is looking for, it is rarely the case that one sees what one is not looking for.

The organizing power of paradigms goes well beyond their effects on particular research projects: paradigms can organize the work of whole communities of scientists and engineers, and not just isolated individuals. They help to define a pattern of common knowledge, goals, methods, and expectations that give a wide range of scientists and engineers in a particular field what seems like a common purpose. Paradigms create communities with shared values and expectations and for this reason they effectively align the efforts of a wide range of otherwise independent scientists and engineers. Wherever they are and whatever they are doing, those scientists and engineers who share the same paradigm are likely to end up, in effect, fishing in pretty much the same way in pretty much the same pond. In these circumstances, it would not be surprising if the fish that different scientists catch in that pond belonged to the same species or to the same family.

The organized research program that scientists and engineers follow means that there may actually be a pattern to innovative activity over time (possibly more evident with the benefit of hindsight than with foresight, and possibly more by accident than deliberate design). One thing may lead to another, one innovation may follow another, one application of a new principle may be followed by a series of further applications of that same basic principle. A technological trajectory is the sequence of innovations that follow each other, all drawing on the same basic scientific or engineering principle(s), each drawing from and then contributing to a cumulatively increasing body of knowledge and expertise. The idea is simply that each innovation in the sequence is not simply an accident, but follows from innovations which have already occurred (and, of course, may lead to more innovations in the future). Different trajectories are typically associated with the different basic scientific principles or the different scientific or technological paradigms from which they have sprung.

It is important not to overplay this idea, not to impose too much of a pattern on the evolution of technologies. For a start, there have always been (and will always be) one-off innovations that come from nowhere (apparently) and lead nowhere. More fundamentally, the blinkered perspective that often comes from relying on hindsight means that it is probably possible to see a trajectory in the evolution of every technology. For scientists and engineers working on the trajectory at the time, things are much less clear. This is particularly so when a trajectory is first established. New trajectories are associated with radical breakthroughs in scientific and engineering knowledge and these are—almost by definition—likely to be a surprise or appear to be 'accidental.' Such break-throughs are likely to lead almost anywhere—or so it certainly seems to the pioneering scientists and engineers associated with the breakthrough at the time.

The pursuit of these possibilities leads people to go shooting off in all directions; some of these possibilities will lead to more breakthroughs which create more possibilities, while others lead nowhere. As time passes, the choices that people have made will lead the technology to develop in certain directions, and the fact that each breakthrough creates possibilities for further break-throughs (and the knowledge and expertise to create them) will give that evolution a cumulative, path-dependent flavor. A process in which each possibility explored leads to the creation of more possibilities will lead to something that looks like a tree whose dense lattice of branches is built up around trunks and main limbs.

Figure 11.1 shows a stylized version of this idea. An original breakthrough in understanding in a new scientific area creates a new avenue for exploration—a main trajectory. Movement along this trajectory opens up other research possibilities—labeled 'the 1st branch' and 'the 2nd branch' in the figure. These, in turn, open up further possibilities. Each of these in turn leads ultimately to particular inventions.

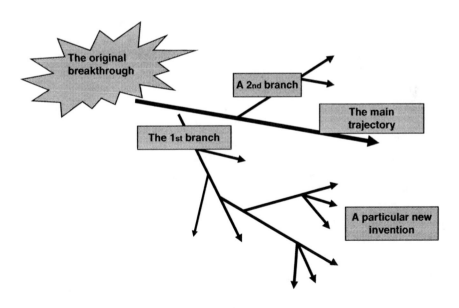

Fig. 11.1 A technological trajectory

Source: Paul Geroski (2003) *The Evolution of New Markets*, Oxford: Oxford University Press.

Develop your Options

The basic branching process suggests that these inventions might come in clusters of related breakthroughs. Thus, the original breakthrough in understanding the structure of atoms at the beginning of the century led to major trajectories in particle physics, cosmology, and chemistry. As scientific and engineering knowledge in each of these areas progressed, further lines of research opened up: the atom was split, the structure of DNA became understood, and so on. Each new area of research has produced a rash of related discoveries, often by different, non-interacting individuals who share only the knowledge of the common branch and its main trajectory.

This discussion might sound theoretical or not applicable to real life but a recent report by the US National Research Council that examined how the key technologies that gave rise to numerous new markets in the last ten years were discovered demonstrates that what we have described here is not far from reality.[2] We reproduce one of the key findings of this Report in Figure 11.2. Note how long it took for the technologies to develop and be commercialized, how scientists from government, universities, and corporate R&D facilities contributed to the development of the technologies, and how the companies that ended up dominating the markets that developed were not even contributing to the key research!

The idea that technologies get discovered along a technological trajectory stimulates a further thought: as the inventions that emerge from different branches are applied in different sectors, their common technological base creates the impression that these sectors are somehow converging. For example, the gradually increasing understanding—and use—of digital technologies has now generated a cascade of innovations in computing and telecommunications whose uses have spilled over into the production of entertainment.

All of this is terribly iffy and imprecise, but it contains within it the seeds of a fairly plausible story that we can use to help explain where new markets come from. The key idea is that of a technological trajectory. If technologies do indeed develop along such trajectories, then it seems clear that they are likely to have something of a life of their own, one which might unfold quite independently of demand. The important point is that the emergence and early development of the trajectory may look like an accident, but once the basic highway that the trajectory is going to follow becomes clear then progress along it is likely to be pretty much self-sustaining, following its own logic at a speed determined primarily by the nature of how scientists and engineers work. From any particular trajectory, all kinds of possibilities arise, all kinds of applications are possible, and so all kinds of new products and services are likely to emerge. The result is that many new innovations that are spun off from any particular trajectory are likely to appear to have been pushed onto the market by the scientists and engineers who have been working along that trajectory. In

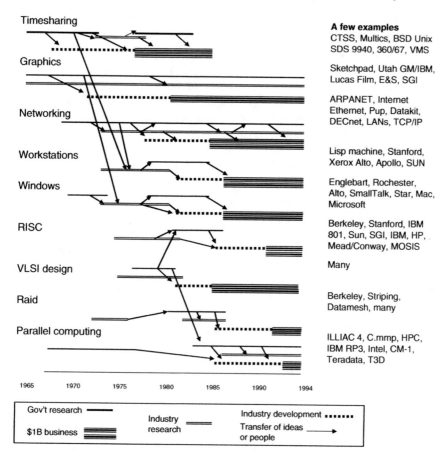

Fig. 11.2 Where key technologies come from

Source: National Research Council, Computer Science and Telecommunications Board (1999) *Funding a Revolution: Government Support for Computing Research*, Washington, D.C.: National Academy Press, 20).

Appendix 11.1, we highlight all this with a prominent example—the development of the internet over the last thirty years.

Big Established Firms Should not Want to Create Radical New Markets

Not only is the innovation process that creates radical new markets impossible to replicate inside a firm but even worse, as we argued elsewhere,[3] the skills and attitudes that big established companies have are not the ones needed for creating new markets. Nor can firms easily adopt the skills of creation because they conflict with their existing skills.

But not everything is bad for established firms! They may not be good at creating radical new markets but the truth be told, they don't need to! That's because the money is not in creating the new market but in scaling it up into a mass market. And that's exactly the area where big established firms have a competitive advantage over younger firms.

Again, to understand the distinction we are making between *creating* new markets and *scaling them up* into mass markets, we must keep in mind the following facts about the structural characteristics of early markets:

First, despite enormous technological and product uncertainty, newly created markets are 'invaded' by hordes of new entrants, sometimes numbering in the hundreds. For example, more than 1,000 firms populated the US auto industry at one time or another, many before the introduction of the Model T in 1908. A total of 14 firms entered this new market between 1885 and 1898; 19 entered in 1899, 37 in 1900, 27 in 1901, and then an average of about 48 new firms entered per year from 1902 until 1910. Amazingly, this surge in firm population happens well before the new market starts growing. This is odd— one would have thought that entry would have been more attractive when the market is large and growing, not before.

Second, not only is the new market flooded with hundreds of new entrants but product variety in the young market also surges to amazingly high levels. In fact, the rate of innovation at the start of a market's life is the highest that this market will ever see. For example, in the early days of the car industry, one could purchase cars powered by petrol, electricity, steam; cars with three and four wheels; and cars with open or closed bodies that came in a bewildering variety of different designs. Cars differed in their suspension, transmission, and brake systems, and in a wide variety of extra or optional features. Not only were there a large variety of different types of cars on the market, but most of the features which marked out the basis of this variety changed rapidly over time. For example, underneath the hood, a continuous stream of innovations led to the development of the four-cylinder engine by 1902, fuel-injection systems by 1910, electric starters by 1912, the V-8 engine by 1914, synchro-mesh transmission in 1929, and so on. In fact, the industry witnessed a wave of innovation between 1899 and 1905 that it never again experienced. Furthermore, these innovations were introduced by a wide range of firms (the dominance of the innovation process by the Big Three occurred later on), and their use diffused rapidly throughout the industry.

Since early markets are small in size and filled with technological and customer uncertainty, it is not immediately clear why we see such a surge in entry and such an amazing variety in products and designs. But the reason becomes obvious enough if we go back to the supply-push innovation process that creates radical new markets.

Supply-push innovation processes have one very important property and this property has a profound impact on how new markets develop. When new innovations are pushed up by supply, they are very underdeveloped. The innovation is typically no more than a list of possibilities and it is anybody's guess as to what the right design is going to be. No one knows what consumers really want and no one knows just what exactly the new technology can do, nor how to economically produce whatever it is that results from the innovation. Anyone's guess is as good as anyone else's, and since there are no real barriers to entry into the as yet underdeveloped new market, there will not, in principle, be any shortage of entrepreneurs who are willing to try out their own particular vision of what the new technology has to offer on the market. Anyone who understands the new technology is, in principle, a potential entrant; anyone enthused by what the new technology might ultimately offer will, in practice, try to become an actual entrant.

Since the basic science and technology is so new, no one is really sure where it is going. Each entrant is, of course, absolutely certain that they are on the right course, but no independent, objective observer would place their bets in any direction. Since there is scope for many different opinions about what the technology can do, there is scope for many different types of new products, for many experiments with that technology. For each possibility there is likely to be an entrant, and each entrant is likely to have several goes at developing the new technology into a new product. The result is market research in real time: a wild and turbulent phase of entry, innovation, and, for most of these early colonizers, exit. The upshot of all of this is that supply-push innovation processes are unlikely to produce a single new product or service. Rather, the nature of how science-push innovations are developed means that they are likely to burst onto the market in a variety of forms. That is, when new technologies emerge, they are likely to do so in a confused and disorganized manner, in a flood of different product or service variants that embody different ideas about what consumers might really want and what might be possible to produce in an economic manner.

Eventually, the wave of entry subsides and is in turn followed by what is sometimes a sharp, sudden, and very sizeable shakeout that leads to the death of most of the early pioneers. The shakeout is associated with the emergence of a 'dominant design' in the market, an event that signals the beginning of growth in the industry.

The dominant design is a basic template or core product that defines what the product is, and what it does. It is a consensus good that commands the support of a wide range of early consumers (even if it is not their first preference); it is a product standard that sends signals to suppliers upstream, retailers downstream, and producers of complementary goods everywhere. Finally, it is a platform good that allows different manufacturers to offer differentiated versions of the product without destroying the consensus or requiring new complementary goods.

The importance of the emergence of a dominant design is that it is the decisive step in establishing a new market. It signals the emergence of a standard product that is capable of forming the basis of a mass market. For the many potential consumers who have yet to enter and make a choice, it signals the end of choice and, therefore, reduces their risks. A successful dominant design almost always triggers massive entry by consumers into the market, and ushers in the early heavy growth phase that most markets undergo.

The emergence of a dominant design is important for a second reason. The hundreds of early pioneers who entered the new market on the basis of different product designs die soon after the dominant design emerges. On the other hand, the champion whose product forms the basis of the dominant design often develops substantial and very long-lived 'first mover' advantages from being the product champion. *Notice, however, that most of these so-called 'first movers' were not, in fact, the first into the market.* All of them were preceded by many, now forgotten, entrepreneurial start-ups whose work formed the foundation upon which these rather later entrants built. These 'first movers' were first only in the sense that they were the first to champion the particular product variant that became the dominant design. They were first when the market emerged (not when the product emerged), and this, of course, is why they ended up with most of the profits.

It is important to emphasize three points from this:

- first, note that very few of the original entrants (i.e. the pioneers) survive the consolidation of the market—most disappear, never to be heard of again;

- second, the consolidators who win in the end are almost never the first into the new market. Their success is based on *not* moving fast but on choosing the right time to move—and that is rarely first;

- third, the things that consolidators do—such as entering at the right time, standardizing the product, cutting prices, scaling up production, creating distribution networks, segmenting the market, spending huge amounts of money on advertising and marketing—are exactly the kinds of things that create what we (somewhat inaccurately) call 'first mover advantages.' By doing these things, consolidators create buyer loyalty, get pre-emptive control of scare assets, go down the learning curve, create brands and reputation, and enjoy economies of scale benefits—all of which give them the advantage versus potential new entrants. Thus, even though pioneers are chronologically first into the market, consolidators are the 'real' first movers—they are the first to the market that counts: the mass market!

The upshot of all this is that the companies that end up capturing and dominating the new-to-the-world markets are *almost never the ones that created these markets*: Mr Ford did not create the car market but the Ford company ended up capturing most of the value in that market in its first one hundred years of existence; Procter & Gamble did not create the market for disposable diapers but it is P&G that ended up harvesting most of the value out of the mass market for disposable diapers that blossomed in the last fifty years; and General Electric did not create the CAT scanner market, yet it was GE that made most of the money out of this market. It turns out that when it comes to new-to-the-world markets, this is more the norm than the exception. Given this fact, why would any company want to *create* a new market? Surely, the advice we should be giving companies is how to scale up and consolidate new markets, not how to create them.

What does all this Mean for Established Companies?

The innovation process that creates radical new markets cannot be replicated inside the modern corporation. In addition, established firms lack the basic science knowledge and entrepreneurial skills to succeed when it comes to radical innovations—those that create radically new markets. Nor do they have the necessary cultures, structures, and attitudes to be good pioneers in these markets.

It is for these reasons that that recent academic work has proposed an 'open-innovation' model for companies that want to create radical new technologies.[4] The idea is to find ways to access and exploit outside knowledge and research while liberating internal expertise for others' use.

But we'd like to propose another option for big established companies. This option is to recognize that the challenge of becoming a successful pioneer of radical and disruptive markets is too formidable for established firms. They should leave this task to 'the market'—the zillions of small, start-up firms around the world that have the requisite skills and attitudes to succeed at this game. Established firms should, instead, concentrate on what they are good at—which is to consolidate young markets into big mass markets. After all, big firms have established one thing in their history: they are good at consolidating new markets. And being a consolidator has given them access to 'first mover' advantages—advantages that the vast majority of pioneers never got close to realizing.

215

Develop your Options

Practically what this means is that instead of spending valuable resources and managerial talent on growing new disruptive businesses inside, established companies should aim to create, sustain, and nurture a network of feeder firms—of young, entrepreneurial firms which are busy colonizing new niches. Through its business development function, the established company could serve as a venture capitalist to these feeder firms. Then, when it is time to consolidate the market, it could build a new mass-market business on the platform that these feeder firms have provided.

A similar point has also been made in a slightly different context by Meyer and Ruggles. Building on their consulting experiences, they argue that:

it does seem that some companies, and some people, are better at reconnaissance [the scouting out of new market opportunities and technological possibilities] than others. They pan for gold in the same streams as many before them but come back with the nuggets no one else spotted. So shouldn't we study those experts closely to find out how they do it—and then codify their secrets into a replicable process that we can impose on our own organisations? We used to think so . . . But increasingly, our attitude is shifting. We now warn companies, 'Don't try this at home.' Like many activities that involve talent and tacit learning, reconnaissance requires an inherent feel for the work and lots of practice. Not many companies can claim that inherent strength; nor can they devote much time to practicing, given that their day-to-day work is exploitation, not exploration.[5]

Such a specialization of labor already exists in creative industries such as the theater, movies, book publishing, and the visual and performing arts. According to Caves, firms in creative industries are either small-scale pickers that concentrate on the selection and development of new creative talents or large-scale promoters that undertake the packaging and widespread distribution of established creative goods.[6] Similarly, Meyer and Ruggles argue that a small but rapidly growing industry has emerged, made up of companies whose specialty is exploration.[7] Mature firms are increasingly outsourcing their exploration needs to these firms, choosing to focus their attention on growing the ideas into mass markets. Finally, Quinn points out that strategically 'outsourcing' innovation is now an accepted practice in a number of industries including pharmaceuticals, financial services, computers, telecommunications, and energy systems.[8]

Such a 'network' strategy has several advantages over the 'grow it inside' strategy: it allows the firm to cover more technologies and more market niches; it enables the feeder firms to compete with each other while allowing the parent company to benchmark one against the other—something very important in new technology areas; it is easier to manage because it bypasses all the problems of trying to manage two conflicting businesses simultaneously; and it has all the traditional benefits of outsourcing.

Therefore, the right way forward for established, mature firms is *not* to build their own new business inside and then consolidate it when the time is right. Rather, they should maintain and manage a feeder system of colonizer businesses—very much what pharmaceutical companies are doing with biotech and what Unilever is doing with new consumer products. Then, when the time is right, they should move in for consolidation and scaling up. This is the area where the mature corporation has unique advantages over the start-up firms. This, therefore, is the area where it should focus its attention.

We are aware that this cuts against the grain of much of the thinking of the last few years, which aimed to make established corporations 'more entrepreneurial' by developing the cultures and structures of the younger, start-up firms. In our view, this is misplaced advice. It's like advising a 70-year-old man how to train to win at the next Olympics—it simply won't happen! What the mature market leaders ought to focus on is gaining access to the ideas generated by the start-up firms and then scaling them up to create mass markets. It seems to us that by trying to be ambidextrous, established companies risk being 'stuck in the middle.' What they need to do is focus on the area where they have an advantage—and that is on consolidating good new ideas drawn from niche markets into new and valuable mass markets.

Appendix 11.1: The Innovation Process that Brought us the Internet

Possibly the most prominent new markets that are currently coming into being are those based on the internet. These new markets owe their birth to a number of technologies that have been discovered in the past forty years, the combination of which has given rise to what we call 'the internet.' But how were the discoveries of the technologies underlying the internet made? Were they driven by clear customer demand and were they developed as a result of a master plan and a coordinated series of actions?

The origins of the internet lie in research on the development of computer networking in the early 1960s. Several strands of complementary work fed into the ultimate development of the internet but arguably the key ones were a series of generic research projects largely supported by the US Department of Defense (the DoD for short) which were motivated by a desire to economize on scarce computer resources. The DoD also supported key work on 'packet switching' using digital technology, research that tried to design reliable and efficient communications networks which would be less vulnerable to attack than centralized telecommunications networks.

Under the auspices of the Defense Advanced Research Projects Agency (DARPA for short), the first computer network—christened ARPANET—made its appearance in the late 1960s and grew quickly in the early 1970s. It was eventually replaced by NSFNET in 1990. Nowadays, numerous networks exist, ranging from very small ones linking one or two computers (called local area networks, or LANs for short) to networks of LANSs. What is—or became—the

Develop your Options

internet started out as a link between institutions. ARPANET initially connected three universities, a consulting firm, and a research institute. By the early 1980s, however, the number of host computers numbered in the hundreds, passing the 1,000 mark in mid-decade and swelling well past 100,000 in the late 1980s before exploding into several millions early in 1990 (the number of internet host sites worldwide rose from 8.2 m in 1995 to over 43 m in 1999).

It is, however, one thing to link computers by telephone lines (or whatever) and quite another to tell them how to communicate with each other when they have been linked up together. As a consequence, much of the interesting history of the internet is really a story about the development of software. There were, arguably, three major developments that turned the ARPANET network into the internet that we all currently know and use. Each of them fundamentally redefined the nature of the networks that were used at the time; each was also in the nature of a 'killer application', a piece of software designed for a particular purpose which rose above several competing alternatives to sweep the market. In a sense, each redefined the internet by introducing new uses or applications, and, at least partly as a consequence, bringing in many new users and suppliers.

By all accounts, the first big breakthrough came in 1973, when two DARPA engineers developed TCP/IP, a protocol that enabled different networks to connect with each other and exchange 'packets' of data. Although it was not the only protocol of this type developed at the time, it had the twin virtues of being free and very reliable. ARPANET switched over to TCP/IP in 1983 and by 1984, it was adopted (and actively sponsored) by the NSF (National Science Foundation) as the standard for its national university network. As a consequence, by the 1990s TCP/IP had become the dominant protocol for virtually all networking.

Many people who are deeply immersed in the technology regard TCP/IP as the glue which holds the internet together. However, most of the rest of us think of the internet as the 'World Wide Web', the catchy name given to the network which began to emerge following the development of the HTML and HTTP protocols at CERN in Switzerland in 1991. They facilitated the sending of graphics between computers and the creation of 'links' which directly take users to other HTML documents.

The web was first designed for the use of scientists, and the main obstacle to its widespread adoption by businesses and, ultimately, by people like you and me was that travelling on the web was not easy. To get onto the net, consumers need software that can search out, retrieve, and display HTML documents. Mosaic was the first internet browser that solved this problem, and created the potential for the internet to evolve beyond being just a toy for scientists to play with. It was developed in the early 1990s, but was rapidly overtaken by Netscape's browser a year or two later (which, in turn, was eclipsed by Microsoft's Internet Explorer in much disputed circumstances some years on). The development of search engines and a wide array of other software packages further enhanced the attractiveness of going on the net, and contributed to the surge in uptake which occurred in the late 1990s, a mere twenty-five or thirty years after the first network was constructed.

There are a number of markets associated with the advent of the internet: markets for particular types of hardware or software, markets for access to the internet, and, of course, markets which are conducted on the internet. More broadly, the basic digital technology underlying the development of the internet has brought other new markets into being (mobile phones, digital television, and so on), and seems to have induced a convergence across formerly independent sectors like computing, telecommunications, and entertainment.

The development of the technologies underlying the internet seems to have opened up numerous new markets, creating many commercial possibilities which various e-entrepreneurs have been quick to take advantage of. In fact, much of the public perception of the net has less to do with the net itself than with the fuss created by the efforts of everyone—consumers and all sorts of producers alike—to clamber onto it.

Making sense of all of this is not easy. For our purposes, the technical development of the net is somewhat less interesting than the business development of the net. But it is important to note three points here: first, it is the discovery of the various technologies underlying what we call 'the internet' that has led to the creation of a number of new markets, such as markets for particular types of hardware or software, markets for access to the internet, and, of course, markets which are conducted on the internet.

Second, the technologies associated with the internet, both hardware and software, were developed in a haphazard way without a clear customer need driving them: no one involved with the technology in the early days had any idea that things would end up where they are today, no one had a master plan that linked the development of new client–server relations between users and mainframe computers to the possibility of booking a hotel room by computer from a mobile phone. This apparently unplanned, unsystematic development of the underlying technology seems to have largely been a consequence of how the work was done, and by whom (mainly scientists and engineers in research institutes and universities in this case). Even the major early user, the US Department of Defense, took a remarkably hands-off attitude towards the research work sponsored by DARPA, rarely insisting that it be linked explicitly to defense needs and giving it a blue skies mandate.

Finally, it is worth noting that the basic technologies underlying the internet emerged from a group of individuals who were both users and producers who devised these technologies for their own uses. It took quite some time, however, for the technology to be adapted for the wider needs of a general market, and it took quite some time for that general market to emerge (i.e. more than fifty years). When it did emerge, however, it seems to have taken off extremely rapidly. The path that formally brought the internet into our homes is littered with the corpses of promising start-up firms too numerous to count and the relics of almost as many now forgotten would-be killer applications.

Notes

The ideas in this chapter have been developed jointly with my late colleague Professor Paul Geroski and are presented in more depth in our book *Fast Second: How Smart Companies Bypass Radical Innovation to Enter and Dominate New Markets*. San Francisco: Jossey-Bass, 2005.

1. There is a second reason why big established firms cannot create radical new markets: they do not have the skills and attitudes necessary for creating such markets. Worse, they cannot simply adopt the necessary skills and mindsets because they conflict with their existing skills and attitudes. We explored this reason in more detail in C. Markides and P. Geroski (2003) 'Teaching Elephants How to Dance and Other Silly Ideas,' *Business Strategy Review*, Autumn, 14 (3): 47–51.

Develop your Options

2. National Research Council, Computer Science and Telecommunications Board (1999) *Funding a Revolution: Government Support for Computing Research.* Washington, DC: National Academy Press.
3. Markides and Geroski, 'Teaching Elephants How to Dance and Other Silly Ideas;' C. Markides and P. Geroski (2003) 'Colonizers and Consolidators: The Two Cultures of Corporate Strategy,' *Strategy + Business,* 32 (Fall): 46–55.
4. Henry Chesbrough (2003) *Open Innovation.* Boston: HBS Press; Andrew Hargadon (2003) *How Breakthroughs Happen.* Boston: HBS Press.
5. Christopher Meyer and Rudy Ruggles (2002) 'Search Parties,' *Harvard Business Review,* Aug.: 14–15.
6. Richard Caves (2002) *Creative Industries: Contracts between Art and Commerce.* Cambridge, Mass.: Harvard University Press.
7. Meyer and Ruggles, 'Search Parties.'
8. James Brian Quinn (2000) 'Outsourcing Innovation: The New Engine of Growth,' *Sloan Management Review,* Summer, 41 (4).

Part III

Lead the Change

12   Leading in the Knowledge Economy

Rob Goffee and Gareth Jones

Highly talented people who are able to create disproportionate amounts of value from organizational resources are increasingly important. How you lead these 'clever' people is one of the keys to succeeding in the knowledge economy.

Sir Martin Sorrell, chief executive of the world's largest communications services company, WPP, is as forthright as he is imposingly well briefed. 'The only reason for this company to exist,' Sorrell told us matter-of-factly when we talked at WPP's London headquarters, 'is to leverage economies of knowledge.' He paused, before adding: 'One of the biggest challenges is that there are diseconomies of scale in creative industries. If you double the number of creative people, it doesn't mean you will be twice as creative.'

Leveraging economies of knowledge is also high on the agenda of Franz Humer, chief executive and chairman of the Swiss-based pharmaceuticals giant Roche, which employs 68,000 people worldwide and sells its products in 150 countries. WPP's 70 operating companies employ 65,000 people in 950 offices in 92 countries. Humer and Sorrell are poles apart, in terms of their industries, styles, and personalities. Yet, their comments to us echoed uncannily. 'In my business of research, economies of scale don't exist. Globally today we spend $4 billion on R&D every year. But I could spend $9 billion and my research wouldn't necessarily be any better: it could even be worse. I could spend $2 billion, but I don't know which two billion to take out. In research there aren't economies of scale, there are economies of ideas,' observed Humer.

We have spent the last twenty years researching the issue of leadership; in particular, what followers want from their leaders. We have interviewed hundreds of leaders all over the world and many of their followers. Of the people we have spoken to, many work for leading players in the knowledge economy—organizations like WPP, Roche, PwC, Electronic Arts, Cisco Systems, Crédit Suisse, Novartis, KPMG, and the British Broadcasting Corporation (BBC). Their observations were as fascinating as they were challenging. The more we talked to them, the more we became intrigued by what leadership means in these sorts of organizations and the challenges it poses for those, like

Lead the Change

Martin Sorrell, Franz Humer, and indeed thousands of their colleagues all over such organizations, who may aspire to and provide leadership.

Our interviews have been wide ranging. We have covered the leadership of individuals whose peculiar skills and knowledge make them vital to organizational success. Equally intriguing has been our exploration of the dynamics of high-performance teams in knowledge-based businesses. Finally, we have been concerned to elucidate the impact of leadership on the creation of organizational cultures which nurture and promote intellectual capital. As always we have been concerned to explore the relational aspects of leadership. We have counted the followers' observations as at least as important as those of the leaders.

The rise of the knowledge economy has been written about extensively, of course. The business world, most experts agree, is undergoing a transformation from a mass production system where the principal source of value was human labour to a new era where the principal component of value creation, productivity, and economic growth is knowledge. The scale of that transformation is now becoming apparent. Baruch Lev, an accounting professor at New York University, has calculated that intangible assets—ranging from patents and know-how to a skilled workforce—now account for more than half of the total market capitalization of public US companies.

The consulting firm McKinsey & Company has divided American jobs into three categories: 'transformational' (extracting raw materials or converting them into finished goods); 'transactional' (interactions that can be easily scripted or automated); and 'tacit' (complex interactions requiring a high level of judgement). In the last six years, the number of tacit jobs has grown two and half times as fast as the number of transactional jobs and three times as fast as employment in general. Tacit jobs now account for some 40 per cent of the US labor market—and 70 per cent of the jobs created since 1998. A similar process is under way in other countries around the world.

There are two clear implications of this change. The first is that intellectual capital—everything from patents and trademarks to software and ideas—has become a key source of value. The second is an increasing dependence within the organization on the people who generate that intellectual capital. We call them 'clever people;' and they operate in the clever economy.

What both Sorrell and Humer are grappling with on a daily basis is a challenge that is central to economic and social progress in the twenty-first century: How do you corral a group of extremely smart and highly creative individuals into an organization, and then inspire them not only to achieve their fullest potential as individuals, but to do so in a way that creates wealth and value for all your stakeholders—customers, shareholders, and the wider community? In short: how do you lead clever people?

Who are 'Clever People'?

The first and most obvious point to make is that clever people are not simply those with the highest IQ or the most impressive academic qualifications (although many of them do score highly on these two measures). Clever people are highly talented individuals with the potential to create disproportionate amounts of value from the resources that the organization makes available to them. Precisely what they do, of course, depends on the context (as we briefly discuss below). In pharmaceutical companies they carry out scientific research and produce ideas for new drugs; in professional services firms they solve complex client problems; in ad agencies they understand customers, brand values, and craft highly innovative communications that connect the two. Typically they are a scarce and valuable resource able to bring creativity, innovation, and complex problem-solving skills to all they do.

There is a continuum between individuals who can create value more or less alone, to those dependent on teams, and yet others who need the complex support systems of large organizations. For example, there are many highly talented individuals who are capable of producing remarkable results on their own—that is to say outside of an organization. These stand-alone clever people include artists, musicians, and other free agents. However, even talented musicians need others to play with—and if they are

Box 12.1 Cleverness in Context

We have argued that cleverness is not simply an innate property; it has to be understood in context. There are two broad ways of conceptualizing organizational context—through an examination of structure and culture.

For example, contrast the structure of a large accounting firm with its emphasis on certification as a prerequisite for practicing, and an advertising agency, where the power or originality of ideas on their own may give you a voice. The former is likely to have protocols and more or less systemized definitions of quality. In the latter there will be more improvisation and the production of 'crafted,' unique, solutions. It would be hard to lead in the law firm or accounting practice without demonstrating certification in the core competence. Or, more precisely, such shared competence forms a platform on which leadership assets can be built.

In the advertising agency or the TV company you could lead where your key skills are complementary. For example, the leader might handle the commercial relationships with clients, while the ad men write great copy.

Culturally, it is clearly different to be clever in driven, almost ideological organizations (Genentech, Google, Cisco) by comparison to organizations which cherish individual excellence. A famous business school which we studied produced this illuminating comment; 'I love working here. I go to work to be alone.'

In the former, cultivating long-term teamwork and inculcating deep adherence to core organizational values will be key leadership challenges. In the latter, the key challenge is creating space to promote individual excellence. In cultures like this leadership is sometimes described as akin to 'herding cats.'

classical musicians they need whole orchestras and the support systems which enable them to play. In this article our emphasis is on talented individuals who need an organizational context in order to achieve their full potential. Think, for example, of a research scientist working on a new cancer drug. He or she cannot work effectively without research funding and facilities such as a laboratory. Or, think of an advertising executive who needs the resources to make and broadcast a TV commercial or, increasingly, create an online marketing campaign.

The clever people we are talking about require a symbiotic relationship with an organization. They may not always realize this fact, or be especially pleased about it, but it is true nonetheless. Herein lies a paradox that is at the heart of leading clever people (more about this later).

The challenge for leaders such as Sorrell and Humer is to be the organization of choice for these people. Fail to do so and you encourage them to walk into the open arms of your competitors.

The starting point if you are to effectively lead clever people is to better understand their key characteristics. Not every clever person has all of the following characteristics. As we shall show later, cleverness must always be contextualized. However, our research suggests that the key attributes of clever people are:

- Their skills are not easily replicated. If they were, then they would not be the scarce resource they are. In a sense, they are closer to the craft skills of the medieval period than they are to the standardized skills which characterized the Industrial Revolution. And just like the medieval craft worker who was motivated to do great work, their relationship with their organizations is equally fragile.

- Their knowledge is tacit (by this we mean that it is embedded in them and in their networks). If it was possible to capture their knowledge within the organizational fabric, then all that would be required would be better knowledge management systems. It isn't. (In fact, one of the great disappointments of knowledge management initiatives to date is their failure to capture clever knowledge.) It is useful to distinguish what they know, how they came to know it, and with whom they share it: a set of distinctions captured in the contemporary reference to intellectual and social capital.

- They are smart enough to be in the right place—and they know it. They will find the organizational context where their interests will be most generously funded. When the funding dries up, they have several options. They can move on to somewhere where resources are plentiful. Others dig in and may engage in elaborate organizational politics to ensure that their own pet projects are indulged.

- Unlike some who are driven to reach the top, they may not be hierarchically aspirational (indeed, many are resistant to the notion) but they are often organizationally savvy because they are so driven by their own obsessions. This also means they are likely to be motivated by factors other than money and power. Typically, they are driven by highly specialist interests and knowledge. This can range from the Nobel Prize-winning research scientist to the music producer recording classical music on original instruments.

- They challenge the status quo and therefore are often sources of creativity in organizations. This can make them uncomfortable if they feel as if they are in a subordinate role. It can also make them difficult to lead. And yet it may be worth the effort—from both sides. For the clever pharmaceutical researcher who together with the team discovers a new drug can potentially bankroll the entire organization for a decade.

- They are well connected to other clever people. In other words, they are plugged into highly developed knowledge networks—who they know is often as important as what they know. We can distinguish between the extent to which they develop their sense of identity from organizational membership or from their wider occupational connections. It is this which explains the centrality of networks to clever people. It's not just the cognitive benefits that they gain from networking, it's that they construct their sense of self from the feedback generated by these extra organizational connections.

But beyond these characteristics, the way to identify clever people is this: *typically, they say they do not want to be led nor to lead others.* This is the central paradox we referred to earlier. But in our experience, neither of their assertions is really true. They do want to be led—indeed they require leadership if they are to achieve their full potential—and they have the ability and motivation to lead others. But in both cases it is a special sort of leadership.

Typically, the clever people we have observed vocalize a disdain for the language of hierarchy and organization because their identity derives from their expertise not their position. It is not uncommon, for example, for clever people to be completely indifferent towards organizational titles. Leaders who seek to use such titles or hierarchical promotion to motivate them are likely to be met with cold disdain. Yet the same clever individual may care fiercely that their status within their profession is acknowledged. They will be totally unmoved by promotion to Vice President of Research, but insist on being called Doctor or Professor. Or consider the case of journalists or TV program makers—they wish to cling to their craft skills: writing articles and producing beautiful programs. Try to promote them to editor or head of drama and they will display a strong desire to stay close to the 'real work.'

We were told this delightful and revealing story by the chairman of a major news organization. It concerns the observed behavior of a globally famous news journalist—an exemplar of the very clever, rather skceptical journalists who drive the news business. He will always give you to understand that he is deeply suspicious of everything the 'suits' are up to and really doesn't understand why they don't just help in the newsroom rather than lounging around in board-rooms. But the reality is rather different—he is astute about the way the company is being led and the strategic direction it is taking. While publicly expressing disdain for the business side of his organization, he privately asks penetrating questions about relationships with important customers and growth prospects. He is also an outspoken champion of the organization when outside it with politicians, other media colleagues, and with customers. You cannot sit him down in a strategy meeting with a sixty-slide Powerpoint presentation but you would be wise to keep him informed of key developments in the business.

Even at large professional services firms like PwC and KPMG those pro-moted into management positions will seek to sustain their presence with key clients in the market. The point to realize is that they are part of a professional community that bears no resemblance to the internal organizational chart. It is this external community and not their job title that confers status.

Because they are passionate about their knowledge and their professional community clever people need organizations to deliver their desired outcomes. The brilliant software engineer requires time and money to produce a new program; the TV documentary maker requires resources to make their award-winning film; the research scientist requires lab facilities to develop a new drug; the investment banker requires financial backing to negotiate the merger deal. All require external resources and recognition to validate their work.

The Challenge of Leading 'Clevers'

Based on our observations, we believe that the growing importance of clever people in the knowledge economy poses a huge challenge for companies. Our research suggests that leading clever people requires a very different style of leadership from that traditionally seen in many organizations. In our experi-ence, getting the best from clever people requires many of the traditional leadership virtues, such as excellent communications skills and authenticity. But it also requires leaders to demonstrate some additional qualities. To lead clever people effectively, you have to do the following.

Acknowledge the Diversity of their Knowledge

Clever people have a distinctive and valuable knowledge base of their own. They see themselves as not dependent on others. The leader must, therefore, start by acknowledging their independence and difference. If leaders do not do this, they fail at the first base. But, and it is an important caveat, the leader's job is to make them understand their interdependence. For example, most innovation requires complex and high-performance teams—this is as true in investment banking as it is in pharmaceuticals. Recognizing the symbiotic nature of the relationship is critical to both the individual and the organization.

Integral to this is recognizing the diversity of intellect. Clever people need the freedom to pursue their hunches—and not all their hunches will be right. This is the leadership equivalent of the strategic maxim: make more than one big bet. Consider the San Francisco-based biotechnology company Genentech. The company has had a stellar performance in recent years, outperforming many of the so-called Big Pharma companies. Helped by blockbuster products such as Avastin, a drug used to treat colorectal cancer, Genentech's stock price doubled in 2005. At one point in December 2005, Genentech's market capitalization was $102 billion, making it the 20th most valuable company in the United States. The company has also won plaudits for its distinctive culture and ability to attract the brightest research scientists in the world. In 2006 it topped *Fortune* magazine's annual ranking of the *Best Company to Work For*. What is less well known, however, is that Roche has a controlling stake in Genentech, and at one point owned the biotech star outright.

As Franz Humer explains: 'Roche owns 57 per cent of Genentech. There was a time when we owned 100 per cent, but I insisted on selling 40 per cent on the stock market. Why? Because I wanted to preserve its different culture. In research there aren't economies of scale, there are economies of ideas. And I believe in diversity of ideas diversity of culture; diversity of origin; diversity of behaviour; and diversity of view.'

If he had one global director of research, Humer explains, then he would have one clever person placing all the research bets for Roche and Genentech. But by diluting Roche's ownership, Genentech retains its research autonomy. Roche also owns 51 per cent of a Japanese company, Chugai; again, Humer insists that the Chugai research director decides on his research programs, and Roche makes its own decisions. The three companies place different bets.

My people in the Roche research organization decide on what they think is right and wrong. I hear debates where the Genentech researchers says this program you're running will never lead to a product. You are on the wrong target. This is the wrong chemical structure—it will prove to be toxic. And my guys say no, we don't think so. And the two views never meet. So I say to Genentech: you do what you want and we will do what we want at Roche and in five years' time we will know. Sometimes you will be right and sometimes we will be right.

That diversity of culture, and thinking and of leadership, is the most challenging task I have, because there are always pressures within a large organization to unify and to direct from above. If we exceed our research budget, the people at Roche say you should acquire 100 per cent of Genentech and then we could stick to the budget. And by the way they wouldn't need their own investor relations and we could cut down on this and that and the other. And I say, yes but we would also cut down on our future.

Humer recognizes that neither he nor anyone else has a monopoly on wisdom. The successful organization in the clever economy is predicated on diversity. In the mass production economy it was predicated on sameness.

Exhibit Competence

Clever people do not expect that their leader's knowledge should match their own. But they do expect that the leader is clearly and demonstrably an expert in their own field. Sometimes the knowledge is in a similar or related field of expertise; other times it is completely distinctive. The economist Laura Tyson served in the Clinton administration and has since led London Business School as its dean. 'You must help clever people realize that their cleverness doesn't mean they can do other things. They may overestimate their cleverness in other areas so you must show that you are competent to help them.'

Surprising juxtapositions of knowledge are often the most powerful. Sir Martin Sorrell, for example, is an accountant in a creative world. In WPP, he runs an organization full of creative talent. 'I am seen as the boring, workaholic accountant and as a micro-manager,' he willingly concedes. 'But I take it as a compliment rather than an insult. Involvement is important. You've got to know what's going on.' Anyone receiving a visit from Sorrell can expect some tough, one-to-one questioning—on the numbers as well as the creative side of the business. Sorrell's difference reminds people that, central though creativity is, WPP is a creative *business*.

Talking to Sorrell's colleagues, the other thing they note is his permanent state of dissatisfaction. He is justifiably proud of WPP's success, but constantly reminds people that 'there's an awful long way to go.'

Sorrell's skills and approach are what WPP needs. His expertise in bottom-line business nitty-gritty complements the clever creatives who are the cornerstone of WPP's success.

Consider another example. The former marketing director of a leading British beer brewer was a man called Tom Nelson. Although he was not an expert on traditional brewing techniques or real ales, he was known throughout the organization as 'Numbers Nelson' for his grasp of the firm's marketing performance. His fame was based on an almost uncanny ability to quote how many barrels of the company's beer were sold the day before in a given part of the country. Nelson's mastery of the firm's sales was both acknowledged and respected. He was not a brewing man, but he was demonstrably a marketing man. This was enough to establish legitimacy even though the knowledge base was rather different.

Contrast Michael Critelli, the CEO of Stamford, Connecticut-based Pitney Bowes. The company, which is best known for making postage meters, holds many patents based on the research and development it carries out in new technology. The careful management of its intellectual property is important to the company's future. Critelli, a former lawyer, holds a number of patents in his own name. This gives him credibility with his clever people.

Also using a similar knowledge base when he was chairman of GlaxoSmithKline, Richard Sykes, a talented scientist, insisted on being called Dr Sykes. The title gave him respect within the professional community that his clever people belonged to in a way that being the chairman of a major multinational pharmaceuticals company did not.

However, a leader who demonstrates technical knowledge in the same area as the clevers can run the risk of getting it wrong. The former England national soccer coach Glenn Hoddle asked his star player David Beckham to practice a particular maneuver. When Beckham couldn't do it, Hoddle—once a brilliant player himself—said, 'Here, I'll show you how.' He performed the maneuver flawlessly, but in that moment he lost the team. The other players saw it as a public humiliation of Beckham. Hoddle was subsequently named 'chocolate' by his players because they believed that he thought of himself as 'good enough to eat.'

Win Resources and Give them Space

Clever people want and need lots of resources; they are expensive to support. They need labs, libraries, equipment, training grounds, etc. You could argue that all your staff want you to win resources for them. What's peculiar about clever people is that they perceive their own work to be so important that it must always be well resourced. They are prone to obsession and it is from their obsessions that organizations can generate the most value. It is this characteristic which can make them extremely difficult to lead, for if you are unable to win the requisite resources they come to believe that they cannot succeed in your organization. The final irony is that having won the resources they require, they will then ask you to leave them alone.

The Virgin Group is famed for creating entrepreneurial space to let clever people just get on with it. Head office is very small and the default mode is to let talent try things—as long as some clear financial limits are understood. There is even clearer recognition that if you encourage the 'clevers' to pursue their obsessions you must absolutely not assume that everything will work.

For example, Google, the eponymous creator of the world's favorite search engine, prides itself on letting its people do their own thing. The Mountain View, California-based technology company is the most recent example of tradition that originated in organizations like 3 M and Lockheed—which allowed employees to pursue their own pet projects in the firm's time. Reflecting the entrepreneurial spirit of founders Sergey Brin and Larry Page, everyone who works at the company can spend one day per week on their own initiatives. Known as '20 per cent time,' staff can spend one day a week on start-up ideas within Google, also known as Googlettes. (Genentech has a similar policy.) The kind of innovation speed this generates puts large bureaucratic organizations to shame. The Google-affiliated social networking website Orkut is just one example of a business project that started out life as a Googlette.

Google is great place to work to start with. At the Googleplex, Google's headquarters in California, there is the massage center, free valet parking, a hair salon, the roller hockey games in the car park, and a concierge service. But, better still for the clevers, Google has a very democratic approach to innovation. Anyone can pitch in with ideas. The company has a number of active email lists, one just for ideas. Ideas are collected and prioritized on Google's idea equivalent of the pop charts—the Google Top 100.

But the clever economy is not the sole preserve of the young—far from it, in fact. At Crédit Suisse's private banking arm, for example, the complex relationships nurtured over time with high net worth clients are very rarely the prerogative of young executives. On the contrary, in order to be given the space to explore and discover the sophisticated solutions they require the organization looks for experience and depth.

Nor are clevers always easy to spot. Some media organizations which like to think of themselves as innovative and creative betray distinctly conservative approaches to the way clever people are led. They divide people into clever creatives or merely administrative support staff. Not surprisingly, they never liberate the full intellectual potential of their people.

BBH (Bartle Bogel and Hegarty) doesn't make this mistake. It has for long been regarded as one of the most creative ad agencies in the world. It now has offices in New York, São Paulo, Singapore, Tokyo, Shanghai, and London. And yet at the heart of its corporate culture is the maxim—respect ideas wherever they come from. Many of its most successful executives started as assistants but they were still given the space to grow and express their cleverness.

Be an Umbrella

Clever people see the administrative machinery of the organization as a distraction from their key value-adding activities. So they need to be protected from the organizational 'rain.' If the leader gets this right, they establish exactly the right kind of relationship with the clever people—demonstrating the ability to facilitate performance in inevitably political contexts. In an academic environment this is the dean freeing the star professor from the burden of departmental administration; at a newspaper this is the editor allowing the investigative reporter to skip editorial meetings; in a multinational fast-moving consumer goods company it is the leader filtering requests for information from head office so that transformational marketing can take place. The pharmaceutical industry is full of such examples, since not every drug can go into full development and there are inevitable organizational politics around the key decisions. The most effective leaders in this context radiate rapport with the clever people while managing organizational realities.

At Genentech, for example, CEO Art Levinson, a talented scientist in his own right, is fiercely protective of his clevers. When Avastin failed in early clinical trials in 2002, Genentech's share price dropped by 10 per cent overnight. Faced with that kind of pressure, some leaders would have pulled the plug on Avastin, but not Levinson. Instead, he and his senior managers knew the science well enough to know that their clevers were close to a breakthrough. Levinson protected them from the rain. Avastin was eventually approved in February 2004 and in the first three-quarters of 2005 had sales of $774 million.

And standing four square behind Levinson is Roche CEO Franz Humer. Leadership of clever people, Humer acknowledges, is especially difficult in hard times. 'You can look at Genentech now and say what a great company,' says Humer, 'but for ten years Genentech had no new products and spent between $500 and $800 million on research every year. In those bad times, the pressure on me to close it down or change the culture was enormous. As the leader you have to believe in your convictions at times like that. I believe in diversity. And as long as I run this company that will be the basis on which it is built.'

Think back also to the discovery of DNA. Crick, Watson, and their colleagues spent ten years producing no results of any substance. Yet, their leaders believed in their abilities and stoutly defended them from harsh funding realities. They batted away intrusive enquiries from the university bureaucracy. In truth they may even have created the impression that more progress was being made than was really the case. They backed their judgement. The result was one of the most significant scientific breakthroughs of the twentieth century.

Encourage Failure

Any organization that strives for high levels of innovation and creativity— exactly the area where clever people make a big difference—must recognize the necessity for failure. In pushing the frontiers of knowledge, clever people live on the perennial edge of failure. Better that than mediocrity or passive acceptance of the status quo. Not all innovations can work. For every successful new pharmaceutical product, there are dozens of failures, for every hit record, hundreds of duds. The leader of clever people must recognize this, acknowledge it with the followers, but at the same time, distinguish between the inevitability of failure associated with innovation and straightforward error. The former may even require celebration while the latter stimulates a whole range of coaching, feedback, even confrontation techniques more normally associated with performance management.

Consider another pharmaceuticals example, involving GlaxoSmithKline. When three high-tech antibiotics in the final stages of clinical trials all failed, Richard Sykes responded by sending letters of congratulations to the team leaders thanking them for killing the drugs and encouraging them to move on to the next challenge. This is inspired leadership of clever people. (Gore (Goretex) people celebrate when they stop work on a failed project.)

Another great example is Diageo's development of the alcoholic drink brand Smirnoff Ice. Detailed analysis of customer data indicated a potential gap in the market for an alcoholic beverage with particular appeal to the younger market. Diageo experimented with many potential products—beginning with the more predictable combinations: rum and coke, rum and blackcurrant, gin and tonic, vodka and fruit juice. None of them seemed to work. At the eleventh attempt they tried a riskier combination: vodka and lemonade; and Smirnoff Ice was born. It is a product that has fundamentally changed its market sector.

Similarly, consider the magisterial Italian tenor Luciano Pavarotti. He was signed by the record label Decca who recognized his extraordinary talent and charisma. But it took more than ten years for Pavarotti's work to command wide public recognition—at least among the record-buying public. He could easily have been written off as a recording failure. Decca recorded him singing with pop stars like Zuchero, Andrea Bocelli, and Jovanotti—all aimed at bringing him to a wider market. In the end, he became Decca's major revenue earner. This enabled Decca to continue experimenting with new kinds of music and to launch the famed *Entartete Musik* series of music banned by the Nazis.

Give Direction: Motivation is Not an Issue

One of the key characteristics of the clever people who inhabit our organizations is that they are frequently driven—often around their own goals and not those of the organization. The key leadership challenge therefore becomes not the traditional one of motivating employees but rather of making sure your clever people are roughly aligned in their aims.

As Martin Sorrell says: 'The critical issue at WPP is getting the 65,000 people who work for the company to face in the same direction. If we can do that then there is no limit to what we can achieve together.'

How does a leader do that with clevers? 'I have learned that if you want them to turn right, then you have to tell them to turn left,' says Sorrell; 'they are always looking to prove you wrong.'

As Sorrell's comments suggest, 100 per cent alignment is impossible. What the leader must provide, however, is coherent shared meaning. This is the organizational glue which makes the task of leading clever people just that little bit easier. Whatever you are in business to achieve it is vital that it is both clearly communicated to the clevers and also that it is worthy of their talents. Google's motto is: 'Do no evil.' Genentech's slogan is: 'In business for life.' These are highly meaningful to the clever people within the two companies.

At BBH the obsession is with the quality of their creative work itself—the capacity to generate marketing communications which can transform whole consumer categories, like their path-breaking Audi and Levi's commercials. The last two years have simply been called 'The Year of the Work.' As you walk the floors of their central London office you can smell that motivation is not an issue.

Of course, creating meaning is relatively easy if you are producing life-saving drugs, or society-changing new technology, but what about less racy industries such as insurance or banking? In our experience, great leaders can find the meaning and significance in every business. Insurance companies are in the business of making our lives safer—and reducing the risk. They help you get your car repaired after it is vandalized, or get your roof fixed in time for Christmas. Banks help us buy a house, and put our kids through college. Our observation of successful leaders in the clever economy is that they excel at finding and communicating an overarching sense of meaning to the clever people on whom their success rests.

Recruit Clevers

Clever people require a peer group of like-minded individuals. This means that leaders must be highly selective about who they recruit. Universities have long understood this. Hire a star professor and you can be sure the young aspiring Ph.D.s in that subject will flock to your institution. They want to work with and be inspired by someone they admire.

The same magnet effect works in creative industries. In January 2007 when the Russian conductor Valery Gergiev took over from Sir Colin Davis as the principal conductor of the London Symphony Orchestra, leading musicians beat a path to his door. Or think about the transformational recording of *The Three Tenors*—Dominguez, Pavarotti, and Carreras. This brought classical music to a new mass audience. Of course these operatic greats were attracted to working with each other, but an equally powerful element was that none of them would have wanted to be excluded.

The same applies in business. In the investment banking world, everyone watches where the cleverest choose to work. Goldman Sachs for example cherishes its reputation as the home of the brightest and best. Those who seek to overtake them must position themselves as places where cleverness thrives. At Microsoft, Bill Gates has always sought out the cleverest software programmers. From the start, Gates insisted that the company required the very best minds. Microsoft calls them 'high IQ people,' and has always understood that they act as a magnet for other clever people. On occasions, Gates intervened personally in the recruitment process. Say, for example, a particularly talented programmer needs a little additional persuasion to join the company, he or she receives a personal call from Gates. Very flattering—and effective.

Exactly the same techniques are used by Art Levinson, the charismatic CEO of Genentech. Genentech also goes further to ensure it attracts people who fit the company's clever profile. Before it hires clever people, it screens them to ensure that money and organizational status are not their primary motivations. Landing a job can involve five or six visits to the firm. If a candidate asks too many questions about salary, job title, and personal career advancement, they will be shown the door. However, remember—clever people can learn to play clever games! The point is to distinguish between a learnt script and authentic motives.

Listen to the Silences

The legendary jazz pianist Bill Evans played with some of the greatest musicians of the twentieth century including Miles Davis, John Coltrane, and Cannonball Adderley. Evans steadfastly refused to look at the keys as he played. He explained this puzzling behavior by saying that it enabled him to concentrate on listening to the others. Rather more cryptically Thelonious Monk remarked, 'Don't listen to the notes I play, listen to the ones I don't.'

For a non-specialist to accurately gauge the context in an environment populated by clever people requires highly acute situation-sensing skills—that is, the ability to judge morale, commitment, and individual motivation in an area where the leader's knowledge base is already stretched. One highly effective way of overcoming the intrinsic difficulties of this situation is to identify and relate to an informed insider from within the phalanx of clever people: someone willing to communicate the issues directly with you.

This is especially true for newly recruited leaders. Parachuting in at the top and accurately reading an organization is difficult. In the early stages leaders need interpreters to make sense of the silences. One leader we spoke to admitted that initially he found the quarterly meetings with R&D baffling. Some of the projects under discussion that seemed to be going nowhere were allowed to continue. The new leader could not understand what criteria were being used to make decisions. It took an insider—someone who had worked in R&D for years—to privately explain the subtle nuances.

'They helped me to read between the lines, to read the silences, and the winks and nudges,' he explains. 'This individual understood how the clevers worked and although he was frustrated by it, he knew how to get things done—and was prepared to act as my interpreter: to explain how he had achieved it. I learnt a lot from him.' We should be clear the leader is not looking for a sycophant, it's much more like the anthropologist seeking a well-placed insider who is both able to interpret the culture and sympathetic to those who seek to understand it.

Be Accessible

Effective leaders of clever people are relentlessly listening to their needs. They have to. 'The ideas of clever people are so present to them that they cannot understand why they may not be present to you—now!' reflected one leader we interviewed.

Martin Sorrell's rapid response to emails is legendary within WPP. His message is clear: I am available. You are important. As he told us: 'If someone contacts you, there's a reason. It's got nothing to do with the hierarchy. It doesn't matter if they're not a big person. There's nothing more frustrating than a voicemail and then nothing back. We're in a service business.'

David Gardner, former European CEO of the computer games company Electronic Arts (EA), made a point of regular visits to each of the EA European offices, listening to as many people as he could—all over and beyond the organization: the sales force, office staff, engineers, and customers. He deliberately avoided being captured by the local senior executives.

Recognition from Outside

It is of course a standard piece of advice for leaders to use a wide recognition range. But for those leading clever people, there are different issues of recognition. While they still require internal recognition they are most turned on by recognition from outside—by the award of Oscars, Grammys, awards for the best paper in research literature, architectural prizes. In other words, recognition from that wider group of clever people with whom they really identify.

Lead the Change

The British Broadcasting Corporation (BBC) prides itself as an organization full of clever program makers and world-class investigative journalists. These are extremely difficult people to lead. It's very important to both allow and encourage them to seek the recognition from outside that they crave. Awards, such as the BAFTAs (from the British Academy of Film and Television Arts) and the SONYs (for excellence in radio), are yearly highlights for many—and to win one the highlight of your career. The leadership challenge becomes building organizations which allow your clever people to gain the recognition from outside that they most cherish. Indeed, organizations may aggressively promote the interests of their own in pursuit of such prizes. They lobby the influential—knowing that creating an environment which fosters recognition

---

Box 12.2 William Shockley and the Traitorous Eight

The failure to lead clever people can be costly. Consider the salutary tale of William Shockley. Shockley was a British-born research scientist who worked at the Bell Labs during the post-war period developing the transistor. In 1947 Shockley was recognized as the co-inventor of the transistor, and in 1956 he was awarded a Nobel Prize. In 1955, he left the Bell Labs to found his own company Shockley Semiconductor Laboratory situated in Palo Alto, California. His academic reputation attracted some of the finest minds in electronics to his company. These included Robert Noyce and Gordon Moore (of Moore's Law fame), who went on to co-found Intel.

Shockley was blessed with a brilliant mind. He was described by Bob Noyce as a 'marvellous intuitive problem solver,' and by Gordon Moore as having 'phenomenal physical intuition.' But unfortunately for Shockley his leadership skills fell far short of his intellectual brilliance.

On one occasion Shockley asked some of his younger employees what he could do to help enthuse them. Several expressed a wish to publish research papers. So Shockley went home, wrote a paper, and returned the next day offering to let them publish the paper in their own names. Well meant but not well led.

In another example Shockley instituted a secret 'project within a project' at the company. Although there were only 50 or so people working at Shockley Labs, when some of the group were employed to work on Shockley's new idea—which according to Shockley had the potential to rival that of the transistor—they were not allowed to discuss the project with other colleagues. It wasn't long before rumblings of discontent at Shockley's leadership style were fanned into the flames of mutiny.

The situation deteriorated and a disenchanted group left to found Fairchild Semiconductors in 1957. Fairchild went on to revolutionize the world of computing through its work on the silicon transistor. As importantly, it threw off a slew of talent who went on to start up some of the best-known companies in Silicon Valley. Intel (Bob Noyce and Gordon Moore), Advanced Micro Devices (Jerry Sanders), and National Semiconductor (Charlie Sporck) were all spin-offs from Fairchild.

Shockley's poor leadership of clever people inadvertently laid the cornerstone of Silicon Valley. First he had brought together a group of the best scientists in the field of electronics, many of whom might not have otherwise remained in the San Francisco area. Second, he had created the conditions necessary to provoke his brilliant employees to leave and start up on their own.

If ever there was a case study of how not to lead clever people this is it. Talented staff who possess special skills are particularly difficult to keep happy. Today, clever people are only too aware of their market value—it's posted in 101 places on the net. Clever people often have a low boredom threshold. Fail to challenge them intellectually or inspire them with an organizational purpose, and in an era of employee mobility they will walk out the door. Are you opening the door?

---

from outside may be a critical retention tool. Misread the signals, provide the wrong type of recognition, or fail to align around purpose and you can lose your most valuable clever people as William Shockley discovered to his cost (see Box 12.2).

Create a Simplified Rule Environment

All organizations have rules but clever people thrive under two particular circumstances. First, a relative absence of rules: that is to say, a few clear rules which are universally enforced. They will react badly to the miasma of bureaucratic rules characteristic of many large organizations—despairing of head office and its capacity to tie them down. Second, the rules need to be ones that they agree to—for example, rules around safety in pharmaceutical companies, risk rules in banks, integrity rules in professional services firms. Sociologists often call these rules *representative* rules and they are precisely the ones that clever people respond to best.

In 1995, when Continental Airlines realized it had to reinvent itself or face certain death by bankruptcy, its leaders gathered employees in the company's parking lot in Houston, Texas. They then dumped piles of old company policy manuals in a large metal trash can, doused them with gasoline, and set the whole thing on fire. 'We knew the company couldn't survive—and it certainly couldn't succeed—if we didn't get rid of all those rigid rules and procedures,' President Greg Brenemann explained. 'Our people had to be thinking of new ways to compete, they had to be fast on their feet, and they had to be empowered to do the right thing. No list of regulations was going to make that happen.' (Since the bonfire, incidentally, Continental's performance has repositioned it atop a most difficult industry.) A well-known example of a company which simplified its rules is Southwest Airlines which lit a bonfire of detailed rules in an attempt to create an empowering culture. At the BBC, a publicly funded organization, Greg Dyke, then director general, discovered a mass of bureaucratic rules, often contradictory, which produced an infuriating organizational *immobilisme*. Nothing could be more calculated to discourage the clever people on whom the reputation and future success of the organization depends. Dyke launched a campaign with the irreverent title 'Cut the Crap'—encouraging the liberation of creative energy and at the same time exposing those who had blamed the rules for their own inadequacies.

In the clever economy the leadership challenge is to create a simplified rule environment which leaves room for the expression of intellectual power. One extremely worrying consequence of the fallout from corporate scandals like Enron and Worldcom is the proliferation of an ever more invasive regulation of our economic lives. For example, the task of auditing, some claim, has been reduced to the endless ticking of boxes. Clever people won't stay in such an environment and the paradoxical outcome will be that the real quality of the audit process will deteriorate.

There is a further complication which leaders must be aware of. 'A lot of clever people are not clever in social dynamics,' observes Laura Tyson. 'They lack emotional intelligence, a repertoire of social skills to influence things. Because they can't figure out how to influence things this way they sometimes look for rules to protect them.' Clever people sometimes create an excessively complex rule-driven environment in a doomed attempt to control the behavior of other people who they don't trust. The leader's challenge therefore is to create a culture of trust. Ian Powell—leader of PWC's advisory businesses in the UK—has striven to build high degrees of empathy between partners in different areas of the business. They may be doing different things but they have developed the capacity to see the world through the eyes of their colleagues and their respective clients. When this takes place they are less likely to seek security in a blanket of rules.

Clever Conclusions

As the migration to the clever economy continues apace the issues raised here become pressing. If leaders cannot grasp that some of their fundamental assumptions about people's attachments to organizations no longer hold then the flight from organizations will continue. The fundamental issue is to reconceptualize the psychological contract. Clever people—even in their fifties—don't stay for the pension.

One final point that relates to the paradox identified earlier. A peculiar characteristic of these clever people is that even when you're leading them well, they may be unable or loath to recognize your leadership. The organizational work you as the leader are carrying out remains on the fringes of their radar. So when you get feedback from them, don't be surprised that the best you may hear is that you don't get in the way too much.

Further Reading

Barley, S. R., and Kunda, G. (2004) *Gurus, Hired Guns and Warm Bodies: Itinerant Experts in a Knowledge Economy.* Princeton: Princeton University Press.
Davenport, T. H. (2005) *Thinking for a Living: How to Get Better Performance and Results from Knowledge Workers.* Boston: Harvard Business School Press.
Glen, T., Maister, D. H., and Bennis, W. G. (2002) *Leading Geeks: How to Manage the People Who Deliver Technology.* San Francis Co: Jossey-Bass.

Goffee, R., and Jones, G. (1998) *The Character of a Corporation*. New York: Harper Collins.

—— —— (2006) *Why Should Anyone be Led by You? What it Takes to be an Authentic Leader*. Boston: Harvard Business School Press.

Lorsch, J. W., and Tierney, T. J. (2002) *Aligning the Stars*. Boston: Harvard Business School Press.

13   The Leader's Prison

Robert Galavan and John Cullen

Conducting long-term strategic planning in a fluid and uncertain world; controlling organizations while attempting to remain flexible; stewarding employees through processes of change whilst maintaining one's credibility; motivating whilst keeping an eye on profitability; and remaining nimble-minded while crafting innovative futures. The demands of leadership are simultaneously delightful and daunting, which is probably why more books, research theses, and articles are published on the subject than any other aspect of business or management.

However insurmountable the challenges of leadership may appear, many senior managers meet the demands and some even manage to do so with style! Others, no matter how hard they try, regardless of their brilliance or past achievements, fail. Why is this? A scan of the business sections of the popular press would doubtlessly provide the 'correlation' oriented student with enough data to apparently answer this question. Successful businesses, it would seem, rise to their lofty heights because of the efforts of talented management teams. Despite the difficulties of emerging technologies and the vagaries of the markets, these select groups have managed to step with grace through the war-torn industry and emerge with the spoils. On the other hand, organizations that fail to remain competitive are often the victims of failures within the market in which they operate and not because of a lack of management talent.

A student of human behavior will quickly recognize this relationship between success and leadership, and failure and circumstances, as a self-serving attribution. That is, we as humans have an innate tendency to believe good things happen because of our actions and bad things happen because of factors outside of our control. To believe otherwise would be to accept that we were the cause of our own problems. But even if what we observe in the pages of the business press is self-serving, we cannot simply dismiss it. Could it be true that managers create success, but circumstances cause failure? As with most management issues, the response will be sometimes and it depends. In some cases it is the market, in some cases the leader, in some the organization, and even occasionally the government! The important thing for us to know is what causes leaders or their organizations' environments to be more or less influential. Central to our explanation of this is an understanding of the level of *discretion* available to leaders in any given situation.

It is broadly accepted that, to some extent, leaders matter to the performance of their firms. The widely publicized pay rates of senior executives, the growth of a global search and headhunt industry, and the attention paid by the contemporary organization to talent development are surface indicators of these beliefs, underscoring a deeply, often tacitly held conviction that quality of leadership is instrumental to sustainable growth. Of course, while this is the generally accepted view in contemporary management circles, it could be argued that it would seem less than beneficial for leaders to make any alternative claim. On the other hand researchers, unencumbered by the limitations of their practitioner subjects, have a well-established (even if not well read by management practitioners) school of thought that argues to the contrary. It articulates that managers really don't matter very much. Proponents of this view, who are broadly categorized as population ecologists, take a somewhat Darwinian perspective, explaining corporate performance as a function of fit between the organization and its environment.[1] Organizations are, from this perspective, too large, slow, cumbersome, political, and socially embedded for mere leaders to influence them much and so, if organizations find that they are a poor fit for their changing markets, they simply die out and are replaced by a better-fitted species. The only solution available to managers and to organizations in this scenario is to engage in regular cycles of 'creative destruction,' where the entire organization is radically redesigned from top to bottom with the aim of continually readjusting itself to meet rapidly changing industry environments and customer needs.[2] This view, of course, is closely aligned to the perspective that all organizations, over their lifespan, are engaged in cycles of quiet evolutionary periods which are disrupted by a significant challenge or leadership crisis which demands a short, sharp period of revolutionary change.[3]

The counter-claim is that managers really do matter and that leaders can and do change the course of their organizations and so materially affect their performance and in some cases make profound differences that change the industry. In this counter-claim, even leaders facing the most intractable of problems such as crime on city streets can and do make a difference. Take, for example, Rudi Giuliani who is widely credited by the press as having cleaned up the streets of New York in the 1990s. Surely if the tenuous powers of a city mayor can be enacted to effectively lead the diverse and complex organization of city bureaucrats and police, then leaders must matter. But this would be to presume that it was in fact Giuliani or indeed anyone in the city organization that managed to reduce the crime rate in New York. At least one notable award-winning economist, the Harvard-educated Stephen Levitt, disagrees.

He, rather controversially, offered an alternative explanation for the reduction of crime in New York in the 1990s as an effect of legalizing abortion in the USA following the *Roe* vs. *Wade* case in 1973. He posits that rather than congratulating Giuliani for his efforts we can see that 'legalized abortion led to less unwantedness; unwantedness leads to high crime; legalized abortion, therefore, led to less crime.'[4] In other words the teenagers of the 1990s who might have become criminals were simply never born. While this explanation may be viewed as morally outrageous, if it has even a semblance of truth, then Giuliani's success in the war on crime is at least partly due to a change in his organization's environment and not simply the result of his leadership. Taken in the extreme, he got lucky by being in the right place at the right time and took credit for the inevitable.

The risk in following the course of this argument is that we get caught in the rather academic and black and white divide of whether managers do or don't matter. A more pragmatic course is to perhaps try to understand the circumstances in which leaders have a greater or lesser effect. Phrased slightly differently, we are trying to understand the extent of the constraints on a leader's discretion. Broadly speaking, these constraints come in at least two forms:[5] the operating environment and the organization itself.

Let us consider in the first instance the operating environment which, for commercial organizations, can usually be described by the concept of its industry. In some cases, the industry will confer more discretion on a leader than in others. Take for example the differences between the software industry and the forestry industry. If we consider just three factors that affect the discretion afforded to these industries, product commoditization, demand stability, and capital intensity, we can easily identify the software industry as a high-discretion industry and forestry as a low-discretion industry (see Table 13.1). The net effect is that managers in the software industry have a greater latitude of action and so firm performance in the software industry is relatively more affected by managers and less so by the industry conditions. In the case of the forestry industry (in Ireland) managers can do relatively little about the market price of logs and so are constrained in their actions. On this basis, forestry managers are prisoners of their industry while software managers roam free.

TABLE 13.1 Discretion in different industries

	Software	Forestry
Product commoditization	Low	High
Demand stability	Low	High
Capital intensity	Low	High
Overall discretion	**High**	**Low**

The second form of constraint on a manager's discretion is the organization itself. Large organizations with limited slack resources and powerful cultures constrain their leader's discretion. We can see the effect of how culture constrains discretion in the print industry. Over the past two decades the market and the technology for printing has changed enormously. Many organizations built on craft traditions with powerful and long-standing union agreements were understandably slow to change. As the markets tightened, their slack resources dwindled, making their operating circumstances even more difficult for them. Many of the firms that prospered in this phase were new start-ups, unencumbered by sunk capital, traditions, and powerful cultures. These new organizations, operating in the same industry, provided the opportunities for their founders to build capabilities that met the emerging market needs, leaving their tradition-encumbered predecessors imprisoned by their organizations' histories. This inability of an organization to change even when alarm bells are ringing loudly that the market is changing has been described as 'cultural lock-in'[6] and is a powerful example that often 'strong' cultures which are allowed to develop, or even are purposefully created, in organizations can eventually become pathological to an organization's own well-being, competitiveness, and sustainability.

Knowing whether an industry, an organization, or both give or constrain a leader's discretion should help us understand the circumstances in which managers matter most, and indeed, the research would seem to bear this out.[7] On average managers in high-discretion contexts matter more than those in low-discretion contexts. But 'on average' isn't much use when we need to consider a specific case. No organization has an average leader. They have real people who lead individual lives and while some industries undoubtedly have inherent constraints, sometimes the constraints are more in the minds of the industry leaders. A lucid example is that of the airline industry which, in a few years in the 1980s, lost more money than it had made in its entire history. It almost repeated this remarkable feat in the aftermath of the 11 September attacks. Its lack of fluid resources, capital intensity, and, apart from infrequent shocks, demand stability provided all of the characteristics of a low-discretion industry. The rules of the game were well established and all organizations followed a similar patter of competition with little variation. This was until Herb Kelleher brought low-cost carriers to the fore in America with Southwest Airlines, followed in Europe by Michael O'Leary's Ryanair, and subsequently Stelios Haji-Ioannou's easyJet. Their subsequent success in this industry is well documented. So how were they able to take on the considerable might of the airline industry and win? Well, one of the reasons was that these new operators were clearly unencumbered by the constraints of their organizations. They developed new organizations and had the discretion to establish different cultures, policies, routines, standards, and processes. Their counterparts, embedded in the full service businesses, were constrained by contracts, relationships, business models, capital structures, pay agreements, and more; and they quickly recognized this. The reaction of some was insightful and they set up 'new' rival organizations such as Buzz and Go that would be unencumbered by their existing conditions and have the discretion to take on the pretenders to their throne. The subsequent success or more to the point lack of success of these organizations is equally well documented. Why though, if the constraints of the existing organizations were lifted, could these fledgling offspring not survive?

The reasons can partly be explained by the third type of discretion constraint, the leaders themselves. While the offshoots of the major airlines benefited from the organizational discretion afforded to them through a lack of established assets, processes, and routines in their new organization, their senior executives were experienced airline people and, while they had the potential to benefit from this discretion, perhaps they were unable to perceive and act on it. On the other hand the leaders of the new low-cost airlines had no such experiential constraints; before entering the airline industry Kelleher was a practicing lawyer, O'Leary an accountant, and Stelios a serial entrepreneur. Rather than being imprisoned by their knowledge of the industry and the rules they couldn't break, they used their innovative capabilities to the full to find new ways of building the most profitable airlines of the twenty-first century. By not being part of the culture of the industry in which they found themselves leaders, they were enabled to think outside the established cultural paradigms of the sector. If we articulate culture as simply the subconscious acceptance of 'the way things are done around here,' and these new industry leaders were not of this culture, we can see they had a greater level of conscious awareness of the way things are *not done* around here, which equipped them with a sensitivity to the potential pathologies of the industry they faced at that point in time.

So we can clearly identify that the nature of the industry matters and the nature of the organization matters. In other words some leaders operate in highly discretionary external and organizational settings and some find, regardless of their efforts, that change proves next to impossible. From this we can take it that it is absolutely essential for leaders to assess the level of discretion available to them in a given situation. Failure to do so will lead to underperformance by not forging ahead with enough gusto when the discretion is available, or wasting energy trying to change things when it is not.

This assessment of course assumes that leaders have the capability to assess the reality they face. First we must ask, without becoming too philosophical, whether it is possible to even know what the reality is. In a world of intangible assets where the balance sheet of leading organizations often accounts for less than 50 per cent of their share value, how can a leader 'know' the resources that are available to him or her and understand the nature of the industry? Even if it is possible to know this reality, do managers have the time and could they handle the complexity involved? Bear in mind that we are now well embedded in an information-saturated world where we are bombarded with views, analysis, and data at a rate that makes it impossible to filter and sift through the continually morphing streams of data that we are presented with in what has been called the 'attention economy.'[8] Leaders, like all of us, need to limit the amount of information that they can process, and this creates what is known as bounded rationality.[9] To cope with information overload, leaders develop internalized approximations of the world they operate in; approximations which might be thought of as personal maps of the business reality that they must grapple with on a day-to-day basis.

These maps are developed over time as leaders gain experience, posit theories of the world they operate in, and test these theories in practice. Of course when testing our theories we have a tendency to look for only the supporting information and discard the rest, thus exposing the possibility of developing inaccurate, but trusted maps. Thus when two leaders face the same 'reality' (environmental and organization discretion) they will interpret this reality differently. They will overlay the complexity of the 'real' situation which they face with their own simplified version of reality in the form of their experientially developed idiosyncratic maps. In this way each leader sees their future options through the lens of past experiences. This allows them to learn from the lessons of the past, but at the same time imprisons their minds within the limits of the map. When leaders operate in circumstances where the future is by and large a replica of their past, those with experience and well-developed maps are likely to flourish. The uninitiated and the naive will have to expend their energy learning costly 'new' lessons. However in circumstances where the future will most likely involve significant change to meet a desired outcome perhaps both in the industry and the organization, these experienced leaders may find themselves disadvantaged. In such situations, the old-timers' demonstrative stories of past failures intended to helpfully teach the inexperienced the lessons of experience are often interpreted as 'holding on to the past' when perhaps new mindsets or maps are needed.

In addition to the embeddedness of thought that these maps create, they create other issues as well. The maps are, by their very nature, deeply personal. Our individual psychological make-up is contributed to by forces and experiences that are not necessarily of our choosing, but which exert phenomenal influence over how we experience reality and the world in which we live. Often these experiences are painful or traumatic and our world-view or personal paradigm develops to help us subconsciously protect ourselves. In particular we are drawn to states of mind and being that reduce pain and tension for us. We can become aware of our world-view if somebody asks us to 'see things from their point of view' or 'take a different' perspective. What they are asking us to consider is an alternative map. However, because these maps are so personal, and function to protect us from reliving difficult and traumatic experiences in the future, we tend to treat any threat to them as a personal threat and lapse into defensive mode. In this mode we try to convince the other person that our map is the 'right' one. They then take this as an assault on their own map and a dysfunctional cycle of arguing about maps rather than exploring reality, ensues. To make progress in situations that require change, and to fully engage with that change, leaders need to be able to engage in a constructive dialogue that stretches and extends the boundaries of their knowledge and the knowledge of others with whom they interact.

This process is problematic for everyone who attempts it; behavioral scientists assert that our core need as human beings is for self-protection. Managers and executives working in organizations in developed economies probably face their cognitive map violation on a much more regular basis than perhaps any other occupation. The reason for this is that they are continually, even relentlessly involved at the coalface of determining what an organization's reality is. In the early 1970s, Henry Mintzberg[10] overturned much of the accepted management theory on how managers actually spend their time, by positing that the vast majority of managerial time is spent in interpersonal communication. If Mintzberg's findings are generalizable to the broader population of managers, they must face challenges from all quarters as to what their organizational reality is, how it is changing, and how future challenges should be met. Key to the 'co-creation' of organizational realities with all stakeholders (organizational actors, shareholders, customers, etc.) is the ability to do something which very often only highly trained counsellors, psychotherapists, and psychoanalysts do; to enter the mindset of the individual or groups with whom they dialogue. Influential psychologists from the 1960s human potential movement, such as Carl Rogers and Abraham Maslow, stressed the importance of developing 'active listening' skills as crucial tools to help overcome conflicts and to create conducive working and living environments. It must be stipulated that this is not a universal requirement though, and extended dialogue in the face of short-term challenges is not always a great idea. In fact it can lead to 'paralysis-by-analysis' at times when direction is most needed. Sometimes a leader needs to impose their vision or map and make it the reality that the organization operates to, and this is particularly the case when employees need a clear picture of what they should do. It has become a cliché that the pace of change is increasing and that globalization is beginning to cause market and societal disruption. Crises are often caused by the emergence of unfamiliar, unstructured situations. During these times, a leader proves their worth by recognizing that it is a crisis, providing a clear and structured analysis of what has happened or is happening, and moves with resolve to implement a solution or a structure to address the challenge which has emerged.

We are reaching a conclusion that while the industry and organizational contexts matter, so too does the leader's perception of these realities; and particularly the leader's perception of their discretion. There are several definitions of what *management* actually is, but when we consider what it is that senior managers actually do, the following one is helpful: managing is 'the creation and maintenance of practical meaning in organised activity.'[11] This definition emphasizes the role that leaders play in offering a clear picture of what organizational realities are, and the practical and purposeful reasons for why they need to create these organizational world-views: to provide a map for the organization to effectively meet its goals.

One of the most interesting findings of Robert Galavan's recent research has been a challenge to the almost total acceptance of the 'fact' that the major influence on leaders' maps, and their perception of the discretion available to them, is their experience. Most students of organizational behaviour will have come across the concept of selective perception[12] in prescribed textbooks. Despite the canonical status of this concept, there is however relatively little support[13] for the original findings that managers selectively perceive issues on the basis of their experiences. In his research, Galavan found that in addition to experience the personality of the manager is at least as and perhaps more potent an indicator of their perceived discretion. That is, when we discount differences based on industry or organization, and even differences based on their personal work and educational experiences, we find that some managers inherently perceive that they have more discretion than others. The implication is that two managers with the same experiences, faced with the same situation, will hold a different perception of the discretion available to them and consequently act differently.

The implications for leaders of these findings are profound. If we need a manager to lead change, not only must we take into account their experience, both personal and industry, but we must also consider the perceptions they hold in relation to the discretion managers have more generally. It is clear from the research that their views will vary widely. We can surmise that when perception matches reality and managers have an accurate understanding of their world this is probably a good thing. If, however, the leader perceives they can do nothing, but the reality is that they can do much, they will miss an opportunity. But recognizing that discretion is available does not mean that leaders need to have all the answers. If leaders can create enough slack in the organization to allow it to respond to the environment it is possible that a learning organization might emerge. If on the other hand a leader perceives that they can create change when in fact the reality is quite different then the outcome is likely to be fraught with difficulties and frustration for everybody involved.

To avoid missed opportunities and the frustration of expending effort to no avail we need to consider how people learn about the world around them.

Lead the Change

In organizational settings getting to 'know' things is a largely a social interpretation process, or in Karl Weick's term 'sensemaking.'[14] Through making sense of the world around us we come not to really know reality, but to move to agree on the premiss for reality—what has worked in the past, and what will work in the future. Once most of the players in the game agree on that reality and play by the rules then all is fine. Economists might explain the 'rules,' people may learn and play by them, then the market will function as expected. This familiar economic modeling of a market scenario, however, is very often different from how markets operate in the real world. These models, at a particular point in time, merely present a good working approximation of how markets operate. Failure to recognize that this is merely an approximation of reality, rather than reality itself, means leaders can fall into the trap of imprisoning their minds and consciously or unconsciously blocking all other options that might have been available to them, options that not only challenge, but change the rules of the game.

Leaders are ultimately prison inmates of one kind or another. The only question is whether it is a high-security or an open prison and the industry characteristics will often give us the answer. The difference between the leader's prison and the criminal's prison is that the leader's bars are sometimes mental constraints and not physical. Leaders can break free of the bars by deciding to do just that. The key element to remember in this regard is, once again, *discretion*. Senior managers who make a real difference to the organizations that they lead are ones who actively choose to confront the limitations that their own world-view places upon them in an effort to transcend the bars that have been built for them. It is interesting to note that topics such as self-awareness and personal development are being articulated with greater regularity in the literature associated with the fields of management development and management learning. These processes are key to assisting leaders in understanding their personal maps, their values, principles, and the internal psychological barriers that might inhibit their personal effectiveness.

One approach to help leaders develop their understanding can be broadly described as *reflective practice*, where leaders are urged to systematically reflect on their own performance, decisions, and reaction to stressful scenarios that may have arisen in their work. The practices associated with this family of approaches are broad and range from group counseling to personal journal keeping, but the aims are the same: to help managers gain an awareness of themselves, their behaviors, and their mental maps in order that they can recognize their limitations and address them through processes of personal development, and also to maximize the talents and skills that they have.

A second approach involves managers developing a deeper understanding of what may have happened to them during their *crucible experiences*.[15] Painful

experiences of failure, reputational damage, even humiliation are valued because, if survived, they strengthen a manager's resolve and develop a much
needed resilience for the turbulent times ahead. Most importantly, they are
essential experiences in assisting the transformation from manager to leader,
as they clearly communicate leadership abilities by forcing individuals to stretch
their intellectual and emotional capabilities. Various leaders are eulogized in
the business context (some even choose to lavish praise on themselves); but it is
interesting to note that leaders who have made their way into popular under-
standings of leadership are ones who themselves have been forced into positions of self-assessment and personal transformation through actual physical
imprisonment. Gandhi, Nelson Mandela, Aung San Suu Kyi, and Anwar Sadat
are individuals who directly confronted their own maps for viewing their
world and their relationship to social reality and, despite the obstacles they
faced, chose to reassess and transform themselves. By being placed in a position where they have effectively lost everything, including their freedom,
leaders who emerge from the crucible experience intact have been through a
process which has radically widened the dimensions of their personal map. The
experience of being imprisoned in a very real sense actually led these leaders to
realize the potential they had for exercising discretion about how they would
conduct their own public professional lives. With just a few anecdotal examples
like this we can say clearly that leaders do matter. But it is perhaps more
important to recognize that some leaders matter more than others and not just
because of the circumstances they found themselves in. In the early days of
Ryanair, a friend of one of the authors of this chapter berated him for using a
case study based on the airline. He was told that they 'knew' the industry, as
they had worked in it, and that you couldn't fly planes at that cost. Luckily for
O'Leary and the other low-cost carriers it appears the entire industry 'knew'
this low cost model couldn't work, and left them to get on with it. Time has
shown very clearly that it does work and now less than a handful of low-cost
carriers account for most of the profits in the global airline industry.

The examples that we have discussed are supportive of the position that
leaders who orchestrated structural change within industries often were unencumbered by the organizational constraints their competitors faced. During
times of change, these leaders exercised the organizational and most importantly the personal perceived discretion available to them. All leaders can expand
their discretion, not through accumulating more facts about the circumstances
in which they find themselves nor better understanding the rules of the game,
although both have value. The real differences come through an engagement
with learning at a deeper level, a level that allows the leader to reflect on the
personal 'truths' they hold and recognize how they are imprisoned by them.

The challenge for leaders is to recognize and act on the discretion the
circumstances offer and then to have the ability to reflect on that 'reality'

through an understanding that this is just their own idiosyncratic view shaped by the facts, but also their personality, beliefs, and learning experiences from the past. The first step in breaking free of the discretion prison is to realize that you are in a prison. Having done this, the most capable leaders will have the personal strength and drive to stick with their view when appropriate, and the humility to learn from others when the time is right. The question for you is which kind of leader will you be? In the final analysis it matters not whether you believe you can make a difference or not—either way you will be right! Think about it—then do something about it.

Notes

1. Michael T. Hannan and John Freeman (1977) 'The Population Ecology of Organizations,' *American Journal of Sociology*, 82 (5): 929–64.
2. R. Foster and S. Kaplan (2001) 'Creative Destruction,' *McKinsey Quarterly*, 3: 40–51.
3. L. E. Greiner (1972) 'Evolution and Revolution as Organizations Grow,' *Harvard Business Review*, 50 (4): 37–46.
4. Steven D. Levitt and Stephen J. Dubner (2005) *Freakonomics*. London: Penguin Books.
5. Donald C. Hambrick and Sydney Finkelstein (1987) 'Managerial Discretion: A Bridge between Polar Views of Organizational Outcomes' in B. M. Staw and L. L. Cummings (eds.), *Research in Organizational Behavior*. Greenwich, Conn.: JAI, 369–406.
6. R. Foster and S. Kaplan (2001) *Why Companies That Are Built to Last Underperform the Market: And How to Successfully Transform Them*. New York: Doubleday Books, 16.
7. Sydney Finkelstein and Donald C. Hambrick (1990) 'Top-Management-Team Tenure and Organizational Outcomes: The Moderating Role of Managerial Discretion,' *Administrative Science Quarterly*, 35: 484–503.
8. T. H. Davenport and J. C. Beck (2001) *The Attention Economy: Understanding the New Currency of Business*. Boston: Harvard Business School Press.
9. R. M. Cyert and J. G. March (1963) *A Behavioral Theory of the Firm*. Englewood Cliffs, NJ: Prentice-Hall.
10. H. Mintzberg (1975) 'The Manager's Job: Folklore and Fact,' *Harvard Business Review*, 53 (4): 49–61.
11. J. Burgoyne (1988) 'Management Development for the Individual and the Organization,' *Personnel Management*, June: 40–4.
12. D. C. Dearborn and H. A. Simon (1958) 'Selective Perception: A Note on the Departmental Identification of Executives,' *Sociometry*, 21: 140–4.
13. Robert Galavan, Andrew Kakabadse, and Nada Kakabadse (2003) *The Pivotol Role of Perceived Discretion in Top Teams: Setting a Research Agenda*. London: British Academy of Management.

14. K. E. Weick (1995) *Sensemaking in Organizations*. Thousand Oaks, Catif.: Sage Publications.
15. W. G. Bennis and R. J. Thomas (2002) 'Crucibles of Leadership,' *Harvard Business Review*, 80 (9): 39–45.

14   Nurturing Innovation Hot Spots

Lynda Gratton

Imagine you are standing on the very peak of a mountain, looking through thermal-imaging goggles that show the extent of energy in the landscape. Imagine that the terrain stretched out before you is the organization. As you look through your heat-sensitive goggles, the terrain appears green. Daily work is happening in a predictable way—people are going about their business, and little excitement or energy beyond the norm is being generated. As you continue to watch, suddenly, in the distance, you see a flare of bright orange and red erupting. This flare could emerge in many places. It could be a workplace, a particular team or department or factory. It could be in a coffee shop, across a hallway, or in a conference. It could even happen across the whole company.

During your career at work you will encounter situations when the inspiration is flowing. Colleagues chip in with great ideas. There is a real feeling of teamwork, a genuine spirit of collaboration and progress. I label such moments *Hot Spots*. They can happen momentarily when a group happens to be together around the coffee machine or they can take place for a prolonged period, even across an entire organization—think of the collaborative and industry Hot Spot created by open software development at Linux.

This is a Hot Spot. It is a moment when people are working together in exceptionally creative and collaborative ways.

Hot Spots occur when the energy within and between people flares—when the mundane of everyday activities is set aside for engaged work that is exciting and challenging. It is at these times that ideas become contagious and new possibilities appear.

As you survey the landscape through your thermal goggles, what do you think causes the changes in energy? Are these fluctuations in energy the result of forces that are part of the everyday work of people, forces that are so deep and so complex that they are impossible to predict, let alone control? Should we simply be passive observers of Hot Spots, looking down from the mountain, or are there actions that we can take to increase the probability of Hot Spots emerging?

These are crucial questions since one of the most pressing issues managers face is how to continue to create energy and passion in their companies. To begin to answer these questions, over the last decade a research team at London Business School has studied commitment, energy, and innovation. In the last three years we have studied over fifty teams in fifteen companies to find out more about these Hot Spots that all of us have experienced at one time or another in our working lives. The results of this study show that there are indeed times, places, and occasions when extraordinary energy arises in an organization, when people from inside and outside the company are able to engage with each other in a way that they have rarely been able to do. When this energy and the resulting excitement are ignited, they have the power to propel teams to work toward goals they never believed achievable.

Hot Spots come into being when our energy and excitement are inflamed through an igniting question or a vision of the future. They are times when positive relationships with work colleagues are a real source of deep satisfaction and a key reason why we decide to stay with a company. As such, they are hugely motivational. Would you work for an organization where there are no Hot Spots? And, they are incredibly productive. Hot Spots are where innovative and industry-shaping ideas are likely to originate.

The trouble is that Hot Spots provide a challenge to the way we have managed and thought about organizations and the people within them over the last 100 years. From scientific management at the turn of the last century to the modern-day call centers, much of our thinking about the role of management has centered on the rules of command and control. Supporting the emergence of Hot Spots requires a whole new set of rules and an entirely new way of approaching the challenge of getting the best out of people.

To take a mechanistic approach to the emergence of Hot Spots is to entirely miss the point of their development. Command and control doesn't work with a Linux software developer working late into the evening for no financial reward. Nor would it work at Google or a whole host of other such companies.

This does not mean that nothing can be done, but our study shows that it takes a more subtle, more nuanced, and I believe more sophisticated approach. It requires unlearning some of the old rules and learning a whole new set of rules. To see what these changes might entail, let us first take a closer look at what happens in a Hot Spot when it emerges. In companies across the world, I have watched Hot Spots flare. I have seen Hot Spots emerge in the teams that network between Poland and Venezuela in the oil giant BP. I have seen an incredibly innovative Hot Spot emerge in Nokia as teams grapple with ways to serve the Asian market. I have watched in awe as the volunteer programmers in Linux created clusters of Hot Spots that are a formidable competitor to Microsoft and have fundamentally reinvented the way we think about organizations. In each of these companies, I have observed over and over again that a Hot Spot flares through the spontaneous combustion of three elements.

The First Element: A Cooperative Mindset

The innovative capacity of Hot Spots arises from the intelligence, insights, and wisdom of people working together. The energy contained in a Hot Spot is essentially a combination of their individual energy with the addition of the relational energy generated between them. As a consequence, the quality and extent of these relationships is crucial to the emergence of Hot Spots, and it is a cooperative mindset that is the foundation of these high-quality relationships. Hot Spots arise because people are excited, willing, and able to cooperate with each other. It is these exciting, skillful cooperative relationships that fuel the exchange of knowledge and insights that ignite a Hot Spot and create innovation.

A key aspect of human potential in Hot Spots is what people know and how they use this knowledge. So in a sense, we can think of a Hot Spot as the sum of all the intellectual capital of the people within it. Although intellectual capital is a crucial aspect of Hot Spots—without it, the Hot Spot becomes dull and tepid—it is not sufficient. The energy flows and ebbs within Hot Spots are just as likely to be caused by emotional capital. This is the emotional insight and ability that people have to adapt and modify their behavior. It is this emotional capital that plays a critical role in self-awareness and self-knowledge. However, the potential energy of a Hot Spot is not simply the addition of the intellectual and emotional capital of all the people who are engaged within it. The effect is a combination effect rather than a simple additive effect. The combination effect occurs as a result of the relationships between people, what we might call the social capital of the Hot Spot. This social capital signifies the depth and extent of relationships within the Hot Spots and the networks of relationships outside the Hot Spot. It is the energy released through these relationships that plays such a crucial role in Hot Spots.

Hot Spots emerge when emotional capital, social capital, and intellectual capital are engaged in a reinforcing cycle. People become energized and excited about sharing knowledge and about what they might learn from others—their intellectual capital is engaged as they become increasingly emotionally involved. As people feel increasingly passionate about something they really care about, they enjoy the emotional contagion when others becoming engaged and excited. Hot Spots become extraordinary opportunities for social capital to be created as friendships and relationships are forged and the people involved feel the pleasure of attachment and intimacy.

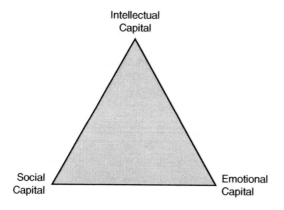

Fig. 14.1 The three aspects of human capital and potential

Where Hot Spots fail, these three aspects of human potential rapidly atrophy. People lose interest, they no longer believe they can learn and develop, and the intellectual challenge is gone. They increasingly withdraw emotionally as the passion of the project wanes and they become increasingly individualistic and uncooperative as relationships cool. Instead of engaging in exciting and skillful cooperation, people become passive or uninterested in each other or even turn competitive and aggressive. Instead of contributing to the learning and innovation of a Hot Spot, they hoard their knowledge and insights, and the level of energy drops to neutral or even dries up entirely. The Big Freeze takes over.

The emergence of the three elements of human potential begins (see Figure 14.1) the process of Hot Spot development. This emergence is in turn dependent on the extent to which individuals value the power of working with others—a cooperative mindset. Without this valuing of cooperation, intellectual and emotional potential are turned inward, to development of the individual, rather than outward, to the development of others and the creation of Hot Spots. Without a deep cooperative mindset, human potential is geared toward producing 'superstars' and all the competitive values associated with them.

Supporting a Cooperative Mindset

Our research shows that there are a number of ways in which executives can increase the probability of a cooperative mindset emerging.

Through Executive Role Modeling

In the teams we studied we found that one of the most important predictors about whether a team was cooperative was the extent to which team members

believed that the senior team of the company are themselves working cooperatively with each other. Even if team members had not actually met the
members of the senior teams of the company, they had heard rumors about
their behavior. So it seems that executive behavior sends clear messages about
cooperative behavior. Role modeling for cooperation starts at the top. When a
senior team is believed to be highly competitive and even dysfunctional then it
is very difficult for other teams in the business to behave in a cooperative way.
At the Royal Bank of Scotland, for example, the practice of CEO Fred Goodwin
to meet with his team every morning sends out a clear signal to the rest of
the company that working collaboratively with each other will be crucial to the
long-term success of the business.

By Cooperative Practices

Next, we found that teams that have a cooperative mindset are more likely to
be found in companies that have what we might call cooperative practices.
There are three cooperative practices that seem to be key. The first is the
practice of selection, in particular the practice of careful selection of people on
the basis of their capacity to work cooperatively with others. This selection for
cooperation is very clear at Goldman Sachs where each candidate to the firm
experiences up to thirty selection interviews devoted to ensuring that highly
energized and talented candidates are also able to work cooperatively with
others. The emphasis at Goldman Sachs is firmly on the 'we' rather than 'I.'
The second cooperative practice is induction and on-boarding. This practice is
so crucial because the first thirty days in a company seem to be critical to
establishing a cooperative mindset. With this in mind, companies such as Nokia
place much emphasis on socializing people early into the power of cooperation. They achieve this by emphasizing the creation of cooperative networks,
whilst ensuring that the key mentors and role models in this crucial phase are
themselves cooperative people. Finally, reward practices play a key role in
establishing a cooperative mindset. Whilst team-based compensation can play
a role in supporting a cooperative mindset, of more importance is the removal
of highly individualized, competitive rewards. By removing one of the most
potent barriers to cooperation, senior teams are showing that cooperation is
critical.

By Supporting Communities of Practice

The everyday actions of employees profoundly influence and support the
development of cooperation. Our team study showed that teams in which
people behaved cooperatively with each other were also those that were more
likely to be members of informal communities of practice. Take the consulting
firm PwC for example. We found that many of the highly cooperative team

members also met with each other in a more informal setting in the myriad of informal communities that criss-cross the enterprise. These communities are groups of people who share a common interest and experience. They could be passionate about fell walking, or share common experiences of bringing up young children, or love opera. It is not the topic *per se* that is important. Rather it is the creation of informal cooperative relationships that seem to create a baseline of cooperation such that when people are engaged in a business task, this cooperative culture makes a difference.

The Second Element: Boundary Spanning

A cooperative mindset between people is crucial to the emergence of a Hot Spot—and without it the Big Freeze takes over. Yet whilst a cooperative mindset is necessary for the emergence of Hot Spots, it is not sufficient. What is clear is that it is the type and extent of relationships that seem to make a crucial difference to emergence of a Hot Spot. To understand this better, take a look at Figure 14.2 which describes relationships across two dimensions.

The first way of thinking about working relationships is to consider the *depth of relationships*. When you think about your relationships at work, some will be relationships that are particularly strong, with people you have known for

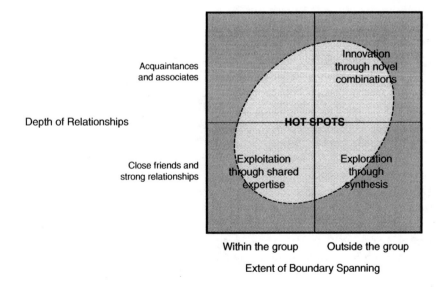

Fig. 14.2 Effects of relationship quality on value creation in Hot Spots

many years. Other relationships are more like associations or acquaintances with people you have known but not known well.

Next, you can think about working relationships with regard to where the other person is located. In particular you can consider where the other person is located with regard to boundaries. We found that the *extent of boundary spanning* differed within Hot Spots. Some relationships are between people who work together in a group—in these occasions there is limited boundary spanning. On the other hand, other relationships span across to people outside of the group, to people in other functions, or even in other companies. In this case, boundary spanning is high as these networks of relationships cross team, function, and company boundaries.

The effects of these relationships on the capacity of the Hot Spot to create business value are shown in Figure 14.2.

This shows the different ways in which value is created in a Hot Spot. Innovative value is created through *novel combinations* of the ideas, knowledge, and insights of people. Value can also be created as people *exploit their shared expertise* within their group or *explore ideas, knowledge, and insights* with people outside their group.

Value creation through exploiting shared expertise. There are times in Hot Spots when the value of the community is created primarily because groups of people have been working together for some time in an activity that has been ignited by a particularly complex or challenging goal. In these circumstances, value within the Hot Spot is created as a result of the members' exploiting and sharing knowledge they already have.

This outcome is unlikely to be unusual or innovative because the members of the Hot Spot know each other well and are probably rather similar in their competencies and attitudes. Hence they are unlikely to learn things from one another that they did not already know. As Figure 14.2 illustrates, although Hot Spots can emerge in this lower left quadrant, in reality they need the stimulation of people from outside the group to flourish in the long term.

Value creation through exploration. Some of the relationships within a Hot Spot are strong ones between people who know each other very well but are located in different groups or functions. These strong boundary-spanning relationships are marvellous opportunities for value to be created as each person explores in depth what the other knows.

Value creation through novel combinations. Relationships between people who know each other well and are located in the same group are important for continuous improvement. However, a significant proportion of the cooperative relationships within Hot Spots span people outside the teams and even outside the boundaries of the company. In Hot Spots, we found marketing people cooperating skillfully with people from sales, people from Poland cooperating skillfully with people from Venezuela, and people within the company cooperating skillfully with customers or partners. These Hot Spots of boundaryless cooperation are particularly adept at the combination of ideas and insights. It is this exploration of novel combinations of insights and ideas that opens the possibility of innovative solutions.

The innovation of these new combinations is most likely to occur under two circumstances: with people who have different mindsets and ways of thinking about the world, and with people who are relative strangers rather than know each other very well.

This may at first seem counterintuitive. Surely in Hot Spots, people know each other well and therefore are more able to be cooperative because they trust each other? In fact, this is not the case. Wonderful long friendships with people who are similar are a joy of life. But they are rarely where innovative ideas arise. The reason is simple: much if not most of the knowledge we exchange in these relationships is already known. We are more likely to talk about what we both know, than about what one of us doesn't know.

These deep, long-term relationships are an important part of our well-being and are indeed crucial to developing trust and respect in Hot Spots. Hot Spots need both the trust and respect of long-term relationships and the insight and novelty of new relationships that cross boundaries. It is this combination that is most valuable.

Creating Boundary Spanning

There is much that can be done to support boundary spanning.

By Encouraging Boundary Spanners

We found that Hot Spots are likely to have a proportion of people within them who are themselves consummate boundary spanners. There seem to be two aspects to this. First, these are people who have in the past ensured that they have themselves worked in various functions, companies, or countries. As a consequence they bring with them wide networks of relationships. Second, these consummate boundary spanners enjoy and are skilled at introducing people to each other. So, for example, they are adept at introducing the people they know in the marketing function to other people they know in the human resource function. Whilst it is inappropriate for everyone to be a boundary spanner, finding, acknowledging, and supporting these people is crucial to Hot Spots.

By Creating Boundary-Spanning Practices

It is also possible for companies to invest in practices and processes that, in an ongoing way, encourage people to share experiences across boundaries.

Nokia is adept at this. Over the long history of the company much attention has been paid to encouraging people to move across boundaries. The career development practices use the notion of the 'big coat' to encourage people to take on responsibilities outside of their immediate area of expertise. The strategy process at Nokia encourages people from across the company to come together every six months to work on key future themes. People throughout the company are encouraged to form working relationships with university departments. As a consequence, across the businesses of Nokia working outside your immediate area of expertise, and forming working relationships with people in other departments and functions, is valued and celebrated.

The same is true at BP where CEO John Browne placed much emphasis on a practice he termed 'peer assist' which encouraged business unit heads to look outside their immediate business for ideas and insights. He even went as far as to support the development of performance management that encouraged business unit heads to agree performance targets with their peers in other businesses.

When innovation through boundary spanning is crucial—as it is for BP and Nokia—then much effort and resources are focused on encouraging and celebrating these activities.

The Third Element: Igniting Purpose

Let us return to the metaphor of the thermal goggles. Imagine that you are sitting on the mountain observing the terrain of the company beneath you and the network of cooperative relationships that criss-cross the company.

These networks of boundaryless cooperative relationships are an essential element of Hot Spots. However, often the energy within them remains latent. Through the thermal goggles, the situation looks green—business as usual. As you watch, you see people meeting each other and engaging in good-natured conversations and activities. Yet the energy remains at the green level. These are not Hot Spots. They remain green, with latent energy, because there is nothing igniting them—nothing that captures people's attention and imagination, nothing that they can all collectively get behind, nothing that releases the latent energy.

We discovered that the flaring of Hot Spots is always accompanied by an *igniting purpose*, something that people find exciting and interesting and worth engaging with. When this igniting purpose occurs, people flock to it—they want to be part of it. As Figure 14.3 illustrates, the igniting purpose can take a number of forms.

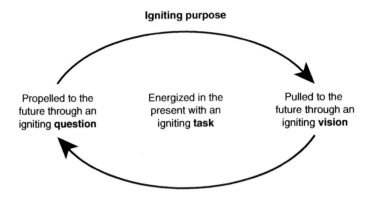

Fig. 14.3 Forms an igniting purpose can take

Igniting Questions

There are occasions when energy is released through the imagination of people being propelled to the future by an igniting question. This is a question that is so exciting and stimulating that people immediately want to engage with it. Some igniting questions are big and expansive, like the one BP CEO John Browne asked of his people: 'How can we, an oil company, become a force for good?'

People throughout BP leapt to answer this question, engaged by the concept behind it and inspired to innovate. The question triggered 'beyond petroleum,' the rebranding and repositioning of BP's core business and innovations involving renewable energy sources. These questions create ignition because, like the idea of an oil company as a force for good—they question the dominant logic.

The very idea of an oil company being a force for good seems to go against the grain. That's why questions like Browne's have rarely been asked before. They encapsulate sufficient excitement and intrigue to awaken people's curiosity and intellectual capital and to stimulate the cooperative relationships that criss-cross the boundaries of the company.

Igniting Visions

Igniting questions invite people to think about the future; the questions essentially propel them into the unknown. However, there is another type of igniting purpose: an igniting vision. Rather than propelling people into an unknown future, this purpose creates an image of what the future could be. Here energy is released by creating a context within which people can collectively imagine what it is they are working toward.

At Linux, the extraordinary innovations around building an open source platform that would enable anyone to access it were triggered by a vision Linus Torvalds had as a graduate student at the University of Helsinki. What ignites the energy of the Hot Spots at Linux is that every one of the thousands of people involved has a vision of what it is they are all trying to achieve.

Igniting Tasks

For some Hot Spots, the latent energy is released by an igniting task that is so interesting, challenging, and potentially developmental that people flock to it spontaneously. At BT, the opportunity to get involved with a task that brought the community and customers into the company was so interesting that over 700 people flocked to it. Igniting tasks are intrinsically motivating; people love working on them.

Laying the Groundwork

Of course, knowing the formula that produces Hot Spots is not the same as being able to create a Hot Spot. In some companies, there are many Hot Spots blazing, while in others, there are few. Why is this the case? Hot Spots cannot be commanded to appear. Performance controls, orders, and directives make little impact. Hot Spots arise through individual and collective choices, when excitement mounts and curiosity is engaged. Hot Spots cannot be simply summoned forth. However, the ground can be prepared, the elements can be put into place, and the igniting questions can be asked. The challenge is that many companies have often unwittingly created an environment where competition and self-interest negate a mindset of cooperation, where 'turf wars' destroy the possibilities of working across boundaries, where dry, tired speech rather than igniting questions is the common parlance, and where a lackadaisical attitude smothers the energy and questioning that might trigger a Hot Spot.

The good news is that much of this can be changed. You can craft a context that favors cooperation rather than competition. You can actively build and support networks of relationships that criss-cross the boundaries of the company. You can create the will and the freedom to ask igniting questions. These elements are marvellous creators of energy. However, to focus this energy and ensure that it actually adds value, you need the fourth and final element: productive capacity.

The Fourth Element: Productive Capacity

Hot Spots that are capable of creating value through innovation are also potentially the most complex. My own research has shown clearly that initially, the

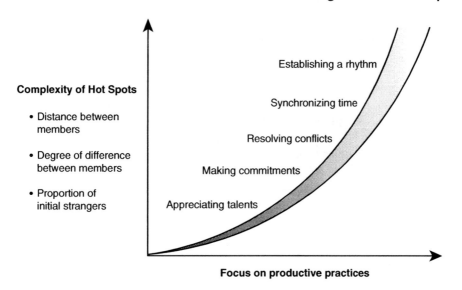

Fig. 14.4 Complexity and productive practices

most productive teams are those located in the lower left quadrant of Figure 14.4—that is, people who work with each other in the same location and have similar skills and attitudes. Those in the top right corner are potentially the most innovative, but they also tend to be less productive. Hot Spots that remained productive did so because the people in them engaged in what we called *productive practices*. Examples of productive practices are illustrated in Figure 14.4.

In the early phases of productive Hot Spots, there is a real emphasis on working on relationships—appreciating the talents of others, learning to make and keep commitments, and resolving conflicts. As the Hot Spot progresses, the type of productive challenge that members face subtly shifts. Whereas previously it was about the relationships between members, it now shifts to members' attitudes to time and rhythm. Hot Spots whose members fail to make this shift in timing and rhythm burn themselves out as the pace of work accelerates. They also become less creative as their time for reflection is overwhelmed by the growing pace of demands. Without these productive practices, the complexity of Hot Spots can be overwhelming, and the energy in the Hot Spot dissipates.

Designing for the Emergence of Hot Spots

Hot Spots emerge on their own; they cannot be controlled and directed. That does not mean that nothing can be done to encourage their emergence. In fact, there are many ways in which you can actively design for the emergence of Hot Spots.

Lead the Change

I have identified a number of key points of leverage through which Hot Spots can be encouraged to emerge. In particular, Hot Spots can be encouraged through subtle shifts in the structure, practices, and processes of your company and the way that decisions are made and resources are allocated. The probability of Hot Spots emerging can be substantially increased through the way tasks are designed, how feedback is given, and the technology used to support the Hot Spot community. The skills, role modeling, and competencies of leaders can play a crucial role, as can the motivation and capability of everyone, and in particular the human capacity and attitude toward spanning boundaries.

In companies in which Hot Spots flourish, executives make use of a large portfolio of these points of leverage to unleash the energy and innovation of Hot Spots. In designing for the emergence of Hot Spots, the ability to recognize and implement best practices from other companies is crucial. However, a word of warning is warranted. Although the search for and adoption of best-practice processes is indeed necessary, it is not sufficient. On the contrary, even though importing and institutionalizing best-practice ideas and processes is important, other types of processes, which I call signature processes, can also be crucial. Indeed, it is your company's unique bundle of signature processes, combined with industry's best practices, that will ultimately create the context in which Hot Spots emerge.

Finding your Own Way to Hot Spots: Signature Processes

I use the term signature to describe the way in which these processes embody a company's character. The term signifies the idiosyncratic, unique, and essentially personal nature of these processes. These signature processes arise from passions and interests within the company, rather than from concepts of best practice from outside the company. So while one task of every executive is to find and adapt best practices—in a sense, to 'bring the outside in'—an added critical task of management is to be able to learn to identify and preserve the company's own signature processes. This added duty might be thought of as the need to 'bring the inside out.'

The distinction between a signature process and an industry best practice is not absolute, however. In particular, if a company's signature processes prove especially advantageous, they may be imitated by other companies so often that they eventually become known as best practices.

Toyota's lean production is an example of a process that began as a signature process for the company. It was capable of creating enormous energy and potential Hot Spots by espousing the values and aspirations of the firm's leaders. Over time, many other companies sought, not always successfully, to adopt the process of lean manufacturing.

266

This subtle but crucial difference between standard best-practice processes and unique signature processes was clear when I took a closer look at the companies in which Hot Spots emerge on a frequent basis. In many of these companies, there are practices and processes that are surprising and intriguing.

When we examined the context that shapes the emergence of Hot Spots at Nokia, we discovered that the company's structural architecture plays a crucial role. At Nokia, it is its modularity which allows frequent restructuring. This structure is unique and has a profound impact on the cooperative mindset of the company. It also affects the precision with which boundary spanning can occur. This modularity is a highly idiosyncratic practice. Best practices suggest that organizational restructuring should take place as infrequently as possible in order to maintain a relatively stable organization and minimize confusion. So why restructure frequently? At BP, 'peer assist' and peer-based bonuses have a critical and positive impact on cooperation and the exchange of knowledge. But again, best practices in performance management require that managers be responsible for what they can personally affect. So why reward people on the performance of their peers who are outside of their own direct line of accountability?

And yet Nokia and BP—both highly successful companies abounding with Hot Spots—adopt processes that differ significantly from general views of best practices. And perhaps even more surprisingly, the executives involved in these processes believe that they are a key part of the company's success.

The reason lies in the idiosyncrasy of these signature processes and in their potential to create the energy to drive high performance. This idiosyncrasy is a direct embodiment, a 'signature,' of the history and values of the company and its top executive team. The combination of values, experience, and passion enables these idiosyncratic processes to flourish against all odds.

Adopting best-practice processes gets a company to a level playing field. Yet the very nature of best practices, drawn as they are from a common pool of industry knowledge, means that the adopters of best practices are always susceptible to being copied by others that catch up with them. In contrast, the signature processes at these companies are so idiosyncratic and so much a part of the organizational heritage and values that the signature processes are difficult for competitors to replicate.

Signature processes develop from the heritage and values of the company, and it is the philosophy and wisdom of the executive team that shape them. At BP, the 'peer-assist' signature process originated not in industry best practices but in the values and beliefs of CEO John Browne and his team. Browne explains the three core premisses of his philosophy: 'that people worked better in smaller units...that any organisation of scale should create proprietary knowledge through learning...[and] that there is a very different interaction between people of equal standing.'

Signature processes are acceptable within the companies in which they develop because very often they have grown as the company grows and are associated with the executive team's passion and values. They are part of the fabric, the ways of behaving, the 'way we do things around here.' So while the task of every executive is to find and adapt best-practice processes from outside the organization to build the strength of the company, an added critical task of management is to be able to articulate the company's signature processes.

This is a difficult task. Executives need skills in developing and encouraging both best practices and signature processes. However, much of what executives have been schooled to do in developing conventional best practices flies in the face of the creation of signature processes. In fact, our recommendations for creating signature processes reverse some of the very prescriptions of best practice. To nurture signature process development, executives should rediscover their heritage and unlock the treasures that have been languishing half-forgotten within the organization, rather than search externally as they do for best-practice processes. Managers should become sensitive to and elaborate on those processes in the company about which people are passionate and become more in tune with the organization's values and beliefs. The challenge in designing for the emergence of Hot Spots is to bring in best practices and discover and shape signature processes that reflect the culture of the company. Without such processes all you will see through your thermal-imaging goggles is the coldness of business as usual.

Further Reading

An overview of Lynda's work can be found at www.lyndgratton.com. There is a flourishing community of people interested in supporting the creation of Hot Spots and bringing energy and innovation to organizations. To join this community visit www.hotspotsmovement.com.

On the Nature of the Cooperative Mindset

There is a vast literature on cooperation and trust. For a very useful overview see:

Fukuyama, F. (1995) *Trust: Social Virtues and the Creation of Prosperity.* London: Hamish Hamilton. This argument is taken further in Nahapiet, J. E., and Ghoshal, S. (1998) 'Social Capital, Intellectual Capital and Organizational Advantage,' *Academy of Management Review*, 23: 242–66.

On Social Capital and Boundary Spanning

For more about the nature of relationships and a deeper discussion of social capital:

Baker, W. (2000) *Achieving Success through Social Capital: Tapping the Hidden Resources in your Personal and Business Networks.* University of Michigan Business School Management Series. San Francisco: Jossey-Bass.

Brown, J. S., and Duguid, P. (2000) *The Social Life of Information*. Barton, Mass.: Harvard Business School Press.

Cross, R., and Parker, P. (2004) *The Hidden Power of Social Networks: Understanding How Work Really Gets Done in Organizations*. Boston: Harvard Business School Press.

A compelling case for the positive impact of high-quality relationships is made in Dutton, J. E., and Heaphy, E. D. (2003) 'The Power of High Quality Connections,' in I. G. Cameron, J. Dutton, and R. Quinn (eds.), *Positive Organizational Scholarship*. San Francisco: Berrett-Koehler.

The genesis of my thinking about boundary spanning can be found in:

Ghoshal, S., and Gratton, L. (2002) 'Integrating the Enterprise,' *Sloan Management Review*, 44: 31–8.

The impact of networks and relationships on the creation and transfer of knowledge and hence on innovation is a fascinating study. For a useful overview see:

Leonard-Barton, D. (1995) *Wellsprings of Knowledge: Building and Sustaining the Sources of Innovation*. Boston: Harvard Business School Press.

On Ignition

Ignition as a force for innovation and creativity has been observed and described by a number of scholars. See for example:

Csikszentmihalyi, M. (1997) *Finding Flow: The Psychology of Engagement with Everyday Life*. New York: Basic Books.

15   The Contrasting Faces
of the Chairman of the Board

*Nada K. Kakabadse, Andrew P. Kakabadse,
and Linda Lee-Davies*

Introduction

Corrupt corporate practices in the 1980s and 1990s meant board processes and procedures became subject to more disciplines to safeguard shareholders. The resulting counterbalance between corporate profitability and protection of shareholder rights yokes the shoulders of the chairman today and influences the leadership of change from the highest organization strata.

This top job tightrope walk straddles internal and external influences of board members and shareholder demands. The chairman must mediate between the political pyramid of power within and the increasingly educated shareholder who is more aware of their rights and how to exercise them.

The changes in corporate governance intended to pull in the belt on the top trousers and restrict the impact of individual pursuit on corporate performance have been initiated, but their success is a matter of debate. With the recognition that an unrestrained CEO and his or her team can be a prime root of corporate excess, the leadership role of chairman is brought into the limelight. The leadership effectiveness of the now more visible chairman is therefore crucial to corporate success.

With the creeping in of numerous regulations, the criticality of compliance makes corporate governance more of a methodical necessity. For some, governance is acquired 'off the shelf.' For others, it is tailored more precisely to the needs of the company. Either way, governance has actually helped place the chairman in the front line not only to tick the boxes but precisely to link key enterprise issues such as 'strategies,' 'change,' 'goals,' 'competitiveness,' 'risk,' 'opportunities' directly to these administrative processes.

With the chairman at the coalface, they may even push the CEO inwards to look after the day-to-day internal affairs. At the very least they sit alongside each other, though it still remains the case that the CEO can be sacked by the chairman.

The governance response to corporate malpractice has clearly complicated matters. Within a framework of ever more intricate corporate governance regulation set out to standardize the practices of firms, this chapter, by looking at the chairman role in detail, highlights a number of interpretations regarding how the leadership role is carried out and understood and how it influences organization outcomes. From different levels of personal discretion to geographical and external factors, there are a number of considerations when trying to pull in a definition of the role as it stands in current climes.

Mapping out the Role of Chairman

Most pundits concur that with the ever greater demand for effective governance and transparency, the quality and capabilities of the chairman are critical to the performance of the organization. However, what are these qualities and are they likely to conflict with each other?

Given the seniority of the role, it is fair to say a forward-thinking mentality is important in terms of the direction the chairman desires for the company, but that would need to be weighed with an open attitude in order to gain the trust of the CEO and the top team to most effectively support them to success. Being approachable enough to court honest opinion would be useful in addition to coordinating the activities of the top team—or is that the CEO's job? That is less than clear as the chairman would need to make a balanced judgement about how far to roll up their sleeves. Just far enough to manage the internal relations, but always at the ready to be wound up and wheeled out to 'nod and grin' with the outside world and to represent the company in the best way possible. No pressure then! And it doesn't stop there.

In the juggling act of managing board activity the chairman must decide the right balance of complimenting or complementing the CEO. The supply of experience they are there to give must be administered in doses appropriate to the situation. Is it a case of back them or sack them? There is no measure on this. Each company will be different and each CEO the same.

As if that were not enough in itself to consider, this is all presuming that the CEO and the chairman are actually two different people.

It is common practice in the UK and Australia for the role of chairman to be separated from that of CEO. This way no one individual can undemocratically influence the firm's strategic and operational decisions. The UK's self-regulatory model of governance makes the chairman ultimately accountable for the activities and personnel of the corporation and in this way all directors are equally responsible for developing and implementing the company's strategy as well as for attending to the governance of the company in Dumas's famous 'one for all and all for one' Three Musketeers culture. This creates a horizontal solidarity between the members of the board as well as a vertical solidarity between them and executive management.

The chairman then, has to create the environment in which this will take place. Facilitating the bonding of the directors and encouraging and enhancing their contribution becomes key in setting up a positive experience where transparency and clear communication is achieved. This is in addition to the more familiar duties of cascading information and quality checking performance levels of people and processes.

In order to achieve all this, the right person for the chairman role then becomes a matter for scrutiny. CEOs migrating into chair position may not be neutral enough. Objectivity may be best delivered through an external candidate.

In the minority of cases, particularly in Australia where the two roles are not kept apart, greater reliance is placed on the board to police the all-powerful chairman/CEO. In contrast role separation is not broadly observed in the USA. The roles of CEO, president and chairman are merged in 76 per cent of US companies. Within the American system, ultimate power lies with the role of president/chairman/CEO and their vision but the price for this is that the chairman carries the full legal and financial responsibility for the company.

In fact there is quite a lot of difference between the practices of the UK and Australia against those of the USA. Governance practice is self-regulatory in the former two but driven by legislation in the USA.

Role duality in the USA has given licence to the chairman/CEO/president to incorporate their personality and personal goals in corporate decision making. Not surprising then that US management and leadership literature has focused on the image of the hero chairman/CEO/president, wielding power to reallocate resources, exercising their personal influence to motivate others to achieve their goals, and building a vision of the corporation's future that is inspirational and shared with enthusiastic followers. It is interesting too that US executive pay for top managerial positions is considerably higher than that of their counterparts abroad.

Despite the US influence across the globe, the rubric of role duality is under attack. The volatility resulting from a one-person rule in terms of human performance, scandals, and temptations makes a good argument for keeping the roles apart. Indeed corporate scandal has influenced the onset of regulation and legislation increasing the legal accountability for any fraudulent behavior.

Together or apart—which is more effective for the company? Whether powerful, independently minded boards are more progressive and effective is unclear. Whether scandal is actually confined to those with role duality is doubtful. However, even if financial effectiveness cannot be attributed to a particular governance structure, the separated structure is taken as most likely to create the environment in which more democratic decisions may occur.

Aside from regulation, increased pressure from shareholders in the wake of public scandal has influenced US boards to introduce the role of 'lead independent director' (LID), to act as the go-between between the chairman/CEO/president and the other board directors. The role comes into its own at times of crisis, when the LID acts as de facto chairman deciding on the future of the CEO.

Contrasting Practices

Having noted the wide level of discretion of the chairman in terms of how they choose to best serve their company and begun to question how that role sits together with the CEO it is clear this is just a scratch at the surface and a number of other influencing factors have to be considered.

The study shows how success is affected by factors such as role boundary, governance application, whether the position is executive or non-executive, and how far chairman accountability extends. Equally, how the chairman links the actions with their driving of the vision, their length of time with the company or in the role, and what counter-influences exist could be factors which matter. Also, what about the actual recruitment of chairmen in the first place in terms of selection criteria as well as where they are geographically? Empirical enquiry confirms that many factors force the face and grace of the chairman.

Role Boundary

It is evident then that where the role of chairman starts and stops is difficult to define. Many influences paint out the parameters of power. These parameters form not just from the ability of the chairman themself but from the existing fabric of the company when they join. The history and culture of the company, and therefore the board itself, start the brushstrokes. The enterprise will already have its own norms and levels of conduct and how changeable these are may be key in deciding the conduct of the commanding character. This is just the beginning and as relationships form, so do further parameters. The level of socialization and quality of communication with colleagues on the board will influence levels of buy-in and cooperation. Each board member will have their own agendas in addition to the corporate one and the chairman has to satisfy both. The management and meeting of these expectations in both directions creates a further dilemma of duality within and power is pushed and pulled until the right mix is achieved for that particular internal environment.

The external environment puts its own push on the parameters of the role. The influence of regulators, legislation, codes of practice, stock exchange conditions, and the demands of institutional investors will each have their own impact.

So, the chairman's contribution is as individual as the company itself and the set of circumstances they find themselves in. This would also be even more evident when viewing the matter from an international perspective. Where the CEO and the chairman are one and the same person as in the USA, the parameters widen further and the diversity of direction is more subject to an individual autonomous input. Role dualities within complicate further the role duality without and individual idiosyncrasies win the day.

Executive/Non-Executive Status

The contribution of the chairman can also be scrutinized in terms of whether they are a full-time or part-time executive or non-executive. Whether executive or non-executive, the principal involvement is attending to the duties of the board, but how far that then reaches will be influenced by whether their status is more involved in executive duties and for how much time they are contracted to provide.

Full-time, particularly executive, chairmen are more involved in the day-to-day affairs of the firm, whereas part-time chairmen place a greater reliance on the quality of relationship and level of trust with their CEO whilst having no executive functions reporting to them.

The level of role delineation (other than in the USA) varies nationally and internationally. In the UK, the chairman emerges as more passive with the CEO dominant but that, again, varies by company. In Australia, the reverse is more likely with, at times, a downgrading of the CEO role to chief operating officer. In the USA, the executive/non-executive distinction would not emerge as a consideration due to the high presence of role duality. In this latter case, it is interesting to note that legal and financial responsibility falls on the shoulders of the CEO and the chief financial officer with, supposedly, the chairman part of the role monitoring the CEO bit despite the fact they are one and the same person.

Accountability Spread

This leads nicely on to how far accountability spreads. The executive/non-executive orientation to the role of chairman obviously reflects in the nature and spread of accountabilities and role duality dictates this further. In the UK and Australia the naturally split roles are policed by the fact that the CEO can always be dismissed by the chairman in addition to working in the glasshouse of corporate governance. In the USA, the weight of legal responsibility lies with the CEO anyway, so even where the roles are more likely merged with that of the chairman, accountability is placeable to an individual rather than a role. Regardless of single or double role, accountability is easy to trace.

Vision

With this accountability spread of the role of chairman, further differences are likely to emerge. In terms of identifying and promoting a vision for the future of the firm, the UK chairmen are more likely to position their board to debate, challenge, and 'sign off' on the vision of the CEO and his or her management team. The 'more passive' UK chairman may be contrasted with the 'more proactive' Australian chairman who is likely to have a distinct involvement in, and perhaps for some outright determination of, the vision of the company. Thus, they take on a stewardship of the vision of the enterprise. As shown later in this chapter, the greater dominance of the Australian chairman emerges as a result of the effect of geographic isolation on recruitment practice.

Where role duality is prevalent, full responsibility for the determination and the driving forward of the vision of the company falls on the shoulders of the chairman/CEO. This brings its own issues in that the board is identified as not sufficiently challenging the figurehead. As a result, healthy debate to reach decisions is more limited.

Recruitment

A further area of interest is also how the chairman arrives at the post. Some companies make a stringent effort to appoint 'home-grown talent' in order to ensure long-term stability. In contrast, Australian firms believe that 'the best' senior management talent is located offshore. Many are British or American with an average shelf life of only three to five years, and so the role providing stability falls to the chairman. Thus, in order to provide for longer-term sustainability, Australians more often appoint chairmen from their own local compatriots. Role duality requires a 'hands-on' approach to both the management of the enterprise and the leadership of the board so an organic journey is more likely as executive track record, executive experience, and managerial skills win over boardroom capability. Having a local knowledge of the USA's economic state and market is the most important consideration.

In the UK, chairmen working separate from, though with the CEO, come from a broader, international reach in terms of recruitment practice. Proximity to Europe and to the USA and the drive for penetration of non-home-based markets require the firm's top executives to display international skill and experience. Therefore, for both CEO and chair roles, the search parameters are broader, encompassing track record, breadth of experience, international exposure, sectoral knowledge, and particularly personal leadership capability. In this case a definite capacity for leadership of the board is essential.

Domicile

Mindful of geographic location as well as their spread of accountabilities and the need for some to attend to operational details, the residence of the chairman comes into play. For the US chairman, being close to the business geographically is just as important as knowing the ins and outs of the business. However, if international weight and pedigree are required then domicile is not such a concern. Travelling considerable distances to board meetings and accompanying the CEO on international tours on behalf of the firm are regarded by the UK chairman as 'part and parcel of the job.' So decision between a wider wisdom and in-house knowledge of the company defines the chairman activity from the start.

Counterbalancing Role

These differences of substance not only concern the range of activities and responsibilities of the role of chairman, but also of the counterbalancing influence to the chairman of the board itself. As seen the room for democratic debate or even outright challenge can vary with role activity mix or just the characters of the chairman and board members anyway. Partly driven by fear of further scandal but also by the realization that the central role of chairman allows for potential domination of the board, an additional role has been deemed as needed to provide a counterbalancing influence to that of the chairman. The role of senior independent director (SID) on UK boards, as stated, is paralleled by an equally deliberately crafted role on US boards, that of lead independent director (LID). In Australia the single source of counter-argument to the Australian chairman is expected from the deputy chairman, though few Australian firms have one.

The role of independent director, however it is acronymed, is a valuable contribution to board dynamics and board functioning. Whether in favor of the independent director concept or not, challenge within the boardroom is essential. Without such independent intervention 'group think' would be prevalent both on boards and on the top team. Such roles offer a quiet defiance.

They are not easy though as challenging the chairman/CEO can be uncomfortable and unwelcome. No matter how appropriate or timely the challenge, a level of discomfort will be experienced by the other board members. In extreme circumstances, no challenge emerges and 'an atmosphere' inhibitive of further discussion prevails. There is a danger then that these skills and experience could be considerably under-utilized and only 'favored' directors may be 'offered' sufficient airtime to express their views in a cherry-picked line. There is, it seems, a big difference between recruiting an independent input and then actually allowing that independence to flourish in a closed-shop type environment. It still falls to the chairman to facilitate this process so it still means the company is subject to their idiosyncrasies.

A shared mindset can flourish virtually undisturbed despite good intention. The counterbalancing capabilities of the board itself are also important. How prepared they are to challenge the chair is as much about their strength within as it is about the approachability and listening ear of the figurehead. How willing teams are to accept different opinions and encourage debate can make the democratic difference. Again, then, it comes back to the figurehead to create the environment in which it is allowable to disagree with others and the chairman too if necessary and for each to respect and value those differences without resentment.

Tenure Effect on Insight

Despite all these differences there is perhaps a common theme across the board—tenure. Those chairmen and board members who consider themselves, and, in turn, are also considered by their board colleagues, to hold a 'deep' insight concerning the value advantage of the firm, its strengths and weaknesses, and why the firm is differentiated from competitors (or not), are usually involved with the affairs of the company and its board for a considerable period of time. High-performing boards would attribute continued success to the chairman being in role for between twelve and fifteen years. A healthy length of tenure can make a significant difference.

Also the longer board members work together, the more meaningful their relationships become and the greater their understanding of the organization and its strength, weaknesses, and idiosyncrasies, the greater the opportunity for the chairman and CEO to evolve a shared mindset concerning the vision for the future of the organization. By being together longer, success breeds success. Further, and contrary to the group think argument, a longer-term developed intimacy of relationship enhances the robustness of conversation. Honest and wide-ranging conversations take place and pertinent issues are raised openly but in such a manner that the relationships are maintained as 'professional and workable.'

277

Ultimately, whatever else, it is the chairman's responsibility to nurture a culture which allows this freedom of speech.

Governance Pursuit

Where the official processes around governance are an influence on the chairman and the success of the company is difficult to pinpoint, the company may well just implement the legalities and transparencies quietly and not make a fuss or alternatively make a fuss but reluctantly do it anyway. Either way, they are in place and add security. Complaints are heard as to cost of implementation and governance viewed as an expensive but necessary irritant. Its well-intentioned appearance, though, may not always result in a high impact on success as with or without it, success is still dependent on the strength of leadership and the functionality of the top team. Administrative controls offer some reassurance but do not push the company forward to make money. The chairman does that.

Conclusion

Or is it the CEO? And so we turn full circle in search of what makes a successful chairman. There are so many variations in practice that common themes are hard to isolate. Not only is each situation different but so is the capability and character of the chairman. It is clear that the role of chairman is influential and powerful in shaping the board, directly or indirectly. This determines, in certain cases, the parameters for judging strategy and, in other cases, the strategy of the firm, and both determine its level of success.

Pulling out to an international dimension some themes began to emerge. At the national level, demographic influences determine the role boundaries and orientation of chairmen. Geographical factors, such as knowledge of home markets, expatriate recruitment, the nature of governance stipulation (voluntary or legislative), role separation or duality, and preference for executive on non-executive status, significantly affect board dynamics, the nature of the chairman/ CEO relationship, and ultimately the effectiveness of the board and the firm.

Above and beyond the particulars of practice within countries, the influence of 'the leader,' namely the individual, irrespective of role held is recognized as the ultimate driving force of the firm. Irrespective of governance practice, irrespective of role separation or duality, one person would seem to determine the success or failure of the enterprise. Those considered to have positive effect display a wide range of styles and approaches, best suited to the situational business challenges facing the company at the time. Those who fail are not adaptable and have only one way of doing things. It is clear that the influence of that one man or woman can so predominate, that corporate governance becomes a secondary concern.

So, despite nationally determined practices and better regulation, despite role delineation (or not) and sound governance application (or not), it is the values, qualities, and behavior of the leader(s) that emerge as a key ingredient to determining firm success. So why focus the attention on boards and the role of chairman? It was the ancient Greeks who defined governance in the form of a person, namely, the *Kyvernitis*—the oarsman or helmsman of the ship who guides the vessel through calms and storms. The term survives today: in Modern Greek, the term for government is *Kyvernisi*. What has not survived, however, is the duality of the leader (the helmsman), namely their influence and also adoption of the necessary disciplines for guiding the vessel or today's modern equivalent, the firm, through a 'storm.'

The modern day *Kyvernitis* is the chairman. The chairman is the bridge between the management and the audit, overseeing and controlling the body of the firm, namely the board. Whatever else, the chairman determines governance pursuit, drives the board, but also is increasingly influential in setting the cultural tone of the organization. In effect, the chairman's influence (as a person) parallels their adoption of governance protocols. It is no surprise, therefore, to discover that those companies considered successful are both better led and display sound governance.

The combination of effective leadership and governance protocol application distinguishes the better-run company. Perhaps one of the more sensitive challenges to face is the changing of the leader(s). In the better-run and better-performing enterprise, it is the chairman (or in the USA, the board) that discusses poor performing CEOs and determines the appointment of their successor. In reality, it is the chairman, less so the board, who determines the nature of CEO performance and either supports the CEO or ensures their departure.

The successful chairman has two positive components, person and protocol. The successful chairman has a number of contrasting faces and combines the right selection of them to obtain the right expression. Their own level of discretion, their relationship with the CEO, the role boundary, whether executive or non-executive, accountability spread, vision, their recruitment, their domicile, allowing a counterbalancing role, the length of time they are in post, and governance pursuit—these all contribute to the alchemy of success in different measure and different combination.

Notes

Our deepest thanks to Lord Tom Sawyer in negotiating access to British chairmen and chief executive officers (CEOs) for the purpose of research. Also, our warmest thanks to Ellen Van

Lead the Change

Velsor, Center for Creative Leadership, North Carolina, USA, for having made possible interviews with some of America's top chairmen and chief executives. Mention must also be made of the efforts of Thunderbird, the International School of Business, Phoenix, Arizona, who also afforded superb access to US chairmen and CEOs. Thanks, also, to Kate Donaghy of Manchester Square Partners, UK, for providing further access to top executives and for her invaluable advice on how to interpret the data. Thanks to David Pumphrey, Partner, Heidrick and Struggles, Australia, for negotiating access to a unique group of top business leaders in Australia. Thanks also to Ruth Barratt for testing our initial findings with UK and US board members.

Above all, we are deeply indebted to the Severstal Group, the Russian Steel company, who have sponsored and financially supported the research reported in this chapter. Their commitment to the promotion of learning acts as an example to others as to what should be part of the nature of a world-class company.

Further Reading

Dearlove, D., and Coomber, S. (2007) 'The Top Chairs,' *World Business*, June, http:// www.worldbusinesslive.com/search/article/661526/the-top-chairs/.

Dulewicz, V., and Herbert, P. (2004) 'Does the Composition and Practice of Boards of Directors Bear Any Relationship to the Performance of their Companies?,' *Corporate Governance and International Review*, 12 (3): 263–80.

Kakabadse, A. (2007) 'Being Responsible: Boards are Reexamining the Bottom Line,' *Leadership in Action* (Centre for Creative Leadership), Mar.–Apr., 27(1): 3–6.

—— and Kakabadse, N. (2007) *Leading the Board: The Six Disciplines of World Class Chairmen*. London: Palgrave.

—— —— and Barratt, R. (2006) 'Chairman and Chief Executive Officer (CEO): That Sacred and Secret Relationship,' *Journal of Management Development*, 25 (2): 134–50.

Nicholson, G. J., and Kiel, G. C. (2004) 'Breakthrough Board Performance: How to Harness your Board's Intellectual Capital,' *Corporate Governance: The International Journal of Business in Society*, 4 (1): 5–23.

16   The Leader as Negotiator

Kathleen Reardon and Andrew McLaughlin

Introduction

> One of the things about leadership is that you're probably constantly negotiating without even knowing it. It's so natural to you that you're doing it all the time.
>
> (IMI Focus Group participant)

Leadership has long been viewed as a trait possessed by exceptional people capable of bringing about change by impressive persuasion, charisma, power, coercion, or some combination of these. Weick sees future leaders as faced with an unknowable, unpredictable world who, in the future, will deal with massive amounts of information changing at near light speed and who cannot be sure that their ideas and perspectives are better than ones they might derive by learning from others.[1] Leaders, therefore, must be more focused on 'updating and plausibility and less on forecasting and accuracy.'[2] Their success in implementing change is dependent, too, on an appreciation for what Weick refers to as 'more migration of decisions to those with the expertise to handle them, and less convergence of decisions on people entitled by rank to make them.'[3]

The Leader's Skill Set

Leadership is no longer, if it ever was, something possessed by a person by virtue of position. It is a set of skills, chief among them the ability to negotiate change rather than dictate it. Governments realize that they need to negotiate with other governments, and businesses understand the need to negotiate with other businesses, yet internally within both government and business, negotiation is typically overlooked as a means of leading significant change.

This contrasts with the popular view of 'great man' leadership and accentuates the importance of communicative abilities: 'Leadership is not the outcome of individual brilliance and glib salesmanship portrayed in the Hollywood version beloved of popular management journals. In reality, it is the outcome of an intensely interactive and collaborative practice.'[4]

In 1961, W. C. H. Prentice wrote an article that captured the connection between leadership and negotiation. He rejected the notion of leadership as the exercise of power or the possession of extraordinary analytical or motivational skills and, instead, defined leadership as 'the accomplishment of a goal through the direction of human assistants.'[5] From this perspective, leadership involves understanding people's motivations, involving them in formulating change, and assuring that their interests and needs are addressed in a way that facilitates the group's purpose. Prentice proposed that leaders succeed because they've learned two basic lessons about people: they are complex and they are different. The leader whose skill permits him or her to respond to these observations is 'better able to create genuinely intrinsic interest in the work that he is charged with getting done.'[6] Perhaps Prentice's perspective did not go so far as to specify negotiation as the means by which leaders acquire human assistance, but the implication can be identified in his writing. Missing is the way that leaders capture the minds and hearts of potential assistants and the steps they take to meet them part way. It conjoins leadership and negotiation, going beyond the need to motivate, to explore what it takes to collaborate in assuring that agreed-upon goals are sought in the interest not only of the organization but of its various constituents as well.

The Cost of Command and Control

Change is not simply envisioned and implemented. Resistance is nearly always a given. Steamrolling over people who resist change is an ill-guided, short-term solution to a long-term challenge. It causes resentment as does moving these people out of the way by demotion, firing, or silencing. As many organizations have also learned the hard way, losing people with important knowledge merely because they disagree with new philosophies or practices can lead to a 'brain drain.' In *Working Knowledge*, Davenport and Prusak describe this situation as it applies to downsizing. They explain what happens to the effectiveness of organizations when owners of essential knowledge are lost:

The cost of losing this knowledge is high, leading to failed processes or the expense of luring back the laid-off workers or buying the equivalent of their knowledge from outside sources. In the post-Cold War retrenchment of the defence industry, for example, many aerospace companies offered buyout packages as part of their downsizing programs. They saw knowledge walk out the door with employees who took the offer, and had to rehire (often at higher consulting rates) the same people they had encouraged to leave.[7]

The 'you're with me or against me' attitude so often unwisely associated with leadership is what prevents most change efforts from proceeding smoothly and effectively.

Coalition and Consensus

Asked what skills will be needed in organizations of the future, Handy emphasized the ability to ally with others:

Key skills will be the ability to win friends and influence people at a personal level, the ability to structure partnerships, and the ability to negotiate and to find compromises. Business will be much more about finding the right people in the right places and negotiating the right deals.[8]

Businesses in the future, Handy added, will be more shapeless. Unlike companies of the past, in which people with roughly the same purpose were bound together, businesses now and for the foreseeable future are more like 'a collection of globules—partnerships and alliances.' Forming partnerships and alliances requires negotiation. New ideas must be sold to stakeholders, bearing in mind their various interests. This means that certain time-honored ways of accomplishing objectives, such as command and control leadership styles, are unlikely to work. Destined to failure is the leader who proves incapable of forming alliances across groups that often hold conflicting views.

In *What Leaders Really Do*, Kotter describes a number of obstacles to effective change and in so doing helps us understand the crucial role negotiation plays in leadership.[9] Among those obstacles are three that indicate the importance of negotiation in formulating and implementing change. These are:

- not creating a powerful enough guiding coalition,
- not removing obstacles to the new vision, and
- not anchoring changes in the corporate culture.

The production of a guiding coalition is especially important to change as it includes people in the process. Kotter proposes the development of coalitions that represent people at all levels of the organization. No group should be excluded, especially ones viewed as potentially hostile. Kotter warns that often the villain of change is closer to the top than is commonly thought. Deciding, for example, that middle managers are likely to be an obstacle causes some leaders to come down hard on the wrong people when what they should be doing is finding ways to involve all levels.

I have found that the biggest obstacles to change are not middle managers but, more often, those who work just a level or so below the CEO—vice presidents, directors, general managers, and others who haven't yet made it to 'the top' and may have the most to lose in change. That's why it is crucial to build a guiding coalition that represents all levels of the organisation. People often hear the president or CEO cheer-leading a change and promising exciting new opportunities. Most people in the middle want to believe that; too often their managers give them reason not to.[10]

Kotter also argues that those leading change often say they are working in teams when they actually have 'a committee or a small hierarchy.' During the stresses of change, he suggests, leaders 'need to draw on reserves of energy, expertise, and, most of all, trust.' None of this is possible without negotiation. People do not trust those who order them about, ignoring or diminishing their potential contributions. They may play along to get along for a while in bogus coalitions, but eventually the change effort will collapse because a true coalition was never formed.

The Leader/Negotiator as Detective

Identifying obstacles to change, the second of Kotter's recommendations relevant to leader/negotiators requires knowing how people who can advance the change process think about it. Do they support it? Do they feel a part of it? Do they have good reason to jeopardize it? Change, no matter how good the ideas behind it, is only as good as the people implementing it allow it to be. Here again negotiation is vital to success. Effective negotiation always involves a period of intelligence gathering during which obstacles are identified along with ways to go around or overcome them. Before commencing interaction, a skilled negotiator learns about the other parties' needs, interests, and concerns (both mutual and divergent), emotionally charged issues, reputations and negotiation styles, claims and evidentiary support, potential paths around resistance, available resources, likely strategies and tactics, and what if anything would cause them to walk away from the table.

Kotter's third obstacle to change, anchoring it in the corporate culture, is also a negotiation activity. Like identifying obstacles, it involves gathering intelligence about ways in which the organization works, often unstated rules, and assuring that the change effort will not fly in the face of these modes of thought and operation. Leaders must take account of their own organization's ways of doing things. Cullen has demonstrated how different sectors in Ireland have distinct cultural requirements for how their leaders negotiate and communicate.[11] Senior managers in commercial organizations, for example, are increasingly recruited to change or develop the organizations they are expected to lead. Coming into a new organization and expecting to change it involves getting to grips with the organizational culture quickly and working with the grain of norms and practices to enact a new organizational reality for its members. It is difficult to imagine a new leader being able to do this without excellent negotiation skills. Similarly organizations in the public and not-for-profit sectors expect their senior managers to be excellent networkers and relationship builders.

Change that displaces all that has come before is not likely to succeed. People need to hold on to something, and often that something is the status quo. 'That's not the way we do things around here' is the kind of resistance those leading change often hear. Then they need to listen. Even the most intelligent people are creatures of habit. Upset too many of those habits and change will not succeed. Negotiate alterations and success is more likely.

Why not just give people information about change in a compelling way? Here again the problem is that people already have ideas formed. They have formulated these ideas over time by learning. Information alone, no matter how compelling, rarely changes ideas. Theodore Roszak, author of *The Cult of Information*, explains that the 'mind thinks with ideas, not with information.'[12]

Information may helpfully illustrate or decorate an idea; it may, where it works under the guidance of a contrasting idea, help to call other ideas into question. But information does not create ideas; by itself, it does not validate or invalidate them. An idea can only be generated, revised, or unseated by another idea.[13]

The Negotiation Style Inventory

The first negotiation skill needed by leaders today is the ability to understand their own negotiation style and that of others. Skilled leaders know their own negotiation style predispositions and are able to determine when and how to stretch beyond them. When a situation calls for a certain type of negotiation leadership, they adapt their own style to those conditions or seek assistance from someone on their team whose style is better suited to the task at hand. This is surely part of the hard stuff of business as there are no manuals to which one might turn for quick answers.

I had a department of about 50 people and the targets were 'non-negotiable.' I was just hit with the targets that we had to deliver operationally... I had to go to my staff and say we need dual ownership today, or we need people to work the weekend, or whatever to deliver [the] specifics, stretch that I'd been forced to accept. And as I got into the role, I got better at negotiating that with them. I got used to negotiating some give-and-take on the targets. I'd go to a meeting with my peers on the management team and I'd get something and I'd come back and I'd say 'They've agreed that if we do this, then next week's target will be reduced by "X."' And then I'd have more credibility with them to negotiate. (IMI Focus Group participant with a primary motivator style)

TABLE 16.1 Negotiation style inventory

For each question, enter an 8 for the response most like you during negotiations, a 4 for the item second most like you, a 2 for the third, and finally a 1. You MUST answer all the questions. There are no RIGHT or WRONG ANSWERS. Respond with what comes first to your mind.

1. When I negotiate, I	focus on my objectives		explore workable solutions		try to understand their thinking		try to avoid arguments	
2. I explain my ideas best by	being forceful		presenting my ideas logically		explaining the implication		relating my points to theirs	
3. When I am confronted, I	react strongly to what is said		explain my position with facts		look for a common ground		give in reluctantly	
4. I describe my expectations	objectively		in complete detail		enthusiastically		amicably	
5. I get my best deals when I	don't make any concessions		utilize my leverage		find creative solutions		am willing to meet them halfway	
6. My objective in negotiation is to	achieve my goal		convince others to accept my position		find the best solution for all		look for an acceptable solution	
7. The way to win an argument is to	be self-confident		be logical		have novel ideas		look for consensus	
8. I prefer information that	is specific and understandable		is complete and persuasive		shows a number of options		helps to achieve rapport	
9. When I'm not sure what to do, I	take direct action		search for possible solutions		rely on my intuition		seek advice from others	
10. I dislike	long debates		incomplete information		highly technical material		having arguments	
11. If I've been rejected, I	persist in my point of view		rethink my position		relate my ideas to theirs		try to salvage the relationship	
12. If timing is important, I	press for a quick decision		rely on critical facts		propose a compromise		hope to postpone the inevitable	
13. When I am questioned, I	answer emphatically		rely on data for my position		respond with a broad question		look at how it affects me	
14. I prefer situations where	I am in control		I can utilize my logical ability		I can explore new opportunities		people are considerable	
15. I negotiate best when	I use my experience		a technical analysis is critical		I can explore many alternatives		I am in a win-win situation	
16. When I am the underdog, I	try not to show any weakness		prepare carefully		try to change the situation		match my needs with theirs	
17. When one is antagonistic, I	stand my ground		reason things out carefully		attempt to rise above the situation		look for ways to reduce the tension	
18. If I'm in a losing situation, I	become more determined		consider all my options		look for ways to turn it around		appeal to their sense of fairness	
19. To achieve mutual gain, I	show a workable solution		clarify everyone's priorities		suggest a mutually beneficial plan		consider both sides of the issue	
20. In negotiating, it is important to	know what each party wants		clearly identify the agenda		start by making a positive impression		recognize that each party has needs	
TOTAL								

Source: © Alan J. Rowe, and Kathleen K. Reardon (Form may not be reproduced without written permission).

Identifying your Style

To assist in this style adaptation needed to negotiate during change, Rowe and Reardon developed *The Negotiation Style Inventory*© (see Table 16.1), which is described at some length in Reardon's book *The Skilled Negotiator*.[14] It is a means of identifying style predispositions. None of us works in just one style but rather a combination of styles. We do, however, have predispositions toward one or two styles and these tend to shape how we communicate with others. Leading by negotiation requires an understanding of both our own style preferences and those of people with whom we intend to form vital alliances.

Style identification is actually a form of *intelligence gathering*, an activity we've noted is imperative to effective negotiation. Understanding how you as a leader tend to negotiate—and then comparing that to the negotiation styles of those on the other side of an issue—provides an indicator of the kind of adaptation that may be necessary in order to convince them to follow your lead or meet you part way.

Once you have assigned an 8, 4, 2, or 1 along each row from strongest to weakest description of you, the inventory is completed. Add the scores in each column. The four numbers at the bottom should sum to 300 if the inventory is filled in as directed and scores are added correctly. At that point, it is possible to identify style preferences. A high score in the left-hand column, indicates a predilection for an *Achiever style*. Achievers usually search for the heart of an issue, moving things along quickly. They have little patience for long-winded logic, and they want to win. They avoid concessions whenever possible. If the highest score was in the second column, the person is inclined to be an *Analytical*. This type of negotiator provides a good deal of data and is inclined to walk people through his or her reasoning step by step. Such negotiators speak in terms of priorities, and if they make concessions, they tend to make them along those lines. The *Motivator* scores high in column three. Such negotiators pride themselves on finding clever, novel ways of reaching solutions. They also express enthusiasm in a contagious fashion. Finally, the *Mediator* is one who scores high in the fourth column. Mediators like to help people find ways to agree. They are inclined to seek compromise or to accommodate so things will work out well for everyone. Most people have at least two styles on which they score relatively high. The means of NSI results often vary by groups, organization, and sometimes by occupation types. In a study using the Leadership Style Inventory, a tool similar to the NSI in type, DePillis and Reardon found significant differences between Irish and American aspiring entrepreneurs.[15] So a low score for an individual on a particular style may not be low for someone who works in his or her field or is influenced by a particular culture.

The scores may be close together, in which case either style is comfortable, or a substantial number of points may separate them. In this case, the style with the highest score is the primary style and the second one is the back-up style. Occasionally, people score closely on more than two. In some cases, they score closely on three styles and very low on one. These people move rather comfortably among the three styles with higher scores, but the final one presents difficulties. Each style type is potentially in conflict with the other types. An Achiever, for example, could become very annoyed with an Analytical, who provides too much data; with a Motivator, who appears to be a dreamer rather than a doer; or with a Mediator, who seems to be looking for happy endings instead of desired, task-related outcomes.

If you didn't have to negotiate, then you could prescribe the rules that everyone had to do their business by, and there would be no need for managers. Constantly, what presents at my door are people who have things outside the norm, that don't fit into the normal standard operating procedures. So, it's all negotiation in terms of, 'What do I do with this?' You might be asking people to do things that are not within the job description, and what do they get in return for that? So I think it's constant . . . you're a negotiator whether you like it or not. (IMI Focus Group participant with primary analytical style)

If you're a manager and you deal with a senior team of professional, qualified, experienced people, your entire style of leadership is very rarely, except in crisis situations . . . going to be directive. It's going to be consensual . . . You might put something on the table and may not have interacted in the agenda yourself. Maybe [you're] not showing where you're taking strategy, but looking for other people to input and working out as you go along what your strategy is and what you want them to buy into. By allowing them to be a part of that, you can commit them to it and you're also going to get the benefit of their knowledge. And you're sort of sizing them up and looking at how committed they are to plans, and what their approach is—and they're also telling you their personal agenda. (IMI Focus Group participant with a primary motivator style)

Style Stretching

There are many occasions when neither you nor a team member is the right style fit for a negotiation. In such cases those who can stretch or flex to a different style will succeed where those who are less flexible will fail. This is one area where one size does not fit all and the person with the most style flexibility will be the most powerful. Examples are given in Figure 16.1 of how to stretch from one style to a different style to speak the psychological language of the other party.

It's important to know how to stretch to communicate with someone whose style differs from one's own. The chart above indicates how a style type needs to be altered to adapt to a different one. If stretching to another style is difficult

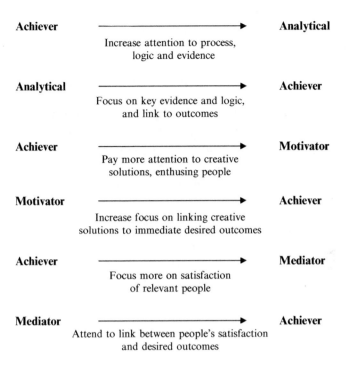

Fig. 16.1 Stretching to a different negotiation style

it is prudent to be accompanied by a team-mate who can stretch or for whom the style in question is a comfortable one. This versatility in style is one advantage of team negotiations. When a negotiating team is balanced in terms of the styles that are represented, the person whose style best meshes with the counterpart can take the lead, at least when differences arise.

If you recognise where your skills are and, more to the point, if you recognise where your weaknesses are, and you surround yourself with people who are strong in those areas, you actually have done a very good thing . . . Looking at myself I see in different situations I would use the analyser style, the motivator style, the mediator style and the achiever style because . . . I would see all four in myself all the time. It just depends on the situation I'm in. (IMI Focus Group participant with a primary motivator style)

The Importance of Framing

The second negotiation skill important to the leader is the ability to frame and reframe as negotiations proceed. Leaders need to consider, when informing their employees of 'the facts,' that when confronted with information the mind seeks to make sense of it by calling on connections to what is known. So change proposals need to be *framed* in a manner that makes them consistent with how employees think. Framing is a means of connecting change to something employees understand and appreciate. Skilled negotiators seek to understand how others with whom they are dealing make sense of their world. Organizational culture is one clue of how employees think as a group. Important too is knowledge about how employees as individuals make sense of information, especially ones who are opinion leaders. For example, will they consider information about proposed change consistent with their roles in the organization or a threat to those roles? Important as well is the extent to which information about change is consistent with employee views of what is ethical and appropriate.

Most organizations conceptualize themselves as active learners. Garvin describes learning organizations as those that 'cultivate the art of open, attentive listening.'[16] Unfortunately, Garvin explains, learning organizations are not built overnight. It takes time, starting with the fostering of an environment that is conducive to learning. All the more reason to avoid rushing into change prior to the opening up of boundaries between employees so that ideas can be exchanged and new ones developed. The organization of 'learning foras' allows leaders of change to learn from employees the limitations of their plans, as well as which steps and alterations may be needed to make change palatable to those upon whose shoulders success or failure rests.

I was responsible for leading the development of the work force in [a service area] and I could have framed it in a language of standardisation, benchmarking and all that, but that wasn't how I saw it. I saw an opportunity to take a workforce that was unskilled, that was maybe struggling with good motivation in a working environment, and to support them through adequate training and organisational structures... Putting out a programme around that, there was no resistance. There was consultation about what people's needs were, what their wants were, and there was a huge groundswell of support for it. (IMI Focus Group participant)

The conversation below is a further example of how an astute negotiator can frame a position to be more palatable to his or her counterpart.

Susan: I can't accept your proposal. Not at this point, anyway.
Paul: Why such rigidity?
Susan: What you call rigidity is actually caution. I haven't refused your proposal; I've merely indicated that accepting it at the moment isn't possible.
Paul: I worked on it for two weeks and you want to drag out a decision?
Susan: I want to give all the work you did the thoughtful consideration it deserves, rather than slip into premature judgment that won't serve either of us.[17]

Susan relabels her actions in a manner less threatening to Paul. The actions he categorizes as rigidity, she calls caution. What he considers to be dragging out a decision, she redefines as deserved, thoughtful consideration. Listen to skilled negotiators and you will hear this kind of relabeling or reframing. They do not overdo it, but they do take notice when labels threaten to harm their efforts, and they quickly shorten the shelf life of such labels.

The Importance of Versatility

The third critical negotiation skill important to leadership is flexibility. Effective leaders always attempt to add choices and to invent options for mutual gain. Effective negotiators do not let the past determine their present and are not ruled by routine. They practice the art of fast forgiveness for past transgressions and rely on well-formed ideas about the outcomes that they seeking. They focus on interests always stressing the limitations of fixed positions. They put in the extra effort it takes to be sensitive to their surroundings and notice not only how things are the same but also how they are different. It is this attention to differences, in particular, that keeps them alert. People generally do not pay attention to the same old things, so people who are not alert to subtle, otherwise unexpected differences walk around each day half asleep.

It is largely in times of uncertainly that most of us pay more attention. For example, Ellen Langer explains, we pay attention to the sounds our new car makes but soon tune them out.[18] We may tune back in when the car makes a loud grinding noise, by which time it is too late to do minor repairs. Skilled negotiators do not stop listening and observing. They pay attention to subtleties and intentionally look for distinctiveness in people and events that others fail to notice. As a result, they are not caught unaware when things change.

Unskilled negotiators routinely abdicate their responsibility to communication and negotiation by allowing themselves to slip into verbal and non-verbal habits that make them predictable and easy targets for the more alert. Expertise in negotiation requires versatility in word choice, emotional expression, and non-verbal gestures. It calls for thinking of ways to get things done that others neglect. Figure 16.2 shows how skilled negotiators use techniques to keep their minds open to options. Mind mapping, developed by Tony Buzan, is one way to do this. In this Figure is a mind map of a negotiation developed by Reardon to explain how mind mapping can work when negotiators have reached an impasse.[19] By thinking in terms of options instead of insisting that an idea be followed exactly as the leader has in mind, avenues open by which others' interests can be considered and utilized in determining the best option.

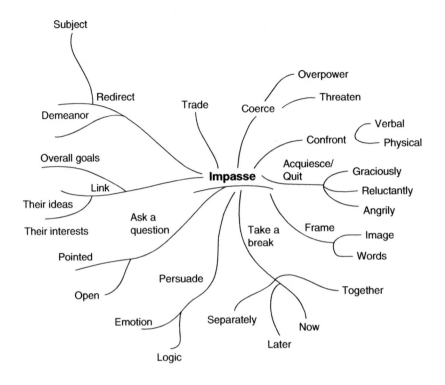

Fig. 16.2 Negotiation mind map: opportunity elaboration

Additional Skills to Become a Better Leader/Negotiator

In addition to negotiation style, framing, and versatility skill development, leaders wanting to derive benefits from the ability to negotiate should also learn the following.

Train Yourself to Effectively Gather Intelligence

The politics of the situation gives you your power to negotiate, and once you understand what the politics are, and who you can influence and negotiate with, you can get into it much more quickly. . . . I'd be suggesting to somebody coming into a new environment now, if I was doing this, that they spend the first couple of weeks just networking and getting to know people: their areas of expertise and power, and what's important for them and get the politics as quickly as possible. Because if you do that, you're actually in a very much stronger position to say what you need, and what you want, and what you understand. (IMI Focus Group participant)

Much of who we are conspires in our unconscious to limit choice. Negotiation at its best involves acute awareness of and adept management of such constraints. Negotiators use the predictability of others to inform their choices while endeavoring to avoid providing their counterparts with the same advantage. Skilled leaders follow steps to assure that they have adequately studied the situation at hand, how the other side thinks on key issues, and what actions they are likely to take.

Below are various forms of intelligence important to assess before proceeding to negotiate:

- Interests—mutual and divergent;
- Concerns—mutual and divergent;
- Emotional issues;
- Primary claims;
- Evidentiary support—strengths and weaknesses;
- Potential avenues around resistance;
- Style compatibility considerations.

It is widely accepted that an understanding of each party's key interests and how they align is crucial. How one achieves this understanding has received less attention. Typically, sophisticated intelligence gathering involves asking strategic questions and observing how they are answered. Most people are not very good liars. Many are uneasy providing only part of the truth. When they are attempting to deceive, their bodies provide clues. Astute intelligence gatherers take notice of these clues. Could information being withheld at this point prove valuable? If this is likely, the next step is to ask questions or disclose information that enables you to test the waters.

Robert Redford, actor, director, producer, and founder of the Sundance Institute—an incubator for independent films—described for the *Harvard Business Review* the importance of identifying the other side's interests:

I learned that the corporate powers that be aren't going to be interested in the fruits of your labor and passion unless you are adept at understanding their agenda and speaking their language. You must always present yourself more conservatively than you privately feel you are. You can't be forceful, loud, confrontational, or declarative. You have to sell what you have on their terms.[20]

'Selling on their terms' means knowing the other parties' interests, their desires, their deep-seated beliefs, and what they're likely to do. It means understanding and appreciating how they communicate, the ways they position their ideas, and their negotiation styles.

Lead the Change

Prioritize Issues and Develop Contingency Plans

When negotiators identify goals too far afield of what can be achieved, they set themselves up for disappointment or failure. Former Mayor of New York Rudi Giuliani writes:

Whenever I approach a problem, I seek the solution that's most favourable but does not overreach. There is no fail-safe formula for knowing where that line is. Leaders seem to develop a sense of it. Those who can't don't stay leaders for long.[21]

It's important to be aware of an important form of a contingency goal known as BATNA, a *best alternative to a negotiated agreement*. A BATNA, according to Roger Fisher and William Ury, answers the question 'What will I do if we can't come to an agreement that meets my needs?'[22] If it becomes clear that your ideal outcomes and all contingencies are not attainable, the BATNA is the answer. Skilled negotiators realize that if they have something else they can do if all else fails, all of their eggs are not in one basket. They have an option on which to fall back—and thus they avoid a sense of failure.

Managing the Power Balance

Another negotiation skill important to leadership is identifying and utilizing power. So much of what occurs in negotiation is rooted in perceptions of who has power. What is power, and how do you get it? Power does not exclusively accrue from status, wealth, or expertise. All of us have the ability to create power. Skillful negotiation requires the rare ability to look carefully and mindfully at what one brings to the table.

Leaders should ask themselves, 'What does the other side want that I have?' 'What might they want if they knew I could provide it?' Power is, in many respects, in the eye of the beholder. Astute negotiators know this and are therefore not thrown off stride by the status of their counterparts or by any other indicator of static power. They craft their own power and thereby increase the odds of a profitable negotiation.

Skillful negotiation isn't about sending the other side away unfulfilled or longing for better treatment. There is no talent to that and little long-term reward. For skilled negotiators, heavy-handed use of power is a device of last resort. Authority is not half as valuable as respect. A senior executive of a Los Angeles-based defence company once told one of the authors, 'I've seen supervisors with authoritative power alone get only what they ask for from people. Consequently, they have to expend much more energy to accomplish their work because they have to think of every move their people will make. Supervisors with respect find that people offer to do more and take on more responsibility, which in turn lightens the management load.'

Respect is crucial to negotiation. If the other side regards you as a fair and worthy counterpart or opponent (and if they too are fair people), the outcome of negotiation is likely to be positive for both parties. However, if they are not fair minded or if they are operating under duress, it may be necessary to win respect based on ability to gain advantage. 'The only thing these guys understand is power' is a common phrase in business in reference to such situations. It's no fun to work in those situations, and it is equally joyless to negotiate with such 'guys.' There are times when power is clearly defined. People in the inner circle of most companies have such power. The CEO of a company typically has more power, in a sense, than the people who work for him or her. The negotiator who has resources clearly desired by the other side (who 'holds the cards,' so to speak) has power. When there is some degree of ambiguity as to who holds the most important resources, however, power can be negotiated. In most cases, reality and perception collide. It is not enough to believe that you have more or less power. The key is to discover what matters to those on the other side and then to shape their perceptions of you and your resources in ways that cause them to consider you powerful. This is not easy to do, but is a key component of leadership.

If as Handy and Kotter argue coalitions are increasingly important to business, the ability to find ways to allow each person in a group to have and exert power is critical. Power is rarely permanently owned and when leaders act as if it is, often they find that others seek to take it from them. By contrast leaders who empower others to achieve their own goals as well as those of the group create win-win outcomes. Such leaders negotiate power rather than possess it. They recognize the interdependence of people, including their own with those who work with them.

Notes

The authors would like to thank Professor John Mangan, University of Hull, and John Cullen, Dublin Institute of Technology, for their early collaboration on this project. We would also like to thank Chris Noblet MBA for his editing expertise and creative insights and the participants on the IMI's M.Sc. in Organizational Behavior (Class of 2005) for their generosity in participating in focus groups and completing Negotiation Style Inventories©.

1. K. Weick (2001) *Managing the Unexpected: Assuring High Performance in an Age of Complexity.* San Francisco: Jossey-Bass.
2. Ibid.
3. Ibid. 93.
4. Michael Shiel (2004) *IMI Handbook of Management.* Dublin, Oak Tree Press, 408.
5. W. C. H. Prentice (2004) 'Understanding Leadership', *Harvard Business Review,* Jan.–June.

6. Ibid. 104.
7. Thomas H. Davenport and Laurence Prusak (1998) *Working Knowledge: How Organisations Manage What They Know.* Boston: Harvard Business School Press, 43–4.
8. Charles B. Handy (2002) *The Elephant and the Flea: Looking Backwards.* London: Arrow Books Ltd., 75.
9. John P. Kotter (1990) 'What Leaders Really Do,' *Harvard Business Review,* May–June.
10. John P. Kotter (1998) 'Winning at Change,' *Leader to Leader,* 10 (Fall): 28.
11. John Cullen (2004) 'Identifying Sectoral Management Cultures through Recruitment Advertising,' *Leadership & Organisation Development Journal,* 25 (3).
12. T. Roszak (1994) *The Cult of Information: A Neo-Luddite Treatise on High Tech, Artificial Intelligence, and the True Art of Thinking.* Berkeley and Los Angeles: University of California Press.
13. Ibid. 88.
14. Kathleen Kelley Reardon (2004) *The Skilled Negotiator: Mastering the Language of Engagement.* San Francisco: Jossey-Bass.
15. E. DePillis and K. Reardon (2007) 'The Influence of Personality Traits and Persuasive Messages on Entrepreneurial Intention: A Cross-Cultural Comparison,' accepted for publication, manuscript, University of Hawaii at Hilo.
16. A. David Garvin (1998) 'The Processes of Organisation and Management,' *Leadership and Organisational Studies,* Summer.
17. Reardon, *The Skilled Negotiator,* 127.
18. Ellen J. Langer (1990) *Mindfulness.* London: Collins-Harvill.
19. Reardon, *The Skilled Negotiator,* 51.
20. B. Fryer and D. E. Meyerson (2002) 'Turning an Industry Out: A Conversation with Robert Redford,' *Harvard Business Review,* May: 9.
21. Rudolph W. Giuliani (2002) *Leadership.* New York: Hyperion, 273.
22. Roger Fisher and William Ury (1991) *Getting to Yes: Negotiating Agreement Without Giving in.* 2nd edn. New York: Viking Penguin.

17 Gaining Strategic Advantage through Talent Management

Jay A. Conger

Without a strong bench of well-aligned and talented leaders, few firms can expect to realize their strategic aspirations. In this chapter, we examine this critical foundation to strategy execution—a firm's talent bench and the processes that develop it. We outline the specific practices that distinguish firms which successfully realize their strategic ambitions through rigorous talent management approaches. That said, these firms are a distinct minority. Most companies do not have well-honed, comprehensive initiatives to fully harness the capabilities of their managers and executives. Instead talent management is often a haphazard and opportunistic set of uncoordinated events. As a result, ambitious strategic goals can stall without a reservoir of the right talent.

In this chapter, we begin by examining today's talent markets and the challenges they pose. This discussion sets the stage for why talent management has become such a critical issue for most companies. From there, we describe the overarching aim of 'best-practice' talent management systems and the underlying design philosophies that characterize these systems. This discussion helps to explain why certain practices have emerged as 'best practices' in the field. We then turn to examining the actual practices of organizations that are considered world class at talent management. These individual practices are well integrated with one another and provide a highly disciplined approach to talent management. In other words, the best-in-class firms take talent development very seriously. It is a core competence of the organization—no different from world-class marketing or operations capabilities.

Today's Talent Challenge: Mobile and Demanding

Readers might be asking themselves why talent management has become such a popular topic among corporate leaders today. The simple answer is that talent—especially in the era of knowledge work—has 'two legs.' It is highly mobile. In contrast to past decades, today's successful managers and executives possess an unsurpassed level of mobility. There are several driving forces. One of the most influential is the search firm industry. Within the last two decades, the search industry has risen in size and power as the movers and brokers of talent.[1] The research arms of the leading search firms compile vast directories of management talent and track the latest changes in the organizational charts to see who might be available for opportunities. Each year, they move tens of thousands of managers across firms in every industry. In addition, career opportunities around the world are now easily identified on company and public internet sites. Job posting sites such as Monsterboard.com have significantly enhanced the visibility of opportunities and in turn mobility. As a result, many small and medium-sized companies can now target the same kinds of talent that have been historically reserved for large firms. These smaller firms can attract talent with greater opportunities for increased responsibility, impact, and wealth.

Another powerful facilitator of mobility is a change in attitudes among the younger generations of managers. Witnesses to the massive downsizing initiatives of large corporations in the late 1980s and 1990s, younger generations have little commitment to the traditional notions of corporate loyalty. Their belief is that loyalty is no longer rewarded in kind. Instead it is assumed that only by moving among different firms can an individual gain greater rewards and responsibility. In other words, opportunities for upward mobility are seriously limited by remaining in a single firm over one's career. This belief aided by search firms and the internet has accelerated company hopping. For example, the average high performer may change companies a couple of time during a career. Some estimates suggest that today's average executive will have worked in five organizations over their career.

Organizations that have world-class approaches to talent management understand profoundly this challenge. They have developed processes that select, develop, and retain the most talented individuals they can find. They understand that there are two critical constituents of talent management: their organization and their individual employees.

The Twin Aims of Talent Management

The aims of an effective talent management system are twofold. The first is to serve the needs of the organization by helping to provide a *continuous* and *deep supply* of the *right* talent to achieve the firm's strategic objectives. In essence, the system must have effective processes along four critical dimensions of the talent lifecycle: selection, development, performance management and rewards, and retention. In addition, the ideal talent system helps the corporation to plan for emerging needs at all leadership levels. It also effectively translates the firm's strategic objectives into the performance objectives and standards of the organization. Managers receive clear messages about what types of performance and behaviors will be measured and rewarded.

The second objective of an effective talent management system is to serve the employees. As noted, individual high performers will always have external opportunities to go elsewhere. An effective talent system helps to keep these individuals challenged and motivated to pre-empt their migration to external opportunities. In other words, *retention* and *development* are critical goals. High performers who find themselves stuck in jobs which they perceive as inadequate are prime targets for headhunters. In contrast, the best systems help talent to develop their potential through timely moves to opportunities that match their needs and complement their current skill set. The best systems also provide challenging opportunities and developmental feedback on performance and potential. They enable talented people to move on a faster, or at least more appropriate track. Finally, they help individuals to avoid derailment throughout their careers.

How do the best firms succeed at these two fundamental objectives of talent management? They are guided by a design and operating philosophy that promotes ease of system use, a developmental mindset, ownership by the most senior leaders, processes that cascade deep into management ranks, and rigorous metrics that encourage proactive interventions. The next section explores these design parameters in more detail.

Parameters Underlying 'Best-Practice' Talent Management Approaches

There are a number of fundamental principles shaping the design features of 'best-practice' approaches to talent management. First, they are designed to be simple and easy to use by executives and line managers. All participants—not just those running the systems—have easy access. This feature is critical for building both acceptance and constructive reliance on the system. Data is secure but open to those who need it. They are non-bureaucratic processes. There is a unified approach to talent management to ensure consistency between different business units and geographic areas and to maintain objectivity across the organization. The overall approach is *developmentally* oriented rather than simply replacement or succession oriented. In other words, the processes behind the system are more concerned with the continuing growth and development of an employee rather than with his or her ultimate job title.

The most effective systems actively involve the very top officers of the organization. The CEO and his or her executive team are committed sponsors-proactively participating in determinations of talent and next steps for development of their talented employees. Best-practice systems are also effective at spotting gaps in talent and identifying essential 'linchpin' roles within the organization. Linchpin positions are those jobs which are critical to fulfilling the firm's current strategic objectives as well as its aspirations. These positions and the individuals who can fill them merit and receive regular and extensive attention.

Best-practice talent management approaches still do the job of monitoring succession, enabling the organization to make certain that the right people are moving into the right jobs at the right time and spotting gaps in talent early on. The most effective systems therefore incorporate frequent checkpoints throughout the year. These checkpoints monitor who is where and where they should be going next. This function is built into the system to spot an issue before it becomes a problem.

Finally, well-run talent management operations are continually reinvented. Best-practice companies refine and adjust their systems as they receive feedback from line executives, experience shifts in the company's strategy, monitor developments in technology, and learn from other leading organizations. For example, the computer manufacturer Dell reduced the degree of computerization for talent management data in response to feedback from the field. To avoid the ever-present danger of becoming bureaucratized and mechanical, best-practice systems therefore actively incorporate dialogues and debates about talent and about the development process. There are continuous 'conversations' about what is needed for the future of each candidate, about who should be where, and when. There are continuous conversations on the part of the guardians and designers about the planning process and how its utilization can be improved.

The Practices That Distinguish the 'Best-Practice' Talent Management Approaches

Beyond the critical design parameters mentioned above, there are seven practices and processes that form the backbone of a world-class talent management system. These include: (1) alignment of the talent strategy to the organization's overarching strategy, (2) senior-level sponsorship and HR 'process' ownership, (3) identification and effective deployment of key linchpin positions, (4) rigorous talent identification processes, (5) strong developmental linkages that accompany talent identification, (6) multiple stakeholders assessments with developmental feedback, and (7) rigorous tracking and feedback metrics. Each of these practices will be discussed below.

Strong Alignment between the Organization's Strategy and its Talent Strategy

Talent management occupies a key position as an interface between the human resource function and the strategic direction of the organization. The company's overarching strategy, its marketplace strategies, and its talent strategy must be intertwined. Talent management then becomes a vital resource in anticipating the future needs of the organization in terms of finding, assessing, developing, and monitoring the human capital required by the organization's strategy. Several key questions must therefore be asked when making talent decisions for the organization. What are the strategic objectives of the company in terms of marketplaces and geography? What are the implications of that strategy for talent development? In turn, what should be the talent strategies of the firm? And how do these translate into our talent systems?

For this 'translation' to work, there has to be a close partnership between the senior executive ranks and the human resource function. They are partners in understanding what the business strategy is and in preparing company-wide talent to meet the demands of that strategy. For example, what types of skills and capabilities will be needed as we enter new markets or geographies or grow and reinvent our existing businesses or develop adjacent markets? What types of developmental assignments will be needed most in the future as the firm unfolds its strategy ahead? Talent systems must be tightly linked to strategic objectives of the firm to be effective and to be credible. Thought has to be given to being responsive to emerging threats and opportunities and the implications of that for a talent strategy.

Senior-Level Sponsorship and HR 'Process' Ownership

The sponsors and 'owners' of talent management processes are critical to their usefulness and acceptance. Sponsorship must be at the very top, both at the most senior level of the corporation and at the top of functions and operating units. The mindset of Procter & Gamble's CEO A. G. Lafley captures this dimension: 'Nothing I do will have a more enduring impact on P&G's long-term success than helping to develop other leaders.' At best-practice firms, senior leaders are actively involved in the process. For example, at Dow Chemical, talent management was designed with the active involvement of the CEO, the vice president of human resources, and the workforce planning strategic center. At other best-practice companies such as General Electric or Pepsico, the CEO is the key sponsor for talent management, and a senior management committee of vice presidents steward the process at the corporate level. Sponsorship can take various forms but it always involves a serious time commitment on the part of the CEO and their executive team. For example, at the Sonoco Corporation, the top eight executives including the CEO, the vice president of HR, and the top group vice presidents meet annually for a week to discuss talent management. This is typical of companies whose senior teams are committed sponsors of talent management.

Without this level of critical support by the very top, talent management can end up a more mechanical process. Sensing that it is simply a tangential activity, line executives will vary widely in their commitments to the development of their own talent. Operating groups and functions can hide and hoard their talent. Limited attention will be given to developmental assignments.

Ideally, the board of directors is also involved. They must be familiar with the firm's talent management processes. It is important that they be knowledgeable about succession candidates at the executive level and not simply at the CEO level. The ownership of the system, however, is shared among the business heads who are the line champions. Line management owns the deliverables and is held accountable for the outcomes of the talent processes. Periodic reviews by the senior executives and divisional heads ensure that the system continues to reflect the needs of the corporation. Corporate Human Resources is the 'owner' of the processes and tools.

Effective Identification and Deployment of Linchpin Jobs

Best-practice talent systems inventory the key positions across the organization from the executive level down to the director level. These are the positions considered critical to the success of the organization and its successful implementation of the strategy. They involve important skills which are often difficult to fill and involve coordination with other parts of the organization. They could include regional management, key functional assignments, general management in a small business unit, or key staff assignments.

The more effective systems focus intensively on specific linchpin positions—a select set of jobs that are essential to the long-term health of the organization. As William Rothwell[2] points out, linchpin positions are 'strategically vital leverage points...which when they are left vacant...the organisation will not be able to meet or exceed customer expectations, confront competition successfully, or follow through on efforts of crucial long-term significance.' They are typically difficult to fill, rarely are individual contributor positions, and usually reside both in established areas of the business and those that will be critical to future success. In a professional services firm, for example, the partners managing critical industry sectors such as healthcare would be in linchpin positions, as would be partners managing growth sectors such as biotech. In a technology organization, linchpin positions might be general managers running businesses building adjacent markets. These positions require broad business perspective and experience and entrepreneurship. By monitoring the pipeline for these jobs, companies can focus development programs on ensuring an adequate supply of appropriate talent.

Rigorous Talent Identification Processes

The fourth dimension is selection or identification of talent and the establishment of talent pools. The more effective systems base their assessments directly on the leadership and organizational competency models that are developed for each level. There is no universal competency model for the entire organization but rather there are multiple models, which vary by function and level. Furthermore, best-practice companies tend to use fewer competencies, feeling that simplicity and focus are stronger advantages than comprehensive efforts. Ideally, these models also contain 'derailing attributes' which provide to participants a set of red flags or reminders of the types of behaviors to avoid. In addition to competencies, there are tiered assessments of the readiness of an individual to be moved into a next position. These are staggered by 'readiness today,' 'readiness in the near future,' and 'readiness a year or two down the road.' People who might be ready to move into linchpin positions are identified. For the very top positions, there are position-specific determinations, but for the levels below, there are talent pools to ensure flexibility when it comes to needs.

After using the tools within the talent process to identify future leaders, the next challenge is to organize the high-potential talent pools. Talent pools increase the visibility of talent among the business units and provide a starting place for making decisions about talent movement. The size and scope of talent pools differ among organizations. For example, Dell uses two distinct pools, Eli Lilly uses four corporate pools, and Sonoco Products uses eight different pools. Within Dell's two pools, one is focused on talent at the corporate level while the other exists to classify talent at the business unit or functional levels. Employees designated as global corporate talent are profiled and reviewed by the Office of the Chief Executive and consist of individuals (fewer than 100) with the capability to run significant portions of a function or business and able to leverage skills or experience on a global basis. Further, Dell tracks the movement and development of the global corporate talent pool on a quarterly basis and reports the results to the Office of the Chief Executive. Similarly,

Dell's business units also have functional high-potential programs that identify talent deeper within their organizational structures. Unlike the global corporate talent pool, the functional high potentials are generally not reviewed during the Office of the Chief Executive presentations.

At Eli Lilly, the first two talent pools are the general manager and product team leader pools. They are composed of individuals who have cross-functional talent and can lead multiple disciplines. The third pool is for individuals who need an international assignment added to their experience base. The last pool moves individuals from function to function and develops behaviors. Individuals nominated for this pool must have at least director potential and must be supported by his or her home function.

Strong Developmental Linkages

The fifth dimension of an effective talent system is its developmental linkages. In other words, the system successfully identifies how positions are tied to an individual manager's development along with the superiors associated with those positions. It is critical that jobs identified for promotions have specific opportunities related to development. If a position is for a general manager role in Shanghai, then what are the developmental opportunities that might lead up to that job? Stretch assignments should be focused on developing talent for specific jobs. An effective talent system identifies shortages or gaps in the types of developmental experiences and jobs and is constantly working to increase the number of these. Finally, best-practice companies typically employ a wide range of developmental activities to engage leaders and extend their capabilities. While they believe that job assignments are the most significant developmental activity, many offer mentoring, coaching, and action learning along with educational programs to complement learning on the job.

Multiple Stakeholder Assessments with Developmental Feedback

The individuals who evaluate 'high potentials' and decide who gets promoted into what positions are major stakeholders in any succession management system. Multiple levels of assessors need to be involved. It is not simply an individual's superior who participates in the review, but also the superior's superior, and peers who possess a cross-functional perspective of a candidate's capabilities. Increasingly subordinates and external or internal customers are also involved in the assessment process.

Reviews include developmental dialogues with talent regarding their career interests and goals and the constraints they see. Individuals being assessed also receive information about suggested activities for further growth. These are complemented by individual developmental and career planning so that each participant is engaged to do reflective work. All of this is supplemented with feedback, such as 360-degree feedback, and coaching on the candidate's overall effectiveness in a particular job and his or her overall readiness to move to the next assignment.

The reviews and talent assessments of individual managers are rolled up the organization to assess the number of high potentials, how many of these are well placed, how many are ready for developmental assignments in the near term, and where there are critical talent gaps and vulnerabilities. These reviews eventually reach up to the executive level so that the senior team has a good sense of the talent below them. For example, at the Bank of America, CEO Ken Lewis meets every summer with his top twenty-four executives to review the organizational health of the business. In two- to three-hour sessions with each executive he probes the financial, operational, and people issues that will drive growth over the next twenty-four months, with the majority of time spent discussing the organizational structure, key players, and critical roles necessary to achieving the company's growth targets. These meetings are personal in nature, with no presentation decks or thick books outlining HR procedures. But they are rigorous. Business leaders come to the sessions with a concise document (three pages or less, to ensure simplicity) describing the unit's strengths and weaknesses in its talent pipeline. During these conversations, they make specific commitments regarding current or potential leaders—specifically identifying the next assignment, special projects, promotions, and the like. Lewis follows up with the executives in his quarterly business reviews, to ensure that they've fulfilled their commitments. In one of these talent review sessions last year, for example, one executive made a pitch to grow his business unit at a double-digit clip. This would require some shifts among top talent and a significant investment in building the sales and distribution workforce. Lewis agreed, and a year later in the talent review meeting, he requested specific progress reports relating to the change, checking that people had been put into the right roles and that the sales management ranks had been filled out.

Rigorous Tracking and Feedback Metrics

Effective tracking in a talent system monitors progress and turnover. It records and analyses exits of individuals who are talented and gaps at certain key levels and jobs, particularly linchpin jobs. Two types of data are traditionally collected: *quantitative* data in terms of statistics of turnover and placement rates, and *qualitative* data which analyses why people are leaving, common problems that participants face in terms of their development and career progress, and dilemmas in using the talent management system. Ideally, the tracking system also highlights the gap between planned assignments and actual assignments. This assessment enables top management to see whether or not the system is actually working according to the principles that guide it.

The use of technology for tracking in talent management varies widely within the best-practice organizations. Yet, web-based systems seem to offer great potential for worldwide access and large-scale integration of data. For instance, Dell has moved from more extensive, global software applications to a much simpler MS Excel workbook to organize data. The tracking process must be easy, accessible, and in an understandable format.

In terms of metrics, there are generally two types: *individual* metrics, which rate the candidate on performance versus perceived potential, and metrics for the *overall system*, which highlight the number of openings that are successfully filled internally by the talent management system. The latter highlights the number of individuals who are selected on the list of high potentials and who ultimately obtained jobs related to a targeted development assignment. There are also important metrics on diversity and cross-functional assignments that show how the organization is fulfilling key goals involving under-represented segments of the workforce and general management development through multiple functional assignments.

Finally, there should be tracking systems and metrics that allow sponsors and owners to determine whether or not the talent system is working effectively to develop an adequate supply. For example, firms such as Dow and Eli Lilly measure the portion of key jobs that are filled by insider versus outsider candidates. Both firms believe that going outside the organization on a regular basis for key talent indicates that talent management is not working properly. Conversely, if all openings are filled by internal candidates, an organization might worry about not getting enough new perspectives into the ranks.

Conclusion

At the foundation of the shift toward an integration of the strategic ambitions of a firm with its talent management process is a belief that talent is a direct determinate of the successful accomplishment of the firm's strategy. To succeed at talent management, the organization's leaders must therefore have a true 'talent mindset.' This belief sets up a mandate for the organization—to get, promote, and keep leadership talent. They must feel comfortable talking about their A-level talent as well as their low performers. Top performers must be rewarded with great opportunities, stretch assignments, and top-performing bosses. At the same time, immediate action must be taken to address low-performing talent. Many organizations instead have a tolerance for lower performers. But these individuals have important ramifications for talent management beyond the traditional measures of performance such as productivity. Sub-par talent can block key developmental positions. They may hamper the overall talent management process as their failure to develop subordinates properly can drive away high-potential people. They can profoundly demotivate talent. In closing our discussion, one of the most important underlying lessons is that good talent management is possible only in an organizational culture that encourages candour and a developmental mindset at the executive level. It also depends upon a deep comfort with differentiating individual performance and in turn a corporate culture where the truth is more highly valued than politeness or tolerance for average or poor performance.

Notes

1. R. Khurana (2004) *Searching for a Corporate Savior: The Irrational Quest for Charismatic CEOs*. Princeton: Princeton University Press.
2. W. J. Rothwell (2001) *Effective Succession Planning*. New York: AMACON, 172.

Further Reading

Conger J. A., and Fulmer, R. (2003) 'Developing your Leadership Pipeline,' *Harvard Business Review*, Dec.

Fulmer, R. M., and Conger, J. A. (2004) *Growing your Company's Leaders: How Great Organizations Use Succession Management to Sustain Competitive Advantage*. New York: AMACON.

Michaels, E., Handfield-Jones, H., and Axelrod, B. (2001) *The War for Talent*. Boston: Harvard Business School Press.

Ready, D., and Conger, J. A. (2007) 'Make your Company a Talent Factory,' *Harvard Business Review*, 85 (6): 68–77.

Index

Index

Index

Index

Index

Index

high-velocity environments 175
high-volume consumer products 192
hobby experience 53
Hoddle, Glenn 231
Hon Hai 152
Honda, Sochiro 163
Honda 163–4
Hong Kong 184
hopes and aspirations 97
horizontal solidarity 272
Hot Spots 254–69
hotels 102
hothouses 175
Hounsfield, Godfrey 192
household appliances 155
Houston 93, 239
HPSU (High Potential Start-Up)
  companies 29, 30, 31
HTC 155
HTML (hypertext mark-up language) 218
HTTP (internet protocol) 218
human capital 301
human resource management 97–110
  new approach to 118
  process ownership, senior-level sponsorship
    and 301–2
Humer, Franz 223, 224, 229, 230, 233
humiliation 231, 251
hunches 229
hypermarkets 141

IBM 71, 72, 93, 197
ice-making 184–5, 190
ICT (information communication
    technology) 31
  advances in 150
  rapid changes in 134
IDA (Industrial Development Authority) 16
ideas 51, 107, 116, 118, 193, 224, 225, 254,
    281, 283, 285
  best-practice 266
  economies of 223, 229
  generalizing 104, 105
  generally contested 119
  innovative 261
  'new public management' 117
  novel combinations of knowledge 260
  requirements of business units 108

respect for 232
sharing across boundaries 104
start-up 232
successful exploitation of 191–2
unthinkingly imitated 120
identity 227
  unique 105
ideology 121
idiosyncratic investments 62
idiosyncratic maps 247
IFSC (International Financial Services
    Center) 33
igniting purpose 262–4
IKEA 151, 156–7, 158
IMD 17, 21
IMI Focus Group 281, 285, 288, 289,
    290–1, 293
imitation 120, 186, 192
  competitive 49
  rapid 50
Immelt, Jeff 94
immersion 140
imports 13
incentives:
  collaboration 25
  fiscal 23
  moving production 153
  reduced 62
  specific 15
income statements 72, 75, 76, 107
incomes policy 16
incumbents:
  defensive 192
  expanding 59
independent advice 124
India 20
indicators 20
  see also performance indicators
indigenous industry realignment 27–33
indirect labor 107
induction 258
industrial development 16
industrial networks 150
industrial products 29
industrial relations 98, 121
Industrial Revolution 226
industry employment 32–3
industry evolution 64–6

318

Index

Jovanotti 234
just-in-time systems 45, 48, 159

kaizen 107
Kaplan, S. 199
Karlsson, C. 150
Kelleher, Herb 245–6
Kennedy, John F. 172
Kerry Group 28
key customers/accounts 103, 106
Khrushchev, Nikita 172
kill ratios 167
Kim, Chan 50
Kingspan 28
knock-on effects 33
know-how:
  accumulated 156
  strengthening 25
  superior production 157
  tacit 154, 156, 158
knowledge-based sectors 20
knowledge economy 31
  leading in 223–41
knowledge exchange 267
knowledge management initiatives 226
knowledge networks 227
knowledge sharing 108, 256
knowledge spillovers 22
knowledge transfer 149
Kogut, B. 149
Korean War 167–8
Kotter, John P. 283–4
KPMG 223, 228

labor productivity 18
  financial savings 102
  modern manufacturing sector 26
Laffey, A. G. 301
LANs (local area networks) 217
laptops 59, 155
  exploding 143
lay-offs 282
  impending 154
  major 158
leadership 98, 102, 126, 278
  definite capacity for 276
  demands of 242–53
  negotiation and 281–96
  political, weak 115
  reinforcement of values 125

relational aspects of 224
researching the issue of 223
role of chairman 270
special sort of 227
strategic 193
leadership traits 175, 177, 179
leading players 65
lean production 266
learning 140, 149, 281
  environment conducive to 290
  ideas formulated 285
  open-minded 117
  proprietary knowledge through 267
  team 104
  tracking 105
learning curves 62, 152–3
learning from experience 45
legislation 272
legitimacy 125, 230
  loss of 125
  readily undermined 112
Lego 62, 157–8
LeMay, Gen. Curtis 172
Lev, Baruch 224
leverage 104, 105, 110, 150, 163, 194, 195,
  286, 303
  economies of knowledge 223
  key points of 266
  strategically vital 302
Levinson, Art 233, 236
Levitt, Stephen 243–4
Levi's 235
Lewis, Ken 305
liabilities 76
liberalization of trade 120
licensing 65, 191
LID (lead independent director) role
  273, 276
light-emitting diodes 191
Limerick 30
linchpin positions 300, 302–3
Linde, Carl von 184, 185
linear approach 164–5
Linux 255, 264
living standards:
  higher 21
  opportunity to improve 18
locational distribution 20
logistics 78, 149
London 232, 235

Index

Index

Index

Index

SMEs (small- and medium-sized
    enterprises) 28–9, 298
  equity and seed capital to 31
Smirnoff Ice 234
soap manufacturers 53
social capital 226
  extraordinary opportunities for 256
social networking 60, 135, 137, 143
social skills 240
socialization 112, 126, 273
socio-economic circumstances 118
socio-economic variables 140
soft options 172
software 185, 224, 244
  global applications 306
  open source 264
  programming 166–7, 174–5, 177, 228, 236
  proprietary 65
software development 71, 198, 255
Solectron 155
solid state lighting 191
Sonoco Corporation 302, 303
SONYs (awards for excellence in radio) 237
Sorrell, Sir Martin 223, 224, 230, 234–5, 237
South East Asia 153
South Korea 149, 157
Southwest Airlines 239, 245–6
Soviet MiG-15 plane 167–8
Soviet Union 172
special-interest groups 135, 143
specialists 123, 227
specialization of labor 216
speed 102, 120, 121
spillovers 22, 23–6
'spin' 112, 176
spin-outs 30
spinning off entities 194
sponsors 300, 301–2, 306
Sprint 61
stability 22
  long-term 275
staff associations 124
Stamford 231
standard architecture/components 65, 154
start-ups 29–31, 58, 167, 214, 245
  mature corporation has unique advantages
    over 217
  performance 179
  see also HPSU companies
state intervention 14

steady state conditions 190–3, 194, 198,
    200, 202
strategic advantage 297–307
strategic choices 57, 58, 59, 60, 194
  winner-take-all game 66–7
'strategic churn' 27–33
strategic convergence 50
strategic investments 22, 71
  improvement in generating revenues 76
  joint ventures and alliances 75
strategic literacy 107
strategic partners 109–10
strategic planning 118, 124, 165,
    166, 168
  careful 163
  long-term 242
strategic position 85
strategic public management 112, 113–19
strategic unity 106–7
strategy 22
  cost leadership 85
  disastrous 57
  the financial footprint of 69–96
  formulating 69
  iterative approach to 163–83
  long-term 150, 152, 155, 160, 164
  market entry 71–2
  marketing 132, 134, 143
  multi-channel 136
  options available 38
  talent 301
strategy innovation 39, 48, 106
  importance of considering 49–50
  opportunities for 49, 53
  potent source of ideas for 51
  radical 38
strategy loops 165–71, 178, 180
  rigorous and frequent revision into 179
stretch assignments 304
style (governance) 118
  identifying 287–8
  stretching 288–89
style (product) 53
subassemblies 153
sub-component manufacturers 66
subsidiaries 23, 136
  relocation to low-cost countries 25
  spillover of entrepreneurs 30
subsidies 45
substitute industries 53, 54

328

Index